MONETARISM

# Studies in Monetary Economics

*Editors*

KARL BRUNNER
STANLEY FISCHER

*Associate Editors*

RUDIGER DORNBUSCH
PIETER KORTEWEG
THOMAS MAYER

Volume 1

NORTH-HOLLAND PUBLISHING COMPANY
AMSTERDAM · NEW YORK · OXFORD

# Monetarism

*Edited by*
JEROME L. STEIN
*Professor of Economics, Eastman Professor of Political Economy*
***Brown University***

1976

NORTH-HOLLAND PUBLISHING COMPANY
AMSTERDAM · NEW YORK · OXFORD

ISBN North-Holland for this series 0 7204 0560 2
ISBN North-Holland for this volume 0 7204 0357 X
ISBN American Elsevier for this volume 0 444 10001 1

*Publishers*

NORTH-HOLLAND PUBLISHING COMPANY
AMSTERDAM · NEW YORK · OXFORD

*Sole distributors for the U.S.A. and Canada*

AMERICAN ELSEVIER PUBLISHING COMPANY, INC.
52 VANDERBILT AVENUE
NEW YORK, N.Y. 10017

**Library of Congress Cataloging in Publication Data**

Main entry under title:

Monetarism

(Studies in monetary economics; v. 1)

Based on a conference sponsored by the National Science Foundation.

1. Monetary policy – Congresses. 2. Fiscal policy – Congresses. I. Stein, Jerome L. II. United States. National Science Foundation.

HG221.M79 1976 332.4 76-4559
ISBN 0-444-10001-1 (American Elsevier)

PRINTED IN THE NETHERLANDS

## INTRODUCTION TO THE SERIES

This new series will publish books of interest to students and researchers working in the fields of macro-economics, monetary theory and policy, banking and the operation of financial markets. It is intended that works of empirical emphasis will be included in the series along with theoretical contributions. Publications will include research monographs and the proceedings of significant conferences. The editors welcome submissions of manuscripts for inclusion in the series.

**CONTENTS**

## PREFACE

Events in the 1970's have shown the profound limitations of the current state of macroeconomic theory. It was no longer the case that economists in policy-making positions could draw upon the existing theory with confidence, to help them solve the serious problems troubling the national economy. Two examples suffice to justify these statements. In the 1972 Economic Report of the President, the Council wrote:

> The problems of managing fiscal policy or monetary policy or both have apparently been underestimated. It may well be that more has been promised than can be delivered with existing knowledge and instruments. Certainly there is need for much additional research. [p. 112]

Again in the 1974 Economic Report, the Council searched in vain for a theoretical answer to their problems. They wrote:

> There is no simple explanation for this price behavior which was the most extraordinary in almost a generation and which confounded the Council and most other economists alike. [p. 65]

Since the state of the theory was unsettled, all sorts of ad hoc factors were adduced to account for this phenomenon. Political, psychological, institutional and sociological "explanations" were invoked regularly. This was equivalent to accounting for yesterday's movement of the Dow–Jones index but being unable to forecast what it will be next week.

Fortunately the National Science Foundation, acting through James Blackman and Daniel Newlon, was anxious to encourage scientific research in the area of macroeconomic theory. Thereby, the academic community would endeavour to provide the theory appropriate to the needs of those in policy-making positions. The conference which gave rise to this volume was supported by the National Science Foundation. To be sure, more questions were raised than were answered; but the movement is in the right direction. May it continue.

JEROME L. STEIN

*Brown University*
*Providence, R. I.*

September, 1975

## INTRODUCTION

## The Monetarist Criticism of the New Economics

Jerome L. STEIN*

### 1. The Monetarist Position

Monetarists have challenged the New Economics' understanding of the economic mechanism; and the monetarist controversy has been the central issue in macroeconomics. Many distinguished economists have participated in the monetarist controversy. It was Karl Brunner who first coined the term "monetarism". Although neither the monetarists nor the neo-Keynesians constitute monolithic groups, the intergroup differences are far greater than the within group differences in emphasis and nuance. Karl Brunner, drawing upon his work with Allan Meltzer, described the common core of the monetarist position as a series of propositions.

> First, monetary impulses are a major factor accounting for variations in output, employment and prices. Second, movements in the money stock are the most reliable measure of the thrust of monetary impulses. Third, the behavior of the monetary authorities dominates movements in the money stock over business cycles. [Brunner (1968, p. 9)]

These propositions are supported by the following empirical evidence gathered by Brunner and Meltzer, Milton Friedman and Anna Schwartz and others.

> (i) Federal Reserve Actions dominate the movements of the monetary base over time; (ii) movements of the monetary base dominate movements of the

*I am indebted to the following for valuable criticisms of earlier drafts: G. Borts, K. Brunner, P. Cagan, M. Friedman, U. Funke, M. Goodfriend, E. F. Infante, B. McGrath, A. Meltzer, W. Poole, A. Schwartz, R. M. Solow and J. Tobin.

money supply over the business cycle; and (iii) accelerations or decelerations of the money supply are clearly followed by accelerations or decelerations in economic activity. [Brunner (1968, p. 24)]

Thomas Mayer ("The structure of monetarism", *Kredit und Kapital*) surveyed the spectrum of views espoused by those who identify themselves as monetarists and showed that propositions accepted by one subset of monetarists need not be accepted by another subset. A monetarist could be a Democrat or a Republican. Conceivably he could be a Socialist but not a Marxist, because a monetarist believes that the monetary authority rather than the private sector is primarily responsible for variations in output and employment, and that the price system is an efficient allocator of resources.

Monetarists are policy oriented. Their major propositions are a series of empirical observations, whose validity is still the subject of dispute, rather than a theory in direct opposition to neo-Keynesian analysis. A neo-Keynesian could accept Brunner's propositions that: monetary impulses are a major factor accounting for variations in output and employment and that movements in the monetary base dominate movements in the money supply over the business cycle. Nevertheless, there are several propositions advanced by monetarists which are inconsistent with neo-Keynesian analysis. These propositions, propounded by Milton Friedman, are as follows.

Monetary policy is effective and fiscal policy is not effective in controlling inflation. Fiscal restraint, measured by the full employment surplus or deficit, for example, can have little effect in reducing the rate of inflation unless it is accompanied by a reduction in the rate of monetary expansion.

> Government spending may or may not be inflationary. It clearly will be inflationary if it is financed by creating money that is, by printing currency or creating bank deposits. If it is financed by taxes or by borrowing from the public, the main effect is that the government spends the funds instead of the taxpayer or instead of the person who would otherwise have borrowed the funds. Fiscal policy is extremely important in determining what fraction of total national income is spent by the government and who bears the burden of expenditure. By itself, fiscal policy is not important for inflation. What is important is how the spending is financed. [Friedman (1973, p. 29)]

Instead of having two instruments, monetary and fiscal policy, to control the rate of price change, monetarists claim that only the former is efficacious. This view is fundamentally different from that held by neo-Keynesians, as is shown below.

Another controversial statement by Friedman is the following:

> I regard the description of our position as 'money is all that matters for changes in *nominal* income and for *short-run* changes in real income' as an exaggeration but one that gives the right flavor of our conclusions. [Friedman (1974, p. 27)]

The monetarists at the Federal Reserve Bank of St. Louis claim that fiscal policy *per se* will only exert an ephemeral effect upon the level of nominal income. At the end of five quarters, the effect will have disappeared completely. This claim, that velocity is independent of fiscal policy during that span of time, is inconsistent with neo-Keynesian theory.

Neo-Keynesian theory is a highly developed method of analysis which is featured prominently in almost every textbook in macroeconomics. On the other hand, there is no monetarist theory *per se* which is taught and which can be contrasted with neo-Keynesian theory. In fact, there is a pervasive view that the monetarists have a "black box" and have not explained the causal mechanism which could imply the propositions advanced by Friedman or the Federal Reserve Bank of St. Louis. Robert Rasche wrote:

> On the one hand, we are left without a clearly specified analytical framework for the monetarist approach which can be contrasted with the well developed static income determination model. On the other hand, and even more importantly, there is no general model which can produce the post-Keynesian model as a particular case, and the monetarist and classical models as alternative cases. Such a framework is useful in order to discriminate between alternative hypotheses and to construct empirical tests which have the potential to refute one, or both, positions. [Rasche (1973, p. 15)]

Tobin was anxious to resolve these controversies and wrote:

> If the monetarists and the neo-Keynesians could agree as to which values of which parameters in which behavior relations imply which policy conclusions, then they could concentrate on the evidence regarding the values of those parameters. I wish that these articles had brought us closer to this goal, but I am afraid they have not. [Tobin (1974, p. 77)]

The purposes of the Brown University conference on monetarism, which gave rise to this volume, were to: evaluate the existing empirical evidence concerning these issues, resolve the theoretical problems posed above and agree on statistical tests which could help us determine which view of the world was correct, the neo-

Keynesian or the monetarist. The reader can evaluate the papers published here in terms of their success in resolving these issues. Four main papers were discussed at the conference.

Franco Modigliani and Albert Ando examine the theory and evidence concerning the impact of fiscal actions upon nominal income. They are concerned with the short- and medium-run (i.e., two to three years) impact of a pure macroeconomic fiscal action, which is not accompanied by any change in the time profile of the money supply, upon the time path of money income. Non-monetarists claim that an increase in real government expenditure will lead to a significant rise in nominal income lasting for several years. By contrast, the reduced form estimates derived at the Federal Reserve Bank of St. Louis imply "that the response reaches a puny peak by the second quarter, and disappears altogether by the end of two years". For this reason, Modigliani and Ando are concerned with what happens to nominal income in the first three years. They first review some monetarist and non-monetarist hypotheses concerning the channels whereby fiscal policy affects nominal income. Then they show why the empirical evidence provided by the reduced forms used by the St. Louis Bank are "grossly unreliable and/or irrelevant". This paper is discussed by Robert Gordon, Lawrence Klein and Anna Schwartz.

Karl Brunner and Allan H. Meltzer formulate an aggregative theory for a closed economy. They state three necessary attributes of a monetarist theory: (a) The long-run position to which the economy moves is determined by stocks, particularly the stock of money, and not by flows.[1] (b) The adjustment to a change in money involves substitution between money, other assets and new production. (c) The economic system is stable. The body of their paper consists of two parts. First, they develop a model and describe the conditions for equilibrium in the markets for assets and output. Second, they examine the effects of monetary and fiscal policies and the financing of the deficits and surpluses upon interest rates, prices and output.

They contend that the relative responses of the economy to monetary and fiscal policies cannot be reduced to propositions about the slopes of *IS–LM* curves. Therefore, the Keynesian paradigm is of limited value. Moreover, in a closed economy with no growth, there cannot be full stock–flow equilibrium with an unbalanced budget. For this reason, the government budget balance condition is an integral part of their model. They conclude that: "A maintained fiscal position does not induce steady inflation or deflation whether financed entirely by debt or by base money". This paper is discussed by Rudiger Dornbusch, Thomas Mayer and Robert Rasche; and there is a reply by the authors.

My paper is designed to fill the void noted by Rasche and is concerned with what is inside the "black box". It is a development of my earlier dynamic model [Stein

[1] On this point the reader may also consult Niehans (1974).

(1974)] in a way which can produce the neo-Keynesian results as a particular case and the monetarist results as an alternative case.

Endogenous variables are: the unemployment rate, the rate of price change, the real wage, real balances per unit of capital, the expected rate of price change, the nominal rate of interest and taxes. Control variables are: the rate of monetary expansion, real government purchases per unit of capital and the ratio of government interest-bearing debt to the money supply. I determine the trajectories of the unemployment rate and the inflation rate resulting from changes in policy variables. The price level does not necessarily converge to a constant. There is a natural transition from the impact effects to the cumulative effects and the model is dynamically stable.

The crucial coefficient is $P_5$: the effect of a rise in the ratio of government bonds to money upon the real excess demand for goods per unit of capital. If that coefficient is non-positive ($P_5 \leqq 0$), monetarist results are obtained. Otherwise, ($P_5 > 0$), neo-Keynesian results are derived. An empirical test is proposed and undertaken to determine which empirical specification is inconsistent with the data. Carl Christ, Jürg Niehans and Robert Solow discuss this paper; and then I reply.

James Tobin and Willem Buiter develop the work of Solow and Blinder and address themselves to the long-run effects of fiscal policy on aggregate demand. Does an expansionary fiscal policy *per se* raise aggregate demand permanently or only temporarily? They examine this problem within a Pigovian stationary state, where account is taken of adjustments in the stocks of capital and other assets. Supply constraints are generally disregarded, by assuming that there is always labor available to produce the output demanded. Their conclusion is that an increase in government expenditure either leads to: a new long-run equilibrium with a higher real income in the stable case, or to an explosive increase in income and interest rate in the unstable case. The strong monetarist proposition, that expansive fiscal effects on aggregate demand are only transitory, crucially relies upon an interest inelastic demand for money. "A fiscally driven expansion could, of course, occur but vanish if the short-run *LM* curve is not vertical while the long-run *LLM* curve is vertical. We are not aware that this argument has been made."

If there is always full employment but flexible prices, the "new long-run equilibrium, after a permanent increase of government expenditures, has a larger real income and capital stock but lower price level and interest rate. But such equilibria are stable, if at all, only if price expectations adapt fairly quickly to price experience." There is, however, no guarantee that the economic system is stable. Phil Cagan, Stanley Fischer and Milton Friedman discuss this paper; and there is a reply by James Tobin.

## 2. The Short-Run Quantity Theory of Money

Just prior to the Brown University conference, the volume edited by Gordon (1974) was published. The focal point of that volume was the dispute between Milton Friedman and James Tobin. A brief analysis of that dispute, and the position taken by the monetarists at the Federal Reserve Bank of St. Louis, will provide the background for the papers contained in this volume.

Friedman argued that changes in the growth of the money supply are the major causes of changes in the growth of nominal income over long periods of time. The monetarists at the Federal Reserve Bank of St. Louis took an ostensibly similar, but in reality a different, position. They regressed the quarterly change in nominal *GNP* upon lagged values of the quarterly changes in the money stock and the nominal values of high employment Federal expenditures. On the basis of data from 1959I to 1969IV, they concluded the following from their reduced form equation.

> The pattern of the coefficients indicates a large and rapid influence of monetary actions on total spending relative to that of fiscal actions. Changes in high-employment expenditures, with the money stock held constant, first have a positive influence on total spending, but the influence becomes significantly negative after three quarters. Fiscal actions, unaccompanied by changes in money, have little net effect on *GNP* over five quarters. [Andersen and Carlson (1970, pp. 11)]

Their conclusion that fiscal policy has only an ephemeral effect on nominal *GNP* is at variance with neo-Keynesian economics, and is a reassertion of the short-run quantity theory of money. According to the latter, "in the short-run nominal income is proportional to the supply of money, although changes in nominal income may affect output as well as prices" [Tobin (1974, p. 85)]. If the St. Louis results were correct, then fiscal policy would have a very short-lived effect upon the income velocity of money.

According to the neo-Keynesian *IS–LM* analysis the short-run quantity theory is valid only if the *LM* curve is vertical: the demand for money is interest inelastic. Tobin was explicit on this point.

> First, let me explain what I thought the main issue was. In terms of the Hicksian language of Friedman's article I thought (and still think) it was the shape of the *LM* locus. . . . It will be vertical if the demand for money is wholly insensive to interest rates. [Tobin (1974, pp. 77–78)]

Were the demand for money $L(Y)$, where $Y$ is nominal income, variations in nominal income would be accounted for by variations in the *LM* curve; and fiscal policy *per se* would exert no systematic effect upon nominal income. Neo-Keynesians reject this rationale for the monetarist position because, of all the issues in monetary economics, there is overwhelming evidence in favor of the proposition that the demand for money is negatively related to the rate of interest.

Since the overwhelming evidence is inconsistent with a vertical *LM* curve, the neo-Keynesians reject the short-run quantity theory described above. An equality between the short-run growth of nominal *GNP* and the rate of monetary expansion is deemed to result from a situation where the nominal rate of interest is fixed by the monetary authority and the demand for money is $L(r)\,Y$, where $r$ is the interest rate. If the monetary authority does not fix the interest rate, then nominal income and the money supply will grow at different rates.

Modigliani and Ando, in their paper below, attempt to explain the results of the St. Louis reduced form equation. They argue that the reduced form gives highly biased estimates of the true structural relations. Consequently, the St. Louis study cannot be considered as convincing evidence supporting the short-run quantity theory. Andersen and Carlson have failed to convince Modigliani and Ando that fiscal policy cannot affect the income velocity of money over a period of a year or more.

Several monetarists have claimed that another difference between their and the neo-Keynesian analysis concerns the transmission mechanism connecting a change in the quantity of money to the change in nominal income. Keith Carlson, at the St. Louis bank, wrote:

> One of the more interesting issues relating to the monetarist–fiscalist controversy is the assumed nature of the transmission mechanism. Even though Brunner lists the transmission mechanism as a separate issue in macroeconomics, it seems that the transmission issue is in a focal point as far as the controversy is concerned. [Carlson (1974, p. 14)]

Tobin completely rejected that view, in a postscript to his comment on Friedman's paper. Not only does the monetarist view of the transmission mechanism conform to Tobin's portfolio approach to monetary theory, but it is inconsistent with the long-run quantity theory of money that real magnitudes are in long-run equilibrium independent of the nominal quantity of money.

> ... [Friedman] argues that monetary shocks affect demands for goods and services by setting in motion complex, interrelated chains of asset substitutions and revaluations. If portfolios are to absorb greater quantities of money, prices

> of other assets – not just Treasury bills and corporate bonds but equities and used cars – must change, mostly rise. Increases in the values of existing stocks of physical assets, or titles to physical assets, encourage the production of new goods of the same type or of close substitutes.
>
> Now this scenario is quite standard. It is one which 'neo-Keynesian' monetary economists have been teaching and expounding for years. It is, for example, the principal point of my own "portfolio" approach to monetary theory. Neo-Keynesian econometric models, notably the Federal Reserve–M.I.T.–Penn model, link monetary policy via financial markets and intermediaries to the markets for producer capital, houses and durable goods.
>
> The puzzle is how Friedman could think that his account of the transmission mechanism supports monetarist conclusions. On the contrary, emphasis on portfolio substitutions suggests, for example, (1) that there is no unique relation between any monetary aggregate and nominal income, (2) that non-monetary events – fiscal policies, shifts in asset preferences, revisions of expectations – will also affect the attractiveness of accumulating physical assets, and (3) that the market does not automatically put full changes in inflation expectations into nominal interest rates. [Tobin (1974, pp. 88–89)]

For these reasons, Tobin was incredulous that some monetarists should claim that the nature of the transmission mechanism accounts for the differences between them. Modigliani and Ando, in their paper below, concur with Tobin. Whatever differences there are between the monetarists and the neo-Keynesians are not due to the nature of the transmission mechanism.

## 3. The Long-Run Quantity Theory and Effects of Fiscal Policy

In their *Monetary History of the United States*, Milton Friedman and Anna Schwartz relied upon the long-run quantity theory presumption that changes in the quantity of money *per se* have a negligible effect upon the growth of real income. Non-monetary forces are "all that matter" for changes in real income over the decades. Supporting evidence for that view is that there were roughly similar rates of growth of real output during the decades 1882–1892 and 1903–1913, although prices declined at a rate of two percent p.a. in the former period and rose at a rate of two percent p.a. in the latter period. "If these figures can be trusted," write the authors [Friedman–Schwartz (1963, p. 187)], "the rate of price change over several cycles had little or no connection with the associated rate of growth of output."

Friedman denied that the fundamental difference between him and the neo-Keynesians concerns the slope of the *LM* curve. In his view they arrive at different conclusions because neo-Keynesians emphasize the impact effects of monetary and fiscal policy whereas he emphasizes the cumulative, or steady state, effects. The differences between them are empirical rather than theoretical: how important are first round (impact) effects compared to the cumulative (steady state) effects. Friedman is unequivocal on this point.

> One way to characterize the Keynesian approach is that it gives almost exclusive importance to the first-round effect. This leads it to attach importance primarily to flows of spending rather than to stocks of assets. Similarly, one way to characterize the quantity-theory approach is to say that it gives almost no importance to the first-round effects. The empirical question is how important the first-round effects are compared to the ultimate effects. [Friedman (1974, p. 147)]

> At any rate, the issue between us clearly is not and never has been whether the *LM* curve is vertical or has a positive slope. [Friedman (1974, p. 142)]

Friedman reasons within the framework of the long-run quantity theory. This theory asserts that: "real magnitudes are in long-run equilibrium independent of the nominal quantity of money, so that nominal magnitudes – prices, money incomes – are simply proportional to the nominal quantity of money" [Tobin (1974, p. 85)].

Tobin responded that the long-run quantity theory of money is theoretically deficient. The effect of a change in the money supply upon the price level is not invariant to the way in which the stock of money is changed. An open-market operation will produce a different effect than will a transfer payment. Drawing upon the literature in money and growth,[2] Tobin explained his objection to the long-run version of the quantity theory.

> The strict quantity theory applies only if there is a single exogenous monetary variable which is "money" except for a factor of proportionality, for example, reserve requirements. Much monetary theory, modern as well as ancient, has developed from a model in which government debt and the monetary base are one and the same. But in a model with various kinds of government liabilities, time as well as demand obligations, it is easy to show that the real equilibrium – for example, capital intensity and the marginal productivity of capital – depends on the proportions in which these liabilities are supplied. . . . Monetary policy has . . . real consequences. [Tobin (1974, p. 17)]

[2] For an analysis of the neoclassical, Keynes–Wicksell and synthesis models of money and growth, see Stein (1971, chs. 1, 3–4, 5, resp.).

In their paper below Tobin and Buiter examine the *cumulative* effects of fiscal policy. They claim that a "characteristic monetarist proposition is that pure fiscal policy does not matter for aggregate real demand, nominal income and the price level". They examine a stationary state when both stocks and flows are in equilibrium, and examine the validity of the "characteristic monetarist proposition" within the context of such a model. Their conclusion is that "nothing in the analysis of this paper suggests that expansionary fiscal effects on aggregate demand are only transitory .... Interest-inelasticity of demand for money seems to be crucial for the strong monetarist proposition after all."

To be sure, there is a difference between the impact and cumulative effects of fiscal policy. Tobin and Buiter "... considered the long-run effects of fiscal expansion in an economy with full employment and flexible prices. Here there is a striking difference between impact and ultimate effects. The new long-run equilibrium, after a permanent increase of government expenditure, has a larger real income and capital stock but lower price level and interest rate. But such equilibria are stable, if at all, only if price expectations adapt fairly quickly to price expectations." Tobin and Buiter conclude that a rise in government expenditures, financed through a sale of bonds, tends to raise the price level in the short run, and lower it in the long run. The long-run quantity theory is not valid.

As an empirical proposition, Friedman claims that variations in the rate of price change are dominated by variations in the rate of monetary expansion. To be sure, variations in the growth of the debt and fiscal variables may contribute to variations in the rate of price change. However, Friedman (1974, p. 148) argues, there has been no systematic evidence produced to support the assertion that these non-monetary effects are significant. Viewed in this manner, the differences between Friedman and Tobin are empirical rather than theoretical.

Brunner and Meltzer examine both the impact and cumulative effects of fiscal policy, and arrive at different conclusions than do Tobin and Buiter. Brunner and Meltzer show that fiscal policy has real and nominal effects in the short and long run. "Our discussion ... shows that the expansive effect of an increase in ... [real government expenditure] is eroded in the long run by the operation of the wage adjustment process. Eventually, the adjustment of the stock of real capital converts the initial expansion of output into a decline of long-run output. Prices are higher in both the short and long run relative to the price level in the initial equilibrium."

A reconciliation of the long-run conclusions of these authors is a subject for further research.[3]

[3] See Blinder and Solow (1973) and (1974).

## 4. Fiscal Policy, the Rate of Inflation and Unemployment

Policy questions illuminate theoretical differences among economists. A basic tenet of neo-Keynesian economics is that there is a fiscal policy multiplier in excess of unity. If tax rates were reduced and the resulting deficit were financed with the sale of bonds, the *IS* curve would shift to the right. Since the *LM* curve is positively sloped, both the level of real income and the interest rate would rise. The potency of fiscal policy in raising the level of real income, or in reducing the level of unemployment, depends upon the magnitude of the shift of the *IS* curve and the slopes of both the *IS* and *LM* curves.

Neo-Keynesian analysis, reflected by the *IS–LM* paradigm, usually treats the price level as exogenous[4] or as an algebraic function of output. This theoretical orientation carried over into the early large-scale econometric models.

> The first large econometric models of the 1940's and 1950's had relatively little to do with prices and wages. Since they were early attempts to quantify Keynes' analysis of the income expenditure stream, their emphasis was on real *GNP* and employment. As late as 1960, one of the major U.S. models did not have price or wage equations. In the late 1950's the authors of another model reported that for all practical purposes price and wage movements were independent of real variables in their model. [de Menil and Enzler (1971, p. 277)]

As a result, the multipliers related policy variables to real variables such as output or employment, and ignored feedbacks between price and output effects.

In 1970, the Federal Reserve Board and Social Science Research Council organized a conference on the econometrics of price determination. The papers presented at that conference represented the progress that had been made in incorporating price and wage equations into the major econometric models. James Tobin evaluated the results of that conference. Suppose, he wrote, that:

> an economist attended the conference hoping to distill from the papers presented a simple working model of wage and price determination that summarized the conventional wisdom of the assembled experts. . . . What would he write down, or tell his students, or report to his policy-making superiors on his return? I think

[4] Alan Blinder and Robert Solow (1973, p. 324) wrote: "The *IS–LM* model usually treats the price level as exogenously fixed, and we shall adhere to this convention. However, it should be noted that we do this strictly for simplicity. There are no real difficulties in . . . allowing the price level to be endogenously determined."

he would be able to place his findings in the framework developed from the following four equations.[5]

There is a price adjustment equation, a wage change equation, a price expectations equation and an equation representing normal utilization. Let $\pi \equiv D \ln p$ be the rate of change of the price level $p$, $W$ be the nominal wage and $U$ be the unemployment rate.

Equation (1) is the price determination equation. The rate of price change is the sum of two elements: (i) the growth of the nominal wage $DW/W$ in excess of the long-run growth of productivity $g$, and (ii) a function of the difference between the current unemployment rate $U$ and the expected normal value $U_e$,

$$\pi = \frac{DW}{W} - g + f(U - U_e); \qquad f(0) = 0, f' < 0. \tag{1}$$

The wage determination equation (2) is a Phillips curve, where the coefficient of the expected rate of price change $\pi^*$ is less than unity, the partial derivatives of the $h(U, DU)$ function are negative, $D \equiv \mathrm{d}/\mathrm{d}t$,

$$\frac{DW}{W} = \alpha_{21}\pi^* + \alpha_{23} g + h(U, DU). \tag{2}$$

Price expectations are based upon past rates of price change, as described by

$$\pi^*(t) = \sum_{i=1}^{\infty} \alpha_{3i}\,\pi(t-i); \quad \sum \alpha_{3i} = 1, \quad \alpha_{3i} \geqq 0. \tag{3}$$

Similarly, the expected or normal value of the unemployment rate is based upon past rates of unemployment, as described by

$$U_e(t) = \sum_{i=1}^{\infty} \alpha_{4i}\, U(t-i); \quad \sum \alpha_{4i} = 1, \quad \alpha_{4i} > 0. \tag{4}$$

> These four equations form a subsystem of a complete model that given an initial price history is capable of determining prices, price expectations and wages. Unemployment, past and present, and the rental cost of capital can be taken as exogenous to the subsystem. [Tobin (1971, p. 6)]

The rate of price change is described by equation (5), based upon equations (1) and (2) above,

$$\pi = \alpha_2\pi^* - (1 - \alpha_{23})g + h(U, DU) + f(U - U_e). \tag{5}$$

[5] Tobin (1971, p. 5). I am not using Tobin's notation, but am describing the equations on his pp. 5–12.

Suppose that price expectations change slowly so that $\pi^*$ is relatively constant during the period considered.

There are many multipliers in this set of models: a money multiplier $A_M = \mathrm{d}U/\mathrm{d}M$, a government expenditures multiplier $A_G = \mathrm{d}U/\mathrm{d}G$, a tax rate multiplier $A_T = \mathrm{d}U/\mathrm{d}T$, etc. All of these multipliers reflect shifts of the *IS* and *LM* curves in the real income (unemployment) and interest rate space. A rise in government purchases of goods or a reduction of tax rates, even when the deficit is financed by the sale of long-term government bonds, will raise the level of real income and reduce the unemployment rate. This is the meaning of a fiscal policy multiplier. For example, let there be a rise in government purchases of goods or a reduction in tax rates $\tau$. According to equation (5), the rate of inflation will be raised.

$$\partial\pi/\partial G = (h_1 + f')\,A_G > 0, \tag{6a}$$

$$\partial\pi/\partial\tau = (h_1 + f')\,A_\tau < 0. \tag{6b}$$

Fiscal policy, unaccompanied by a change in the rate of monetary expansion can affect the rate of inflation in these models.

There are two other noteworthy implications of these models. An incomes policy, which reduces the growth of nominal wages, can successfully reduce the rate of inflation without a reduction in the rate of monetary expansion. Moreover, a restrictive fiscal policy can offset the inflationary effects of a high rate of monetary expansion. Therefore, inflation is not necessarily a monetary phenomenon in this class of models. On the other hand, monetarists claim that:

> To have a significant impact on the economy a tax increase must somehow affect monetary policy – the quantity of money and its rate of growth. . . . Whether deficits produce inflation depends on how they are financed. . . . If, as so often happens, they are financed by creating money, they unquestionably do produce inflationary pressure. . . . If they are financed by borrowing from the public, at whatever interest rates are necessary, they may still exert some minor inflationary pressure. . . . However, their major effect will be to make interest rates higher than they would otherwise be. [Friedman (1974, pp. 139–140)]

Tobin could not accept this position as being correct. He asked (1974, p. 87) why the accumulation of Treasury bills, resulting from deficit financing, is of no consequence for the price level while the financing of the deficits with currency inflates prices proportionately. Friedman replied that:

> . . . evidences of government debt are largely in place of evidences of private debt – people hold Treasury bills instead of bills issued by, for example, U.S.

> Steel. The total nominal volume of debt grows by . . . much less . . . than the size of the deficit. Moreover, even this growth is offset by two other factors: the increase expected in future tax liabilities accompanying the growth of the government debt . . . and the reduction in the physical volume of assets created because of lowered private investment. [Friedman (1974, p. 142)]

The specific dynamics whereby Friedman's scenario unfolds were not made explicit in terms of a model. For that reason, the differences between him and Tobin were unresolved.

Friedman did not claim that the entire set of monetarist propositions is deducible from an explicit model. In fact, he stated that both the *IS–LM* neo-Keynesian paradigm and the quantity theory framework have serious deficiencies. Neither is fully capable of explaining the empirical phenomena nor, of accounting for the variables that are significant in the other theory. Prior to this conference (November 1974), Friedman stated that the unresolved problems were as follows:

> Both [theories] regard each equilibrium position as characterized by a stable *level* of prices or output. Neither explicitly introduces changing prices or changing output into the formal analysis. [Friedman (1974, pp. 43–45)]

> The key need to remedy the defects common to all the models I have sketched is a theory that will explain (a) the short-run division of a change in nominal income between prices and output, (b) the short-run adjustment of nominal income to a change in autonomous variables, and (c) the transition between this short-run situation and a long-run equilibrium. [Friedman (1974, p. 48)]

A useful monetarist or neo-Keynesian theory must contain the unemployment rate (or level of real output) and the rate of price change as state variables. The level of nominal income would follow as the product of the rate of output and the price level. The theory must explain what parameters determine whether fiscal policy *per se* can be effective in controlling the rate of inflation, without assuming that the demand for money is interest inelastic or that nominal wages and prices are fixed. These were the objectives of my paper.

I concluded that the crucial coefficient was $P_5$, the upward shift of the *IS* curve minus the upward shift of the *LM* curve resulting from a rise in the quantity of government bonds. Neo-Keynesians results occur if $P_5$ is positive. Friedman's results occur if $P_5$ is zero. Suppose that the level of real government purchases per unit of capital rise to a higher level and are financed entirely through bond sales. Assume that there is an equilibrium rate of unemployment. What are the scenarios in the two cases?

If $P_5$ were zero, then the *acceleration* of real government purchases would lead to a lower unemployment rate and a higher rate of price change. Consequently, there is a rise in the growth rate of nominal *GNP*. When real government purchases of goods stabilize at the higher level, the rate of price change is brought back to the old equilibrium level: the rate of monetary expansion less the growth of effective labor. The unemployment rate returns to the equilibrium level. Nominal *GNP* will be higher than it was before the rise in real government purchases, but will continue to grow at the same equilibrium rate equal to the rate of monetary expansion. Velocity will stabilize at a higher level than before; and there will only be a temporary rise in the rate of price change. These results are consistent with Friedman's views.

If $P_5$ were positive, then different results would occur. The *acceleration* of real government purchases of goods produces the same results as in the previous case. When the level of real government purchases stabilizes at the higher level, the rate of price change will recede from its peak but will stabilize at a rate above the original equilibrium. Eventually, the unemployment rate will converge to its equilibrium rate, but it will take a longer time than it did in the earlier case. The growth of nominal income will reach a peak and then decline to a higher rate than prevailed before the rise in the level of real government purchases of goods per unit of capital. Nominal income will move to a higher trend line with a larger slope than before.

Within the framework of my dynamic model, I have generated either monetarist of non-monetarist results depending on the value of the $P_5$ coefficient. There are, however, differences between my intermediate-run results and the long-run results of Tobin–Buiter which should be reconciled in subsequent research.

This volume raises at least as many questions as it answers and should serve as a program for further research.

## Bibliography

Andersen, L. C. and K. M. Carlson, 1970, A monetarist model of economic stabilization, Federal Reserve Bank of St. Louis Review 52, no. 4, April.

Blinder, A. S. and R. M. Solow, 1973, Does fiscal policy matter?, Journal of Public Economics 2, pp. 319–337.

Blinder, A. S. and R. M. Solow, 1974, in: The economics of public finance (Brookings Institution, Washington, D.C.).

Brunner, K., 1968, The role of monetary policy, Federal Reserve Bank of St. Louis Review 50, no. 7, July.

Carlson, K. H., 1974, Monetary and fiscal actions in macroeconomic models, Federal Reserve Bank of St. Louis Review 56, no. 1, Jan.

deMenil, G. and J. J. Enzler, 1971, Prices and wages in the FR–MIT–Penn econometric model, in: O. Eckstein (1971).

Eckstein, O., ed., 1971, The econometrics of price determination (Board of Governors of the Federal Reserve System, Washington, D.C.).
Friedman, M., 1973, Money and economic development (Praeger, New York).
Friedman, M., 1974, A theoretical framework for monetary analysis, in: R. Gordon (1974).
Friedman, M. and A. Schwartz, 1963, A monetary history of United States (Princeton University Press, Princeton).
Gordon, R., ed., 1974, Milton Friedman's monetary framework (University of Chicago Press, Chicago).
Niehans, J., 1974, Monetary policy with full stock adjustment, Zeitschrift für Wirtschafts- und Sozialwissenschaften 1, pp. 17–43.
Rasche, R., 1973, A comparative static analysis of some monetarist propositions, Federal Reserve Bank of St. Louis Review 55, no. 12, Dec.
Stein, J. L., 1971, Money and capacity growth (Columbia University Press, New York).
Stein, J. L., 1974, Unemployment, inflation and monetarism, American Economic Review LXIV, no. 6, pp. 867–887.
Tobin, J., 1971, The wage–price mechanism, Overview of the conference, in: O. Eckstein (1971).
Tobin, J., 1974, Friedman's theoretical framework, in: R. Gordon (1974).

Chapter 1

# IMPACTS OF FISCAL ACTIONS ON AGGREGATE INCOME AND THE MONETARIST CONTROVERSY: THEORY AND EVIDENCE*

Franco MODIGLIANI and Albert ANDO

with the assistance of J. GIANGRANDE

## 1. The Issues

After many years of sharp and sometimes acrimonious controversy between the monetarists and their sympathizers on the one hand, and the "non-monetarists" on the other, over the effects of monetary and fiscal actions on aggregate income, some consensus seems finally emerging at least over what to disagree about: the main significant area of remaining disagreement seems to be over the *short- and medium-run* impact of *pure macro fiscal actions* on *aggregate money income*. The monetarists (hereafter the "m"s) hold, in Friedman's words that it "is certain to be temporary and likely to be minor" (1972), while the non-monetarists (the "n-m"s) hold that it must be substantial – at least for a good many quarters. Since our purpose here is to contribute to a clarification of the issues, it is well to start by spelling out the operational meaning of the four italicized expressions.

(i) By a *macro fiscal action* we mean an exogenous action of the treasury changing expenditure or receipts, that is, specifically: (a) a change in the quantum of goods and services purchased by the (federal) government ($G$), or (b) a change in the rate of taxation and transfers. The term thus excludes many other events which affect current dollar receipts and expenditures, such as increases in outlays due to changes in the price level, or a change in tax receipts due to changes in real and/or money income. For the "n-m"s, these events should have no significant causal effects on real or money income.

* The contribution of Ando and Giangrande, and the cost of computations necessary to the preparation of this paper was supported by the National Science Foundation grant GS-32383X to the University of Pennsylvania.

To conserve space, our discussion will focus on one specific macro fiscal action, namely a maintained change in $G$; however, the results can be readily generalized to the case of tax changes.

(ii) By *pure* we mean that the fiscal action does not give rise to a change in the money supply. Operationally, we define the *impact* of the fiscal action as the difference between the path of money income ($X\$$) of two economies which are identical in all other respects (initial conditions, policy variables, other exogenous variables) except for the fiscal action. The impact of the fiscal action on any variable $Z$, $t$ quarters after the stimulus, will be denoted by $\Delta * Z_t \equiv Z_t' - Z_t$ when $Z_t'$ and $Z_t$ are, respectively, the values of $Z$ in the economy subject to the shock and in the comparison economy. Of course, the behavior of $\Delta * Z_t$ will in general not be independent of the date at which the experiment is performed.

From the point of view of tying the fiscal with the monetary policy, the most suitable definition of money aggregate would be the monetary base: however, for practical purposes, we find it more convenient to use $M_1$. This should not make a major difference, and may even be more suitable when account is taken of the interest elasticity of demand for currency, which, together with fractional reserve, would tend to make $M_1$ respond to the demand for it, for a given base. In other words, taking $M_1$ as given should strengthen the monetarist case.

(iii) By *short- and medium-run* we mean a period of two to three years. To be sure, this span is arbitrary but it is chosen in the light of two considerations. First, many "n-m"s, and certainly the authors, would agree that, *given time enough* (and provided the system is stable), as increase in real government expenditure is likely to crowd out entirely some other component of expenditure, with the result that the initial increase in income will, eventually, largely disappear, at least in real terms [cf. Modigliani (1971), Ando (1974)]. And they would also agree that the same conclusion holds for the increase in income resulting, initially, from the rise in consumption consequent upon a reduction in taxes. Insofar as money income is concerned, we would expect to find some permanent effect, since the crowding out of other components is achieved largely through a rise in prices and in the entire family of interest rates, which must increase velocity, and, hence, increase money income, given $M_1$ However, this effect would probably be small and is even somewhat uncertain as it depends on the extent to which private net worth consists of money fixed outside debt. Thus, there is no significant disagreement on the proposition that, by the time a new "long-run equilibrium" is reached, the macro fiscal actions will have no significant effect, at least on real income. However, in the "n-m"s view, this long-run equilibrium outcome will require a very long time (if not forever); it is, therefore, hardly more than a *curiosum* which tells us nothing about the response in the span relevant to the design of policy – say the first one to three years. For the "n-m"s in this initial span, the response will rise to a sizeable peak and will remain consistently positive. By contrast, many monetarists seem to take quite seriously the implications of the St. Louis reduced form estimates implying that the response reaches a puny peak by the second quarter, and disappears altogether by the end of two years. Hence, the real controversial issue concerns what happens in the first three to, say, twelve quarters.

(iv) Finally we want to concentrate on $X\$$, again to focus on points of maximum difference. The "n-m"s have always recognized that, if $M_1$ is constant, $G$ will crowd out some investment so that the impact of $G$ on $X$ will, at some point, decline, and this might even occur in short order. However, since the crowding out arises from an increase in interest rates, there must initially be a rise in $X\$$. This would come about in part from a rise in prices, though only in part, since prices could not rise unless there was an expansion of $X$ and employment. But because the "n-m"s (and perhaps even "m"s) hold that prices are sluggish – especially downward – even if the effect on $X$ should be shortlived, the effect on $X\$$ must be fairly lasting. Thus if the St. Louis coefficients were estimates of effects in real terms the "n-m"s might conceivably accept them as an outside possibility. But an unreconcilable disagreement arises over the implied impact on $X\$$.

In what follows, we propose to make one more attempt at reaching some consensus that pure fiscal actions do have an appreciable effect on money income (i.e., multipliers well above unity) in the short and medium run. To this end we will start by reviewing "n-m"s, and some "m"s, hypotheses about the individual links and their interaction and the empirical evidence supporting these hypotheses. Next we will endeavor to show why the empirical evidence provided by the St. Louis type reduced forms is grossly unreliable and/or irrelevant.

## 2. The Non-Monetarists Model and Empirical Evidence

We find it convenient to use the structure of the MPS model to illustrate the "n-m" position both for the sake of concreteness and because it facilitates the task of mustering the supporting empirical evidence. To be sure, not all of the "constituents" for whom we purport to speak would agree with every detail of our formulation, but we do believe that they would broadly agree with its essence, at least qualitatively.

Before examining the response of $X\$$ to $G$ implied by the MPS, it is useful to review some of the earlier models, in part, because this helps to set the MPS structure in perspective and, in part, to show how the difference between monetarists and non-monetarists has narrowed down in time, in part, no doubt, through learning from monetarists' contributions.

### 2.1. *The Earliest Keynesian Model*

In the earliest text-book version, the multiplier was given by the well-known formula

$$\frac{\mathrm{d}X\$}{\mathrm{d}G} \equiv \frac{\Delta * X\$}{\Delta * G} = \frac{1}{1 - c(1 - \tau)}, \tag{1}$$

where $c$ is the m.p.c. and $\tau$ the marginal tax rate. $\Delta * X\$$ denotes the limiting value taken by $\Delta * X\$_t$ when (if ever) it has stopped changing. The common-sense of (1) is that income must rise enough to provide extra saving equal to the increase in the government deficit ($\Delta * G - \tau\Delta * X\$$). Allowing for a gradual response of $C$ to $X$, some time would be required for this rise to occur, but, once reached, it would be maintained. This result would, of course, be applicable only if: (i) the interest rate, rather than $M_1$, were kept constant ("permissive monetary policy"), and (ii) there were no response of $P$ to $X$ (so that $\Delta * X = \Delta * X\$$), which could make sense, at best, if there was plenty of slack in the economy.

### 2.2. *The IS–LM Paradigm*

If $M_1$, rather than $r$, is kept constant, but the other assumptions are maintained, one obtains the classic formula

$$\frac{\Delta * X\$}{\Delta * G} = \frac{1}{1 - c(1 - \tau) + H}, \qquad H = \frac{I_r L_y}{L_r}, \tag{2}$$

which epitomizes the Hicksian rendition of the General Theory: income must rise to the point where the increase in saving offsets the higher deficit minus the fall in investment crowded out by $\Delta * G$. Because the response of $I$ to $r$ would be gradual, the equilibrium position (2) could be reached only after a substantial stretch of time. On the other hand, the gradual response of the demand for money to $r$, might speed up the process, by causing some initial overshooting of $r$ [cf. Tucker (1968)].

## 2.3. *Wealth Effects*

Formulae (1) and (2) still neglect the effect of wealth ($W$) in the consumption function. As shown in Modigliani (1971), once we allow for $W$, formula (1) would have to be changed to

$$\frac{\Delta * X\$}{\Delta * G} = \frac{1}{\tau}, \tag{3}$$

that is, income would have to rise enough to make the deficit disappear; for, as long as there was a deficit, $W$ and $C$, and hence $X$, would continue to rise. Note that equation (3) had already been derived by Christ (1968) without allowing for $W$, but that was under the assumption that the deficit was entirely financed by money creation.

Similarly, one can readily establish that, allowing for wealth effects, (2) is changed to

$$\frac{\Delta * X\$}{\Delta * G} = \frac{1}{\tau + H},^{1} \tag{4}$$

i.e., income must rise enough so that the incremental budget deficit equals the displaced investment. But the attainment of this equilibrium level would require a very long time (especially since the increase in $r$ will have a negative impact on $W$). Hence a long-run equilibrium formula like (4) is already of rather questionable relevance for an analysis of short-run response. This conclusion is reinforced by the consideration that once we take into account the effect of $\Delta G$ on investment, we must also allow for acceleration effects on all durable goods – plant, equipment, housing consumers durables. These effects, being transient (if the system is stable), are almost sure to result in over-shooting and may dominate the initial response.

## 2.4. *Wage–Price Effects*

Yet even formula (4) is not the relevant one for it still ignores the effect of the rise in $G$ on wages and prices. The "n-m"'s by and large accept the view that ceteris paribus, the rate of change of money wages, and hence of prices, is larger if unemployment is lower (which is consistent both with the view that the longest-run Phillips curve is vertical and that it is not). It then follows, as pointed out,

[1] This formula ignores the effect of the interest on the debt and tax revenue therefrom, which is quantitatively small but introduces some further complications.

e.g., in Modigliani (1971) and Ando (1974), that, in the longest run (and provided the system is stable), $\Delta * X$ must approach zero. For, as long as it is positive, prices must rise faster than they would have in the absence of $\Delta * G$, causing $\Delta * P$, and hence $\Delta * r$, to be positive. This in turn, would keep reducing all interest elastic components of aggregate demand, such as investment and consumption (via $W$). Thus, in the end $\Delta * G$ must "crowd out" an equal amount of other components of demand, or

$$\frac{\Delta * X}{\Delta * G} = 0. \tag{5a}$$

On the other hand, as noted earlier, we would expect $\Delta * G$ to cause a *permanent* increase in $X\$$ – in the sense that the effect would hold in the new long-run equilibrium – because the increase in $r$, needed to produce the crowding out, produces a permanent increase in velocity. The permanent effect is given by

$$\frac{\Delta * X\$}{\Delta * G} = X\$ \quad \frac{1}{P}\frac{\Delta * P}{\Delta * G} = \frac{1}{H}, \tag{5b}$$

where $H$ is defined in (2), except that $I_r$ must now be thought of as measuring the responsiveness to $r$ of all components of (real) private demand, and not just of investment. Even this conclusion should be readily acceptable to monetarists since it was clearly stated by Friedman (1972), though in the specific context of a pure tax increase: ". . . the lowered interest rate resulting from the federal government absorbing a smaller share of annual saving will reduce velocity; the transition to the lower velocity reduces spending for a given money stock. . ." The only puzzling thing about the above passage is that the acknowledgment of a once and for all reduction in $X\$$ for a given $M$ was used to support the statement quoted earlier that "any net decrease in spending from these sources is certain to be *temporary*".[2] (Italics supplied).

But we must emphasize once more that, at least according to the parameter estimates of the MPS model, the limiting position described by (5a) and (5b) is relevant, at best, in the proverbial Keynesian long run.[3]

[2] The only way to reconcile the two passages is to suppose that Friedman is confusing the effect of the tax on expenditure with its rate of change. The rate of change of expenditure will be negative only temporarily, namely in the period of "transition to the lower velocity", but, at the end of the transition, the level will stay permanently lower.

[3] In addition, (5a) and (5b) are only approximately valid for they do not take into account all relevant effects. For instance (5b) neglects the possibility that a portion of private wealth might take the form of net money fixed assets: allowing for this possibility would add to the denominator a term consisting of the elasticity of private demand with respect to private wealth times the share of wealth represented by money fixed claims – thus reducing the permanent effect. Similarly, one should allow

### 2.5. *The Short- and Medium-Run Response*

As is apparent from the above, in our view, none of the multiplier formulae just reviewed is of much relevance for the problem on hand, which is the response in the first two or three years. However, they help to call attention to the various mechanisms that contribute to shape the short-run response of money income. They can be summarized as follows:

(i) *The direct effect of* $G$, which, being a component of $X$, must contribute at least \$1 (per dollar), in the opening quarters.

(ii) *The induced consumption effect* which results from the increase in net of tax income: all the leading hypotheses maintain, and the evidence confirms, that, in an uncertain world, the response of consumption (to be distinguished from consumer expenditure) to a change in income is quite gradual, especially if income includes profits. The permanent income hypothesis leads to a Koyck type distributed lag of indefinite length. In the MPS, relying on the life cycle hypothesis, the distributed lag extends over a finite but substantial period – the past three years. Thus, if the consumption multiplier were the only mechanism at work, we would expect the response to continue to build up for a substantial period tending according to (1), to a limiting value of about 1.5 (since $c \simeq 0.66$ and $\tau \simeq 0.5$). Note also that mechanism (i) and (ii) will be reduced by the marginal propensity to import, estimated at somewhat over 0.10 in the MPS.

(iii) *The accelerator mechanism*: the timing here is more difficult to judge on *a priori* ground, but one would expect the build-up of durable goods, including consumers' durables, to service the larger demand, to occur gradually, except in the case of inventories and possibly consumers durables. On the other hand, if the system is stable, this effect must, at some point, reverse itself.

(iv) *The price effect* which will make $\Delta * X\$$ larger than $\Delta * X$. It must be remembered, in this connection, that, in order to make our analysis conform with the St. Louis approach, we must define $\Delta * X\$$ as the change in the value of *GNP* and not the value of the change, i.e., $\Delta * (X\$) = P \cdot \Delta * (X) + X \cdot \Delta * P$. As $P$ rises, the second term can make a large contribution relative to the first. Just how fast this

*Footnote 3 continued*
for the fact that the displacement of investment by government expenditure would tend to reduce the capital–labor ratio, and hence $X$, at least as conventionally measured. Taking this effect into account would tend to make $\Delta * X/\Delta * G$ negative and to increase the price response given in (5b).

effect builds up clearly depends on the extent of slack in the economy. The evidence suggests that there are significant lags in the response of wages to unemployment, of prices to wages, and finally of wages to prices; indeed it is this kind of lag that accounts for the stagflation of 1970–1971 and of today. Accordingly the increase in $P$ should tend to occur gradually, but to become important within the span with which we are concerned, particularly if the rate of employment is high to begin with.

(v) *The wealth effect* which tends to increase consumption through the higher level of wealth resulting from a larger flow of saving. However, one should expect this effect to contribute negligibly over the run with which we are concerned.

(vi) *The Hicksian crowding out effect* which starts with the rise in interest rates resulting from the rise in *X$*, in the face of an unchanged supply of money. The beginning of this process may be related, in monetarist style, to the additional borrowing by the government to finance the incremental deficit. However, it must be remembered that the extra borrowing is matched by an equal flow of incremental saving; hence, the reason for the rise in $r$ must finally be traced to the need to induce the public to transact a larger volume of business with the same cash balance. This strain, and consequent rise in $r$, increases as the secondary effects listed above contribute to expand *X$*. The initial impact of the strains in the money market falls on the short rate which may rise fairly fast, since the available evidence suggests that the demand for money adjusts slowly to $r$; but the adjustment of the long rates may be expected to be a good deal more sluggish (since they reflect expectations of many future short rates). Finally the rise in the long rates will adversely affect private demand. The channels through which this effect occurs in the MPS are quite varied, as the monetarists prescribe. There are a dozen interest rates and capitalization rates for money fixed as well as equity streams, and every endogenous component of demand responds to at least one rate, except state and local government purchase of services, and (regretfully) inventories. However, the response takes time, though the speed varies for different components.

(vii) *The Pigou–Patinkin "outside debt" effect.* The rise in prices will also have an adverse effect on consumption insofar as money fixed public debt constitutes a significant portion of net worth – which is not the case for the U.S. In part, for this reason, this effect, which is crucial in Patinkin's analysis, is likely to contribute only to a minor extent, at least in the medium run.

On the whole, the evidence suggests that the main contractive mechanism, (vi) tends to work more slowly than the major expansive ones, (i), (ii), (iii). Hence one would expect the response to grow for at least the first few quarters; somewhat later, real output will turn down (if the system is stable) through the combined effect of the accelerator and higher interest rates, and it is hard to say a priori which would play the larger role (nor would this be independent of initial conditions); on the other hand, $\Delta * P$, and hence $\Delta * X\$$, should continue to rise after $X$ peaks through the term $X\Delta * P$, and should remain substantial even when $\Delta * X$ dwindles to zero or first turns negative (something one would hardly expect much before two to three years).

In the light of the above, one should find hardly surprising the results presented in figure 1. Figure 1a shows the response of money *GNP* ($X\$$) and of real *GNP* ($X$) and its components to a maintained change in government expenditure on goods ($GG$) implied by the MPS. Figure 1b shows the response of interest rates and prices. The data are obtained from a simulation in which $G$ was increased by 1 billion in 1958.1 ($M_1$ constant). In figure 1a, the top $\Delta$-curve represents

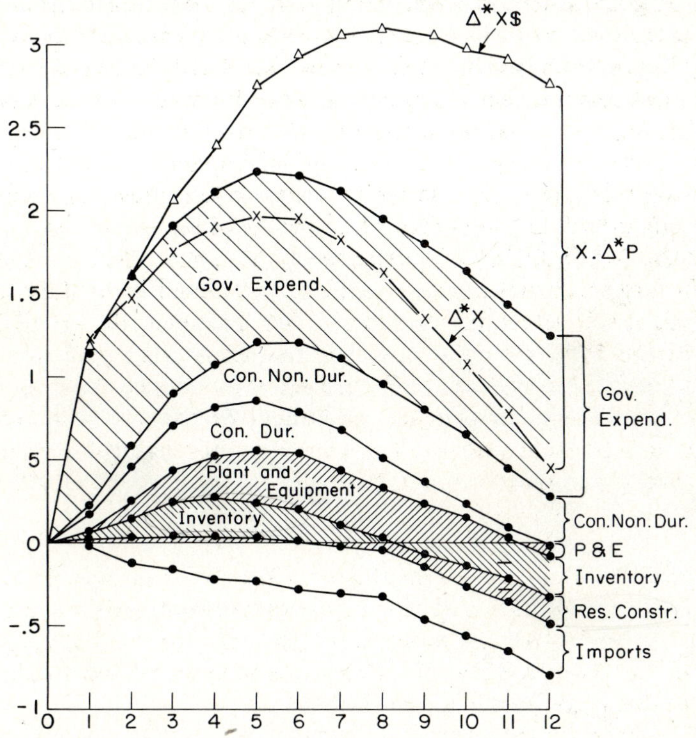


FIGURE 1a. Response of money *GNP* ($X\$$) and real *GNP* ($X$) and its components to a one billion maintained change in *GG* (government purchase of goods), based on MPS – initial conditions of 1958. 1.

$\Delta * X\$$; $\Delta * X$ is represented by the $X$-curve which is also the sum of the individual real components. Some of these components are positive and they cumulate to the upper dotted curve; some are negative and they cumulate to the bottom dotted curve. The $X$-curve is the algebraic sum of the positive and negative components and thus falls inside the upper dotted curve. Finally, the distance between the $X$-curve and the $\Delta$-curve measures the price effect.

A few points are worth noting about the chart. First, the peak response, in real terms – $X$-curve – is reached fairly early, in about 5 quarters. It is around 2, a figure similar to that reported for other models. This is larger than can be accounted for by equation (2), because of the accelerator mechanism. The role of this mechanism can be inferred also from the rise in the investment components, which are also the first to peak: inventory in quarter 4, consumers durables in 5, and equipment in 6. This suggests that the major mechanism causing the early end of the expansion is the accelerator. However, there is little doubt that the Hicksian crowding out mechanism also begins to work early contributing to the fall of investment, and is important in pushing the response down after the peak. This can be seen, e.g., from the fact that several investment components turn negative (i.e., fall below what they would have been without $\Delta * GG$) when the $X$ response is still quite positive; this happens for residential construction as early

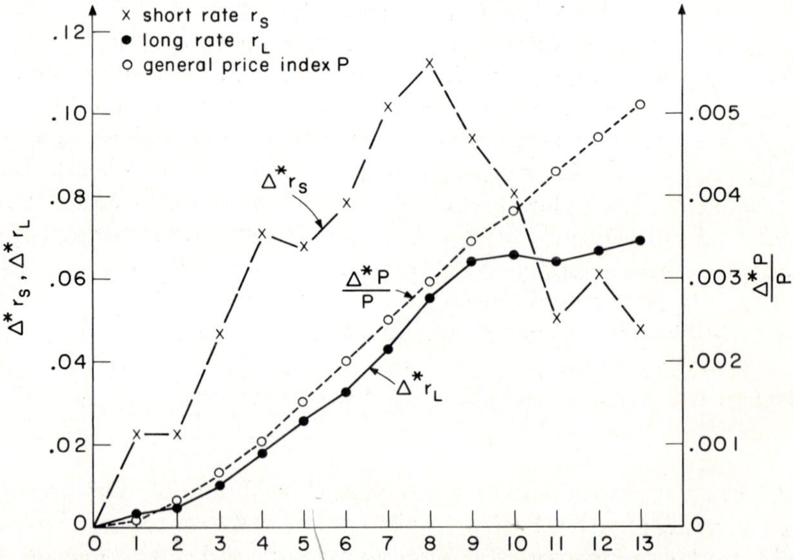


FIGURE 1b. Response of selected intensive variables to a one billion maintained change in $GG$ (government purchase of goods), based on MPS – initial conditions of 1958.1.

as quarter 7, for equipment in quarter 11 and consumers durables in 12. Finally, the price effect, $X \cdot \Delta * P$, behaves pretty much as expected: $\Delta * P$ grows slowly at first but it continues to rise well after $X$ has peaked; thus $\Delta *X\$$ reaches its peak some three quarters later than $\Delta * X$ (in quarter 8), and by the end of three years, it is still substantial, though by then $\Delta * X$ is close to zero.

It should be stressed that, especially because of the price effect, according to the MPS, both the $\Delta * X\$$ and the $\Delta * X$ path can vary substantially, depending on initial conditions. Indeed in a simulation in which the *GG* shock was applied in 1966.1, the response is found to be explosive. Nonetheless, the results reported in the chart are fairly typical of those obtained at least in the years preceding the Vietnam war.

Having thus established why it is impossible to make any sense of response patterns of the type implied by the St. Louis estimates, we must proceed to review some of the mechanisms most commonly advanced by monetarists, or their interpreters, to account for a very small and purely fleeting response even of $X\$$.

## 3. Some Monetarists Mechanisms and Their Weaknesses

### *3.1. The Role of Wealth in the Demand for Money*

Some monetarists might claim that in our reasoning we have failed to take into account the role of wealth in the demand for money and that, if we had, our conclusions would be radically different. Indeed the increase in wealth generated by the deficit, and its financing through public debt, must lead to a prompt rise in the demand for money. Since $M_1$ is constant, the result must be an increase in interest rates which will greatly speed up the crowding out effect. Indeed, Blinder and Solow, in a well-known paper (1973, p. 330), have concluded that if $Lw$ is large enough "fiscal policy does not work" and as a result of $\Delta GG$, "income falls cumulative and without limit". We propose to argue that this monetarist conclusion must be rejected for three reasons: (i) even if $W$ enters the demand for money, $\Delta * X$ must still be positive for a good while, and this holds a fortiori for $\Delta * X\$$; (ii) theory suggests that, with well-functioning capital markets as in the U.S. in the postwar period, $W$ should *not* enter the demand for money; and (iii) empirical evidence supports this theoretical conclusion. We will take up these points in turn.

(i) Clearly $r$ cannot rise unless $W$ rises; but $W$ cannot rise unless saving increases, which requires a rise in $X$! Put a little differently, if the deficit induced by $GG$ immediately displaces an equal amount of $I$, $W$ would remain constant and, therefore, $r$ would not rise and could not displace $I$. Thus we must first have a rise in $X$; then the gradual accumulation of $W$ can raise $r$ and begin to affect $I$; there is absolutely no reason why this process should work any faster than the Hicksian one; and, certainly once the rise in $X$ has caused higher prices, $\Delta * X\$$ can be counted upon to be positive for quite a while. The contrary conclusion reached by Solow and Blinder is due in our view to many shortcomings of their analysis which have been partly pointed out in Ando (1974). But, for present purposes, their critical shortcoming is that, in the model used to establish the above mentioned conclusion, they have neglected price effects, and, more seriously, they have failed to recognize that wealth includes not only the public debt but also the stock of capital. In addition, they define the multiplier quite unusually as the limiting value taken by $\Delta * (X)$ when the deficit vanishes, rather than when $\Delta * X$ ceases to change. The latter condition, in turn, requires that $\Delta * W$ should also be stationary, and not that the deficit be zero. Had they avoided these shortcomings, they would have found that, under their assumption of slack resources and given $P$, $\mathrm{d}X/\mathrm{d}G$ does have a finite value which is a generalization of (4), namely

$$\frac{\Delta * X}{\Delta * G} = \frac{1}{\tau + H + (S/C_w)(1 - c)(1 - \tau)}, \quad S = \frac{I_r L_w}{L_r} > 0. \tag{6}$$

This formula is obtained by making use of the condition that, in the limit, the rate of saving in the economy experiencing the increase in $G$ must return to the same as in the comparison economy. Note that (6) implies that the final effect of $\Delta * G$ is to permanently increase the deficit and reduce the rate of investment. The right-hand side of (6) must be smaller than that of (4) (as long as $c < 1$), so that the $L_w$ does imply a smaller multiplier; nonetheless (6) must be clearly positive.

(ii) In an appendix to Ando and Modigliani (1974), Ando and Shell have established that, with well-functioning markets, and in the presence of a short-term asset involving no risk of principal, the demand for money must depend only on the short-term rate and the volume of transactions (as well as on transaction costs), but must be independent of either wealth or $\dot{P}$. In the MPS, the money demand equation does not contain wealth because we could find no evidence that it had a significant effect; the Ando–Shell results support this specification.[4]

[4] The measures of transaction used in the MPS model – *GNP* for demand deposits and consumers' expenditure for currency – do not explicitly take into account transactions on wealth account. In the course of estimating the money sector, we did initially include one variable providing at least a partial measure for such transactions [see Modigliani, Rasche and Cooper (1970)]. This variable was, however, dropped in the final version incorporated in the model because its effect was quantitatively too small to justify the effort of endogenizing it. But we could not find evidence that the wealth transaction effect could be effectively proxied by wealth itself, a result confirmed by the Goldfeld study cited in (iii) below.

(iii) Finally the hypothesis that wealth has no effect on money demand in the U.S. has been confirmed by the exhaustive empirical study of Goldfeld (1973). It is true that Goldfeld finds some mild evidence for an effect of the rate of change of wealth (which he interprets as related to transactions in assets generated by saving). However, extrapolation tests uniformly show that the inclusion of this variable worsens the extrapolation. In any event, this effect could not significantly affect any of our quantitative conclusions, especially since it is, at best, transient.

### *3.2. The Effect of the Increase in Debt on r, via the Composition of Wealth*

Another mechanism claimed by the monetarist and not mentioned by us is the portfolio composition effect: the financing of the deficit raises the ratio of debt instruments to other components of wealth, raising $r$ and thus contributing directly to the crowding out. This argument has been examined with some care and rejected in Ando (1974), to which the reader is referred. It will suffice here to summarize his conclusions:

(i) The issue of debt cannot affect the short-term rate, which, in view of the Ando–Shell argument, depends only on $M_1$ and $X\$$.

(ii) Hence, if the extra deficit is entirely financed by short-term debt, the resulting increase in the supply of shorts and of sure assets relative to the other components of wealth, will tend to *lower* long-term rates and the required rate of return on equity. This effect, of course, contributes to promoting rather than displacing investment.

(iii) Only if the deficit were primarily financed by long-term debt, the effect of the new issue could conceivably be that of raising the required return on capital, though the effect is uncertain.

(iv) Given the existence in the U.S. of a very large short-term market and its extensive use by the government, we can conclude that even this argument is inconclusive and could not be empirically important. Indeed, in the MPS model, this composition of wealth mechanism is ignored because, much as we tried, we could not find a measurable effect.

### *3.3. Conclusions*

We must conclude that none of the monetarists' arguments reviewed provides cause for questioning the "n-m"s results reported in section 2, either qualitatively or quantitatively. The only remaining problem is: how then can we account for the St. Louis results? It is to this last topic that we now turn.

## 4. The Unreliability of the Reduced Form Approach

The St. Louis approach has been frequently criticized because of the specific choice of independent variables. We shall largely bypass this issue here because we do not regard it as the crucial one; if the method is basically unreliable, the choice of variables is irrelevant.[5] Hereafter we find it convenient to measure fiscal action, as in figure 1, by government purchases except that we now lump together expenditures on goods and services ($G$); but no great significance should be attached to this specific choice, other than that of convenience. Indeed, if one runs a "reduced form" (RF) regression using as independent variables $\Delta M_1$ and $\Delta G\$$, one obtains coefficients that look very much like those obtained with other measures of fiscal policy, such as the full employment deficit. This can be seen from the $X$-curve in figure 2a, which shows the RF coefficients of $\Delta G$ current and lagged up to seven quarters estimated over the period 1958.1–1969.4 by a third-degree Almon polynomial – a typical St. Louis specification. It is apparent that the response path, $\Delta * X\$_t$ (the cumulant of the coefficients in the graph) reaches its peak already in the second quarter, and it is quite shallow, but 1.2. It then declines steadily and is practically down to zero by the last quarter. Indeed $\Delta * X\$_8/\Delta * G\$$ amounts to only 0.38, as shown in the legend. It is also apparent that these coefficients bear little relation to those implied by the $\Delta * X\$$ path produced by the MPS simulation reported in figure 1a, which are shown in figure 2a by the $\Delta$-curve. Figure 2b shows RF coefficients of $\Delta M_1$ current and lagged. The $X$-curve gives again the $\Delta M_1$ coefficients of the RF estimated on actual data, and the $\Delta$-curve those implied by a simulation of the MPS model in which $M_1$ was changed by one billion (spread over two quarters), beginning in 1962.1.[6] Again, there is little similarity between the two curves, except that in this case, the RF estimates imply a distinctly larger and faster response.

What should one make of the striking discrepancy between the MPS response and that implied by the RF estimates? Must one conclude that the theory advanced in section 2 is all wrong, and the empirical evidence underlying it is, somehow, irrelevant? In Modigliani (1971), it was suggested that the answer should be negative and the hypothesis was advanced that the discrepancy

[5] This a somewhat different position from that set forth in Modigliani (1971); the shift reflects, in part, the result of research done in preparation for this paper, reported below.

[6] The reason for choosing a simulation with 1962 initial conditions is that for the MPS, the $\Delta*X\$/\Delta*M$ path is much more dependent on initial conditions than the $\Delta*X\$/\Delta G$ path. The pattern produced by the 1962 simulation is more typical of those obtained up to the late sixties, than that obtained in 1958, which is rather more sluggish. The reason for spreading the increase over two quarters is set out in Modigliani (1971, pp. 46–47).

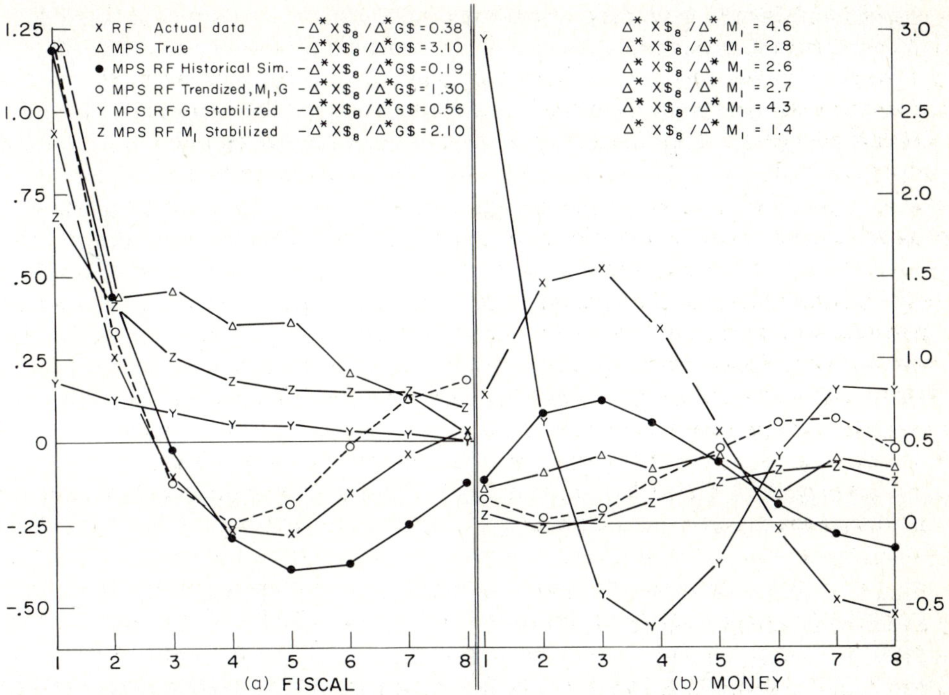


FIGURE 2. True response and reduced form estimates for the MPS model.

results from the fact that, for a system as complex as the U.S. economy, the St. Louis reduced form approach is a very unreliable method of estimating the true response path of *X$* to changes in monetary or fiscal aggregates.

### *4.1. A Test of Reliability Based on Simulation*

The above hypothesis was supported by means of a simulation experiment which was labeled, perhaps somewhat inappropriately, a Monte Carlo experiment. Since there has been a good deal of misunderstanding concerning the nature and implications of this test, especially among monetarists, it may be appropriate to review it here. Basically the experiment was designed to test how well the mechanism built inside a fairly complex "black box" having at least some vague similarity to the U.S. economy, could be estimated by applying the St. Louis RF method to the output generated by the black box. The black box chosen for this experiment was the MPS model, and the output was the time series of dollar *GNP* (*X$*), of *G$* and of demand deposits (*MD*) generated by a dynamic simulation for the period 1958.1 to 1969.4, using as inputs the historical value of *G*, and of the treasury bills rate, *RTB*, as well as of the other policy and exogenous variables. By regressing the value of $\Delta X\$$ so obtained on the current and lagged values of $\Delta MD\$$ and $\Delta G\$$, we can test whether the coefficients of a St. Louis type RF can provide a reasonably close estimate of the "true" response path of *X$* to changes in *G$* and *MD$* which is built into the black box that generated the data, namely the MPS model. The true path is, of course, known with certainty, from the structure of the MPS model and could be conveniently inferred from policy simulations such as those underlying figure 1. It was found that the response of *X$* to *G$* estimated by the RF bore no recognizable relation to the true response of the MPS model which had generated the data (though it showed some mild similarity to the estimates obtained by applying RF to the historical data).

### 4.2. *Some Replications of the Simulation Test*

Figures 2 and 3 report the results of a number of replications of the simulation experiment just described. The first, reported in figure 2, is again based on the MPS and involves only relatively minor variations: (1) to improve the comparability with the St. Louis exercises, the simulation of MPS was carried out taking $M_1$ rather than *RTB* as the historically given monetary policy variable, and (ii) in the reduced form, the monetary variable was also $M_1$ rather than demand deposits.[7]

The coefficients of the reduced form estimated from the output of this simulation, again for the period 1958.1–1969.4, are shown by the black-dot-curve, in figure 2a for government expenditure, and in figure 2b for $M_1$. This curve is labeled "historical" in the legend, because, in the simulation, all policy and exogenous variables are assigned their historical values, as in the Modigliani (1971) experiment. The true typical MPS response, of which the RF coefficients are supposed to be an estimate, is shown in each figure by Δ-curve. It is apparent from figure 2a that there is, again, little recognizable relation between the true response and the RF estimate of this response, e.g., the estimated response reaches a shallow peak in the second quarter and by the eighth quarter is close to zero, in fact even closer to zero than for the RF estimated from actual data – the *X*-curve. In the case

[7] In addition, the version of the MPS used for this paper differs slightly from that used in Modigliani (1971). For present purposes, the only significant difference is in the equation accounting for the market value of corporate shares, a component of net worth. The old equation was found to have unacceptable long-run implications and was re-estimated imposing some constraints on the coefficients. For the current equation, see MPS (1973).

of $M_1$ – figure 2b – the discrepancy between true and estimated response is less striking, though the RF clearly tends to overestimate the early response.

Layton (1972), in the course of pursuing a systematic analysis of the extent and possible sources of bias in RF estimates, replicated the simulation experiment outlined above for three other U.S. models differing widely, in terms of size, complexity, period of estimation, and model structure. These are:

(1) The model by Moroney and Mason [M–M (1971)] – an eight-equation, linear model, with parameters estimated over the period 1953.3–1965.4. It is fairly monetarist in inspiration, with all variables in current prices and the monetary variable consisting of the unborrowed monetary base. For the RF experiment, the output was obtained from a simulation of the model from 1954.1 to 1969.4, and the RF coefficients were estimated by regression for 1958.1–1969.4.
(2) The Kuh–Schmalensee (K–S) model, with 42 behavioral equations, highly non-linear and estimated over the period 1959.1–1969.4. The RF coefficients were estimated by the same method and the same period used for M–M. The money variable is unborrowed reserves.
(3) The well-known Brookings model, probably the largest in existence. The inputs for the RF estimates were obtained from various sources described in Layton, and the sample period was 1953.4–1962.4. Also, because of the nature of the available information, the dependent variable was $\Delta X$ rather than $\Delta X\$$ and the fiscal variable $\Delta G$ rather than $\Delta G\$$.

The results of these tests are summarized in figure 3, taken directly from Layton (except for labelling). Part I of each figure reports the coefficients of the fiscal variable, and part II those of the monetary variable. The true response of the model is shown by the histogram: for the M–M model which is linear, it was computed analytically, for the other two models from simulations. The total response at the end of nine quarters (the cumulant of the coefficients) or $\Delta^*X\$_9$ in our notation, is shown next to the legend. It is worth noting first the broad similarity in the fiscal multipliers implied by the three models and the MPS. Thus by the end of one year the value falls within a range of 0.5, between 2.15 and 2.65; by the end of two years the range is even narrower, between 2.5 and 2.8. On the other hand, the money multipliers cannot be readily compared because of the different monetary aggregates used for the different models.

The dashed curve in figures 3a and 3b and both curves in figure 3c, labelled "historical" in the legend, exhibit the results of the replication of Modigliani's test for each model. Specifically, they show the response as estimated by RF from the output of a simulation in which all policy and exogenous variables appearing in each model assumed their historical value. In the case of figure 3c, two historical RF estimates are reported, one based on a nine quarter lag (light solid line) and the other on 13 (heavy line).

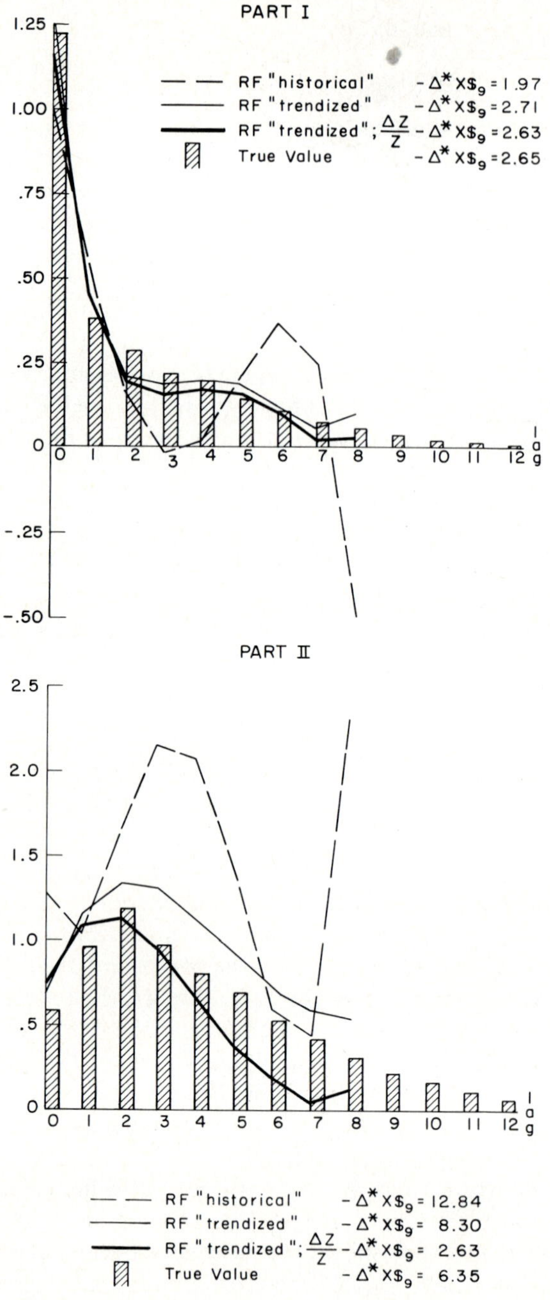


FIGURE 3a. The true and several reduced form implied fiscal (part I) and monetary (part II) multipliers of the Moroney–Mason model – nine quarters.

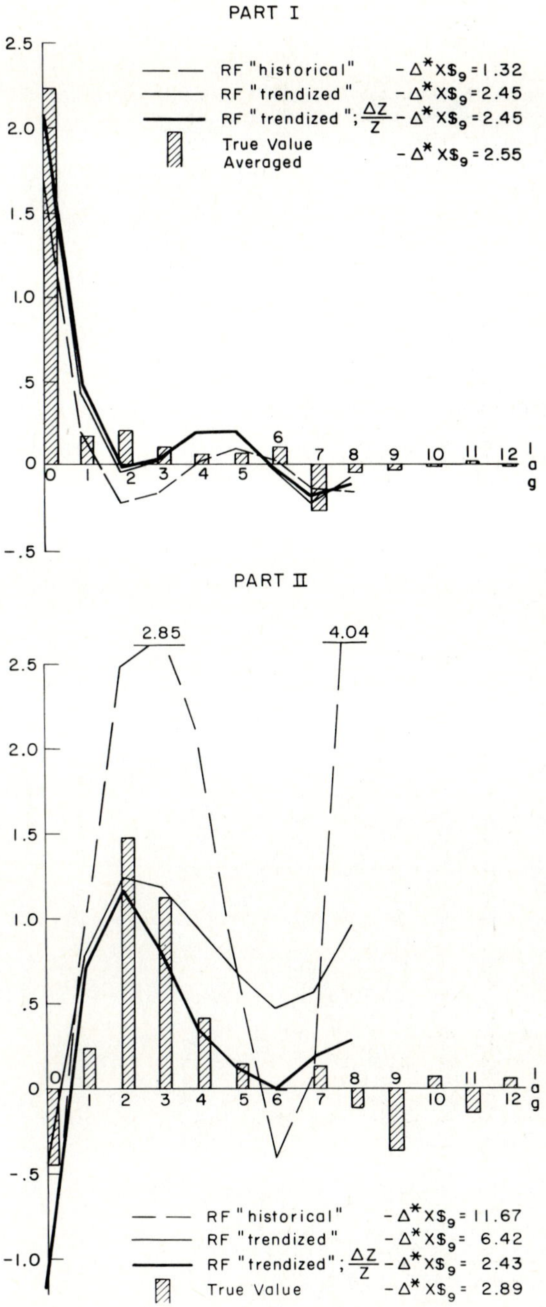


FIGURE 3b. The true and several reduced form implied fiscal (part I) and monetary (part II) multipliers of the Kuh–Schmalensee model – nine quarters.

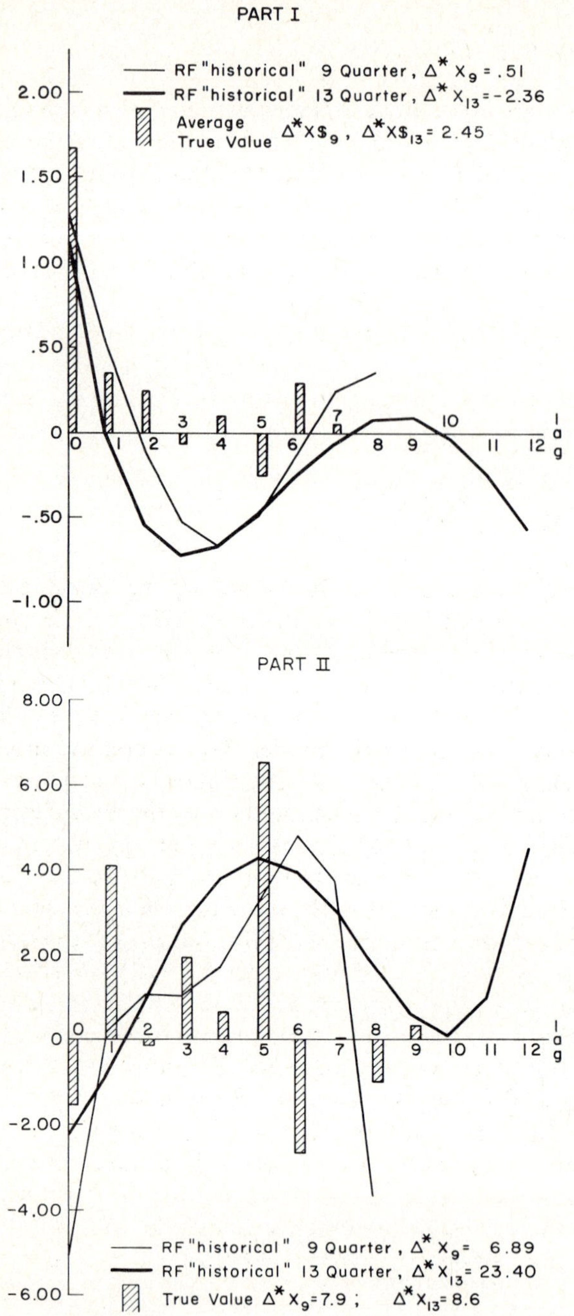


FIGURE 3c. The true and reduced form implied fiscal (part I) and monetary (part II) multipliers of the Brookings model.

It is seen that in every case the RF estimates of the fiscal response tend to underestimate substantially the true response. Thus by the end of the first year the cumulated response estimated by RF is between one half and three quarters of the true response. By the end of the second year, when as already noted, the true response scatters narrowly around $2\frac{3}{4}$, the RF estimate range all the way from nearly 2 for the M–M model, having but two exogenous variables, down to 0.5 and 0.2 for the large-scale Brookings and MPS model. In the case of the money multipliers in part II of each chart, the RF estimates are again generally rather poor; indeed in the case of the K–S model, they are outright wild. Furthermore, they overestimate substantially the true response from the very beginning (with some exceptions for the Brookings model).

### *4.3. An Objection to the Simulation Experiment*

Layton's results just reported are also relevant in answering one plausible criticism that has been levied against Modigliani's simulation experiment. The argument runs as follows.[8] Suppose the true response of the U.S. economy to the monetary and fiscal variables were that implied by the St. Louis RF. The MPS model must then be badly misspecified, in view of the wide discrepancy between these RF estimates and the response implied by the model. To be sure, the model does manage to track reasonably well the historical path of the U.S. economy over the period of the experiment, but this can be accounted for by the consideration that it was estimated over this same period and that with enough ingenuity, and use of degrees of freedom, one can always manage to reproduce a finite set of observations, no matter how false one's model. At the same time, the very fact that the model tracks closely, implies that the output of the simulation used to estimate the RF is *close to the historical path*. It then follows that the RF estimates based on this simulation *must* give rise to coefficients which are close to those of the historical RF and hence very different from the model's response. The discrepancy between the model response and the RF estimate, it is concluded, results from this mechanism and not from any inherent shortcoming of the RF method.

We have never found this argument very convincing since in a ten year dynamic simulation, the MPS model does not track that well. This is especially true of first differences which are always hard to track, especially for the MPS which was designed to account for the level of, rather than the change in, variables. Hence it is pretty far from the mark to assert that the simulation output is simply the historical path.

In any event, Layton's results provide more direct evidence counter to this

[8] The argument that follows has been advanced on several occasions in both oral and written communications, including one by Keith M. Carlson.

argument. We may note, in fact, that two of his models, the M–M and K–S, were estimated just like the MPS over a period which includes the years 1958–1969 which were used to estimate the RF coefficients of figure 3, as well as the RF based on actual data. The argument reported above would then imply that the RF estimates of M–M, K–S and MPS should be close to each other and close to those obtained from actual data. In fact, as in apparent from the charts and from the summary of the results reported earlier, one finds that the three RF are quite different from each other and, except possibly for the MPS, also quite different from the RF based on actual data. Finally the RF estimates are also uniformly very poor estimates of true response paths of each of the three models which are broadly similar to each other. We can conclude, therefore, that the "plausible" argument summarized at the beginning of this paragraph can, in fact, not provide an explanation for the fact that RF based on the models' output provides poor estimates of the models' true response.

What then could account for the poor performance of RF? Modigliani (1971, p. 72) called attention to "severe danger of bias in reduced forms" and listed two likely sources:

(i) the presence of correlation between the policy variables included in the RF regression and other policy and exogenous variables which affect *X$* but are omitted in the RF;

(ii) in the case of the $M_1$ coefficients, the likelihood that, at least at times during the period, "the variable directly controlled by the monetary authority was unborrowed, or free reserves or interest rates", $M_1$ being then an endogenous variable.

More recently, several authors, notably Goldfeld and Blinder (1972), have called attention to another source of difficulties, to wit:

(iii) the reduced form coefficients will be biased insofar as, over the period of estimation, the policy variables included in the RF have been maneuvered for the purpose of economic stabilization.

In the rest of this section, we endeavor to provide evidence that each of these sources of bias does, in fact, play an important role in distorting the RF estimates over the period of observation. In addition, evidence will be adduced that the RF estimates are plagued not only by bias but also by marked unreliability.

### 4.4. *The Effect of Correlation Between the Included Independent Variables and Omitted Exogenous Variables*

Layton (1972) designed and carried out a rather ingenious test to ascertain the role of the correlation between the included policy variables and the omitted exogenous variables, in biasing the RF estimates. It consisted in *eliminating* the correlation by *replacing*, in the stimulation of the models, the historical value of the omitted exogenous variables either by a constant equal to the mean value of the variable (for intensive type variables), or by a time trend fitted to the data (for the extensive variables). It is clear that with this transformation, the first difference of every exogenous variable is basically a constant and hence cannot be correlated with the policy variables, which were kept on their historical path. Unfortunately, the available budget forced Layton to limit the experiment to the two smaller models – the M–M having but two exogenous variables and the K–S having 33.

The RF coefficients estimated on the output of the simulation just described are shown by the light solid curve in figures 3a and 3b. The result, at least for the fiscal variable, is rather dramatic; for both models, the downward bias in the cumulated response disappears and the shape of the RF coefficients fit very closely the true response.

For the monetary variables on the other hand, the fit, while greatly improved, is still not very close and still tends to overestimate the response, especially in the case of K–S. Layton conjectured that this could be due, in part, to the fact that the method described above might not have totally eliminated the correlation. This is because his trends were exponential, and hence the arithmetic increments would still exhibit a positive time trend which would be present also in the included policy variables. To eliminate this last source of correlation, he proceeded to re-estimate the RF coefficients with all variables expressed as percentage changes, $\Delta Z/Z$. The resulting coefficients (multiplied by the mean values of the variable to which they refer to make them comparable with the other estimates), are shown by the heavy solid curve in figures 3a and 3b. For the fiscal variables, there is hardly any change from the previous results; for the monetary variable there is a fair improvement for K–S but less for M–M, as the overestimation is replaced by underestimation.

These results suggest that, at least for the fiscal variable, the correlation with the excluded exogenous variables is a major and, perhaps *the* major source of distortion in the RF coefficients. However, before accepting this conclusion, we must review the results of a replication of Layton's experiment, conducted with MPS. In this experiment, the correlation between included and excluded variables, was eliminated not by changing the *exogenous* variables, à la Layton, but by replacing the historical values of the *policy variables* by exponential time trends fitted to the actual values, plus a randomly drawn additive component. This component was designed to have a substantial serial correlation (0.8), and a variance equal to some chosen multiple, $m$, of the variance of the residuals around trend. Clearly these concocted policy variables could not be *systematically* correlated with the excluded exogenous variables which were kept on their historical paths. The serial correlation and a sufficiently large variance were designed to insure enough lasting variation in the policy variables to affect significantly aggregate output.

In figure 2, the *o*-curve shows the RF estimates for the simulation in which $m$ was assigned a rather large value, namely 9. Somewhat to our surprise, these estimates are seen to bear again very little resemblance to the true structure, and look a lot more like those of the RF based on actual data, even though the simulated path is now quite a bit different from the actual one. Not less surprising, in another simulation with $m = 4$ (and hence a weaker signal), the pattern of the fiscal coefficients (not shown in figure 2) turns out to have the same general J-shape, but the underestimation is distinctly smaller, the total response after nine quarters amounting to 2.7. On the other hand, the $M$ coefficients are quite non-sensical, starting negative and cumulating to $-0.68$! The implications of these results, which at first sight seem inconsistent with Layton's, will be taken up in section 4.7 below.

### *4.5. The Effect of the Monetary Policy Variable Being Different from $M_1$*

To test the relevance of this source of bias suggested by Modigliani (1971) a simulation was run in which the fiscal variables had the same value as in the experiment last described, but *RTB* was replaced by its trend, $M_1$ being then computed from the model. The result was that the $M_1$ coefficients assumed a much more plausible shape, and the total 9 quarter response rose from $-0.68$ to 2.48! Clearly, this can be an important source of RF bias, even if the choice of interest rates as the control variable occurs only some of the time.

### *4.6. The Effect of the Policy Variables Being Actively Used for Stabilization*

As shown by Goldfeld and Blinder one would expect that, if a policy variable is actively used to stabilize $X$, then RF coefficients will underestimate the true response to that variable and, likely, overestimate the response to other policy variables included in RF. To test the importance of this effect in the simulation last described, the fiscal variable $G$ consisting of trend plus random error was replaced by a different series designed to stabilize unemployment ($U$); this series was arrived at by a combination of informal simple proportional and derivative stabilization rules and some judgment. The chosen $G$ maintained unemployment between 3.5 and 4.5%, whereas in the absence of stabilization the fluctuation over the simulation period had been between 3 and 7%. The RF estimates based on this simulation are shown in figure 2 by the $Y$-curve. As expected, the coefficients of the fiscal variable heavily underestimate the true response, those of $M_1$ substantially overestimate it, and neither bear resemblance to the true response.

Finally, the $Z$-curve in figure 2 shows the results of a simulation in which the fiscal variable is trend plus random error with $m = 9$ (as in the first experiment described), while $M_1$ was used to stabilize $U$; because stabilization by $M_1$ alone is somewhat harder to accomplish, we only succeeded in keeping $U$ between 3.5 and 5.5%. The response to $M$ now has a strange shape: it is appreciably lower than the $o$-curve based on a comparable simulation in which neither $M$ nor $G$ were used to stabilize $U$, and as expected, generally underestimates the true response. The clear conclusion is that the Goldfeld–Blinder effect could be quite important.

### *4.7. Overall Unreliability of RF as a Short-Cut to Estimating Structure*

In summary, all the experiments point to the unavoidable conclusion that the RF is a very unreliable method for estimating structure. A glance at figure 2 is sufficient to establish that RF can yield widely different estimates of the structure of the model generating the data. As it turns out, in the experiments we have performed, none of the RF estimates comes even close to reproducing the response of *X$* to $G$ built into the MPS model, and all of them underestimate substantially the response at least beyond the second quarter. This underestimation, however, is happenchance and we have no doubt that, by conducting a few more simulations, we could come up with some RF estimates looking similar to the structure or even overestimating the true response.

The reason why Layton was able to come pretty close to the true structure by merely eliminating the correlation between included and excluded variables, is to be found primarily in the nature of his technique and, to a minor extent, in the fact, that the response he was trying to reproduce came from models having much simpler structure than MPS – let alone the U.S. economy! Having turned the rate of change of the exogenous variables into a constant in his simulation, the system was exclusively driven by the two included policy variables. Since in addition M–M is linear, Layton's method was bound to reproduce very nearly its structure. Failure to reproduce it exactly would only come from forcing the response to be described by a low-order polynomial of 9 terms. This conclusion is confirmed by the fact that his RF correlation ($R^2$) was 0.99. For the non-linear K–S model, another possible source of distortion is that the response varies with initial conditions. This factor was apparently not important as $R^2$ was again 0.99. For the MPS experiment, on the other hand *X$* was buffetted around by the exogenous variables kept on their historical path. Accordingly, $R^2$ is almost universally between 0.45 and 0.65, a range quite comparable to that obtained with historical data. (For our historical RF, $R^2$ is 0.57.) The unreliability is hardly surprising when so much of the movement in *X$* comes from excluded variables.

We conclude that the RF is both a severely biased and quite unreliable method of estimating the response of a complex economy to fiscal and monetary action. This is unfortunate because it really looked like a brilliant short-cut. As it turns out, it has only served to mislead students of macro economics, and to waste efforts in rationalizing its numerical results.

We can only conclude in the same vein in which we concluded our exchange with Friedman and Meiselman many years ago – there are no viable alternatives to the painstaking task of looking inside the black box. When this is done, one cannot fail to conclude that the effects of macro fiscal actions are certain to be long-lasting and likely to be substantial.

## Bibliography

Ando, A., 1974, Some aspects of stabilization policies, the monetarist controversy and the MPS model, International Economic Review 15, pp. 541–571.

Ando, A. and F. Modigliani, 1974, Some reflection on describing structures of financial sectors, With an appendix by Ando and Shell, in: The Brookings model: Perspective and recent developments (North-Holland, Amsterdam).

Blinder, S. and R. M. Solow, 1973, Does fiscal policy matter? Journal of Public Economics 2, pp. 319–337.

Christ, C., 1968, A simple macroeconomic model with a government budget restraint, Journal of Political Economy 76, pp. 53–67.

Friedman, M., 1972, Comments on the critics, Journal of Political Economy 80, pp. 906–950.

Goldfeld, S. M., 1973, The demand for money revisited, Brookings Papers on Economic Activity 3, pp. 577–637.

Goldfeld, S. M. and A. S. Blinder, 1972, Some implications of endogenous stabilization policy, Brookings Papers on Economic Activity 3, pp. 585–640.

Layton, D. H., 1972, An analysis of the bias in the reduced form technique of estimating structural properties of economic systems, Master Thesis (M.I.T., Cambridge, Mass.).

Modigliani, F., 1971, Monetary policy and consumption, in: Consumer spending and monetary policy: The linkages (Federal Reserve Bank, Boston, Mass.).

Modigliani, F., R. Rasche and J. P. Cooper, 1970, Central bank policy, the money supply, and the short-term rate of interest, Journal of Money, Credit and Banking 2, pp. 166-218.

MPS, 1973, Quarterly econometric model equations (obtainable from: EFA, University of Pennsylvania, Philadelphia, Penn.).

Stein, J. L., 1976, Inside the monetarist black box, Chapter 3 of this volume.

Tucker, D., 1968, Credit rationing, interest rate lags, and monetary policy speed, Quarterly Journal of Economics 82, pp. 54–84.

## 1. COMMENTS ON MODIGLIANI AND ANDO

Anna J. SCHWARTZ

The Modigliani–Ando joint paper takes as its point of departure a paper by Ando (1974), so I shall comment first on the latter.

Ando's paper presents a stripped down version of the MPS model, on the basis of which he discusses fiscal and monetary policies in the model in relation to what he regards as the views of monetarists. I shall return to his discussion at a later point. Here I would like to note that there are research differences between monetarists and non-monetarists exclusive of the issue that is the occasion for today's conference. Let me start by observing that the model is not designed to answer the questions that we ask, and it does not include the explanatory variables that we deem important. I think it would be useful if I reviewed the analytical framework that Milton has developed and say something about our empirical work to implement it.

We are interested in the effects on the demand for money and nominal income of changes in the growth of money. All other macro economic shocks are excluded. We trace the cyclical process of adjustment towards a new steady state equilibrium. The key variables we study are aggregate nominal income, its division between output and prices, and interest rates. Our horizon for the short run is not one quarter or one year but the duration of a reference cycle; for the long run, our horizon is several cycles.

We start with a stable demand function for money and a variable nominal quantity of money. We investigate the way in which changes in the nominal quantity of money inpinge on the relatively stable demand function to alter nominal income, prices, interest rates, and output.

For a hypothetical simple quantity theory world in which velocity is a numerical constant, prices are completely flexible, and reactions are instantaneous, the analysis of the interaction of supply and demand is trivial. Price mirrors instantly and perfectly the changes in the quantity of money. Output and the real yield on capital are unaffected, determined by other variables. Yet even in this hypothetical case, the effects of changes in the quantity of money on nominal interest rates depend on anticipated rates of price change and cannot be described without specifying how anticipations are formed.

Alter this hypothetical case in almost any respect and the analysis becomes far from trivial. Make velocity a function of nominal interest rates and let interest rates be a function of anticipated rates of price change, and the theoretical analysis becomes extremely complex. Introduce lags in reaction, and output and real interest rates enter into the reaction process.

In principle, all of the variables are simultaneously determined and the effect of a monetary change on any one, say, nominal income is linked to the way it affects the others, say, prices, output and interest rates. Empirically, we separate the effect of monetary change on nominal income into the component effects on prices and output, and we treat interest rate changes as themselves traceable to earlier monetary change.

We find that the quantity of money is by far the most important variable linked to nominal income. Yields on nominal and real assets exert a significant but much smaller influence, which can itself largely be traced back to earlier monetary changes, so that nominal income can be regarded as largely though by no means exclusively a function of the current and past history of nominal money. There is a pattern of initial overshoot and a subsequent reaction in the coefficients of current and lagged money. We allow for transient effects when there is a movement from one rate of monetary growth to another rate of monetary growth. This involves a once-for-all shift to bring real money balances to the new level appropriate to the new rate of price change associated with the new rate of monetary growth.

The same variables that we have isolated as determining the growth rate of nominal income must of course be linked to the growth rates of prices and output separately, given that the growth rate nominal income is their sum. The question is whether their relation with one or the other component of nominal income is closer than with nominal income itself. If it is, that would suggest that the relation with nominal income is derivative rather than primary. If it is not, that might be either because the primary relation is with nominal income – as the quantity theory with a unitary real income elasticity implies – or because the combination of quasi-independent relations with prices and output into a relation with nominal income produces a cancellation of statistical errors. Our results as a whole are in accordance with the theoretical expectation that nominal income will be more closely related to money than are prices and output separately.

Turning to the rate of growth of output, we regard it as related first to real factors, which tend to change only slowly and determine the secular trend, not cyclical or transitory movements, and second to deviations of nominal income from its anticipated path, which produce deviations of real growth from the path determined by real factors. We neglect the real factors on the ground that wartime apart, they change slowly.

We derive a relation between the discrepancy between actual and anticipated output growth and first unanticipated change in nominal income and second a stock adjustment term for the deviation of the level of real output from its equilibrium level. For unanticipated change in nominal income, we substitute unanticipated monetary growth. We interpret the equilibrium level of output as corresponding to long-run potential output, and use the ratio of actual to potential output as a proxy for the deviation of the level of real output from its equilibrium level.

We then compare various hypotheses:

(a) neglecting vs. including the effect on the rate of change of output of the difference between actual and potential output;
(b) supposing that economic actors treat both anticipated output and anticipated monetary growth as constants;
(c) supposing there are unchanging anticipations for output and adaptive expectations for money;
(d) supposing there are adaptive expectations for both output and money.

We also derive the change in real output as a function of current and past rates of change of monetary growth alone by substituting past monetary growth in the equation for adaptive expectations for both output and money.

We have claculated the parameter values for the United States for all non-war years from such an equation for both nominal income and real output and the implied change in prices. An initially unanticipated rise in monetary growth by one percentage point, maintained at the new level, produces a rise of about $1\frac{1}{2}$ percentage points in the growth rate nominal income in the initial cyclical phase, of which about one half a percentage point is offset in the succeeding four phases. For output, an initially unanticipated rise in monetary growth of one percentage point produces a rise of about four-fifths a percentage point in the initial phase, with subsequent negative values untimately cancelling the initial effect. For the rate of change of prices, the initial effect is about three-fifths of a percentage point, with positive values in phases 2–4 ultimately adding to a sum slightly lower than the percentage point change in nominal income.

Our studies of interest rate changes distinguish three different effects of monetary growth on interest rates, a negative liquidity effect, a positive income effect, and a positive price anticipations effect.

I have said enough, I believe, to indicate the thrust of our research effort. The MPS model is irrelevant. Anyone with an interest in monetary effects would find the model unsatisfactory. Let me cite some examples.

(1) In the model, the consumption function is a flow function only. Yet excess money balances are spent almost exclusively on the purchase of other assets and not on flow consumption. Consumer durable and semi-durable goods are substitutes for money in a household's allocation of wealth. The model does not allow for the direct effects on consumer durable and semi-durable purchases of an increase in the real money stock. Hence the model understates the effect on aggregate expenditure of the increase in real consumer expenditures for a given level of real income and the interest rate owing to an increase in real money balances.

In the Procrustean bed of the model, as Ando (1974, p. 557) writes: "The only way income and output can be increased . . . is through the presence of net worth in the consumption function which keeps rising so long as there are government deficits and/or by a much more indirect channel, in which the supply of money is increased by the increased deficits which reduces the interest rate through the demand for money, and this in turn increases investment through the presence of the interest rate in the investment function." If monetary effects are defined in such a way as to make them indirect, it is hardly surprising that the model will yield weak monetary effects.

(2) In the model, the price level of output given the level of money wage is determined by a mark-up on the minimized average cost. This is not a specification that falls within a monetarist framework. To allocate changes in nominal income between changes in prices and changes in output, the crucial determinant of price change is price anticipations. In an economy in which the rate of change in the general level of prices has been highly stable, anticipations about that rate might be expected to be held with considerable confidence and much new evidence required before participants in the economy came to interpret changes in the nominal demands for their products and services as reflecting changes in the rate of inflation rather than in relative demand. Conversely, in an economy which has experienced frequent and substantial changes in the rate of inflation, participants will readily alter their inflationary expectations. We would expect a change in the rate of monetary growth to be reflected to a greater initial extent in a change in the rate of output growth in the first economy than in the second and a longer period to elapse before the change was fully reflected in prices. Expected variability of prices may be another variable with a significant effect on the fraction of nominal income change absorbed by price rather than output.

Incidentally, while the model includes an equation for the generation of expected rate of change of prices – which enters the equation for the relation between real and nominal short-term interest rates – in a monetarist framework the expected rate of change of prices is misspecified. The equation is not "rational" in the sense that it does not involve the full utilization of the data available to market participants in forming their price expectations. An optimal prediction of inflation is based on information not just on past rates of inflation alone but also on past rates of change in money. On the same grounds, the term structure equation is also misspecified. The rational expectations hypothesis of inflation states that each one period rate of interest is the sum of weighted sums of past realized (a) short-term rates of interest, (b) rates of inflation, and (c) rates of change in money. The autoregressive assumption underlying the model's term structure equation is that (c) can be regarded as zero. Models which omit this variable implicitly assume that information on monetary growth rates is too costly for investors to collect.

Let me now comment on some of Ando's conclusions. He starts out by asserting that "an increase in government deficit without a corresponding increase in the money supply" (p. 555) will be expansionary because "an increase in government deficits is always accompanied by increased income and output through the standard multiplier effects, other things equal" (footnote 11, p. 556). Later on in the paper, he offers a scenario in which complete "crowding out" occurs, but instead of taking 4 quarters, as in the St. Louis model, the effect takes 40 quarters. As Ando says, the timing depends not on theory but on the detailed dynamic characteristics of the system (p. 556), so that monetarists may well conclude that it is the idiosyncracy of the model rather than the real world that is reflected in the timing of the "crowding out".

For example, it is not clear to a monetarist, as it is to Ando, that once prices rise, real money balances will continue to increase consumption. He does not separate out the real money balances effect, combining it with real government debt. In a monetarist framework, negative consumption effects would occur as long as prices are rising with the money stock held constant, and would offset any expansionary effects attributable to the deficit. The accelerator mechanism would be reversed. Figure 1b in the Modigliani–Ando paper shows prices rising from the first quarter. Neglect of the offset on nominal income growth of the real money balance effect may be one factor contributing to the 40-quarter result.

Complete "crowding out" effects occur in the model by suspending the expected rate of change of prices, for then the rise in the short-term market rate also increases the real short rate which in turn must increase the capitalization rate with impacts on investment and the market value of real wealth. However, once the expected rate of change of prices is permitted to increase in the model, there is no guarantee that the real short rate will rise. In a monetarist framework, with the expected rate of change of prices including weighted sums of past realized rates of change of money, with money supply kept constant in the base and shocked paths, the expected rate of change of prices would also be stable, assuming the weight of current monetary growth has a significant impact. Here is one respect in which the scenario for a monetarist would differ from that of a priest of the model.

To a monetarist, Ando's suggestion that a hyper-inflationary situation might occur in response to a fiscal stimulus when the supply of money is kept constant flies in the face of evidence to the contrary over the centuries. Perhaps prices spurted in 1950 on the outbreak of the Korean War before monetary growth accelerated, but it is difficult to identify any comparable experience, much less a condition of hyperinflation, without a monetary stimulus.

Ando pursues the combination of fiscal stimulus and monetary contraction, which he analyzes as producing even higher short-term market rates than otherwise, with a possible policy goal of high enough expected rates of changes of prices to counteract the movement in the short-term market rate, so that the capitalization rate would simultaneously decline. This scenario in a monetarist's eyes neglects the income and price anticipations effects on interest rates and concentrates only on the short-term liquidity effect. Monetary contraction would lead expected rates of change of prices to decline and short-term market rates to reflect both reduced income and price anticipations effects.

To a monetarist, the case that Ando poses in footnote 28 (1974, p. 567), contrary to his conclusion, is no problem for monetary policy. If the expected rate of change of prices is negative and its absolute value is greater than the capitalization rate required to bring about full employment, so that the market rate of interest would be a negative rate, monetary growth *can* change all that. Sustained acceleration of the monetary growth rate through the price expectations equation, properly specified, will change the expected rate of prices from a negative to a positive figure. History has recorded many such shifts.

The model thus does not accommodate monetary effects that are crucial in the real world. Until the priests of the model respond to this challenge, there can be no common ground between them and monetarists.

The Modigliani–Ando paper compares reduced form regression estimates with those implied by simulations of the MPS model and of three other U.S. models. The output of the simulations was used to estimate by the reduced form approach the response of nominal income (real income in one model) to a change in a monetary variable and government expenditures. The fiscal response tended to be underestimated, the monetary response overestimated by the reduced form, and the individual coefficients tended to be unrelated to the response of the structural models. The authors concluded that three sources of bias distort the reduced form estimates over the period of observation and in addition the estimates are unreliable for computing structure.

The underlying assumption of this exercise is that the structural models provide some kind of standard against which to measure reduced forms. Yet the very same shortcomings alleged for reduced forms may also inhere in structural models. Reduced forms are said to be subject to bias because of the presence of association between the policy variables included and other omitted exogenous variables. This assumes that because a model has 8 or 42 or 182 equations there are no "omitted exogenous variables". If $M_1$ is the monetary variable in a reduced form, the estimates are said to be biased because in the structural model the variable is endogenous. To a monetarist, that is not a useful way of dealing with the scientific problem of income determination. For this purpose, the nominal quantity of money can be treated as an exogenous variable, the determinants of which are largely independent of such an endogenous variable as nominal income. This does not mean that the nominal quantity of money is not an endogenous variable from a different point of view. The object is to analyze recursive systems: variables treated as exogenous for one sector should be determined in another sector by variables other than those regarded as endogenous in the first sector. The final source of bias alleged for reduced forms is that if a policy variable is actively used to stabilize income, then reduced forms will underestimate the true response to that variable and overestimate the response to other policy variables included. The assumption here is that fiscal policy was successfully used and hence can explain the limited response of the fiscal variable. What evidence is there for such an assumption?

The reported simulations prove nothing. As the authors themselves state, "by conducting a few more simulations, we could come up with some RF estimates looking similar to the structure or overestimating the true response to almost any desired extent". The point is that even if the reduced form estimates can give a misleading estimate of the structure of the models, that does not tell anyone which estimate is closer to a true picture of the world.

## Bibliography

Ando, A., 1974, Some aspects of stabilization policies, the monetarist controversy, and the MPS model, International Economic Review 15, pp. 541–571.

## 2. COMMENTS ON MODIGLIANI AND ANDO

L. R. KLEIN

It is as a friendly critic, trying to make constructive comment, that I approach the discussion of this paper. The arguments against the use of reduced forms without having derived them from an explicitly estimated structure fits in well with my own point of view about model building. The reduced form approach often looks extremely good on the basis of "fit" to sample data, but often performs poorly in extrapolation and application to new situations. Insofar as monetarism is based on a reduced form approach, it cannot be accepted as having been established in a way that inspires much confidence about its applications.

What has been proved in the Ando–Modigliani paper? It is not that they are clearly right and monetarists correspondingly wrong. They have shown that the St. Louis type results could have been generated from a universe different from that assumed by the monetarists. I do not mean necessarily that reduced form equations with the same coefficients as those found in the St. Louis model were estimated from data generated by an MPS universe, but that relative magnitudes of effects of fiscal and monetary policies similar to those estimated by the St. Louis model, and indeed by monetarists generally, were found in the reduced forms fit to data from an MPS universe. If the world were constructed along lines portrayed by the MPS model, St. Louis conclusions could have been innocently obtained by one who did not bother to estimate the structure. This is the strongest statement that can be made. It is an important one, but it should not be concluded that the St. Louis calculations have been proved wrong in some definitive sense.

It is not surprising that the authors chose to work out the details of their case through the dynamics of the MPS model. It should be stressed, however, that their model has a characteristic that is somewhat different from most non-monetarist models. We can all agree that the usual fiscal multiplier generally rises to a maximum value in the neighborhood of two or three years and then falls, as long as the calculation is made in real terms. Most of the non-monetarist models in the Seminar on Comparison of Econometric Models exhibit this kind of multiplier path, although they may vary a bit as to timing of the peak and amplitude of the fall [see Fromm and Klein (1973)]. They are all sensitive to the degree of monetary accomodation that accompanies the fiscal change. The MPS model parts company, however, with the other non-monetarist models when it comes to calculation of this same fiscal multiplier in nominal terms. In that case, the MPS multiplier also turns down, after a stimulus has achieved its peak impact, but many other models generate price inflation that keeps the nominal multiplier on an expansion path.

This point is especially important in the neighborhood of full employment. Events of recent years have demonstrated clearly that practically all economists, with or without models, underestimated the degree of inflation in the neighborhood of full employment. If we do not know what happens to the price level in this situation we do not have unique estimates of the nominal fiscal multiplier.

Small models in general, and the St. Louis model in particular, have performed poorly in the short run – certainly as short as the dynamic multiplier build-up period being considered here; therefore their multiplier responses can be rejected on the basis of predictive testing alone.

With regard to specific issues in the paper, let me point out that non-monetarists should not agree that induced (non-exogenous) actions of the treasury have no significant causal effects on real money income. I believe that the built-in stabilizers are of enormous importance, quietly doing their work and keeping fluctuations within bounds. They can be just as important as the exogenous effects studied in the paper at hand. Without these effects or with parametric changes in them, the responses would be quite different.

The authors assert that the specific choice of independent variables is not important. They even say that "if the method is basically unreliable, the choice of variables is irrelevant". It is hard to agree with their view. We cannot be sure about the degree of reliability until we have made a careful study with much attention paid to all details, including the choice of variables. In comparing the test results from other models besides the MPS model, the authors refer to the now-dormant Brookings model as the "largest in existence". It is, in fact, rather modest in size compared with new Wharton quarterly and annual models, to name only some of the larger ones.

Finally, I might add that it would seem to be useful to orthogonalize exogenous variables used in experimental calculations. In this way, it becomes easier to assess separate causal influences.

## Bibliography

Fromm, G. and L. R. Klein, 1973, A comparison of eleven econometric models of the United States, American Economic Review LXIII, May, pp. 385–393.

## 3. COMMENTS ON MODIGLIANI AND ANDO

Robert J. GORDON

### 1. Introduction

My most striking impression of the monetarist/non-monetarist debate is a paradoxical convergence of views on a common analytical language describing the determination of income and prices, together with a continuing divergence of policy recommendations in particular cyclical episodes. The first part of this comment explores the nature and causes of the paradox, while the second deals more directly with the empirical evidence in the Modigliani–Ando (M–A) paper – if one accepts their argument that the St. Louis reduced form estimates of the influence of fiscal changes on nominal spending are biased downward, whence emanates the bias? An effective fiscal policy which stabilizes nominal spending by offsetting exogenous shocks must, as an econometric truism, bias toward zero the coefficients on fiscal policy in an equation which regresses changes in nominal spending on, among other things, changes in fiscal policy. But one wonders, in which post-war episodes was fiscal policy so effective?

An initial issue is purely semantic but nevertheless symbolizes the aggressive stance of the monetarists and the defensive stance of their opponents during the past decade: what label is most appropriate for the opponents? The essential problem is an assymetry in the claims of the two groups. Since monetarists have appeared to claim that only money matters, while their opponents have always [at least since Modigliani (1944)] treated *both* monetary and fiscal changes as basic determinants of changes in income, "fiscalist" is an entirely inaccurate label for the opponents. Similarly, the labels "Keynesian" or "neo-Keynesian" connote wage-rigidity and are inappropriate because no serious "monetarist opponent" assumes that wages are fixed, at least in analyses where that assumption matters.[1]

[1] Tobin and his colleague Brainard were attacked by Friedman (1970, p. 21) for their use in several papers of the assumption that prices are rigid. I support Tobin's defense (1972b, p. 80) of the papers criticized and offer both Tobin's AEA Presidential Address (1972a), and a description by deMenil–Enzler (1972) of the wage–price subsector of the large-scale econometric model with which Modigliani

The label "eclectics" is most accurate but also most insulting in a world in which eclectics are often considered soft-headed. So perhaps Modigliani's "non-monetarist" label is least offensive, although it still carries the completely inaccurate connotation (especially for Modigliani) that money does not matter.

## 2. The Paradox of Convergence Without Agreement

### *2.1. Evidence of Convergence*

For years the non-monetarists believed that they were opposing a position which was at least comprehensible within their own theoretical approach; in their classroom teaching based on Hicks' *IS–LM* framework they treated as a special case the absence of fiscal effects on spending when the demand for money is interest-inelastic, and they regarded Friedman's de-emphasis on the interest rate in his early empirical study of the demand for money as the empirical basis for a position which they regarded as extreme.[2] Later Friedman, in a 1966 essay which initially attracted little attention, confused his critics by adopting their *IS–LM* paradigm while simultaneously claiming that "no 'fundamental issues' in either monetary theory or monetary policy" depend on whether the interest elasticity is zero or a negative number smaller than infinity. Since in the *IS–LM* model with flexible prices, fiscal policy leads to a shift in the *LM* curve, the *LM* slope is irrelevant – in more modern terms, Friedman correctly denied the relevance of the *LM* slope for the size of the *real* "crowding out effect". But he never denied the relevance of the *LM* slope for the size of the nominal crowding out effect and explicitly stated that "fiscal policy could alter interest rates and, through them the composition and level of income, and these in turn might affect velocity and so aggregate nominal expenditures" (1966, p. 153). Analytical convergence

*Footnote 1 continued*
has been associated for the last decade, as examples of the theoretical and empirical concern of non-monetarist authors with the determinants of wage and price changes. Below I criticize monetarists for their lack of concern with the specific nature of the short-run price-adjustment process.

[2] Although the empirical paper (1959) never explicitly states that the interest elasticity is zero, it employs a flawed two-stage statistical procedure which simultaneously indicates an a priori presumption that the role of the interest rate is secondary and yields an estimated interest response which, as Laidler (1970) has pointed out, may be statistically biased toward zero. (In place of the usual procedure of multiple regression, Friedman first runs a univariate regression of real per-capita balances on real per-capita income followed by an examination of the correlation between the residual of the initial univariate equation and the interest rate, leading to a downward bias of the interest response if the partial correlation of the interest rate and real per-capita income is positive.)

was complete, and disagreement become entirely semantic, revolving around Friedman's implicit judgment that the effects of fiscal policy on nominal income, which he admitted depend on the *LM* slope, do not consititute a "fundamental issue" in monetary theory.

Although analytical convergence was complete by 1966, the distinction between real and nominal crowding out was not widely understood. As late as 1972 Tobin described as a "characteristic monetarist proposition" the statement that "A shift of the *IS* locus . . . cannot alter nominal income" (1972, p. 78), thus ignoring Friedman's 1966 admission that such a shift *can* alter nominal income. In his rely to Tobin, Friedman repeated his 1966 statement, this time in reference to an increase in tax rates: ". . . the lowered interest rate resulting from the federal government's absorbing a smaller share of annual savings will reduce velocity; the transition to the lower velocity reduces spending for a given money stock . . ." (1972, p. 140).[3]

Not only have the main protagonists converged in their willingness to use the *IS–LM* paradigm in discussions of the determinants of nominal income, they have both selected the expectational Phillips curve approach as the most fruitful candidate for the "missing equation" necessary to determine the division of changes in nominal income between changes in output and prices.[4] Here most of the "movement" of professional opinion has occurred in the non-monetarist camp as the acceleration of inflation in the late 1960's and early 1970's forced acceptance of Friedman's "natural rate hypothesis", a proposition (1968) that expansive monetary and fiscal policy cannot "buy a permanent economic high", since the negatively sloped short-run Phillips curve shifts up as expectations adjust to higher realized inflation rates and in the long run becomes vertical. Acceptance of Friedman's proposition was initially delayed by a conflict between the theoretical appeal of the natural rate hypothesis and the empirical evidence from U.S. post-war data supporting a negatively sloped long-run trade-off curve. Friedman and his followers did not pay much attention to the U.S. empirical findings nor attempt to explain the apparent conflict, since the close contacts of the University of Chicago with Latin America provided them with another set of empirical observations which were consistent with the natural rate hypothesis.

[3] I agree with M–A's interpretation that, in his use of the word "temporary" to describe the effects of the fiscal shift, Friedman should be charitably interpreted as describing as temporary the *change* in spending. The *level* of velocity remains lower permanently.

[4] An expectational Phillips curve is explicitly used by Friedman in his "Theoretical Framework" to determine the dynamic adjustment of prices (1970, p. 49, eq. 45). There is no significant difference between Friedman's equation and the reduced form price equation which would be obtained by combining the wage and price equations of the MPS model, except that in most versions of the latter the elasticity of inflation to changes in the expected rate of inflation is less than the value of unity assumed by Friedman.

And by 1971 the U.S. data no longer allowed statistical rejection of the hypothesis that the U.S. Phillips curve is vertical in the long run.[5]

### *2.2. Continuing Disagreement and the Role of Differing Time Horizons*

Yet, despite gradual convergence of monetarists and non-monetarists on a common analytical language, their policy discussions and recommendations have been diametrically opposed more often than not. Compare, for instance, Modigliani's recommendation that in 1974 higher oil prices should have been at least partly accommodated by a temporary increase in the growth rate of the money supply, with Friedman's opinion in September 1974 that "recent rates of monetary growth are not too low" (1974). Another monetarist Allan Meltzer (1974) also recommended monetary growth rates which were far below those generally recommended by non-monetarists. More recently, Friedman discussed the proposition that tax cuts are an effective cure for recession under the heading "Two Economic Fallacies". Or, in an earlier episode, recall Friedman's (1971) verdict in the face of an anemic rate of recovery of real output in the half-year prior to August 1971 that Nixon's pre-August-1971 economic policies were achieving their goals at a satisfactory pace.[6]

At one time, I believed that the strong disagreement by non-monetarists with many of Friedman's policy pronouncements, despite the analytical convergence in the academic journals, was caused by an inconsistency between "academic journal monetarism" and "news-magazine monetarism", i.e., that in his popular writing Friedman relied more on the simple quantity theory and less on the *IS–LM*–Phillips curve paradigm featured in the academic journal exchanges. When re-examined, however, the *Newsweek* pieces on fiscal policy contain almost exactly the same description of the interest rate effect on cash holding as the journal articles referenced above.[7]

A much more profound explanation of continuing monetarist/non-monetarist disagreement is a difference of time horizon. Although this explanation has been offered previously, e.g., in a two-sentence remark by Modigliani (1975), it deserves

[5] The steady upward drift in estimates of the slope of the long-run Phillips curve is examined in Gordon (1972). In a recent exchange, Lucas (1975) and I (1975) examine models of price adjustment in which the natural rate hypothesis is valid yet which are capable of generating data similar to the U.S. experience in the earlier postwar years which yield statistical estimates of a negatively sloped long-run Phillips curve.

[6] The average annual rate of growth of real *GNP* in the second and third quarters of 1971 was 3.2 percent, below the growth rate generally agreed as necessary to keep unemployment constant.

[7] See especially the discussion of the 1975 tax reduction (1975) and the 1968 tax surcharge [the latter is quoted in (1972, pp. 139–140)].

greater emphasis and attention. Monetarists implicitly evaluate the merits of alternative policies by comparing their consequences in the long run, while non-monetarists place much more weight on the short run. There is usually little doubt of the specific time interval with which non-monetarists are concerned, since their policy evaluations are so often accompanied by quantitative projections based on simulations of large-scale econometric models. The M–A paper explicitly defines the "short and medium run" as a period of "two to three years". It is much harder to decipher the time dimension of monetarist policy evaluations, but I suggest that a non-monetarist reader of Friedman's *Newsweek* columns will find little with which to disagree if he liberally inserts the phrase "after 20 years" next to every statement which initially appears controversial. Consider the controversies which disappear when this technique is applied:

(1) Friedman claims that the changes resulting from fiscal policy financed by borrowing are "temporary and minor" when compared with the same policy shift fiananced dollar-for-dollar by money creation or destruction. A permanent increase in government spending creates a deficit which, when financed by money creation, requires the continual creation of money, the effects of which "after 20 years" are bound to swamp the effects of the same increase in government spending financed by borrowing.[8] If all Vietnam war deficits had been financed by borrowing, and the growth rate of the money supply had not been allowed to accelerate in 1967–1968, monetarists and non-monetarists alike would agree that "after 20 years" the price level would have been markedly lower.

(2) In the expectational Phillips curve framework accepted by both groups a change in nominal income initially is reflected almost entirely as a change in real output, and only gradually as a change in prices. Eventually the price adjustment is "complete", meaning that the effects on real output disappear (ignoring the capacity effects of long-run changes in the capital stock). By implicitly examining the consequences of nominal spending shifts "after 20 years", monetarists can with considerable justification treat real output as fixed and prices as perfectly flexible. With their two-year horizon, however, non-monetarists observe the economy when the price adjustment has barely begun and to a first approximation can treat prices as fixed and real output as absorbing the entire impact of the spending shift. Thus Friedman's much-criticized (1970) distinction between the

[8] Long before 20 years have passed, money creation will cease when enough income-sensitive tax revenues have been generated to eliminate the deficit. M–A's equation (3) yields the same multiplier regardless of the method of finance, but they implicitly ignore the discounting of future tax liabilities which at least dampens and possibly eliminates the increase in wealth associated with an increase in public holdings of government interest-bearing debt.

quantity theory and the "income–expenditure" theory on the basis of their respective choice of fixed real output and fixed prices is not far-fetched for use in distinguishing between monetarists and non-monetarists. For example, I have shown (1975a) that the optimal response of policy to higher oil prices in 1974 would have been a *reduction* in monetary growth if non-oil prices had been perfectly flexible and an *increase* if non-oil prices had been absolutely rigid. The actual recommendations of monetarists and non-monetarists differed in precisely this way and were both optimal if we allow for the difference between a 20-year and two-year time horizon.

(3) In the theory of optimal economic policy, the choice of monetary growth targets depends on the policy-maker's rate of time preference. Consider an economy in roughly the U.S. situation of 1965, with actual and anticipated inflation rates at an optimum, and unemployment at the "natural rate". A policy-maker with a short time horizon might have decided to accelerate monetary growth because he placed high value on the temporary gains of output which would occur before inflation expectations could adjust completely to higher actual inflation, whereas a long time horizon would have dissuaded another policy-maker from monetary acceleration in exactly the same situation. Similarly, in 1970 with actual and anticipated inflation rates well above the optimum, a short time horizon would lead a policy-maker to resist the short-run costs of the output recession necessary to reduce inflation, whereas a long time horizon would place sufficiently high value on the eventual benefits of lower inflation as to swamp the short-run costs of recession. The contrast of Tobin's advice (1971) to "live with inflation" with Friedman's simultaneous approval of Nixon's "Old Game Plan" (1971) is a typical example of a non-monetarist/monetarist disagreement which can be rationalized completely on the basis of differing time horizons.

One might stop here, instructing voters, politicians, and colleagues to be guided by their own internal rate of time preference when choosing between the conflicting advice of monetarists and non-monetarists. But this will not do, since anyone with a non-zero but non-infinite rate of time preference must ask the monetarists to be more specific on the length of the interval before the long run begins. If monetarists act, in Modigliani's words, as if the "long run is around the corner", we still need to know how far it is from here to the corner. The key parameters required to measure this time interval are (a) the slope of the short-run Phillips curve and (b) the speed of adjustment of expectations, which together determine the length of the recession and hence the social cost of an anti-inflationary monetary growth path. Rapid adjustment parameters would allow an early return of the U.S. economy from its mid-1975 situation to "reasonable" unemployment rates even if the growth rate of money were maintained at the average pace of the last five years (6.2 percent), but at the other extreme zero adjustment parameters would maintain inflation at a sufficiently high rate to "use up" almost all of the money created at that growth pace, leaving little remaining to support growth in real output, so that the unemployment rate would continue to rise. Many fair-minded observers would support the monetarist prescription for the continuation of steady monetary growth if they could be convinced that the adjustment parameters were large, and would support the non-monetarist recommendation of temporary but substantial monetary acceleration if the parameters turned out to be small.

Given the importance of evidence on the specific quantitative magnitude of the short-run price adjustment parameters, I find it surprising that monetarist authors have done so little empirical research on price behavior.[9] Yet again, this indifference may implicitly reflect the extreme length of the time horizon of the monetarist – if they are concerned only with the state of the economy 20 years after a shift or shock, they can be excused for their lack of interest in determining whether the price adjustment is complete after 5, 10, or 15 years. But at the same time they should be sensitive to skeptics in the non-monetarist or "uncommitted" camps who may wonder just how long a recession the economy is presently being asked to endure.

## 3. Resolving the St. Louis Puzzle

The version of monetarism represented by the St. Louis money-income regressions is a much "harder-line" version that Friedman's; in the St. Louis regressions fiscal policy has essentially a zero effect on *nominal* income after only four quarters, whereas Friedman since 1966 has been willing to concede a permanent (albeit one-time-only) shift in velocity following a change in government spending or tax rates financed by borrowing. In contrast to the dispute between Friedman and his critics, there is no single interpretation which allows both the St. Louis and MPS government spending multipliers to be correct simultaneously. Instead, we face the following alternatives:

(a) The St. Louis multipliers are an accurate estimate of the truth, in which case the MPS model must be incorrectly specified.

[9] The sole exception is the price equation in the Andersen–Carlson St. Louis model (1970), which adjusts even more sluggishly than my wage and price equations or those in the deMenil–Enzler MPS model (1972). Friedman and Schwartz are including studies of price behavior in the U.S. and U.K. over a long historical period in their forthcoming manuscript, but their approach is not designed to yield the parameters required in the present context.

(b) The MPS multipliers are an accurate estimate of the truth, in which case the St. Louis model must be incorrectly specified.
(c) Multipliers estimated by the St. Louis approach are far from the multipliers implied by artificial data generated from the known structure of any one of several macro models, but there is no proof that any of the latter represent the true structure of the real world.

The first part of the M–A paper examines proposition (a) by searching for specification errors which might rationalize the St. Louis multipliers. Finding no errors, (a) is rejected. The second part demonstrates the validity of proposition (c) and claims that the St. Louis approach is incapable of reproducing a known economic structure, whether or not that structure is "true". In her comment in this volume Anna Schwartz misses the entire point of the second part of the M–A paper by criticizing the specification of the MPS model; but the validity of proposition (c) does not depend in the slightest on the empirical validity of the structural model which generates the artificial data. While Modigliani and Ando may feel deep in their hearts that their MPS model has accurately captured the basic structure of the real world, their paper makes only the "soft" claim that proposition (c) is valid and does not, as Schwartz appears to believe, make any claims about the validity of proposition (b).

### *3.1. Is There a Theoretical Rationale for the St. Louis Multipliers?*

M–A's examination of proposition (a) consists of a search for possible misspecifications in the MPS model. Not surprisingly, none are found. The basic point is that the nominal crowding out effect of higher government spending requires an increase in interest rates to reduce interest-sensitive components of spending, but that increase in interest rates cannot occur unless the nominal demand for money is increased relative to the fixed nominal supply. If the nominal demand for money depends only on interest rates and nominal income, clearly nominal income must rise for crowding out to occur; if in addition money demand depends on wealth, then nominal income must rise to generate the saving which is the couterpart of the increase in wealth. The argument is convincing as long as an increase in interest rates is required for investment to be crowded out; but it would not be valid if instead government spending directly entered the investment or consumption demand function with a coefficient of minus unity. I know of no evidence to support this proposition. Furthermore, monetarists have emphasized the broad spectrum of assets which are substitutes with money, but they have never proposed that implicit yields on consumer goods can rise without a simultaneous increase in explicit yields on financial assets. Thus I fail to find a loophole in this part of A–M's analysis.

Another approach examined by A–M is based on Tobin's analysis of debt management (1971a); if the government borrowing takes the form of long-term bonds, and if long-term bonds and equities are close substitutes, both the long-term bond rate and the capitalization rate must rise together and the demand for investment goods will be reduced. If long-term bonds are at the same time sufficiently distant substitutes to short-term bonds, and if short-term but not long-term rates enter the demand for money function, nominal income and short-term rates could in principle remain constant while crowding out takes place. M–A correctly argue that this line of reasoning cannot explain the St. Louis results in the relevant sample period, since the U.S. government was mainly dealing in short-term debt. One might also add that empirical work on the term structure of interest rates has with relative success applied the hypothesis that long-term and short-term bonds are close substitutes, although this success could simply reflect the absence of major government-engineered changes in the relative supply of long debt during the sample period.

### 3.2. *An Interpretation of the St. Louis Bias*

The major contribution of the M–A paper is its demonstration that correlation between included policy variables and other excluded variables severely biases the estimated St. Louis multipliers and renders useless the reduced form technique. Compare a "true model",

$$\Delta Y_t = \alpha + \sum_i^K \beta_i \Delta M_{t-i} + \sum_i^L \gamma_i \Delta G_{t-i} + \sum_i^N \eta_i \Delta A_{t-i} + u_t, \tag{1}$$

with the truncated version estimated by St. Louis,

$$\Delta Y_t = a + \sum_i^K b_i \Delta M_{t-i} + \sum_i^L c_i \Delta G_{t-i} + v_t, \tag{2}$$

where all variables are measured as absolute dollar changes, $Y$ is nominal income, $M$ is the money supply ($M_1$), $G$ is Federal government spending on goods and services, $A$ is a set of non-stochastic left-out variables, and $u$ is a stochastic error term. Biased estimates of the $b_i$ and $c_i$ in (2) might occur if:

(a) Policy-makers attempt to stabilize $Y$ by offsetting changes in the $A$. If the $u$ are truly stochastic, any attempt by policy shifts to offset $u$ is likely to be futile.

(b) Policy-makers destabilize income by attempting to stabilize interest rates, leading to an automatic positive response of $M$ to movements in $A$ and $u$ if the latter represent shifts in expenditure functions rather than in the demand for money.
(c) Policy variables are correlated with $A$ and $u$ by coincidence rather than by design.

Accepting the basic message of the M–A paper, one nevertheless ask whether it is possible to make any progress in isolating the specific causes of the St. Louis bias. To what extent is the bias due to (a), (b), and (c)? In which particular episodes did policy-makers succeed in stabilizing income? This paper attempts to isolate individual episodes, first, by examining shifts in coefficients in reduced form regressions in which a "shock proxy" is alternatively included and excluded, and, second, by examining simple correlations between policy variables and the shock proxy. Although experiments could be conducted with numerous alternative proxies, the discussion here is simplified by the choice of a single representation of $A$ – the sum of net exports, consumer expenditures on new automobiles, and non-residential fixed investment. Although this trilogy is by no means totally exogenous, its fluctuations over short periods of four to eight quarters are relatively independent of changes in the money supply and government spending, and are affected by the timing of changes in foreign demand, consumer expectations, tax rates and incentives, and other excluded variables.

If (1) above is the true model and (2) is estimated, then there are separate biases for each of the $K$ lagged money and $L$ lagged government spending terms, depending on the correlation of each lagged term with the *net* effect of *all* lagged values of $A$. Examination of the total correlation matrix helps to distinguish among the three explanations of the reduced form bias – (a), (b), and (c) above. For instance, a negative correlation between current $A$ and $M$ or $A$ and $G$ would suggest a stabilizing policy, although in the case of government spending it is rather implausible to believe that a single quarter is sufficiently long for policy-makers to have time to turn the expenditure spigot. A negative correlation between lagged $A$ and current $M$ or lagged $A$ and current $G$ would add credence to the stabilizing policy explanation. On the other hand, a positive correlation between current $A$ and $M$ would tend to support the hypothesis that by pursuing a policy of stabilizing interest rates, the Federal Reserve allowed $M$ to move simultaneously in the same direction as $IS$ curve shifts. Positive correlation between lagged $M$ and current $A$, or lagged $G$ and current $A$, could simply reflect the direct but lagged impact of policy variables on investment and consumer automobile expenditure, while a negative relationship between lagged policy variables and current $A$ could be caused by the negative impact of lagged policy variables on net exports, or accurate forecasting by a policy-maker attempting to stabilize, or sheer coincidence.

The sums of coefficients on lagged $\Delta M$ and lagged $\Delta G$ in St. Louis type regressions are displayed in table 1, lines (1a) and (1c), for five sample periods, respectively: (i) the M–A period, (ii) the total post-Korea era, and three subperiods of the latter – (iii) Eisenhower, (iv) Kennedy–Johnson, and (v) Nixon–Ford. There is no appreciable difference in the monetary and fiscal coefficients between the Eisenhower and Kennedy–Johnson years: the St. Louis conclusion of negligible fiscal multipliers holds equally in both periods. But the results are very different for the Nixon–Ford subperiod, when the fiscal multiplier (albeit only on the borderline of significance) is even larger than that yielded by the MPS model.

Lines (1b) and (1d) show the sums of coefficients on lagged $\Delta M$ and lagged $\Delta G$ when current $\Delta A$ is added as a single additional right-hand variable. In all three subperiods the monetary coefficients decline, fading into insignificance in the Eisenhower period, declining modestly in the Kennedy–Johnson years, and falling negligibly in the Nixon–Ford period. These results are consistent with the hypothesis that during the 1950's the Fed destabilized the economy by actively attempting to stabilize interest rates in the face of *IS* curve shifts, but by 1970 had shifted largely to control of monetary aggregates. The introduction of $\Delta A$ raises the fiscal coefficients in the first two periods (although not to significance) whether due to coincidence or policy design, but reduces them in the Nixon–Ford era.

Similar regressions including lagged values of $\Delta A$ were estimated but are omitted from table 1 to simplify the discussion; the results are similar and indicate that almost all of the impact of $\Delta A$ affects $\Delta Y$ in the current period. Concentration on the relationship between lagged policy variables and current $\Delta A$ allows an inspection of correlation vectors (rather than matrices) in parts 2 and 3 of table 1. Since the long sample period results are simple averages of the very different subperiods, we should limit our attention to the subperiod results.

In the Eisenhower years the major negative correlation between lagged $\Delta G$ and current $\Delta A$ is contributed by lags $t-3$ and $t-4$. Why? As I pointed out long ago (1971), the main variance of $\Delta G$ occurs in the post-Korea 1953–1954 decline of defense spending, and is followed a year later by the unprecedented auto boom year of 1955. This was hardly the result of deliberate counter-cyclical fiscal policy, unless one is prepared to argue that Eisenhower deliberately ended the Korean war in 1953 because his crystal ball informed him that auto sales were destined to boom in 1955! Instead, the causation can be described as "crowding in" induced by a channel other than the interest rate route described by M–A; for instance, the release of resources no longer needed for defense purposes in 1953–1954 induced the Federal Reserve to loosen significantly the quantitative regulations on automobile installment sales. In the 1958–1959 period, $\Delta G$ and $\Delta A$ exhibit a roughly concurrent negative correlation as government expenditures increased during the 1958 recession and fell during the 1959 mini-boom. This can more plausibly be interpreted as deliberately counter-cyclical fiscal policy.

In the Kennedy–Johnson period the negative correlation occurs at lags $t$ and $t-2$, due to a relatively strong roughly concurrent negative correlation between $\Delta G$ and $\Delta A$ during the entire period between 1964.2 and 1968.2. During the first part of this interval (through 1965.3) an interpretation of stabilizing fiscal policy is plausible, as nominal government purchases were maintained constant during the 1964–1965 period of boom sales in autos, exports, and capital goods. One can hardly go further, however, and claim that the rapid acceleration of $G$ after 1965.3 reflected foreknowledge that the auto, investment, and net export expansions had run their course. Instead, the 1966–1967 period exhibits very rapid and dramatic "crowding out" which could perhaps reflect a more rapid effect on spending of rising interest rates than is consistent with the MPS specification. During the Nixon–Ford era fiscal policy was mainly destabilizing, in the sense that government purchases contracted during the declining phase of 1969.1 through 1970.4, and expanded during the first stage of the boom between 1971.1 and 1972.2.

The interpretation of the correlation coefficients between lagged $\Delta M$ and current $\Delta A$ is more consistent with a single mechanism. By attempting to stabilize interest rates and offset the impact of *IS* shifts on velocity, the Federal Reserve allowed $M$ to vary positively with *IS* shifts. By the Nixon–Ford period the positive correlation was lower, indicating a partial but not complete shift to the use of monetary aggregates as instruments. An alternative interpretation is that the positive lagged coefficients on $\Delta M$ simply reflect the direct effect of the money supply on investment and auto sales, but this view cannot explain the decline in the positive correlation and in the bias on the $\Delta M$ regression coefficients across subsample periods.

Overall, there is something in these results for everyone. They are consistent with M–A's interpretation of the St. Louis reduced form bias, yet the fiscal multipliers even in regressions including $\Delta A$ are insignificant in all three subperiods. M–A might rightly respond that my "shock proxy" captures only some of the exogenous impacts with which monetary and fiscal variables are correlated, while monetarists might follow up on my interpretation of 1966–1967 and claim that the crowding out effect is stronger and more rapid than in the large-scale models. The MPS model builders should take seriously the possibility that, in peering into the black box, they have not yet located all of the creeks, tributaries, and rivers which lead from money to income.

TABLE 1[a]

| | $\Delta A$ Variable | 1958.1 – 1969.4 | 1953.1 – 1974.4 | 1953.1 – 1960.4 | 1961.1 – 1968.4 | 1969.1 – 1974.4 |
|---|---|---|---|---|---|---|
| 1. *$\Delta Y$ dependent variable, sum of coefficients on:* | | | | | | |
| (a) $\Delta M$, current and lagged | Excluded | 4.62 | 5.86 | 6.62 | 4.57 | 6.70 |
| | | [6.32] | [13.69] | [2.70] | [4.32] | [1.84] |
| (b) $\Delta M$, current and lagged | Included | 3.73 | 5.11 | 1.87 | 3.64 | 6.61 |
| | | [6.04] | [14.56] | [0.83] | [4.06] | [2.18] |
| (c) $\Delta G$, current and lagged | Excluded | 0.28 | 0.39 | −0.20 | −0.04 | 3.94 |
| | | [0.42] | [ 0.81] | [−0.33] | [−0.05] | [1.37] |
| (d) $\Delta G$, current and lagged | Included | 0.85 | 0.59 | 0.18 | 0.60 | 1.65 |
| | | [1.57] | [ 1.55] | [0.37] | [0.97] | [0.65] |
| (e) $\Delta A$, current only | Included | 0.81 | 0.85 | 0.95 | 0.81 | 0.78 |
| | | [4.89] | [ 7.20] | [4.01] | [3.65] | [2.88] |

| | | | | | |
|---|---|---|---|---|---|
| 2. *Correlation coefficient with* $\Delta A$ *of*: | | | | | |
| (a) $\Delta G_t$ | −0.253 | −0.131 | −0.066 | −0.356 | −0.210 |
| (b) $\Delta G_{t-1}$ | 0.033 | 0.030 | −0.122 | 0.071 | 0.023 |
| (c) $\Delta G_{t-2}$ | −0.178 | −0.051 | −0.021 | −0.328 | −0.020 |
| (d) $\Delta G_{t-3}$ | 0.040 | 0.054 | −0.278 | −0.162 | 0.320 |
| (e) $\Delta G_{t-4}$ | −0.003 | 0.054 | −0.357 | 0.017 | 0.294 |
| (f) $\Delta G_{t-5}$ | 0.038 | 0.025 | −0.069 | −0.000 | 0.082 |
| (g) $\Delta G_{t-6}$ | 0.137 | 0.151 | −0.100 | 0.091 | 0.426 |
| (h) $\Delta G_{t-7}$ | 0.197 | 0.124 | 0.123 | 0.183 | 0.138 |
| 3. *Correlation coefficient with* $\Delta A$ *of*: | | | | | |
| (a) $\Delta M_{1,t}$ | 0.154 | 0.297 | 0.298 | 0.089 | 0.244 |
| (b) $\Delta M_{1,t-1}$ | 0.344 | 0.360 | 0.499 | 0.232 | 0.275 |
| (c) $\Delta M_{1,t-2}$ | 0.338 | 0.329 | 0.413 | 0.171 | 0.247 |
| (d) $\Delta M_{1,t-3}$ | 0.277 | 0.232 | 0.343 | 0.115 | 0.013 |
| (e) $\Delta M_{1,t-4}$ | 0.203 | 0.158 | 0.028 | 0.126 | −0.078 |
| (f) $\Delta M_{1,t-5}$ | 0.157 | 0.149 | −0.114 | 0.123 | −0.035 |
| (g) $\Delta M_{1,t-6}$ | 0.015 | 0.137 | 0.002 | −0.129 | 0.012 |
| (h) $\Delta M_{1,t-7}$ | −0.027 | 0.201 | −0.005 | −0.121 | 0.196 |

[a] Estimation details for part 1: eight-quarter third-degree Almon lags with the level and first derivative of the tail constrained to zero.

[b] $Y$ = Current-dollar *GNP*. $M$ = Currency plus demand deposits. $G$ = Federal government spending on goods and services. $A$ = Net exports plus consumer expenditures on automobiles plus fixed non-residential investment.

## References

Anderson, L. and K. Carlson, 1970, A monetarist model for economic stabilization, Federal Reserve Bank of St. Louis Review 52, April, pp. 7–25.

deMenil, G. and J. Enzler, Prices and wages in the FR–MIT–PENN econometric model, in: O. Eckstein, ed., The econometrics of price determination: Conference (Washington Federal Reserve), pp. 277–308.

Friedman, M., 1959, The demand for money: Some theoretical and empirical results, Journal of Political Economy 67, Aug., pp. 327–351. Reprinted in: M. Friedman (1969).

Friedman, M., 1966, Interest rates and the demand for money, Journal of Law and Economics 9, Oct. Reprinted in: M. Friedman (1969).

Friedman, M., 1968, The role of monetary policy, American Economic Review 58, March, pp. 1–17. Reprinted in: M. Friedman (1969).

Friedman, M., 1969, The optimum quantity of money and other essays (Aldine, Chicago, Ill.).

Friedman, M., 1970, A theoretical framework for monetary analysis, in: M. Friedman et al. (1974).

Friedman, M., 1971, Last readings on the old game plan, Newsweek, Sept. 27.

Friedman, M., 1972, Comments on the critics, in: M. Friedman et al. (1974).

Friedman, M., 1974, Is money too tight, Newsweek, Sept. 23.

Friedman, M., 1975, Two economic fallacies, Newsweek, May 12.

Friedman, M. et al., 1974, Milton Friedman's monetary framework: A debate with his critics, edited by R. J. Gordon (University of Chicago Press, Chicago, Ill.).

Gordon, R. J., 1971, Notes on money, income, and Gramlich, Journal of Money, Credit, and Banking 3 May, pp. 533–545.

Gordon, R. J., 1972, Wage–price controls and the shifting Phillips curve; Brookings Papers on Economic Activity 3, no. 2, pp. 385–421.

Gordon, R. J., 1975a, Alternative responses of policy to external supply shocks, Brookings Papers on Economic Activity 6, no. 1, pp. 183–206.

Gordon, R. J., 1975b, Can econometric policy evaluations be salvaged, in: K. Brunner and A. Meltzer, eds., The Phillips curve and public policy (North-Holland, Amsterdam) pp. 44–58.

Laidler, D., 1970, The demand for money: Theories and evidence (International Textbook, Scranton, Penn.).

Lucas, Jr., R. E., 1975, Econometric policy evaluations: A critique, in: K. Brunner and A. Meltzer, eds., The Phillips curve and public policy (North-Holland, Amsterdam).

Meltzer, A., 1974, A plan for subduing inflation, Fortune 90, Sept., p. 112 ff.

Modigliani, F., 1975, Rediscovery of money discussion, American Economic Review 65, May, pp. 45–88.

Modigliani, F., 1974, A critique of past and prospective economic policies, American Economic Review 64, Sept., pp. 544–577.

Modigliani, F., 1975, Rediscovery of money discussion, American Economic Review 65, May, pp. 179–181.

Tobin, J., 1971, An essay on the principles of debt management, Essays in economics, vol. 1: Macroeconomics (North-Holland, Amsterdam) pp. 378–455.

Tobin, J., 1972a, Inflation and unemployment, American Economic Review 62, March, pp. 1–18.

Tobin, J., 1972b, Friedman's theoretical framework, in: M. Friedman et al. (1974).

Tobin, J. and L. Ross, 1971, Living with inflation, New York Review of Books 16, May, p. 23.

## 4. COMMENTS ON MODIGLIANI AND ANDO

Michael R. DARBY

The paper by Modigliani and Ando suggests that the reduced form approach of the St. Louis equations may give erroneous estimates of the impacts of monetary and fiscal policy on income because of the omission of certain other exogenous variables which are included in various structural models. This point has nothing to do with the structural versus reduced form debate, but only with the proper specification of the list of exogenous variables. Rephrasing their objection to the St. Louis equation in simpler terms does illuminate an area for substantive research.

The St. Louis approach relates a measure $Y_t$ of nominal income to measures of monetary policy $M_t$ and fiscal policy $F_t$,

$$Y_t = a_1 M_t + a_2 F_t + u_t. \tag{1}$$

The variables $M_t$ and $F_t$ and their coefficients $a_1$ and $a_2$ are typically vectors, although this adds nothing to the current discussion. Modigliani and Ando's objection may be summarized as stating that this reduced form omits measures $A_t$ of other autonomous expenditures which are exogenous variables in the structural models. So, a correct reduced form would be

$$Y_t = b_1 M_t + b_2 F_t + b_3 A_t + v_t. \tag{2}$$

If equation (2) is the true reduced form, standard specification analysis applies. It is necessary to estimate the auxiliary regression,[1]

$$A_t = c_1 M_t + c_2 F_t + w_t. \tag{3}$$

So if equation (1) is estimated instead of equation (2), the expected regression result is

$$Y_t = (b_1 + b_3 c_1) M_t + (b_2 + b_3 c_2) F_t. \tag{4}$$

Modigliani and Ando note that $c_1$ is positive and $c_2$ is negative and conclude that

[1] If $M_t$, $F_t$, and $A_t$ are interpreted as vectors, then $c_1$ and $c_2$ are matrices of auxiliary regression coefficients.

the St. Louis equation overestimates the impact of monetary influences and underestimates the impact of fiscal influences.

But the same equations could be interpreted in a much different way. Suppose for a given monetary policy an increase in government spending induces an offsetting decrease in the (supposedly exogenous) "other autonomous expenditures". Indeed on "the" monetarist position there will always be offsetting shifts in other autonomous expenditures which moderate the supposedly powerful effect of government spending. The structure of this larger model is not yet understood, but if it in fact exists it is clear that equations (1) and (3) are both reduced form equations relating endogenous variables on the left to exogenous variables on the right. Equation (2) is only a semi-reduced form equation since the endogenous $A_t$ is on the right-hand side. Equation (4) breaks down the reduced form equation (1) coefficients into direct effects of monetary and fiscal policy ($b_1$ and $b_2$) and indirect effects ($c_1 b_3$ and $c_2 b_3$) operating through changes in the endogenous "other autonomous expenditures". Monetarists are interested in the total – not just the direct – effects of monetary and fiscal policy.[2]

So there is a substantive question here: Is equation (3) a reduced form equation reflecting causal relations or simply a sample-period curiosity without causal significance if government policy were otherwise formulated? The answer of Modigliani and Ando would seem (pp. 19–20) to be that this is a reflection of passive procyclical variations in the money supply and wise contra-cyclical fiscal policy – particularly during the Eisenhower administration! Most monetarists find this position rather tenuous and suspect that "shifts" in the investment and net export functions, for example, are due to causal relations omitted in the models examined. These causal relations may be transmitted for example through omitted relative price effects. The structure and existence of these causal relationships is an area for further substantive research.

[2] The distinction is between $dY_t/dM_t$ and $dY_t/dF_t$ on the one hand and $\partial Y_t/\partial M_t$ and $\partial Y_t/\partial F_t$ on the other hand.

Chapter 2

# AN AGGREGATIVE THEORY FOR A CLOSED ECONOMY*

Karl BRUNNER and Allan H. MELTZER

## 1. Introduction

For more than a generation, aggregative analysis of a closed economy has remained within the confines of the Keynesian framework as interpreted by Hicks (1937). Metzler (1951), Patinkin (1965) and others provided an alternative interpretation of Keynes (1936). Later extensions introduced anticipations and growth without altering the main qualitative conclusions. In both interpretations, the short-run response to monetary and fiscal policy is transmitted mainly by interest rates and depends on properties of the demand function for money and the expenditure function. A large interest elasticity of the demand for money increases the short-run response of output to fiscal policy. A large interest elasticity of consumption or investment expenditure increases the short-run response of output to monetary policy.

The meaning of "interest rates" differs in the two interpretations, and the adjustment processes differ as a consequence. In the common text book version, interest rates are borrowing costs and portfolio adjustment consists of substitution between money and a narrow range of financial assets called bonds. Metzler's financial asset is a composite representing claims to real capital. Bonds are perfect substitutes for such claims, and interest rates are the yield per period of a unit of real capital.

In Metzler's analysis real resources are fixed, so long-run output is fixed. The long-run effects of monetary and fiscal policies are on prices and interest rates. Changes in money change the price level but leave interest rates and real balances unchanged. Open market operations and changes in tax rates transfer ownership

* A first draft was presented at the First Murphy Symposium on Inflation at Tulane University in April 1973. A later draft circulated under the title "Fiscal and Monetary Policy in a Closed Economy". Helpful comments have been received from many readers. We are grateful to all of them and particularly to Pieter Korteweg. We are indebted to the National Science Foundation for continued support of our work.

of claims to streams of real income between the government and the private sector. Interest rates rise in response to open market sales and reductions in tax rates and fall in response to open market purchases and tax increases. Open market operations induce larger changes in the price level than tax changes that transfer securities of equal value, but the effects on real balances are identical. Open market purchases raise the equilibrium price level; open market sales lower the equilibrium price level.

All of the above conclusions are derived from a static model of exchange in which government is, at most, an agency for redistributing income by changing the ownership of wealth. Similar conclusions have been obtained for a growing economy under similar assumptions. In the Hicksian version, the government purchases goods and services. The long-run implications for prices and interest rates of issuing and withdrawing bonds are rarely discussed.

The basic difference between Hicks' and Metzler's analysis of portfolio adjustment reflects a difference in the assumptions about transaction costs. The Hicksian approach makes the cost of adjusting real assets in portfolios infinite. The Metzler approach sets these costs approximately equal to the transaction costs for securities, at or near zero. An intermediate position permitting adjustment of real capital, or claims to real capital, bonds and money seems to us more appropriate for aggregate analysis.

Our version of the monetarist hypothesis analyzes an economy in which costs of adjusting real capital in portfolios are neither zero nor infinite. Finite transaction costs place a wedge between the price of current output and the price of existing real capital. Substitution is not limited to two assets but includes the entire spectrum of assets. Adjustment is not limited to "the interest rate" but includes the relative prices of real capital and financial assets.

In two previous papers (1972, 1974a), we developed a general framework involving interaction between three assets. Wealth owners may accumulate or decumulate each of the assets – money, financial assets, and real capital – and may purchase current output. The economy is closed and, as in most of our discussion here, there is no growth in the stock of real capital, population or effective labor force. Interest rates, the prices of output and real capital are variable, however, and there is a government that purchases goods and services, taxes, finances deficits and surpluses and engages in open market operations.

Several of the conclusions obtained from a model with only two assets do not hold in a three-asset model. We have shown [Brunner and Meltzer (1974a)] that the slopes of the expenditure functions and the demand function for money do not determine the relative size of the responses to fiscal and monetary policies. Contrary to frequent assertions, the major issues in aggregative analysis cannot be reduced to propositions about the relative slopes of the *IS* and *LM* curves.

In this paper, we consider standard propositions about the effects of policy changes in a closed economy. The following two sections present the model, develop conditions for equilibrium on the markets for assets and output, and show that the interaction of policy variables and market variables determine interest rates, prices, output and the government's budget position. Next, we consider the effects of monetary and fiscal policies and the financing of deficits and surpluses. The conclusion examines the main empirical conjectures that separate monetarist and Keynesian views.

## 2. The Framework

In the economy that we analyze, private decisions to hold, acquire or dispose of assets and to consume are made in response to prices and anticipated prices including the prices of current output, existing real capital and the market rate of interest. Government decisions on tax rates, expenditure and the financing of the budget surplus or deficit are summarized in a budget equation. For given tastes, opportunities and anticipations, and given wage rates, the decisions of the government and private sectors determine the level of output, the market rate of interest, the size of the budget deficit or surplus and the prices of real capital and current production. The economy is closed, and the capital stock and money wages are given. At a few points we relax the last constraints and permit the capital stock or money wage to change.[1]

### *2.1. The Output Market*

Three principal equations describe the output market. Equation (1), is an equilibrium condition. Real output produced by the private sector, $y$, is absorbed by the private and government sectors. Real government expenditure, $g$, is set by government. Private expenditure, $d$, depends on prices and wealth, as shown in equation (1′). Equation (1″) describes the pricing behavior of producers. Output prices, $p$, are revised in response to current market conditions expressed by $y$, real capital stock, $K$, efficiency wage rate, $w$, and suppliers' anticipations of prices, $\phi$.[2]

[1] More attention is given to longer-run consideration in Brunner (1974b). The international aspects were integrated in some detail in Brunner and Meltzer (1974b).

[2] There is no labor market in our model. The influence of the labor market on output, prices and other variables come through $w$ and $W_h$, the efficiency wage and the value of current and future income from labor services. In a more complete analysis, $w$ would be replaced by a solution of the labor market equations. Wage rates and interest rates are net of income and other taxes.

$$y = d + g, \tag{1}$$

$$d = d(i - \pi, p, p^*, P, e, W_n, W_h), \quad d_1, d_2 < 0; \quad d_3, \ldots, d_7 > 0, \tag{1'}$$

$$p = p(y, K, w, \phi), \quad p_1, p_3, p_4 > 0; \quad p_2 < 0. \tag{1''}$$

The variables affecting private expenditure are: $i$, the market rate of interest; $\pi$, the rate of inflation anticipated on the credit market; $p^*$, the price level anticipated by purchasers; $P$, the current price of existing real capital; $e$, the anticipated return to real capital per unit of capital; $W_n$ and $W_h$ are, respectively, human and non-human wealth at market value.

Differences between anticipated and actual outcomes affect the output market in a number of ways. The anticipated return to real capital may differ from the real rate of interest received and paid by lenders and borrowers on the credit market. Prices anticipated by purchasers may differ from the prices anticipated by suppliers, and both may differ from prevailing prices. The market rate of interest is related to prices and to anticipated returns, and in long run, steady state equilibrium, satisfies the equation

$$i = (p/P)e + \pi.$$

Elsewhere, the equality need not hold.

Both $W_h$ and $e$ depend on the level of real income and on the tax rates applicable to income from labor and capital. We assume that, for given tax rates, there is sufficient regularity in the distribution of income to permit us to neglect explicit references to the effect of changes in the distribution on expenditure, borrowing, lending or money holding. Human wealth, $W_h$, depends on wages, prices, and the tax rates applicable to income of this kind. Tax rates on non-human wealth affect the expected return to capital, $e$, and the returns received by owners of real assets, $pe/P$.

Non-human wealth at market value is the sum of base money, $B$, government securities held by banks and the non-bank public, $S$, and the stock of capital,[3]

$$W_h = PK + v(i, \tau)S + (1 + \omega)B.$$

$S$ is the face value of the stock of government debt, and $v$ is the market value per unit of debt. The market value of the debt depends on the difference between market and coupon rates, on maturity, and on the tax rates applicable to income from this source. The market value, $v$, depends negatively on $i$ with an elasticity, $\epsilon(v, i)$ dependent on maturity structure; $\epsilon(v, i)$ rises algebraically as the maturity declines. The parameters $\tau$ and $\omega$ represent a vector of tax rates and the net worth

[3] This expression is equivalent to the public's net worth.

multiplier of the banking system, respectively. The latter reflects a Pesek–Saving (1967) effect resulting from a regulated, non-competitive banking system and the real resources invested in the banking system but not included in $K$. The monetary base, $B$, is the total monetary liability of the monetary authorities and is equal to total bank reserves and currency outstanding.

The output market proximately determines real output and the price level for given values of the other variables. Interest rates and asset prices affect the output market but are proximately determined in the asset markets. Money wages, anticipated prices, tax rates and real government expenditure are treated as given. In a closed economy, base money and outstanding securities are cumulated sums remaining from the financing of fiscal and monetary policies. Current changes in the base and the outstanding stock of securities depend on policy decisions and the position of the economy. The remaining component of wealth, real capital, is taken as given until the restriction is relaxed below.

### *2.2. The Asset Markets*

Two asset markets, a credit market and money market, proximately determine the interest rate, $i$, and the asset price level, $P$. Interaction of the credit and money markets redistributes the components of existing wealth – money, government securities (or non-money financial assets) and real capital – among wealth holders until all assets are willingly held. Money is a substitute for securities and real capital, not for securities alone.

The credit market distributes the stock of outstanding securities between banks and the non-bank public and proximately determines the market rate of interest, $i$. Credit is defined as the asset portfolio on the consolidated balance sheet of the banking system and consists of bank loans and the banks' holdings of government securities. The stock of credit is the product of the monetary base, $B$, and the bank credit multiplier, $a$. The latter depends on all of the arguments of the expenditure function,[4] with derivatives shown in equation (2), and on policy variables such as the discount rate and the reserve requirement ratios represented by the dots in the $a$-function. The public's supply of earning assets to banks, $\sigma$, depends on all the variables introduced in our discussion of the output market, and on the outstanding stock of securities, $S$. Equation (2) is an equilibrium condition for the stock of

[4] More complete discussion of the bank credit and money multipliers – and the credit and money markets – can be found in several of our earlier papers. See Brunner and Meltzer (1968, 1974a), Brunner (1974a), or Burger (1972). Equations (2) and (3) can be interpreted as partially reduced forms.

bank credit,

$$a(i, p, P, W_n, W_h, e, \ldots)B = \sigma(i - \pi, P, p, p^*, \phi, e, S, W_n, W_h), \quad (2)$$

$$a_1, a_3, a_4 > 0 > a_2; \sigma_1, \sigma_2 < 0; \sigma_3, \ldots, \sigma_7 > 0.$$

For the public, buying securities is an alternative to repaying loans, and selling securities is an alternative to borrowing from banks. The derivatives of the first six terms of the $\sigma$ function show that prices, anticipated prices and returns affect the two components of $\sigma$ – the public's desired borrowing and the excess supply of securities offered to banks – in the same way. Changes in wealth affect the two components in opposite ways. Hence, the derivatives with respect to wealth are small and of uncertain sign.

The demand for money is not equivalent to the public's supply of earning assets to banks, and the stock of money is not identical to the stock of bank credit. The money market of our analysis proximately determines the asset price level, $P$, and for given values of $p$ and $e$, determines the real rate of return on real capital.

The asset price level is distinct from the price level of new production. Costs of adjustment associated with the acquisition of real capital, and costs of acquiring information about market opportunities, assure that $p$ and $P$ are, generally, not equal. In full long-run adjustment to a steady state, with all costs variable, all opportunities realized, and all anticipations equal to actual values, existing capital sells at reproduction cost, and the real return to real capital equals the expected return, $e$.

Equation (3) is the equilibrium condition for the money market. The stock of money is the product of a money multiplier, $m$, and the monetary base. Interest rates, asset prices and wealth affect the money multiplier and the stock of money by changing the distribution of money between currency and demand deposits and the distribution of deposits between time and demand accounts. Reserve requirement ratios and the discount rate affect the money multiplier by changing the distribution of reserves between required and surplus reserves or by increasing or decreasing borrowing from the central bank.

$$m(i, p, P, W_n, W_h, \ldots)B = L(i, p^*, \phi, e, p, P, W_n, W_h), \quad (3)$$

$$m_1, m_2 > 0; \quad m_3, m_4 < 0;$$

$$L_1, \ldots, L_4 < 0; \quad L_5, \ldots, L_8 > 0.$$

The demand for money depends on all of the arguments of the $\sigma$ function except $S$. However, the properties of the two functions differ. Changes in anticipated prices, the anticipated rate of price change, the anticipated yield on real capital, and the asset price level shift $L$ and $\sigma$ in opposite directions. Moreover, the wealth elasticities of $L$ are considerably larger than the wealth elasticities of $\sigma$.

Our analysis explicitly rejects the traditional Keynesian view that identifies the demand for money with the supply of earning assets of banks [Gramley and Chase (1965)]. Failure to separate the markets for money and credit restricts such analysis – for example, *IS–LM* analysis – to a world in which there are at most two assets. We do not believe it is possible to correctly analyze the adjustment of prices and output to government fiscal and monetary policies without separating the credit and money markets, or alternatively, distinguishing money, bonds and real capital.

### *2.3. The Government Sector*

An understanding of the effects of monetary and fiscal policy requires analysis linking the government budget deficit or surplus and the financing of the budget with the markets for assets and output [Christ (1972) and Silber (1970)]. Changes in tax rates or government expenditure affect the output market directly. Changes in the volume of base money and securities issued to finance the budget deficit also change expenditure, and more importantly, change the position of the asset market. Even a constant, maintained deficit or surplus affects the markets for assets and output. The reason is that the financing of any deficit or surplus alters the nominal stocks of base money and securities and changes the prices of assets and output.

Equation (4) is the government's budget equation. The government's purchase of goods, $pg$, labor services, $\bar{w}lg$, and interest payments (net of taxes), $I(i)S$, are financed by tax revenues, $t(p, y, \bar{w}lg; \tau)$, and by issuing base money and securities. All bonds are issued at par,

$$pg + \bar{w}lg + I(i)S - t(p, y, \bar{w}lg; \tau) = \mathring{B} + \mathring{S}. \tag{4}$$

In a closed economy, most changes in the base and the stock of securities result from the financing of the current deficit or from open market operations.

The government hires labor at the market money wage $\bar{w}$, and pays interest on its outstanding debt. Interest payments depend on the maturity and volume of debt. Expenditure $g$ (or $pg$) the number of workers hired, $lg$, or expenditure for labor services, $wlg$, and the tax rate schedule, $\tau$, are set by policy decisions. We are free to choose either $\mathring{B}$ or $\mathring{S}$ or some combination as an additional policy variable. The proper choice depends on the institutional arrangements prevailing in a given economy. Most central banks and governments do not choose explicitly but, instead, attempt to damp fluctuations in interest rates. Let $\mu$ be the portion of the current deficit or surplus financed by issuing or withdrawing base money, and let $\nu$ be the amount of base money issued or withdrawn by open market operations conducted independently of deficit finance. $\mathring{B} = v$ whenever the budget is balanced. If the budget is unbalanced, $v = 0$ whenever $0 < \mu < 1$. More generally,

$$\mathring{B} = \mu(pg + \bar{w}lg + IS - t) + v,$$

and

$$\mathring{S} = (1 - \mu)(pg + \bar{w}lg + IS - t) - v.$$

We treat $\mu$ as a policy parameter describing the financing of the government budget.

## 3. Interaction of the Budget and the Markets for Assets and Output

Every displacement of the equilibrium position of the credit, money or output market affects the other markets and the budget equation. Every change in the budget position affects the markets for assets and output. Every change in stocks, flows or the budget changes relative prices, tax collections and the amounts of base money and securities issued or withdrawn. In this section, we analyze the interaction of the system and show the conditions for stock–flow equilibrium. Diagrams illustrate the main points.

The position of flow equilibrium must satisfy the equilibrium condition, equation (1), relating actual and desired output or expenditure. Desired expenditure depends on $P$ and $i$. Changes in the stocks – $B$, $S$, or $K$ – affect $P$ and $i$ and shift the position of flow equilibrium, so the flow equilibrium depends upon the position of the asset market.

To take account of the effect of the asset markets on the flow equilibrium, we first solve the asset market equations for $P$ and $i$. The solutions for $P$ and $i$ depend on $p$ and $y$ because the multipliers $m$ and $a$ and the $L$ and $\sigma$ functions depend on prices and output. The dependence on $y$ reflects the presence of $W_h$ and $e$ in the asset equations. Let $\epsilon(i, y|AM)$, $\epsilon(P, y|AM)$ and similar expressions with output price ($p$) in lieu of $y$, denote the elasticities of $i$ and $P$ with respect to prices and output derived from the equilibrium conditions for the asset markets given the position of the output market.[5] Next we substitute the solutions for $i$ and $P$ obtained from the asset market equations into the $d$ function and obtain an implicit function, shown by the $d + g$ line, involving $p$ and $y$. Then we differentiate the equilibrium condition for the output market with respect to $y$ and solve for $\epsilon(p, y|d + g)$, the slope of the $d + g$ curve in figure 1. The slope is the elasticity of $p$ with respect to $y$ obtained from the expenditure and asset market equations. The bars on

[5] The appendix describes the asset market responses discussed in the text.

$\bar{\epsilon}(d, i)$ and $\bar{\epsilon}(d, P)$ indicate that these elasticities include the effect on expenditure of the change in wealth induced by changes in interest rates and asset prices.

$$\begin{aligned}\epsilon(p, y|d + g) = \{1 - (1 - \gamma)[\bar{\epsilon}(d, i)\, \epsilon(i, y|AM) + \bar{\epsilon}(d, P)\, \epsilon(P, y|AM) \\ + \epsilon(d, W_h)\, \epsilon(W_h, y) + \epsilon(d, e)\, \epsilon(e, y)]\} \\ \times \{(1 - \gamma)[\epsilon(d, p) + \bar{\epsilon}(d, i)\, \epsilon(i, p|AM) \\ + \bar{\epsilon}(d, P)\, \epsilon(P, p|AM) + \epsilon(d, W_h)\, \epsilon(W_h, p)]\}^{-1}.\end{aligned}$$

The numerator and denominator depend on the proportion of total output absorbed by government, $\gamma = g/(d + g)$, and on the relative responses of expenditure to asset prices, interest rates and output prices. The elasticity is likely to be negative.[6] The magnitude increases (numerically) as $\gamma$ increases. The rate of use of resources, $y/K$, also affects the size of the elasticity. At low rates of utilization the numerator is smaller than at high rates. The reason is that $\epsilon(i, y|AM)$ and $\epsilon(P, y|AM)$ change with the utilization of capacity and the distribution of income.[7] To simplify the notation, we rewrite the slope of $d + g$ as

$$\epsilon(p, y|d + g) = \{1 - (1 - \gamma)\, \bar{\epsilon}(d, y)\}\{(1 - \gamma)\, \bar{\epsilon}(d, p)\}^{-1}$$

The barred values of the elasticities are defined by the corresponding expressions in the brackets above. The position of the $d + g$ curve depends on anticipations and stocks. The curve is the locus of all $p, y$ combinations satisfying the output and asset market equations simultaneously.

The supply curve ($s$) of output is obtained from the price setting function, equation (1″). The price elasticity of the supply of output increases as capacity utilization increases. The position of the supply curve depends on $K$, $w$ and $\phi$. The slope of the supply curve is denoted $\epsilon(p, y|s)$.

Figure 1a shows a flow equilibrium at the intersection of $d + g$ and $s$. The equilibrium position depends on the stocks of financial assets and real capital, the efficiency wage and anticipations. The size of the financial stocks depends, in turn, on the history of the government's budget and the financing parameter, $\mu$.

In a closed economy with no growth, there cannot be full stock–flow equilibrium

[6] The homogeneity properties of the $d$ function assure that $\epsilon(d, p)$ is large relative to the elasticities with respect to $P$, $W_h$, $W_n$ and $p^*$. The denominator is unambiguously negative. A very large positive value of $\bar{\epsilon}(d, P)\epsilon(P, y|AM)$, substantially greater than unity, is required to turn the numerator negative and determine an ascending "demand" curve. This is unlikely. The $d + g$ curve is an equilibrium position for expenditure, not an expenditure relation as we incorrectly described it in an earlier paper (1974a). J. Marquez-Ruarte pointed out the error. The $d + g$ line is the locus of all combinations $(p, y)$ simultaneously satisfying asset markets and output markets.

[7] The distribution of income changes with fluctuations in income. At low rates of utilization, changes in $y$ have larger effects on $e$ than on $W_h$, while at high rates of utilization, the opposite is true. The elasticities $\epsilon(e, y)$ and $\epsilon(W_h, y)$ are components of $\epsilon(i, y|AM)$ and $\epsilon(P, y|AM)$. On the supply side, $\epsilon(p, y|s)$ rises monotonically with the degree of utilization.

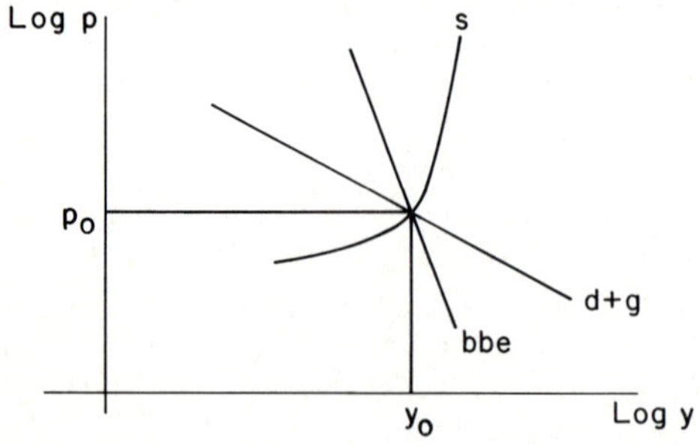


FIGURE 1a

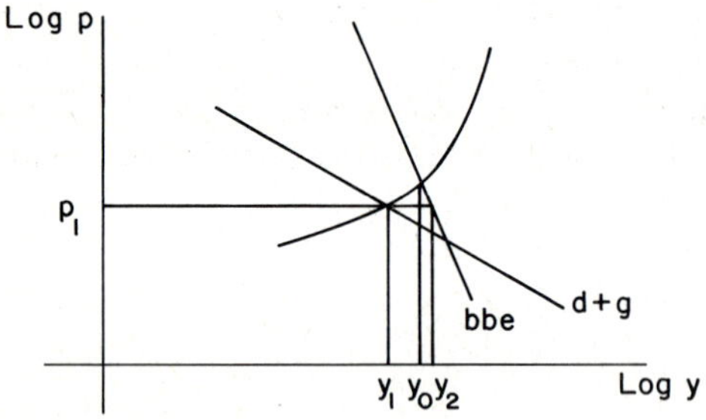


FIGURE 1b

with an unbalanced budget. The relation between the government's budget and the position of the economy is expressed by the balanced budget equation and shown by the *bbe* curve in figure 1. The *bbe* curve is the locus of all $p, y$ combinations that satisfy the asset market equations and the balanced budget equation. To obtain the curve, we substitute the solution for $i$ from the asset market equation into the balanced budget,

$$i = i(y, p, B, S),$$

$$pg + \bar{w}lg + I(i)S = t(p, y, \bar{w}lg; \tau).$$

The position of the curve depends on fiscal and monetary policies. Increases in $g$, $lg$, or $S$ move the line to the right; increases in $\tau$ move the line to the left. The slope of the line, holding $w$ constant, is

$$\epsilon(p, y|bbe; g) = \frac{\epsilon(t, y) - \epsilon(I, i)\,\epsilon(i, y|AM)\,IS/t}{pg/t - \epsilon(t, p) + \epsilon(I, i)\,\epsilon(i, p|AM)\,IS/t} < 0.$$

The elasticity $\epsilon(I, i)$ rises from zero to unity as the average maturity of the debt declines. With a positive wage bill and a positive volume of outstanding government debt, the ratio $pg/t < 1$. The *bbe* line is negatively sloped for all tax revenue functions at least proportional in the price level, i.e., for $\epsilon(t,p) \geqq 1$.[8] If, as we have assumed, government sets the level of real expenditure, $g$, the *bbe* line is relatively steep. If the government directs its fiscal policy at nominal expenditure, $pg$, the elasticity becomes

$$\epsilon(p, y | bbe; pg) = \frac{-\epsilon(t, y) + \epsilon(I, i)\, \epsilon(i, y | AM)\, IS/t}{\epsilon(t, p) - \epsilon(I, i)\, \epsilon(i, p | AM)\, IS/t},$$

and the value of the elasticity is approximately $-1$.

All points on the *bbe* line are, by definition, positions of budget balance. Any price output combination to the right of the line generates a budget surplus, and any point to the left of the line generates a budget deficit. Every budget deficit or surplus requires the banks and the public to increase or decrease holdings of base money and debt, so any departure from the *bbe* line affects the position of the $d + g$ line. Changes in financial stocks change $P$ and $i$ and modify the $d + g$ line. It follows that all points of stock–flow equilibrium must lie at the common intersection of the *bbe* line, the $d + g$ line and the $s$ line. An equilibrium of this kind is shown at $p_0 y_0$ in figure 1a.

### *3.1. Short-Run Equilibrium*

Suppose the output market comes into short-run flow equilibrium with output less than $y_0$, for example at $p_1, y_1$ in figure 1b. With current fiscal policies shown by the position of the *bbe* line, the government budget has a deficit. The size of the deficit increases with the horizontal distance, $y_1 - y_2$, between the position of flow equilibrium at the intersection of $d + g$ and $s$ and the position of budget balance on the *bbe* line at the prevailing price level, $p_1$. A budget surplus forces a reduction in the stocks of base money and securities, and a budget deficit requires an increase in the stocks of these financial assets. The relative size of the changes in each stock depends on the financing parameter, $\mu$, and the speed of adjustment to a balanced budget equilibrium depends on $\mu$ also. As the value of $\mu$ increases, the change in the base and the speed of adjustment to a new equilibrium increase.

[8] A positive slope of the *bbe* line does not alter the main conclusions of the analysis unless the slope of the *bbe* line exceeds the slope of the $s$ curve. For the problem to arise, the share of taxes allocated to interest payments must be so large that increases in output increase interest rates and raise the budget deficit and reductions in expenditure induce ever-increasing budget surpluses.

However, for given $w$, $K$ and unchanged position of $s$, the total size of the adjustment from $p_1\ y_1$ to a position of stock–flow equilibrium declines as $\mu$ increases.

### 3.2. Intermediate-Run Equilibrium

We refer to the resulting stock–flow equilibrium, at an intersection of the $d + g$, $s$, and *bbe* curves, as an intermediate-run equilibrium to emphasize that money wages are constant and $s$ remains fixed. The adjustment to intermediate-run equilibrium involves changes in the $d + g$ line and the *bbe* line. These changes are the responses to the changes in $B$ and $S$ issued to finance the deficit – or retired if a surplus replaces the deficit – in figure 1b.

Financing the deficit increases $B$ and $S$ in the proportion defined by $\mu$. Increases in $B$ and $S$ shift the $d + g$ line to the right. The size of each shift is obtained by differentiating the output market equation with respect to $B$ or $S$ after replacing $i$ and $P$ with their respective solutions from the asset market equations, holding the value of $y$ constant. The two vertical shift elasticities are

$$\epsilon(p, B|d + g) = \Big[- \bar{\epsilon}(d, i)\, \epsilon(i, B|AM) + \bar{\epsilon}(d, P)\, \epsilon(P, B|AM) + + \epsilon(d, W_n) \frac{(1 + \omega)B}{W_n}\Big] \left[\bar{\epsilon}(d, p)\right]^{-1} > 0,$$

$$\epsilon(p, S|d + g) = \epsilon(p, B|d + g) \Bigg\{ \Big[\bar{\epsilon}(d, i)\, \epsilon(i, S|AM) + \bar{\epsilon}(d, P)\, \epsilon(P, S|AM) + \epsilon(d, W_n) \frac{vS}{W_n}\Big] \Big[\bar{\epsilon}(d, i)\, \epsilon(i, B|AM) + \bar{\epsilon}(d, P)\, \epsilon(P, B|AM) + \epsilon(d, W_n) \frac{(1 + w)B}{W_n}\Big]^{-1} \Bigg\} > 0.$$

Both elasticities are positive, so the direction in which the $d + g$ lines shifts is independent of the method of financing the deficit or surplus.[9] The $d + g$ line always shifts in the direction of the *bbe* line, toward a position of budget balance.

[9] A low interest elasticity of expenditure $\epsilon(d, i)$ is clearly not sufficient to eliminate the effect of monetary policy. The sign of the denominator of $\epsilon(p, B|d + g)$ is discussed in the appendix. The sign of the numerator depends on $\epsilon(i, B|AM) < 0$ and $\epsilon(P, B|AM) > 0$. The former is unambiguous; the latter occurs if the interest elasticity of the excess supply of credit exceeds the interest elasticity of the excess supply of money. The signs of the elasticities of $i$ and $P$ with respect to $B$ and $S$ are shown in the appendix. The positive sign of $\epsilon(p, S|d + g)$ requires that in the numerator

$$|\bar{\epsilon}(d, i)\, \epsilon(i, S|AM)| < \bar{\epsilon}(d, P)\, \epsilon(P, S|AM) + \epsilon(d, W_n)\, vS/W_n.$$

The restriction assures that issues of debt to finance expansive fiscal policies increase expenditure and prices. A very large $\bar{\epsilon}(d, i)$ reverses the response of output and prices to debt financed fiscal policy. The stability of the system requires that the inequality above holds.

The size of the shift depends on the relative amounts of base money and debt issued (or withdrawn in the case of a surplus). The larger the value of $\mu$, the larger is the instantaneous shift in the $d + g$ curve. This is shown by the elasticity formulas. The response of the $d + g$ line to a unit change in debt, $\epsilon(p, S|d + g)$, is proportional to $\epsilon(p, B|d + g)$, the response to a unit change in the base. The denominator of the proportionality factor, or ratio, is positive, but the first two terms of the numerator are of opposite sign. The ratio is less than one, so the response of the $d + g$ line to a unit change in the base exceeds the response to a unit change in debt.

The vertical shift in $d + g$ and the slopes of the $d + g$ and $s$ curves determine the position of flow equilibrium to which the system moves in response to changes in $B$ and $S$. We use $\epsilon(p, B|0, AM)$, $\epsilon(y, B|0, AM)$ and similar expressions with $S$ replacing $B$ to denote the responses of prices and output to financial stocks. As before, the responses combine the adjustment of the asset markets and the output market to changes in the financial variables, holding the position of $s$ constant. The 0, $AM$ elasticities define the movement of the flow equilibrium point determined by $d + g$ and $s$ in figure 1.

$$\epsilon(p, B|0, AM) = \frac{-\epsilon(p, B|d + g)\,\epsilon(p, y|s)}{\epsilon(p, y|d + g) - \epsilon(p, y|s)} > 0, \tag{5'}$$

$$\epsilon(y, B|0, AM) = \frac{-\epsilon(p, B|d + g)}{\epsilon(p, y|d + g) - \epsilon(p, y|s)} > 0. \tag{5''}$$

The responses of $p$ and $y$ to $S$ (or $g$) are similar to equations (5′) and (5″); $S$ (or $g$) replaces $B$ in the first term of the numerator.

The response of the flow equilibrium position to a given deficit is a weighted combination of the separate responses of $B$ and $S$ with weights fixed by financial policies. Let $D$ be the cumulated deficit. In a closed economy, the current stocks of $B$ and $S$ record past financial policy,

$$B = B_0 + \bar{\mu}D, \tag{6'}$$
$$S = S_0 + (1 - \bar{\mu})D, \tag{6''}$$

where $\bar{\mu}$ is the mean value of the financing parameter, and $B_0$ and $S_0$ describe stocks of base money and government securities acquired independently of the budget process. $B_0$ and $S_0$ are the values of any prehistoric stocks of base money or securities modified by the cumulated effect of pure open market operations, $v$.

The weighted shift of the $d + g$ curve induced by a deficit (or surplus), per unit, is

$$\epsilon(p, D|d + g) = \epsilon(p, B|d + g)\bar{\mu}\frac{D}{B} + \epsilon(p, S|d + g)(1 - \bar{\mu})\frac{D}{S} > 0.$$

All terms are positive, so the direction of response is independent of current and past financial policies. The magnitude of the response depends on both current and past policies. A large value of $\bar{\mu}$ raises $\epsilon(p, D \mid d + g)$ and the adjustment speed of the flow equilibrium.

The movement to a new flow equilibrium position reduces the initial deficit (or surplus). However, the size of the deficit depends on the distance between the flow equilibrium position and the *bbe* line. The position of the *bbe* line is also changed by the financing of the deficit or surplus and the direction of change depends on the way in which the deficit is financed. The vertical shifts of the *bbe* line, per unit change, are expressed as elasticities. The elasticities are obtained by differentiating the government budget equation with respect to $B$ and $S$ taking into account the effect of price changes on interest rates, holding money wages constant. The numerators of the two elasticities are of opposite sign. The denominators are negative wherever tax revenues are not sufficiently regressive.

$$\epsilon(p, B \mid bbe; g) = \frac{-\epsilon(I, i)\, \epsilon(i, B \mid AM)\, IS/t}{pg/t + \epsilon(i, p \mid AM)\, \epsilon(I, i)\, IS/t - \epsilon(t, p)} < 0,$$

$$\epsilon(p, S \mid bbe; g) = \frac{-[\epsilon(I, i)\, \epsilon(i, S \mid AM) + \epsilon(I, S)]\, IS/t}{pg/t + \epsilon(i, p \mid AM)\, \epsilon(I, i)\, IS/t - \epsilon(t, p)} > 0.$$

An increase in $B$ lowers the *bbe* line, whereas an increase in $S$ raises the line. The size of the change in the *bbe* line depends on the relative sizes of the numerators of the two shift elasticities. With $\epsilon(I, S)$ equal to unity, $\epsilon(p, S \mid bbe)$ probably exceeds $|\epsilon(p, B \mid bbe)|$. At high values of $\mu$, deficits shift the *bbe* line to the left and surpluses shift the *bbe* line to the right. At low values of $\mu$, deficits move the *bbe* line to the right and surpluses move the line to the left.

The speed of convergence to intermediate-run equilibrium and the equilibrium position depend on the value of $\mu$. With $\mu = 1$, the $d + g$ line shifts up when there is a deficit and down when there is a surplus. The *bbe* line shifts the opposite way, down when there is a deficit and up when there is a surplus. The process converges to equilibrium at an intersection of $d + g$, $s$ and *bbe*. In figure 1b, with $\mu = 1$ the *bbe* curve slides down the $s$ curve until it meets the rising $d + g$ curve. For values of $\mu$ near unity, similar movements take place, but as $\mu$ declines the change in the position of the *bbe* curve becomes smaller relative to the change in the position of $d + g$.

We reach a critical value of $\mu$ at which the position of the *bbe* line is fixed. The adjustment to intermediate-run equilibrium is now described by the movement of the $d + g$ curve along $s$. If the intersection of *bbe* and $s$ is a position of long-run equilibrium, the economy returns to long-run equilibrium at unchanged prices and output.

The diagram cannot show a determinate result for low values of $\mu$. The reason is that the *bbe* and $d + g$ lines move in the same direction. Convergence requires that the *bbe* line moves less than the $d + g$ line. Otherwise, the deficit continues and the stocks of financial assets increase forever. Prices rise continuously as $d + g$ chases *bbe* along $s$. The system never reaches intermediate-run equilibrium. At the polar position, $\mu = 0$, if the system does not converge to equilibrium, prices rise with a constant monetary base.

Can there be inflation with a constant monetary base? To show that the system converges to an intermediate-run equilibrium for all values of $\mu$, we substitute in the government budget equation until the equation contains only variables taken as givens in the determination of flow equilibrium. The price level $p$ is replaced by the price setting function. The values of $i$ and $y$ are replaced by their flow equilibrium solutions. The 0, $AM$ elasticities, as in equation (5), describe the properties of these solutions. Further, we use equation (6) to replace $B$ and $S$ with the cumulated deficit and the stocks $B_0$ and $S_0$. We obtain a differential equation relating the current deficit (or surplus) to the cumulated deficit.

$$\mathring{D} = f(D; B_0, S_0, \mu; g, \tau).$$

The stability of the stock–flow system and convergence to intermediate-run equilibrium require that the derivative $f_D < 0$.

The derivative is

$$\frac{\partial f}{\partial D} = \frac{\partial f}{\partial B}\bar{\mu} + \frac{\partial f}{\partial S}(1 - \bar{\mu});$$

$$\frac{\partial f}{\partial B} = \frac{t}{B}\left\{\epsilon(y, B\,|\,0, AM)\left[\epsilon(p, y\,|\,s)\left(\frac{pg}{t} - \epsilon(t, p)\right) - \epsilon(t, y)\right]\right.$$
$$\left. + \epsilon(I, i)\,\epsilon(i, B\,|\,0, AM)\frac{IS}{t}\right\} < 0,$$

$$\frac{\partial f}{\partial S} = \frac{t}{S}\left\{\epsilon(y, S\,|\,0, AM)\left[\epsilon(p, y\,|\,s)\left(\frac{pg}{t} - \epsilon(t, p)\right) - \epsilon(t, y)\right.\right.$$
$$\left.\left. + \left[1 + \epsilon(I, i)\,\epsilon(i, S\,|\,0, AM)\right]\frac{IS}{t}\right\}\right..$$

The necessary conditions for stability and convergence, with any value of $\mu$ are $\epsilon(y, S\,|\,0, AM) > 0$ and a non-regressive tax function. The first condition is discussed in footnote 9 and the accompanying text. The second condition is required to assure $\partial f/\partial S < 0$. The second term of $\partial f/\partial S$ is positive. The derivative remains negative, however, if net interest payments are sufficiently small relative to tax revenues and tax revenues are not overly regressive.

Analysis of stock–flow adjustment to an intermediate-run equilibrium yields four principal conclusions. First, the relative sizes of the shift elasticities $\epsilon(p, B|d+g)$ and $\epsilon(p, S|d+g)$ imply that the *instantaneous* rate of adjustment of output to a budget deficit or surplus increases with the value of $\mu$. Second, the *total* adjustment of output and prices, measured from the initial displacement to the intermediate-run equilibrium, *decreases* as $\mu$ increases. The change along a given $s$ curve reaches a maximum with debt finance, $\mu = 0$, and a minimum with base money finance, $\mu = 1$. Third, any change in $\mu$ changes the equilibrium position of the *bbe* line and therefore affects prices and output. Fourth, maintenance of stock flow equilbrium at constant prices requires a balanced budget and no open market operations. The first of these restrictions assures that $\mathring{D} = 0$; the second maintains a constant ratio of $B_0$ to $S_0$. Both are required for equilibrium in a non-growing economy.

### *3.3. Long-Run Equilibrium*

Money wages cannot be held fixed if prices and output change. The dynamics of the labor market push the system toward a longer-run position determined by long-run output and the long-run *bbe* line. In figure 2 long-run output is shown as a vertical line drawn at $y_0$. The position of $y_0$ depends on productive opportunities, resources, and tastes. The long-run position of flow equilibrium and the long-run position of the *bbe* line depend on the adjustment of money wages. Even in a closed economy with no growth, the long-run position of stock–flow equilibrium differs from the intermediate-run position if prices and money wages change. To reveal the general nature of long-run adjustment, we permit efficiency wages to adjust to market conditions.

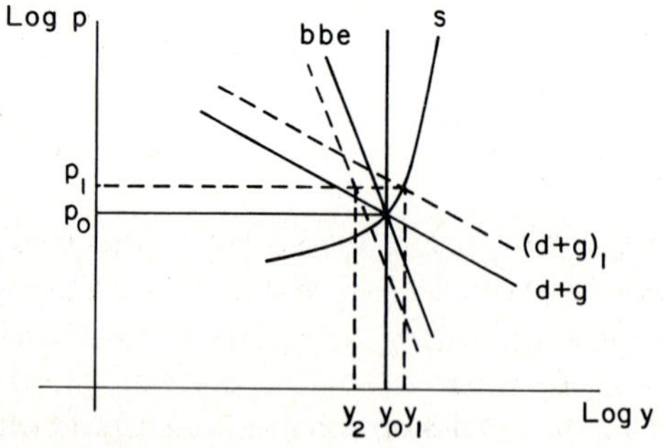


FIGURE 2

The wage adjustment process can be divided into two parts. One links wage movements to prices and completes our analysis of the response to changes in $B$, $S$, and government expenditure; the other develops the general relation between changes in prices, in efficiency wages and in the deviations of output from its long-equilibrium value. Only the first process is discussed here. The second is developed in Brunner (1974b).

The elasticity $\epsilon(w, p)$ describes the (eventual) adjustment of efficiency wages to prices. Adjustment of wages shifts the supply of output and changes the position of flow equilibrium. The response of the $s$ curve is

$$\epsilon(p, w|s)\,\epsilon(w, p)\,\epsilon(p, x|0, AM, s).$$

The responses of the price level and output are

$$\begin{aligned}\epsilon(p, x|0, AM, s) = \{&-\epsilon(p, x|d+g)\,\epsilon(p, y|s)\\ &+ \epsilon(p, y|d+g)\,\epsilon(p, w|s)\,\epsilon(w, p)\,\epsilon(p, x|0, AM, s)\}\\ &\times \{\epsilon(p, y|d+g) - \epsilon(p, y|s)\}^{-1},\\ \epsilon(y, x|0, AM, s) = \{&-\epsilon(p, x|d+g) + \epsilon(p, w|s)\,\epsilon(w, p)\,\epsilon(p, x|0, AM, s)\}\\ &\times \{\epsilon(p, y|d+g) - \epsilon(p, y|s)\}^{-1},\end{aligned}$$

for $x = B, S, g$.

Rearrangement yields

$$\begin{aligned}\epsilon(p, x|0, AM, s) &= \{\epsilon(p, x|d+g)\,\epsilon(p, y|s)\}\,\{\epsilon(p, y|d+g)\\ &\quad\times [1 - \epsilon(p, w|s)\,\epsilon(w, p)] - \epsilon(p, y|s)\}^{-1} > 0,\\ \epsilon(y, x|0, AM, s) &= \{-\epsilon(p, x|d+g)\}/\{\epsilon(p, y|d+g) - \epsilon(p, y|s)\}\\ &\quad\times 1 + [\epsilon(p, w|s)\,\epsilon(w, p)\,\epsilon(p, y|s)]/[den]\},\end{aligned}$$

where *den* is the denominator of $\epsilon(p, x|0, AM, s)$.

With $\epsilon(p, w|s)\,\epsilon(w, p)$ approximately 1,

$$\epsilon(p, x|0, AM, s) \sim \epsilon(p, x|d+g),$$

and

$$\epsilon(y, x|0, AM, s) \sim 0.$$

In the limiting case of flexible money wages, real output is unaffected by monetary and fiscal policies. The instantaneous shift effect of policy variables on output prices is identical to the long-run effect.

The value of the product $\epsilon(p, w|s) \cdot \epsilon(w, p)$ describing the wage adjustment process probably lies between 0 and 1. The results obtained holding the $s$ line fixed correspond to $\epsilon(p, w|s) \cdot \epsilon(w, p) = 0$. This state describes short-run processes and is dominated by the response of output. At the opposite pole the price level absorbs all the effects of wage adjustment, and output is not affected. We conjecture that in the intermediate run, the value for $\epsilon(p, w|s)\cdot\epsilon(w, p)$ produces a noticeable output response. Subsequent wage adjustments strengthen the price response and dampen the output response.

Wage adjustments change little in the dynamics of the intermediate financial stock–flow process. To show this result, we again substitute the solutions from the flow equilibrium system into the deficit function and obtain a differential equation determining the motion of $D$. The main differences from results without wage adjustment are in the properties of the $p$ and $y$ function. With $\epsilon(p, w|s)\cdot\epsilon(w, p) = 0$ the $p$ function was simply the price setting function, whereas it is now a solution function with arguments $B$, $S$ and $g$ and properties established in previous paragraphs. The derivative of the deficit function with respect to $D$ is again a linear combination of derivatives with respect to $B$ and $S$ with weights $\mu$ and $(1 - \mu)$.

$$f_B = \frac{t}{B}\Bigg[\epsilon(p, B|0, AM, s)\left\{\frac{pg}{t} - \epsilon(t, p) + \epsilon(w, p)\left(\frac{wlg}{t} - \epsilon(t, \bar{w}lg)\right)\right\}$$
$$-\epsilon(t, y)\cdot\epsilon(y, B|0, AM, s) + \epsilon(I, i)\cdot\epsilon(i, B|0, AM, s)\,\frac{IS}{t}\Bigg],$$

$$f_S = \frac{t}{S}\Bigg[\epsilon(p, S|0, AM, s)\left\{\frac{pg}{t} - \epsilon(t, p + \epsilon(w, p)\left(\frac{wlg}{t} - \epsilon(t, \bar{w}lg)\right)\right\}$$
$$-\epsilon(t, y)\cdot\epsilon(y, S|0, AM, s) + \left[1 + \epsilon(I, i)\cdot\epsilon(i, S|0, AM, s)\right]\frac{IS}{t}\Bigg].$$

The interaction of wages and prices raises the third component of both derivatives algebraically and lowers the second component algebraically. Both changes narrow the constraints required to assure stability in the case of debt finance. For stability the system may require a minimal value of $\mu$ to prevent the destabilizing influence arising from a numerically small but positive derivative $f_S$. Instability reflects an inadequate financing procedure of the government and becomes most relevant when interest payments are large relative to taxes.

The operation of the wage adjustment process moves the intermediate-run system expressed by the $d + g$, $s$ and *bbe* lines towards an intersection on the vertical long-run output line. Convergence of the system allows us to discuss general directions of longer-run movements by concentrating attention on the intersection between the (long-run) *bbe* line and the vertical long-run output line. Changes in this intersection determine the system's underlying trend movement in prices and output. An examination of longer-run aspects requires a clear description of the long-run *bbe* line.

The line is obtained by replacing $i$ with the solution for $i$ from the asset market ($AM$) equations and replacing $B$ and $S$ by $B_0 + \mu D$ and $S_0 + (1 - \mu)D$. With these changes, the balanced budget equation becomes

$$pg + \bar{w}lg + I\{i[B_0 + \mu D, S_0 + (1 - \mu)D; p, y]\}[S_0 + (1 - \mu)D] = t(p, y, \bar{w}lg; \tau).$$

The position of the line depends on the value of $D$. The slope of the line, with $g$ as a policy variable, is

$$\epsilon(p, y|bbe; g) = \{\epsilon(t, y) - \epsilon(I, i)\epsilon(i, y|AM)\, IS/t\}\{pg/t + \epsilon(\bar{w}, p)\,\bar{w}lg/t + \epsilon(I, i)\epsilon(i, p|AM)\, IS/t - \epsilon(t, p) - \epsilon(\bar{w}, p)\epsilon(t, \bar{w}lg)\}^{-1} > 0.$$

We previously noted that allowing for the adjustment of money wages lowers the denominator numerically; the slope of the *bbe* line becomes slightly steeper. A non-regressive tax revenue function assures that the slope is negative.

The position of the long-run *bbe* line depends on $D$, the cumulated deficit. Once the fiscal policy variables, $g$ and $\tau$, and the parameter $\mu$ have been fixed, the balanced budget determines $D$. This is necessary to assure that in the long-run *bbe* and long-run output, $y_0$, intersect at a price level consistent with the long-run solutions of the output market equations and the government budget equation. The solution for $D$ acts as a scale value that places the *bbe* line at its long-run position.

The value of long-run output depends on opportunities, resources, and tastes. With a stationary population and a constant value of $K$, long-run output $y_0$ and the expected return to capital are fixed. The output and asset market equations determine two ratios and the rate of interest, given long-run output,

$$p/D = \bar{p}(\mu, g, lg, \tau, B_0/D, S_0/D, y_0),$$
$$P/D = \bar{P}(\mu, g, lg, \tau, B_0/D, S_0/D, y_0),$$
$$i = \bar{i}(\mu, g, lg, \tau, B_0/D, S_0/D, y_0).$$

The price-setting function can be used to determine the money wage consistent with long-run equilibrium. This permits the replacement of $w$ in the budget equation by an expression that is linear, homogeneous in $p$. If we now replace $p$ with $\bar{p}D$, $y$ with $y_0$, and $i$ with $\bar{i}$ in the government budget equation, the equation determines a value of $D = D^*$ associated with given fiscal and monetary policy. With proportional taxes, $\epsilon(t, p) + \epsilon(t, \bar{w}lg) = 1$, and $S_0 = B_0 = 0$ the value of $D^*$ is arbitrary. Otherwise, the budget equation determines a unique $D^*$. $D^*$ determines the position of the long-run *bbe* line, and the intersection of the line with $y_0$ determines the price level at which the economy reaches stock equilibrium.

Changes in the intersection between the long-run *bbe* line and long-run equilibrium output, $y_0$, determine the general direction in which the price level changes. Fiscal policy ($g$, $lg$, $\tau$) and monetary policy ($\mu$, $B_0$, $S_0$) affect the relative changes in the position of *both* lines. Increases in the government's absorption of output, $g$, or absorption of labor, $lg$, or lower tax rates, raise the *bbe* line and the price level to which the economy adjusts. Open market operations determine the size of $B_0$ relative to $S_0$, and the choice of $\bar{\mu}$ determines the proportion in which $B$ and $S$ are issued or withdrawn to finance budget deficits and surpluses. Increases in $\bar{\mu}$ lower the *bbe* line and reduce the price level to which the economy adjusts.

In the long run, all costs are variable, capital sells at replacement cost, $p = P$, and the market rate of interest equals the expected return to capital per unit of capital. The system cannot determine values for $\bar{p}D$, $\bar{P}D$ and $\bar{i}$ that ignore these constraints. If the capital stock is fixed and monetary policy sets $\mu$, fiscal policy cannot be predetermined but must adjust to the system. Or, if $lg$, $g$ and $\tau$ are set and $K$ remains fixed, the system determines $\mu$ and $B_0$ or $S_0$.

There is a third alternative. We may choose both fiscal variables, $B_0$ and $S_0$. The long-run conditions $p = P$ and $i = e + \pi$ determine $K$ and $\mu$. All real stocks are then determined endogenously and adjusted to policy variables. The long run level of economic activity is conditioned by the stock of real capital, the labor force, the absorption of labor by the government sector, the amount invested in human capital such as skills and knowledge. These determinants of the level at which $y_0$ settles depend on fiscal and monetary policies. If expenditure, transfer and tax policies and the means of financing deficits and surpluses are set by political or policy decisions, the capital stock, the productivity of capital, and long-run output, $y_0$, must adjust.[10]

## 4. Monetary Policy

The interaction of stocks and flows with the budget deficit or surplus provides a framework within which we can trace the effects of monetary and fiscal policy on prices and output. Population and the capital stock are fixed. There is an efficient long-run output, $y_0$, corresponding to the optimal rate of use of fixed capital and manpower for unchanging tastes, opportunities and realized anticipations. Every departure from equilibrium produces a budget deficit or surplus and requires a decision about the financing of the budget, a choice of $\mu$. The speed of adjustment to a new equilibrium and the characteristics of the new equilibrium depend on the choice. In this section, we analyze the response to changes in

[10] Brunner (1974b) examines these longer-run aspects in greater detail. Discussion of a growing economy requires some minor changes discussed there.

monetary policy – changes in the monetary base. Tax rates and real government expenditure remain fixed. In the following section we analyze the response to fiscal changes – changes in government expenditure and tax rates.

We start from a position of stock–flow equilibrium such as $p_0$, $y_0$ in figure 2. The intersection of the *bbe* line and the vertical line at $y_0$ determines the position of long-run stock equilibrium. The budget is balanced; all stocks are fixed, unchanging and willingly held at prevailing prices and anticipations. The intersection of $d + g$ and $s$ at $y_0$ determines the position of full employment flow equilibrium. Equilibrium positions to the right and left of $y_0$ are admissible positions of flow equilibrium but not positions of full stock equilibrium. In a growing economy, capital and the effective labor force grow; $y_0$ is the rate of output per man with the optimal stock of capital per man. Very little in our discussion depends on the difference between a growing and a non-growing economy, so the capital stock is fixed unless we note the contrary.

Suppose the central bank undertakes an open market operation. A purchase or sale of securities changes $B_0$ and $S_0$, disturbs the asset market equilibrium and thereby changes $P$ and $i$. The initial responses to any change in $B$ and $S$ are weighted sums of the elasticities of $i$ and $P$ with respect to $B$ and $S$. The elasticities and their signs are shown in the appendix. The signs of the elasticities indicate that, initially, asset prices fall and interest rates rise with open market sales. Asset prices rise and interest rates fall with open market purchases. The responses of $i$ and $P$ to open market operations are weighted combinations of the responses to $B$ and $S$. Inspection of the elasticities shows that the responses to changes in the base and to open market operations are approximately equal in modern economies with large outstanding public debt.

$$\begin{aligned}\epsilon(i, 0M0|AM) &= \epsilon(i, B|AM)\, B_0/B - \epsilon(i, S|AM)\, B_0/S < 0,\\ \epsilon(P, 0M0|AM) &= \epsilon(P, B|AM)\, B_0/B - \epsilon(P, S|AM)\, B_0/S > 0.\end{aligned}$$

In an open market operation, $B_0$ and $S_0$ change in opposite directions. Open market operations amplify the response of $i$ and moderate the response of $P$ relative to fiat changes in the base.

An open market operation disturbs the flow equilibrium. The position of flow equilibrium shifts in proportion to a weighted sum of $\epsilon(p, B|0, AM)$ and $\epsilon(p, S|O, AM)$ with weights shown in the previous section. We noted there that the sum is dominated by the response to the base. If we start from full employment, the new position of flow equilibrium is above full employment equilibrium output following an open market purchase and below full employment equilibrium output following a sale. In figure 2, we have shown the response to an open market purchase. Flow equilibrium is at output $y_1$, and there is a budget surplus.

Open market operations also change the position of the *bbe* line. Purchases lower the line by reducing the outstanding stock of securities and interest payments. The response of the *bbe* line reinforces the output effect; the surplus increases as shown in figure 2.

The budget imbalance induced by monetary policy starts a process that restores stock equilibrium. The budget surplus reduces $B$ and $S$. The reductions of $B$ and $S$ shift $d + g$ to the left, reducing expenditure. With $s$ constant, the position of flow equilibrium moves toward the *bbe* line. Output and prices decline. The speed of adjustment depends on the financing of the budget, i.e., on the choice of $\mu$. A large value of $\mu$ raises the rate at which the intersection of $d + g$ and $s$ converges to an intersection with *bbe*. The common intersection is a position of intermediate-run equilibrium.

The position of the *bbe* line depends on the financing of the surplus. If pure open market operations cease, $B_0$ and $S_0$ remain at their new values. Further changes in $B$ and $S$ arise from the financing of the budget and depend on the choice of $\mu$. There is a critical value of $\mu$ that holds the *bbe* line constant. A value of $\mu$ less than the critical value reinforces the effect of the open market purchase on the position of the *bbe* line. The *bbe* line shifts away from the initial position shown by the solid *bbe* line in figure 2. A large value of $\mu$ offsets the downward shift induced by the initial open market purchase. In this case, the broken *bbe* line in figure 2 moves in the direction of the solid *bbe* line.

Fiscal policy $(g, \tau)$ and monetary policy $(\mu, B_0, S_0)$ determine the position of the long-run *bbe* line. The intersection of the long-run *bbe* line and the long-run output line, $y_0$, determines the long-run equilibrium price level. With fiscal policy constant, the long-run equilibrium price level is *lowered* by an open market purchase. And the larger $\mu$ relative to the critical value following the open market purchase, the larger is the decline in the price level.

Figure 2 shows the adjustment. The solid lines are the initial position of equilibrium. An open market purchase raises $P$ and lowers $i$, shifting the $d + g$ curve to the position shown as $(d + g)_1$. The *bbe* line moves down, as shown by the broken line. There is a budget surplus, proportional to $y_1 - y_2$. With money wages and anticipations unchanged, the position of the $s$ curve is fixed. The surplus moves $d + g$ back along the $s$ curve until $s$, *bbe*, and $d + g$ intersect. The intersection is a position of intermediate-run equilibrium. The intermediate-run equilibrium is at an output below $y_0$; the precise location depends on the choice of $\mu$. Money wages gradually adjust to prices, so the efficiency wage declines, and the $s$ curve shifts to the right. Output increases, and prices fall.

Stock–flow equilibrium at output $y_0$ can occur only if the equilibrium price level is fully anticipated by purchasers and producers and embedded in wage contracts. Unless money wages eventually fall during the adjustment to an open market purchase and rise during the adjustment to an open market sale, real output cannot return to $y_0$. With money wages fixed, open market purchases first raise employment, output and prices but adjustment of asset and output markets lowers employment, output and prices. Open market sales have the opposite effects on prices, output and employment.

If there were no adjustment in money wages, real output, or per capita real output, and the price level would be correlated positively. The adjustment of money wages removes the correlation between prices and output, but the price level does not return to its previous value. Output prices and market interest rates are lower at full employment following an open market purchase and higher following an open market sale. The response of interest rates is similar to the conclusion about the effects of open market operations reached by Metzler (1951). The response of prices differs.

All conditions for long-run full equilibrium have not been satisfied at this point. We note that $\epsilon(P, B|AM) - \epsilon(P, S|AM)$ is positive. Asset prices remain higher relative to output prices after adjustment to an open market purchase and relatively lower after adjustment to an open market sale. Since there cannot be full stock flow equilibrium with $P \neq p$, further adjustment is required to reach full equilibrium.

To restore full stock flow equilibrium with unchanged fiscal policy, the composition of expenditure and the size of the capital stock must change. With output prices and market interest rates lower, and asset prices higher, after adjustment to an open market purchase, investment increases relative to consumption, so the capital stock increases. Open market purchases increase the equilibrium stock of capital, or capital per man, and open market sales reduce the equilibrium stock of capital. Long-run output, $y_0$, depends on the capital stock and changes as the capital stock changes.

Changes in the *bbe* line and the level of long-run output imply that the adjustments following an open market operation do not return the economy to the previous equilibrium. In the equilibrium reached after full adjustment of *bbe* and $y_0$ to an open market purchase, output, or output per man, is higher and prices are lower. Open market sales reduce equilibrium output and raise prices. In the long-run prices and output are negatively related. After full adjustment, real balances and the stock of real capital are complements; bonds and real capital are substitutes.

The qualitative conclusions from our analysis of the long-run adjustment to an open market operation do not depend on whether equilibrium is disturbed by the purchase or sale of securities, as in Metzler (1951) and Patinkin (1965). Suppose, as is customary, that money is distributed by airplane, destroyed in a furnace, delivered like milk, or withdrawn by vacuum cleaner. Each of these operations changes $B_0$ and, therefore, the relation of $B_0$ to $S_0$. The position of full employment stock–flow equilibrium depends on $B_0$ and $S_0$ and changes as either magnitude changes. The signs of $\epsilon(i, B|AM)$, $\epsilon(P, B|AM)$ and $\epsilon(p, B|O, AM)$ are the same as the corresponding elasticities with respect to open market operations. Money wages must *fall* to restore full employment following an increase in the base and must *rise* in the full adjustment to a decrease in the base. The equilibrium capital stock is higher following an increase in base money and lower following a decrease. Prices and real output are negatively related in the long-run response to a change in money just as in the case of an open market operation.[11]

To this point, we have assumed that the government maintains real expenditure and keeps tax rates unchanged. The size of the budget deficit or surplus, at each price–output combination, depends on these assumptions. For a given tax rate schedule a policy of maintaining constant nominal expenditure, *pg*, produces a larger deficit when the base is reduced and a larger surplus when the base is increased relative to the deficit or surplus when fiscal policy holds *g* constant.

Maintaining constant nominal government expenditure, *pg*, increases the contribution of policy to the stability of aggregate real expenditure. The countercyclical increases in debt and money induced by shifts in expenditure are larger than under the policy of keeping *g* constant. Moreover, the shift in the position of the *bbe* line is larger algebraically per unit change in *B* but smaller numerically. The size of the shift in the *bbe* line induced by a change in the base is

$$\epsilon(p, B|bbe; pg) = \frac{-\epsilon(i, B|AM)\, \epsilon(I, i)\, IS/t}{\epsilon(i, p|AM)\, IS/t - \epsilon(t, p)} < 0,$$

The elasticity $\epsilon(p, S|bbe; pg)$ is algebraically and numerically smaller than the elasticity for fixed *g*. A policy of maintaining constant *pg* lowers the absolute value of the response of the equilibrium price level to changes in money. If remains true, however, that changes in money change the equilibrium stock of real capital, output, prices and real returns.

## 5. Fiscal Policy

Monetary policy consists of setting reserve requirement ratios, discount rates and choosing values of $\mu$, $B_0$ and $S_0$. Fiscal policy consists of setting government expenditures and tax rates. Fiscal policy determines the relative sizes of the private and public sectors and the distribution of income.

[11] A qualification to these propositions is that an initial increase in *B*, with *S* unchanged, followed by a financial policy of maintaining $\mu = 1$ restores the previous equilibrium. This is the analogue of a fiat change in money when the government budget equation is acknowledged.

Policies interact. The speed of adjustment to changes in monetary policy depends on a fiscal decision, the decision to maintain constant real or nominal government expenditure. The size of the "automatic" or "built-in" stabilizers increases, at any deviation from full employment output, if the maintained fiscal policy holds nominal expenditure constant. The response to a change in tax rates or real government expenditure varies with the method of financing the resulting deficit or surplus, the choice of $\mu$.

In this section, we analyze the response to changes in $g$ on short- and long-run equilibrium. To separate the effects of fiscal and monetary policy, we assume throughout this section that $\mu$ remains constant at the prevailing value of $B/S$. Base money and securities are issued or withdrawn in proportion to the ratio of $B$ to $S$ prevailing before the fiscal change. $B_0$ and $S_0$ are constant also.

Every change in $g$ (or $\tau$) disturbs both the flow equilibrium and the stock equilibrium. Per unit percent change in $g$ the $d + g$ curve shifts by an amount

$$\epsilon(p, g|d + g) = -\gamma/[(1 - \gamma)\,\bar{\epsilon}(d, p)] > 0.$$

The denominator is negative, as discussed previously, so an increase in government expenditure raises prices and output, and a reduction in $g$ lowers prices and output. The size of the response depends on the distribution of expenditure between the government and the private sector. The larger is $\gamma$, the larger is the relative size of the government. The size of the response of prices to fiscal policy on the output market increases as $\gamma$ increases.

The change in the stock equilibrium position depends on the method of financing the resulting deficit or surplus, the value of $\mu$, on the tax revenue function, and on the choice of $g$ or $pg$ as a budget or expenditure policy. Holding $g$ constant at the level reached after the change induces a much larger shift in the stock equilibrium position than holding nominal government expenditure constant. The reason is that with real expenditure constant the price level must rise or fall until the private sector releases or absorbs an amount of real output equal to the change in $g$. Holding $pg$ constant, following a change in real expenditure, distributes the effect of the induced price change between the real expenditure of the government and private sectors. The effects of the alternative policies on the stock equilibrium position is shown by comparing the changes in the position of the *bbe* line,

$$\epsilon(p, g|bbe; g) = \frac{-[pg/t]}{pg/t - \epsilon(t, p) + \epsilon(I, i)\,\epsilon(i, p|AM)\,IS/t} > 0,$$

$$\epsilon(p, g|bbe; pg) = \frac{-[pg/t]}{-\epsilon(t, p) + \epsilon(I, i)\,\epsilon(i, p|AM)\,IS/t} > 0.$$

The relative responses to the two types of expenditure policy depend only on the denominators. The denominator of $\epsilon(p, g|bbe; pg)$ is approximately unity, so the ratio of the two elasticities is approximately equal to

$$(pg - t)/-t = IS/t,$$

the ratio of interest payments to tax collections. At current values, the policy of holding $g$ constant raises the response of the price level to fiscal changes by a factor of 9 or 10.

An increase in $g$ raises both the $d + g$ line and the *bbe* line. The relative magnitude of the two vertical shifts determines the system's subsequent adjustment. If the shift of the $d + g$ line exceeds the shift of the *bbe* line, the flow equilibrium at an intersection of $d + g$ and $s$ lies to the right of the *bbe* line. The financial stock–flow equilibrium on *bbe* associated with the new level of $g$ is below the new flow equilibrium position. The increase in $g$ produces a *surplus*, lowering $B$ and $S$ and driving the $d + g$ line back to the *bbe* line. If the response of the *bbe* line is larger than the response of $d + g$, the new flow equilibrium occurs below the new *bbe* line. There is a budget deficit. The resulting deficit accelerates $B$ and $S$, expands output and raises prices. The additional increases in $p$ and $y$ are responses to the financial consequences of the deficit.

The position of intermediate-run stock–flow equilibrium reached after adjustment to the change in $g$ and the resulting deficit or surplus depends on the slopes of the $d + g$, $s$, and *bbe* curves and on the size of the shifts, $\epsilon(p, g|d + g)$ and $\epsilon(p, g|bbe)$. Both the slope and the position of the balanced budget equation depend on the choice of budget policy – constant real or nominal expenditure. Moreover, the slope of the price setting function depends on capacity utilization. All that can be said without considering relative orders of magnitude is that, for given anticipations, money wages and stock of capital, stock–flow equilibrium lies at higher output and prices following the adjustment to an increase in $g$ and at lower output and price level following a reduction in $g$.

With constant anticipations and money wages, expansive fiscal policy lowers real wages; and fiscal contraction increases real wages (per efficiency unit). The change in real wages is a main reason that stock–flow equilibrium can be achieved temporarily at a position above or below full employment. Restoring real wages to the level of the previous full employment equilibrium by changing money wages does not restore the price level that prevailed at the previous full stock–flow equilibrium. The *bbe* line and therefore the position of stock equilibrium has changed. If, as we have assumed, real or nominal expenditure and $\mu$ are maintained, the price level remains higher than in the previous equilibrium following an increase in $g$, and prices remain lower after a reduction in $g$. The magnitude of the price change depends, of course, on the choice of expenditure policy.

The economy cannot return to full stock–flow equilibrium if asset prices and output prices are unequal. Increases in *g* raise *p* and, generally, lower *P* and increase *i*. The changes in *P* and *i* are a consequence of the redistribution of income and the effects of the redistribution on the credit and money markets. The changes in *P*, *i* and *p* assure that the intermediate-run stock–flow equilibrium reached following adjustment to a change in *g* is not maintained. Even if money wages remain unchanged, the stock equilibrium and the flow equilibrium cannot persist. The increase in *p* and reduction in *P*, following an increase in *g*, leaves the price of existing assets lower than the price of current output. Any increase in money wages further increases prices and interest rates and lowers asset prices. To restore full equilibrium, the distribution of expenditure between consumption and investment must change. An increase in consumption and a reduction in investment moves the economy toward equilibrium, the capital stock (or capital per man) is smaller following an increase in *g* and larger following a reduction in *g*. For the

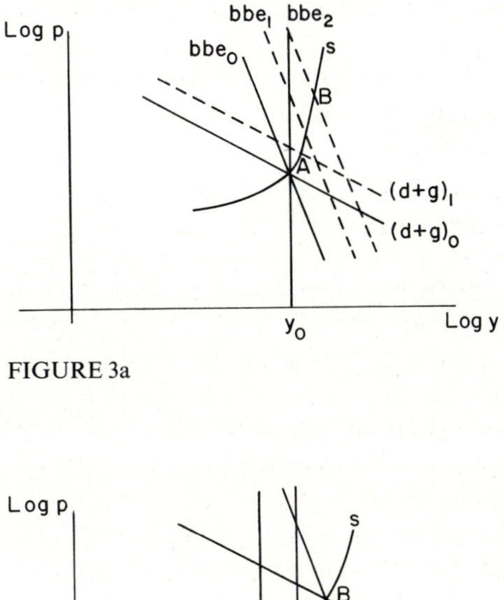


FIGURE 3a

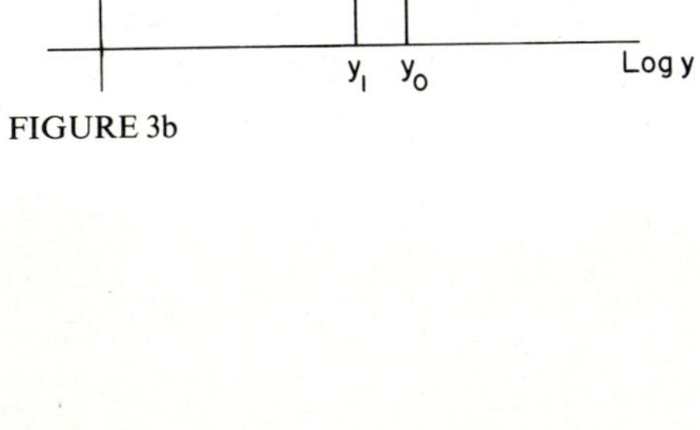


FIGURE 3b

longer-run adjustment of the price level to a change in $g$, the effects on *bbe* and long-run output are reinforcing. The level of prices is positively related to $g$.

Fiscal policy has short-run, intermediate-run and long-run effects. Figure 3 brings out aspects of these adjustments. We start from a full stock–flow equilibrium, at the intersection of the solid lines in figure 3a. The budget is balanced; and the flow markets are in equilibrium at long-run output equal to $y_0$. An increase in $g$, with $\mu$, $B_0$ and $S_0$ given, raises the *bbe* line to $bbe_1$ and the $d + g$ line to $(d + g)_1$. Comparison of the two responses to $g$ shows that $\epsilon(p, g|d + g)$ is a small fraction of $\epsilon(p, g|bbe; g)$. The size of the relative shifts assures that the flow equilibrium at the intersection of $(d + g)_1$ and $s$ is to the left of $bbe_1$. The government budget is in deficit. Point $A$ shows the short-run flow equilibrium.

The financing of the deficit gradually moves the $d + g$ line to the right. With fixed $B_0$ and $S_0$, and $\mu$ below the critical level, the cumulated deficit, $D$, moves the *bbe* line to the right along the $s$ curve. The economy reaches point $B$, a position of intermediate-run equilibrium at the intersection of $bbe_2$, $s$ and a $d + g$ curve. Output and prices are higher. The movement from the initial position to $A$ is the pure fiscal effect of fiscal policy and the movement from $A$ to $B$ shows the financial effect of the same policy.

The system does not remain at the intermediate-run position, $B$. Output at $B$ is above the long-run level; wages and prices rise, and the $s$ line moves to the left. A further round of financial stock–flow adjustments moves the flow equilibrium system along a northwesterly path toward the intersection of the long-run *bbe* line and the new level of long-run output, $y_1$, in figure 3b.

Fiscal policy has real and nominal effects in the short and in the long run. Our discussion of figure 3 shows that the expansive effect of an increase in $g$ is eroded in the longer run by the operation of the wage adjustment process. Eventually, the adjustment of the stock of real capital converts the initial expansion of output into a decline of long-run output. Prices are higher in both the short and long run relative to the price level in the initial equilibrium. A reduction in $g$, depresses real output in the shorter run but increases long-run output of the private sector. Prices are lower following the reduction in $g$.

Similar conclusions are obtained from the analysis of changes in tax rates. Increases in tax rates reduce output prices, interest rates and asset prices and raises real wages in the short run. The size of the price and interest rate changes depends on expenditure policy. A policy of maintaining constant nominal expenditure induces smaller changes in the position of stock equilibrium than a policy of maintaining constant real expenditure. Full adjustment to an increase in tax rates is not completed until money wages fall and asset prices are again equal to output prices. The composition of real expenditure changes to adjust the capital stock.

## 6. Monetarist Implications and Conjectures

What makes our theory a monetarist theory instead of a Keynesian, neo-Keynesian or quantity theory? We trust that the careful reader finds many points at which we do not differ from other economists, including economists who would not christen their theories "monetarist". Often, labels remain, sustained by the intellectual laziness that postpones careful examination of implications and propositions long after hypotheses have changed and distinctions have blurred. There is, therefore, reason to end this paper by pointing to the characteristics that we regard as "monetarist", if a label is to be assigned, and to point out also the relation of the implications and conjectures to the hypothesis.

A theory is not a monetarist theory unless three conditions are met. One, the long-run position to which the system moves is determined by stocks, particularly the stock of money, and not by flows. Stocks and flows interact, but in the longer run, flows adjust to stocks. Two, the adjustment to a change in money involves substitution between money, other assets and new production. Adjustment is not confined to a narrow range of assets, called bonds, or a single price, "the" interest rate. Changes in money modify relative prices and initiate a process of substitution that spreads to the markets for existing capital, securities, loans and current output. Three, the economic system is stable. Cumulative movements of prices or output result mainly from the decisions or actions of governments not individuals or private institutions. The private sector has a stabilizing influence, so that the economy adjusts to any maintained policy.

Together, or separately, we and other "monetarists" have made these statements, or similar statements, for many years. Contrasts and conflicts between "monetarists" and non-monetarists are most apparent in policy recommendations or criticisms and discussions of past and future courses of action. These discussions reveal differences in analysis and interpretation of events that cannot be reduced to differences about the slopes of standard *IS* and *LM* curves of Hicks' or the similar curves of Metzler's analysis, as is often suggested [Okun (1971) and Samuelson (1969)].

The transmission of monetary changes, in our analysis, does not depend on the interest elasticities of the demand for money and expenditure. The relative interest elasticities that matter are the interest elasticities of the money and credit markets. As long as the credit market response to interest rates exceeds the money market response, increases in the base raise the prices of real assets and reductions in the base lower asset prices. Moreover, a small response of expenditure to interest rates, "elasticity pessimism", has no implication for the effectiveness of monetary policy. Monetary policy affects expenditure by changing interest rates and asset prices, so the combined effects of the changes, not the separate effects, determines the response of expenditure.

The difference in implications reflects differences in the transmission or adjustment process. In Hicksian analysis, real capital is locked in portfolios and is not affected by the substitution and adjustment processes. There are markets for money and bonds, but Walras' law is used to eliminate analysis of the bond market. The money market remains as the only relevant asset market. In Metzler's interpretation, real output is fixed and all non-monetary assets are perfect substitutes, so a single asset price or interest rate is all that is required for the analysis of substitution between money and other assets.

Metzler's analysis clarified a number of outstanding issues. However, he did not analyze positions other than long-run full equilibrium or permit prices of existing assets to differ from replacement costs. To move beyond his analysis, we assume that bonds and claim to real capital are not perfect substitutes. The money market is supplemented by another asset market, the credit market.[12] Asset prices join interest rates in the transmission of monetary (and fiscal) changes. Once these changes are made, the response of assets and output to policy variables becomes more pervasive than in Keynesian models.

Long-run positions of stock–flow equilibrium are adjustments to the position determined by past policies, real resources, tastes, opportunities and realized anticipations. The accumulated effects of past policies determine the outstanding stocks of money and debt. Fiscal policy determines the size of budget deficits or surpluses and monetary policy determines the distribution of stocks of financial assets between money and debt. If fiscal and monetary policies remain fixed, long-run equilibrium requires adjustment of the prices of assets and output and the stock of real capital. In the long run, government securities and real capital are substitutes; base money and capital are complements.

The price level and real output settle at a position determined by the stocks of money, debt and capital, for given resources, tastes and opportunities. In stationary, long-run equilibrium the budget must be balanced and the stocks of money and debt unchanging. We show that, if the system is stable and there are reasonable restrictions on the tax revenue function, the economy converges to an equilibrium for any combination of debt and base money issued or withdrawn to finance budget deficits or surpluses.[13] The principal long-run effects of maintained

[12] The real capital market is related by Walras' law to the credit and money market. The choice of the two markets involves no logical issue. It reflects a judgment about a useful strategy for empirical research.

[13] The qualifications apply to fiscal policy financed by debt issues. The response of real output to a change in debt depends on a combination of negative and positive responses $\bar{\epsilon}(d, i)\ \epsilon(i, S|AM) +$

government policies are on the level of prices, the distribution of output between consumption and investment expenditure and the level of output at which the economy reaches equilibrium, not on the existence of equilibrium. The private sector adjusts to any set of maintained government fiscal and monetary policies.

Of particular interest is the response to a maintained change in real or nominal government expenditure financed entirely by issuing debt. Our analysis implies that the interaction of stocks and flows brings the budget into balance at a constant price level, under the conditions reiterated in footnote 13. Fiscal changes induce once and for all adjustments of the equilibrium price level, long-run equilibrium output and the stock of capital.

A maintained fiscal position does not induce steady inflation or deflation whether financed entirely by debt or by base money. The main differences between money and debt finance are on the level of long-run output and prices and on the speed of adjustment to equilibrium. The speed of adjustment to a deficit rises with the ratio of base money to debt issued (or withdrawn in the event of a surplus). The long-run price level is *lower* and output is higher the larger the ratio of base money to debt accumulated in the financing of deficits and surpluses and resulting from open market operations.

The stability of the private sector, one of the principal monetarist conjectures, is an implication of our stock flow analysis. Keynesians typically assume that the private sector is unstable. Waves of optimism or pessimism, stable Phillips curves and the "autonomy of the wage unit"[14] determine the rate of inflation. Any proposition asserting that prices or wages move independently of current and past market conditions and the values of financial variables is inconsistent with the monetarist proposition and with our analysis. The evidence is not conclusive but we believe that the weight of the evidence, including the evidence from large econometric models, supports us.

The stability of the private sector supports another of the principal monetarist propositions. Inflation (or deflation) can occur, in our analysis, only if some impulse is maintained. A one-time change in base money, government expenditure, tax rates, debt, or anticipated real returns produces at most a one-time adjustment of prices. Inflation or deflation cannot occur unless some impulse is

*Footnote 13 continued*
$\bar{\epsilon}(d, P)\ \epsilon(P, S|AM)$ that must be non-negative if the system is stable. Also a slightly progressive tax revenue function may be required to balance the budget at the higher or lower interest payments resulting from the financing of fiscal policy solely by issuing or withdrawing debt.

[14] An explicit statement of the "autonomy" of prices and wage movements is in a recent paper by Lerner (1974). He argues that excess demand creates inflation and deficient demand creates depression (at unchanged prices or wages). Therefore, if one observes "stagflation" one necessarily has a demand deficiency. But, we also require recognition of a supplementary force driving prices independently of market conditions.

maintained. We observe secular increases in the share of output absorbed by the government sector in many countries, but we have not observed sporadic increases capable of explaining observed inflation or deflation. Nor do we know of any evidence of steady changes in the expected return to capital or the monopoly positions of unions and corporations that is capable of explaining current or past rates of price change. The absence of such evidence is inconsistent with the eclectic–agnostic view and the "special factors" explanations of inflation and deflation. Evidence showing the effect of monetary growth on inflation and deflation is consistent with our analysis, supports our hypothesis and the monetarist proposition that the monetary impulse is the dominant impulse in inflations or deflations.

The three conjectures constitute the core of monetarism, but they are not the only monetarist propositions. Differences between monetarists and some Keynesian and eclectic economists are not limited to conjectures about the impulses initiating major changes in prices and output, or the processes transmitting such changes from one market to another, or the stability of the private sector. There are differences in methods also. Monetarists have not developed large-scale econometric models – models with twenty or more behavior equations – to analyze or predict aggregate behavior. The reason is that many Keynesians treat allocative detail as central to an explanation of aggregative behavior, and monetarists do not. Nowhere in our discussion of short- and intermediate-run adjustment did we find reason to mention the distribution of output between consumption and investment or the many kinds of consumption and investment spending. For us, the distribution of private expenditure is determined by relative prices and wealth in response to monetary and fiscal policies. The distribution is not invariant. In the long run, fiscal policy determines the absolute size of the government sector and the relative size of the private and the government sector. Both the stock of private capital and the level of long-run output change inversely to the size of the government sector and the stock of securities. Changes of this kind have important long-run but not short-run effects on output and the price level.

On the asset market of our analysis, the excess supply of government securities and the excess supply of money simultaneously determine the asset price level and the market rate of interest. The allocation of credit by type of loan or securities plays no role and has no effect on aggregates. In large, econometric models, and in policy discussions, many Keynesians assign importance to the allocation of credit. Selective credit controls, changes in the stock of mortgages, and other changes in the distribution of financial assets have effects on the composition of spending and on aggregate output. "Credit rationing" and institutional practice are used to justify these hypotheses and policy recommendations.

Once again, the difference in analysis reflects a difference in the roles assigned to relative prices. To us, "credit rationing" means that the empirical counterpart of the term "price" often includes the terms and conditions of a contract or agreement. The adjustment of relative prices includes such changes in terms. Changes in terms and conditions under which borrowing and lending occur change the allocation of financial assets but have very little effect on the allocation of real resources and no effect on total spending.

A century of assertions has not produced any reliable or persuasive evidence that the phenomenon called "credit rationing" affects the composition of spending or its total. The absence of such evidence is support for the monetarist proposition and our hypothesis that assign no role to allocative detail.

Discussion of the conjectures and implication dividing economists, and their relation to the formal analysis of the paper, can be extended. Perhaps enough has been said to justify our contention that monetarism is *not* a set of empirical conjectures about the slopes of *IS* and *LM* curves or a proposition denying any effect of fiscal policy.

## Appendix: Some Asset Market Responses

(1) Response to the base,

$$\epsilon(i, B|AM) = -\frac{\epsilon(MM, P) - \epsilon(CM, P)}{\epsilon(CM, i)\cdot\epsilon(MM, P) - \epsilon(MM, i)\cdot\epsilon(CM, P)} < 0,$$

$$\epsilon(P, B|AM) = -\frac{\epsilon(CM, i) - \epsilon(MM, i)}{\Delta},$$

where $\Delta$ is the same denominator as in $\epsilon(i, B|AM)$. The components of the expression defining the two elasticities are

$$\epsilon(CM, i) = \epsilon(a, i) - \epsilon(\sigma, i) > 0, \qquad \epsilon(MM, i) = \epsilon(m, i) - \epsilon(L, i) > 0,$$

$$\epsilon(CM, P) = \epsilon(a, P) - \epsilon(\sigma, P) > 0, \qquad \epsilon(MM, P) = \epsilon(m, P) - \epsilon(L, P) < 0.$$

Inspection of these expressions yields the following interpretation:

$\epsilon(CM, i)$ the interest elasticity of the excess supply of "bank credit" or earning assets,

$\epsilon(MM, i)$ the interest elasticity of the excess supply of money.

A similar interpretation applies to the two elasticities with respect to $P$.

The following inequality is the basic order constraint of our analysis,

$$\epsilon(CM, i) > \epsilon(MM, i) > 0.$$

The reader should note that with $\epsilon(CM, i) = \epsilon(MM, i)$ the extended range of substitution relations induced by changes in $B$ becomes irrelevant. Debt and real capital remain less than perfect substitutes, and our analysis of fiscal policy is unaffected.

(2) Response to government securities,

$$\epsilon(i, S|AM) \sim \{\epsilon(MM, P)/\Delta\}\,(S/aB) > 0,$$

$$\epsilon(P, S|AM) \sim -\{\epsilon(MM, i)/\Delta\}\,(S/aB) > 0.$$

The approximations ($\sim$) denote that minor effects of wealth are omitted.

(3) Response to $p$,

$$\epsilon(i, p|AM) = -\{\overset{-}{\epsilon(CM, p)}\cdot\overset{-}{\epsilon(MM, P)} - \overset{-}{\epsilon(MM, p)}\cdot\overset{+}{\epsilon(CM, P)}\}/\Delta > 0,$$

$$\epsilon(P, p|AM) = -\{\overset{+}{\epsilon(CM, i)}\cdot\overset{-}{\epsilon(MM, p)} - \overset{+}{\epsilon(MM, i)}\cdot\overset{-}{\epsilon(CM, p)}\}/\Delta < 0,$$

where

$$\epsilon(CM, p) = \epsilon(a, p) - \epsilon(\sigma, p) < 0, \quad \epsilon(MM, p) = \epsilon(m, p) - \epsilon(L, p) < 0.$$

The sign for $\epsilon(P, p|AM)$ is based on the order condition $0 > \epsilon(CM,p) > \epsilon(MM,p)$. Note that $|\epsilon(P, p|AM)| < 1$.

(4) Response to $y$,

$$\epsilon(i, y|AM) = -\{\overset{-}{\epsilon(CM, y)}\cdot\overset{-}{\epsilon(MM, P)} - \epsilon(MM, y)\cdot\overset{+}{\epsilon(CM, P)}\}/\Delta > 0,$$

$$\epsilon(P, y) = \{\epsilon(CM, i)\cdot\epsilon(MM, y) - \epsilon(MM, i)\cdot\epsilon(CM, y)\}/\Delta,$$

where

$$\begin{aligned}\epsilon(CM, y) &= [\epsilon(a, W_h) - \epsilon(\sigma, W_h)]\,\overset{+}{\epsilon(W_h, y)} \\ &\quad + \overset{-}{[\epsilon(a, e) - \epsilon(\sigma, e)]}\,\overset{+}{\epsilon(e, y)} < 0, \\ \epsilon(MM, y) &= \overset{-}{[\epsilon(m, W_h) - \epsilon(L, W_h)]}\,\overset{+}{\epsilon(W_h, y)} \\ &\quad + \overset{+}{[\epsilon(m, e) - \epsilon(L, e)]}\,\overset{+}{\epsilon(e, y)} \gtrless 0.\end{aligned}$$

## Bibliography

Brunner, K., 1971, A survey of selected issues in monetary theory, Schweizerische Zeitschrift für Volkswirtschaft und Statistik 107, pp. 1–146.

Brunner, K., 1974a, A diagrammatic exposition of the money supply process, Schweizerische Zeitschrift für Volkswirtschaft und Statistik 109, pp. 481–533.

Brunner, K., 1974b, Inflation, money and the role of fiscal arrangements: An analytic framework for the inflation problem, Conference on the New Inflation (Milan, June 24–26, 1974).

Brunner, K. and A. H. Meltzer, 1968, Liquidity traps for money, bank credit and interest rates, Journal of Political Economy 76, pp. 1–37.

Brunner, K. and A. H. Meltzer, 1972, A monetarist framework for aggregative analysis, Proceedings of the First Konstanz Seminar on Monetary Theory and Monetary Policy, Kredit und Kapital (Duncker & Humboldt, Berlin) pp. 31–88.

Brunner, K. and A. H. Meltzer, 1974a, Money, debt and economic activity, Journal of Political Economy 80, pp. 951–977.

Brunner, K. and A. H. Meltzer, 1974b, Monetary and fiscal policy in open, interdependent economies, in: E. Claassen and P. Salin, eds., Paris–Dauphine Conference on Monetary Theory, forthcoming in this series.

Burger, A., 1972, The money supply process (Wadsworth, Belmont, Calif.).

Christ, C., 1972, A simple macroeconomic model with a government budget restraint, Journal of Political Economy 76, pp. 53–67.

Gramley, L. and S. Chase, 1965, Time deposits in monetary analysis, Federal Reserve Bulletin 51, pp. 1380–1406.

Hicks, J. R., 1937, Mr. Keynes and the "classics": A suggested interpretation, Econometrica 5, pp. 147–159.

Keynes, J. M., 1936, The general theory of employment, interest and money (Macmillan, New York).

Lerner, A. P., 1974, From the treatise on money to the general theory, Journal of Economic Literature 12, pp. 38–42.

Metzler, L., 1951, Wealth, saving and the rate of interest, Journal of Political Economy 59, pp. 93–116.

Okun, A., 1971, Rules and roles for fiscal and monetary policy, in: J. Diamond, ed., Issues in fiscal and monetary policy: The eclectic economist views the controversy (DePaul University Press, Chicago, Ill.) pp. 51–74.

Patinkin, D., 1965, Money, interest and prices, 2nd ed. (Harper & Row, New York).

Pesek, B. and T. Saving, 1967, Money, wealth and economic theory (Macmillan, New York).

Samuelson, P., 1969, The role of money in national economic policy, Controlling monetary aggregates (Federal Reserve Bank of Boston, Mass.).

Silber, W. L., 1970, Fiscal policy in IS–LM analysis: A correction, Journal of Money, Credit and Banking 2, pp. 461–472.

## 1. COMMENTS ON BRUNNER AND MELTZER

Rudiger DORNBUSCH*

### 1. Introduction

The work by Brunner and Meltzer over the last fifteen years has become an important part of monetarism and macroeconomics. From their earlier work on the transmission mechanism[1] to the more recent work on an integrated macroeconomic model,[2] they have given consistent emphasis to a unified view of the operation of the economy, the sources of disturbances, and the patterns of responses. The model that has evolved exhibits considerable analytical detail, in particular in the modeling of the asset markets. That detail is designed primarily to provide a framework for the analysis of specific effects in the asset markets – say, disintermediation induced by inflation in the presence of regulatory constraints on the banking system – and is less critical to an analysis of the broad macroeconomic problem of the determination of output and prices. It will therefore be helpful to separate out in the form of a brief exposition the main elements of the Brunner–Meltzer model (B–M) as it pertains to these issues. In section 2, accordingly a restatement of the key features of the B–M model is provided. In the third section, I extend the analysis to a steady-state model that is implicit in some of the B–M conjectures and that further highlights important aspects of their approach. In section 4, finally, some comments are offered and the question is raised to what extent the B–M model is "monetarist".

### 2. The Brunner–Meltzer Model: An Exposition

In this section I propose to develop a brief exposition of the B–M model. In so doing, I shall not consider those aspects of the model that arise from steady-state

*I am indebted to Karl Brunner, Thomas Mayer and Michael Mussa for their very helpful comments on an earlier draft and for a number of specific suggestions that I have followed.

[1] See Brunner and Meltzer (1963).

[2] Such models are developed in Brunner (1974) and Brunner and Meltzer (1972, 1974).

inflation and trend growth.[3] I shall attempt to modify the treatment somewhat to accord with the standard macroeconomic literature, and to do so it will be helpful to derive the reduced form aggregate demand function the properties of which, together with the budgetary process, form the core of the B–M model.

The model will be analyzed in terms of the asset markets – the markets for money, debt, and capital – and the goods market. The exogenous variables can be grouped into two sets. One set comprises the money wage rate and the physical stock of capital – along with technology and the like – and is considered given at a point in time. Another set of exogenous variables, again parametrically given at a point in time, is at the discretion of the government. This set, summarized in the vector $z$, contains the tax structure, $t$, real government spending, $g$, the nominal stock of public debt, $S$, and the nominal quantity of base money, $B$,

$$z = z(t, g, S, B). \tag{1}$$

For given values of these exogenous variables, we determine at a point in time the equilibrium prices of goods and assets as well as the level of real output. Along with the determination of current prices and the rate of supply, we determine the rate at which the government, through the budgetary process, creates assets and the rate at which the money wage rate and expected prices are revised. These changes in the state variables govern the dynamics of the system.

The analysis distinguishes four time periods differentiated by the state variables that are allowed to adjust. To study the impact or *short-run* effect of disturbances, all state variables are held constant. In the *intermediate run*, financial asset supplies are endogenous but the capital stock and money wage rate are held constant. In the *long run*, the money wage rate is fully endogenous and an invariance of output along with budgetary balance characterizes that state. There is a *final run*, or steady state, in which the capital stock is endogenous and in which the detail of fiscal and financial interventions affects the productive structure of the economy.

### *2.1. The Asset Markets*

A key feature of the B–M model is a distinction between debt and real capital; capital, or equity, and debt are imperfect substitutes and are therefore not aggregated into "bonds" in the manner that has proved so convenient in the Hicksian apparatus summarized in the *LM* schedule. Rather, we have to distinguish now three assets and accordingly require to study the equilibrium in asset

[3] Issues of steady-state inflation and trend growth are not raised in the paper under discussion here but are developed in an essentially similar framework in Brunner (1974).

markets in terms of two separate markets. Since it will be convenient to study alternative pairs, we lay down here all the equilibrium conditions although it should be obvious that, because of the budget constraint attaching to asset demands, only two equilibrium conditions will be independent.

In the market for debt, the supply of loans by the banking system has to equal the stock of public debt outstanding plus the private sector's net demand for loans, $V$,

$$a(i, \ldots)B = S/i + V(r, i, W), \tag{2}$$

$r$ = the yield on equity,
$i$ = the yield on debt,
$B$ = the monetary base,
$W$ = nominal wealth,
$a$ = the bank asset multiplier,
$S$ = the number of permanent income streams yielding each a dollar a year indefinitely,

and where nominal wealth is equal to the value of the capital stock, $PK$, plus the value of the public debt, $S/i$, plus the monetary base, $B$,

$$W \equiv PK + S/i + B. \tag{3}$$

It is assumed that an increase in the yield on debt (or loans which are assumed to be perfect substitutes for debt) raises the banks supply of loans as would an increase in the monetary base. The public's demand for loans is an increasing function of the yield on capital and a decreasing function of yield on debt. An increase in wealth, following B–M, is assumed to raise the private sector's desired net indebtedness or, equivalently, to reduce the private sector's demand for debt holdings.

Equilibrium in the money market requires that the equilibrium supply of money, $mB$, be equal to the demand for nominal balances,

$$m(i, \ldots)B = L(r, i, W). \tag{4}$$

The bank money multiplier, $m(\cdot)$, is an increasing function of the yield on earning assets, while the demand for money is a decreasing function of the yield on both debt and capital. An increase in wealth, on the contrary, raises the demand for money. Finally, in the capital market equilibrium requires that the existing stock of capital be held or that the value of the capital stock, $PK$, be equal to the nominal demand for equity, $E$,

$$PK = E(r, i, W). \tag{5}$$

The stock of capital, $K$, is given and the price of capital assets, $P$, is endogenous. The demand for equity is an increasing function of the yield on equity and of wealth and a decreasing function of the yield on debt.

To close the model of the asset markets, we require a determination of the yield on equity. The yield on equity, $r$, is defined as the ratio of nominal earnings to the price of a unit of capital,

$$r = pe(w/p, K)/P, \tag{6}$$

$e$ = real rental on capital,
$p$ = the price of output,
$w$ = money wage rate,
$P$ = the price of capital.

From equation (6), the yield on capital is an increasing function of the price of output and a decreasing function of the price of capital. Alternatively, using (6) we can write the price of capital as a function of the yield on capital and the price of output,

$$P = pe/r = \pi(p)/r, \qquad \pi \equiv pe(w/p, K). \tag{7}$$

Using the relation between the price of equity, the yield on capital and the price of output, we can rewrite the wealth definition in terms of (7) as

$$W \equiv \pi(p)K/r + S/i + B. \tag{8}$$

From (8) we observe that the price of output will have effects in the asset markets through wealth: an increase in the price of output raises nominal wealth and thereby creates an excess supply of equity and loans and an excess demand for money at initial asset yields.[4]

Consider next the equilibrium in the asset markets for a given level of output prices, $P_0$, and given values of asset supplies. In figure 1 we show the asset market equilibrium schedules, having imposed the assumption of gross substitutability. Along *LM* the money market clears, along *KK* the capital market is in equilibrium, and along *SS* the market for debt and loans is in equilibrium. To characterize the nature of disequilibria off the curves, we note that at point $A_1$ there is an excess supply of money, an excess supply of debt, and an excess demand for capital.

Consider next the effect of variations in the price of output on the equilibrium asset yields. An increase in the price of output at the initial yield on capital will

[4] This effect does not depend on the assumption that the wage rate is fixed. The latter assumption serves rather to reinforce the effect since it implies that the nominal value of capital rises proportionately more than the price of output due to the increase in the real rental on capital.

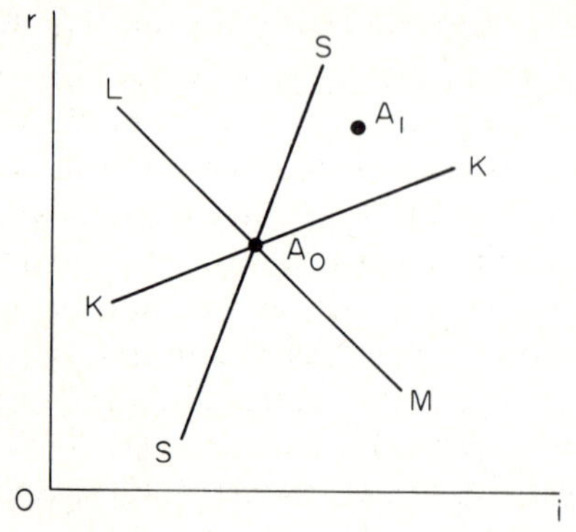


FIGURE 1

raise the value of the capital stock and hence wealth. The increase in the value of capital and wealth will create an excess supply of capital and debt and an excess demand for money. To eliminate this disequilibrium, the yield on both debt and capital will have to rise. In terms of figure 1, the market equilibrium schedules shift to intersect at point $A_1$.[5]

In figure 2, we consider the effect of an increase in the public debt. An increase in the public debt will create an excess demand for money and capital and an excess supply of debt or equivalently an excess demand for loans. The excess

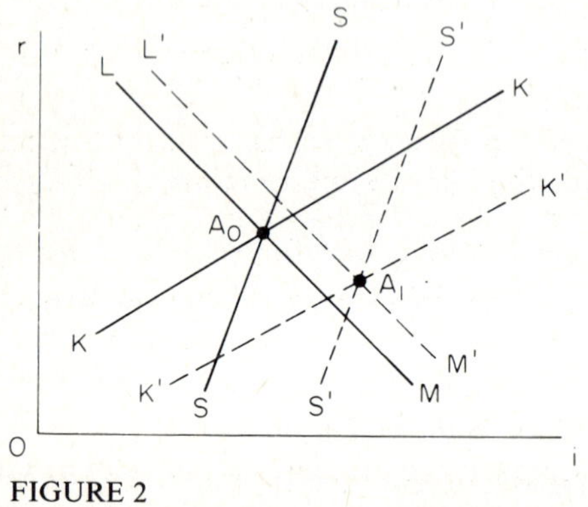


FIGURE 2

[5] The assumption that an increase in wealth raises the private sector's desired indebtedness is of relevance here since it implies that the *SS* schedule shifts to the right, thereby contributing to the unambiguity of our conclusion. If an increase in wealth, on the contrary, caused the private sector to purchase rather than issue debt there would be an excess supply of debt, the *SS* schedule would shift to the left and the equilibrium yield on debt could fall.

supply of debt arises from the increase in debt directly and from the effect of higher wealth on the desired indebtedness of the private sector. The excess supply of debt, therefore, is in excess of the increase in the public debt to the extent that the private sector in response to higher wealth increases their desired indebtedness with a view of using the proceeds to increase their holdings of money and equity. The remaining disequilibrium is resolved by an increase in the yield on debt and a change in the yield on capital the direction of which is ambiguous without further restrictions. The relevant restriction that will determine the direction in which the equilibrium yield on capital will move concerns the *relative* substitutability between assets and the *relative* size of the wealth effects on asset demands. Following B–M, we show in figure 2 the case where money and debt are closer substitutes than debt and capital so that the equilibrium yield on capital falls and the equilibrium price of equity rises.[6] The fact that in the B–M model an increase in the public debt raises stock prices is a key feature of their model and is one they share with Tobin (1961, 1969) and that differentiates their treatment from the body of thinking that would draw a distinction between money on one hand and all other assets on the other hand. The latter line of thinking implicitly assumes a relatively high substituability between debt and capital and would imply that an increase in debt would raise the yield on both debt and capital, although raising the yield on debt relative to that on capital.

Finally, consider the effect of an increase in the monetary base. This will create an excess supply of money – the money multiplier exceeds the marginal propensity to hold money out of wealth – an excess demand for capital, and an excess supply of debt. The equilibrium yields on both debt and equity will therefore decline.

The conclusions of the preceding paragraphs are summarized in the reduced form solutions that express *equilibrium* interest rates as functions of asset supplies and the price of output,

$$r = \alpha(p, S, B, \ldots), \quad \alpha_p > 0, \quad \alpha_S < 0, \quad \alpha_B < 0, \tag{9}$$

and

$$i = \beta(p, S, B, \ldots), \quad \beta_p > 0, \quad \beta_S > 0, \quad \beta_B < 0. \tag{10}$$

The value of wealth, too, is determined by the equilibrium condition in asset

[6] The relative shifts in the *KK* schedule and *LL* schedule depend on both the wealth effect and the responsiveness to the yield on debt. At a constant yield on capital, the *KK* schedule will shift more than the *LL* schedule the larger the wealth effect on capital demand relative to money demand and the smaller the responsiveness of capital demand, as compared to money demand, with respect to the yield on debt.

markets, and we can write equilibrium wealth as a function of the output price level and asset supplies. The effect of various parameter changes on *equilibrium* real wealth is somewhat ambiguous,

$$W/p = \phi(p, S, B), \qquad \phi_p > 0, \quad \phi_S > 0, \quad \phi_B > 0. \tag{11}$$

We will follow B–M in assuming that an increase in the price of output or the stock of debt raises wealth. The effect of an increase in the base on real wealth is unambiguous since here the quantity increase is accompanied by a decline in asset yields and hence an increase in asset prices.

This completes the dicussion of asset markets, and we can now proceed to use these equilibrium reduced forms in the determination of goods market equilibrium.

### 2.2. The Goods Market

In the goods market we assume in the short run, because of a fixed money wage, that the supply of output is an increasing function of the current price of output,

$$y = y(p/w), \qquad y' > 0. \tag{12}$$

The demand for output will depend on asset yields, real wealth, and real disposable income, $\bar{y}$,[7]

$$d = d(r, i, W/p, \bar{y}). \tag{13}$$

In addition, the government spends on real output at the given rate, $g$.

Real disposable income is an increasing function of the level of output and a decreasing function of the level of prices if taxation is progressive on nominal income.

Equilibrium in the goods market requires that the supply of output equal private aggregate demand plus real government spending,

$$y(p) = d(r, i, W/p, \bar{y}) + g. \tag{14}$$

If we further impose the condition of simultaneous asset market equilibrium, we can use the equilibrium asset yields and real wealth derived in the preceding section and substitute into the aggregate demand function to obtain the *reduced*

[7] We depart here marginally from the B–M model by including real disposable income rather than non-human wealth as an argument in aggregate demand. The variable is included in order to have taxes show up somewhere and without the need to raise the issue of the capitalization of labor income.

*form aggregate demand*, $x$, that embodies asset market equilibrium,

$$d(\alpha, \beta, \phi, \bar{y}) \equiv x(p, S, B, t), \qquad x_p < 0, \quad x_S > 0, \quad x_B > 0. \tag{15}$$

In assigning restrictions to the effects of output price changes and debt changes on (reduced form) aggregate demand we have used further restrictions on the relative magnitude of yield and wealth effects. The assumption that an increase in the price of output lowers real aggregate demand arises because the combined effects of higher real taxes and higher asset yields dominate the (possible) positive wealth effects. For the case of an increase in debt the situation is considerably more ambiguous since now the yield on debt increases as does wealth while the yield on equity declines. It is assumed here that the yield on debt does not dominate and that accordingly an increase in debt will *raise* aggregate demand.[8] We note next that an increase in the monetary base will quite unambiguously raise the level of aggregate demand since such a change raises wealth and lowers asset yields. Finally an open market operation – a purchase of debt and sale of money – has a net expansionary effect on aggregate demand. This is another way of noting that while an increase in debt is expansionary with respect to aggregate demand the effect is small relative to the expansionary effects of a monetary increase.

In figure 3 we show, following B–M, the short-run equilibrium of the system for given values of all the state variables, in particular, supplies of debt and base and the money wage rate. The aggregate demand curve is shown downward sloping as a function of the price level, while the supply schedule is upward sloping, given the money wage rate.[9]

Consider next the budget. The real budget deficit, $D$, is equal to the excess of government spending plus debt service over real tax collections,

$$D = g + S/p - \theta, \tag{16}$$

where real tax collection is an increasing function of real income plus income from

[8] The ambiguity that surrounds the effect of an increase in debt on aggregate demand, given that the asset market(s) clears, is not peculiar to the B–M model but actually obtains, too, in the standard Keynesian model where the wealth effect in the demand for money will raise the interest rate at the initial level of income, thereby depressing aggregate demand while at the same time the wealth effect on expenditure will tend to raise aggregate demand. The larger the direct wealth effect relative to the interest rate effect the more expansionary is a debt increases. See, for a further discussion Blinder and Solow (1974, pp. 52–55).

The reader will note too, that in assigning an expansionary effect to debt issue B–M decidedly do *not* espouse the view that debt-financed increases in government spending are ineffective because of crowding-out effects resulting from the debt issue. On the contrary in the short run the debt issue reinforces the effects of higher government spending. The long-run effect will, however, involve crowding out. For a further discussion see below section 3.

[9] For early use of such a graphical representation, see Tobin and Hall (1971) and Marschak (1965).

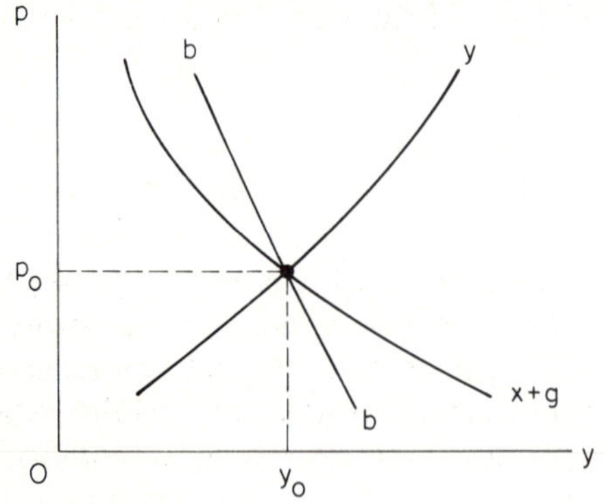


FIGURE 3

debt which is part of the tax base. If the tax structure is progressive on nominal income, an increase in the price level will raise real taxes. Finally, the parameter $t$ denotes the tax structure,

$$\theta = \theta(y + S/p; p, t), \qquad \theta_1 > 0, \quad \theta_2 \gtreqq 0, \quad \theta_3 > 0. \tag{17}$$

In figure 3 we show the schedule bb along which the budget is balanced, given the tax structure, the level of real government spending, and the number of consols outstanding. The schedule is negatively sloped since an increase in the price level raises real taxes while it lowers real government outlays by reducing the real value of interest payments. We require therefore an accompanying decline in real income in order to lower real taxes. The position of the *bb* schedule is determined by the tax structure, government spending, and the debt outstanding.

When the budget is not balanced, the resulting disequilibrium will be financed by increasing or decreasing the stocks of debt and/or base outstanding. Budgetary balance is obviously not necessary in short-run equilibrium and in fact is the prime element of the dynamics in the B–M model. The budgetary imbalance feeds assets into the system which in turn moves the equilibrium position over time.

As part of intermediate- and long-run equilibrium, we assume on the contrary that the budget is balanced. The only distinction between intermediate- and long-run equilibrium in fact lies in the supply of output. We assume that in the short and intermediate run output is supplied according to (12), while in the long run, because of wage flexibility, output is independent of the price level and equal to $y_0$. Accordingly, in the long run we have a vertical supply curve.[10] This

[10] There is a further difference in the long run that is suppressed by the reduced form in (15). In the long run, the real rental on capital is independent of the price level and therefore an increase in the price of output has a smaller effect on real wealth and asset yields. This will not, however, change any conclusions.

completes the discussion of the model, and we can now turn to some applications to illustrate its implications.

## 2.3. Comparative Statics

Consider now the effect of an increase in government spending assuming that any budgetary imbalance is entirely financed by money creation. We show in figure 4 the effect of increased government spending as a shift in the aggregate demand for goods and as a shift in the balanced budget line; the latter shifts to the right since budgetary balance requires higher real taxes to match the higher level of real government spending.

The impact effect of the increased spending is to move the system to point $A_1$, where goods and asset markets clear and where both the price level and real output have risen. Furthermore, at point $A_1$ we have a budget deficit so that the nominal quantity of base money is expanding.

The expansion in the monetary base, by (15) raises aggregate demand at each level of prices since it causes asset yields to decline and real wealth to rise.[11] It therefore shifts the aggregate demand schedule upward over time until the intermediate-run equilibrium at point $A_2$ is reached. At that point, real taxes

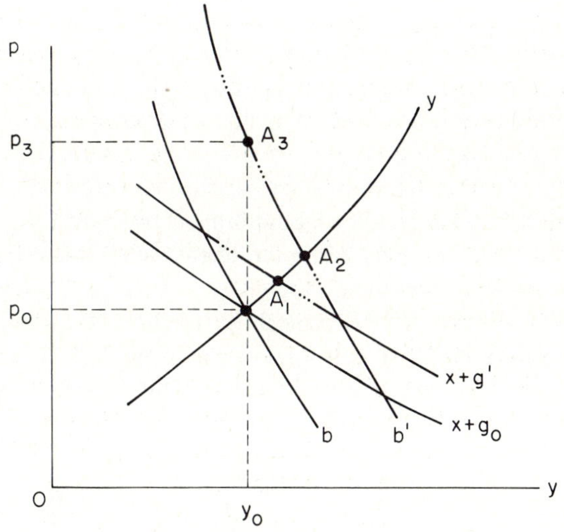


FIGURE 4

[11] We are using here the properties of the reduced form aggregate demand function developed in section 2.1 above.

have risen sufficiently, and the real value of interest payments has declined enough for the budget to be balanced. In fact, the economy would remain at that point if it were not for wage flexibility.

The flexibility of wages implies that over time the supply schedule shifts upward, or better, rotates and becomes in the long run a vertical schedule at the level of output $y_0$. This has the effect of raising prices further and reducing output until a long-run equilibrium at point $A_3$ is reached.

The manner in which the economy accommodates an increased level of real government spending is by an increase in the price level. An increase in the price level will serve to balance the budget through a higher real tax yield from progressive taxation of nominal income and through reduced real debt service. The goods market will be cleared via a price increase by crowding out private real aggregate demand.

It is perhaps peculiar that in our formulation the long-run equilibrium is determined exclusively by the long-run level of output and the balanced budget line but is entirely independent of private behavior such as aggregate demand or asset demands. There are several reasons. First, the interest rate on debt is excluded from the budget constraint by the assumption that all debt issue is in the form of consols so that no refunding is required and therefore the issue price – related to the rate of interest – does not appear.[12] Second, the long-run level of output is assumed independent of the tax yield. Third, the tax yield is dependent only on the level of output but is independent of microeconomic details that are aggregated away.

Assume now that rather than financing the budget by money creation it were financed by creation of debt. The impact effect of increased government spending would be identical both in terms of the shift in aggregate demand and the shift in the balanced budget line. The impact effect of increased government spending is therefore entirely independent of the mode of financing. The stability problem arises, however, the moment we actually start creating debt. Now both the aggregate demand schedule *and* the balanced budget line shift to the right; the latter will shift because of the increased debt service as part of government outlays. This raises then the question of stability – the question whether the balanced budget line outruns the aggregate demand schedule.[13]

[12] B–M actually use a broader assumption where the maturity structure of the debt is finite and accordingly they would use the full system to determine the long-run level of prices.

[13] The stability of the system with debt-financed deficits can be determined as follows. The *equilibrium* short-run price of output is a function of the parameters, in particular, the stock of debt outstanding: $p = \bar{p}(S, B, g, t, \ldots)$. The rate of increase of debt is equal to the deficit, or $\dot{S} = i[\bar{p}(g - \theta) + S]$, where the equation is evaluated at the balanced budget equilibrium. Taking

If debt-financed deficits raise a stability question while money-financed decifits conspicuously do not, then we can be sure that mixed financing, in the right proportions, will be consistent with stability. To the extent that the debt component of deficit financing shifts the balanced budget line to the right, we can conclude that the long-run price effects of a given increase in government spending are larger the higher the share of debt creation in the budget-financing process. This point can be ascertained from inspection of figure 4. The intuition is simply that we now require a larger price change to reduce the real value of the larger debt service liability that is created in the transition period.

### 3. Steady-State Equilibrium

The model of the very long run, in which the capital stock itself is endogenous, is not developed in the B–M model except for some conjectures and two key features of such a model:

(i) Capital and output are the same in the sense that their prices are equalized, i.e., $P = p$.
(ii) Capital and debt are perfect substitutes and accordingly their real rate of return is equalized. In the absence of inflationary expectations this implies $i = r$.

This section is designed to fill the gap in B–M's treatment. Such an extension is of interest because it provides an interesting perspective on the implications of the budgetary process. In the shortest run, the manner in which the budget is financed – by debt or money creation – is of no consequence. In the very long run, the manner in which it is financed is all important for the real structure of the economy. Emphasis on this point and conjectures about the role of debt in this long-run context are an important aspect of the B–M model and approach.

We shall assume a neoclassical one-sector technology so that for a given labor force the equilibrium stock of capital, and hence the rate of output, is a decreasing function of the rate of interest,

$$y = y(K), \qquad r = r(K). \tag{18}$$

*Footnote 13 continued*
the derivative of that equation, we have

$$\mathrm{d}\dot{S}/\mathrm{d}S = i\left[\bar{p}'(g - \theta + \theta_1 S/\bar{p}^2 - \bar{p}\theta_2) + 1 - \theta_1/\bar{p}\right].$$

For stability we want the expression to be negative. This is the more likely, given that $\bar{p}' > 0$, the larger the initial excess of tax receipts over spending, $g - \theta$, and the more progressive the tax structure.

The equilibrium conditions characterizing the asset markets can be developed entirely in terms of the money market because of the assumed perfect substitution between debt and equity,

$$m(r, \dots)(B/p) = L(r, W/p), \tag{19}$$

where real wealth, $W/p$, is defined as

$$W/p \equiv K + B/p + S/rp. \tag{20}$$

The rate of increase in the capital stock will equal the excess of output over consumption expenditure, $c$, plus government spending, and in the steady state will equal zero,[14]

$$\dot{K} = y(K) - c(r, W/p, y-\theta) - g = 0. \tag{21}$$

Finally, for budgetary equilibrium we require that the budget deficit, $D$, be equal to zero so that there is no net creation or destruction of financial assets,

$$D = g + S/p - \theta(y + S/p, p, t) = 0. \tag{22}$$

Equations (18) to (22) define the steady-state equilibrium of the model. Several important characteristics of that long-run equilibrium should be noted:

(i) In the long run, money is not neutral in the sense that a doubling in the nominal quantity of money leaves all real variables unchanged. This is so because there are systematic non-homogeneities built into the system. These non-homogeneities arise in part from the public debt and in part from progressive taxation of nominal income. In fact, it will be true that a doubling in both the nominal stock of debt and money will have real effects unless the tax structure is defined relative to real income.

(ii) There is a further sense in which homogeneity is relevant. Even if the tax structure does not give rise to non-homogeneities, we require restrictions on the manner in which the budget is financed in order to achieve long-run neutrality from changes in the nominal supplies of assets. In particular, the financing process

[14] The reader will note that in (21) we have shifted from aggregate demand, used so far, to consumption spending, $c$. The reason is that in a one-sector model we do not have an independent investment function. In fact, investment is identically equal to the excess of output over consumption plus government demand. An alternative treatment, perhaps more in line with the short-run model, would be to assume an explicit two-sector model such as developed in Foley and Sidrauski (1971) and Mussa (1976). While the detail of the productive structure, no doubt, affects the particulars of comparative statics the present structure would seem adequate for the points to be made.

has to be able to undo the real affects of a change in the composition of assets. Thus an open market purchase of money and sale of debt would have no long-run real effects if the budget was entirely financed by money creation. In the long run, the nominal quantity of debt and money would increase in the same proportion and leave the real equilibrium unaffected, provided $\theta_2 = 0$.

(iii) Comparative static analysis across long-run equilibria requires that we specify which of the assets, base or debt, is endogenous or equivalently whether transitory budget disequilibria are financed by money or debt. The stocks of base and/or debt are endogenous in the long run. This very important point is an implication of the budgetary process which makes at least one of the assets fully endogenous. To put the same point in a slightly different manner: the authorities can fix the quantity of money or the quantity of debt but not both – unless, of course, the tax structure is changed along with the change in parameters.

Consider now the question whether this model indeed generates the B – M conclusion that an increase in government spending eventually raises prices and lowers the capital stock and output? This question can be analyzed with the help of figure 5. The money market equilibrium is represented by the downward-sloping *LM* curve along which the nominal quantity of debt and money are held constant. The schedule is downward sloping since an increase in the capital stock via the wealth effect and the lowering of interest rates creates an excess demand for money that has to be compensated by a lowering of the price level. The balanced budget schedule, for the initial level of government spending, debt, and tax structure, is shown as the $D_0 = 0$ schedule. It is downward sloping since an in-

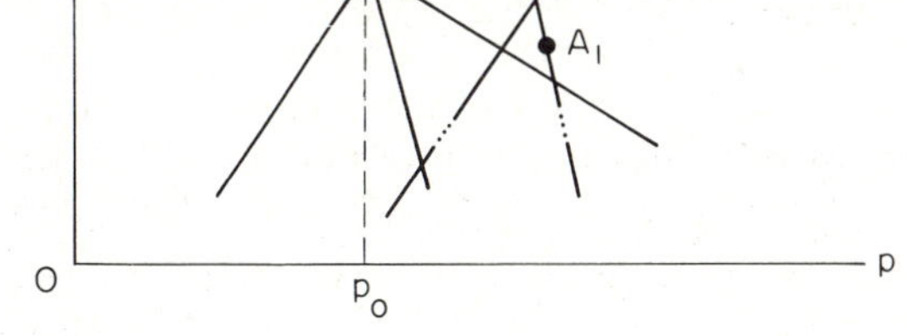


FIGURE 5

crease in the capital stock raises the tax base, and hence collection, and therefore requires a lower price level so as to raise the real value of the debt service liability.[15] Finally, along $\dot{K} = 0$, the capital stock is stationary. That schedule is positively sloped on the assumption that an increase in the capital stock raises consumption demand, via interest and wealth effects, relative to the level of output and therefore causes capital to be decreasing unless compensated by the expenditure-reducing effect of an increase in the price level.

The initial full equilibrium obtains at point $A_0$, with the markets clearing and stationary stocks of capital and financial assets. An increase in the rate of government spending will shift the balanced budget line to the right to $D_1 = 0$ since a higher price level and therefore lower real debt service is required to compensate for the higher real spending. The zero investment schedule shifts similarly to the right since at $A_0$ the higher real government spending reduces capital investment by exactly that amount.

The position to which the economy will move in the long run will depend both on how the budget deficit is financed and on the relative response of consumption and the budget to changes in the price level – the relative shifts of the $D$ and $\dot{K}$ schedules. In figure 5 we consider the case of money finance in which case the economy will move in equilibrium to a lower stock of capital and a higher price level. To note this point, we just need to recognize that the deficit at point $A_0$ will cause money creation which shifts to the right both the $LM$ and $\dot{K}_1 = 0$ schedules until they intersect along the balanced budget line.

For the case shown in figure 5, it is true that the long-run effect of increased government spending is to depress output and raise prices as, indeed, B–M suggest. This need not, however, be the case as can be noted from the alternative where the $D$ schedule shifts relatively more than the $\dot{K}$ schedule – the budget is less responsive to price level changes than consumption expenditure. In that case we may end up with a higher price level and a higher stock of capital and flow of output. This case is more likely the less progressive is the tax structure.

Consider next the case where some of the budget deficit is financed by debt creation. The analysis now becomes significantly more cumbersome because the balanced budget line, too, will shift with debt issue. A relatively simple case, though, is provided by the assumption that the proportions in which the budget is financed by money and debt are such that the $LM$ schedule will stay put. Equivalently, the budget financing is *neutral* in its portfolio effects. Given that assumption, the new long-run equilibrium must lie along the initial $LM$ schedule. By inspection of figure 5, it is obvious that the new equilibrium will imply a higher

[15] We assume for the present that $\theta_2 = 0$.

price level and lower capital stock than point $A_1$. This is so because the debt issue will shift the balanced budget line from $D_1 = 0$ up and to the right.[16]

From the preceding analysis, we can infer that the steady-state reduction in the capital stock and output will be larger the larger the share of the budget that is financed by debt creation. It is true, too, that instability becomes more likely the larger that share.

## 4. Comments

In these comments I shall focus on three essential issues raised by the B–M model. They are, respectively, the adequacy of discussing their model in terms of comparative statics, the need for disaggregation, and the extent to which their analysis can be judged "monetarist".

### *4.1. Dynamics, Stability, and Comparative Statics*

The B–M analysis of the process of adjustment of the economy relies essentially on a comparative static analysis. The economy adjusts to a disturbance over various runs where for each run a further state variable is treated as endogenous or a further constraint is imposed. Thus, in the short run all state variables other than the one causing a disturbance are treated as given; in the inter run financial assets are endogenous; in the long run money wages and expectations adjust; and in the final-run equilibrium the stock of capital itself is endogenous. The problem with such a formulation is that in fact most of the described states would actually never be observed because the state variables are *jointly* endogenous. To put the same point somewhat differently, we note that capital accumulation, wage revisions, and budget financing are concurrent processes. This implies that in terms of comparative statics we can only study the impact effect of a disturbance and the steady state but not the intermediate and long run. Alternatively with a complete dynamic specification the entire equilibrium path of the system can be considered.

There is a further respect in which the splitting up of essentially concurrent processes is misleading, and this concerns the stability properties of the model.

[16] If the budget was entirely financed by debt creation, the *LM* schedule must shift down and to the left in the financing process. The case of mixed finance such that the *LM* schedule stays put is therefore a benchmark case in between a deficit that is entirely money-financed and one that is entirely debt-financed; it is in this sense that the financing is "neutral".

If, in fact, revisions in money wages and capital accumulation occur concurrently with budget financing, then the appropriate dynamic system is not restricted to the goods market equilibrium conditions and the evolution of financial asset supplies but rather is to be augmented by a theory of investment and a wage formation process as part of the dynamic model.

Such an extension has two implications. One is that the B–M model does not possess enough "allocative detail" to discuss the actual time path of the economy and is therefore limited to statements that can be made relative to the static equations that govern the impact effect and the steady state. Contrary to B–M, their neglect of a distinction between consumption and investment spending is a shortcoming rather than a superior method.[17]

A second implication concerns their inference that "the economic system is stable" and that "cumulative movements of price or output result mainly from the decisions or actions of governments, not individuals or private institutions. The private sector has a stabilizing influence, so that the economy adjusts to any maintained policy". There is quite obviously no support in the B–M model for such a statement. There is surely little doubt that for a sustained period of time the motion of the economy can be entirely dominated by capital formation and expectations or, for that matter, that shifts in private behavior can induce budgetary imbalance.

A final remark in the context of dynamics and stability concerns the adjustment of the economy to a debt-financed budget deficit. B–M show, by imposing sufficient conditions on the structural equations, that the system may be stable provided an increase in debt expands aggregate demand. It is not obvious why one would want to restrict behavior, somewhat arbitrarily perhaps, to generate stability under all kinds of experiments. In particular, why should the economy not blow up if the government persistently feeds debt into the system? The answer, in all likelihood, is that the economy would come to expect the debt creation and that the relevant system of behavioral equations changes to accomodate the systematic behavior of the government.

No doubt, B–M are aware of the above limitations of their model and in fact are arguing, implicity, that their modeling of the economy reflects empirical judgments about the relative speeds and dominance of various processes and about the relative contributions to stability of the government and the private sector. Viewed in this perspective the private sector is relatively stable and aggregate demand changes and the budgetary process are dominant relative to the influence of expectations and capital accumulation in the initial phases of a disturbance induced by a change in government spending. It is important for an understanding of the

[17] See, however, Brunner and Meltzer (1974, p. 46).

present paper to remember that these empirical judgments that characterize much of the B–M work are implicit in their modeling.

### *4.2. Aggregation in Asset Markets and Channels of Transmission*

A key feature of the work on macroeconomics by B–M has been an emphasis on disaggregated asset markets – a distinction between debt, money, and capital. Their models have the feature that "substitution is not limited to two assets but includes the entire spectrum of assets. Adjustment is not limited to 'the interest rate' but includes the relative prices of real capital and financial assets". They further claim that "contrary to frequent assertions, the major issues in aggregative analysis cannot be reduced to propositions about the relative slopes of the *IS* and *LM* curves".

I believe it is important to distinguish two separate and distinct issues. One concerns the value added of disaggregated asset markets as opposed to the judicious aggregation using the concept of "the rate of interest" to reflect a broad range of substitution across financial and real assets. If such an aggregation is possible – and it is if debt and capital are relatively close substitutes – the issue is one of exposition and there is considerable advantage in the use of aggregation. The second issue is concerned with the *reduced form* aggregate demand function and the question whether the only channel of transmission is the interest rate or whether, in addition, wealth effects act on real aggregate demand. This issue is substantitive, indeed, but I am certain entirely uncontested at the theoretical level and in more recent empirical work.[18]

Consider first the question of aggregation in asset markets. For that purpose assume for a moment that money, debt, and capital were gross substitutes, as B–M do. Assume, too, contrary to B–M, that debt and capital were relatively close substitutes so that an increase in debt raises the equilibrium yield on *both* debt and capital. We have shown above already that an increase in the price of output – and therefore an increase in the value of capital – would raise the yield on both assets and that an increase in the base would lower the yield on both. It follows, therefore, that the yields on both debt and equity would, for the relevant experiments, move in the same direction so that we could without any loss of generality talk about "the rate of interest" as a function of the relative quantities of money and other assets where, for the purpose

[18] See, for example, Modigliani (1971). That such agreement has been achieved is perhaps largely due to theoretical work on the consumption function and perhaps the limited effects of transitory tax cuts.

of discussing the *level* of the yield structure, we aggregate debt and capital and oppose it to the monetary base. For purposes of determining *relative* asset yields, we will be concerned with the composition of assets between capital and debt, and we know that an increase in the quantity of debt relative to capital will raise the yield on debt relative to that on capital. If need be, we can therefore go behind the aggregate concept of "the interest rate" and enquire into allocative detail such as relative interest rates.

The concept of "the rate of interest" is therefore in no manner incompatible with a broad spectrum of assets and a wide-ranging substitution effect induced by changes in the relative supplies of assets. It certainly takes account, too, of changes in the relative prices of assets since these are reflected in changes in their rates of return. In fact, the aggregation of all non-monetary assets and a consequent distinction between money and all other assets strikes me as far more "monetarist" an approach than the B–M procedure.[19]

I should like to question briefly what such an aggregtion would do to the B–M conclusions. The only change I can see would be in the effect of a change in debt on the price of capital or the rate of return on capital. B–M assume that the debt issue will cause an increase in the value of stocks while the approach suggested above implies the obverse. The proposed aggregation does not, however, affect any of the substantive conclusions concerning the effects of policies on prices and output. This is so because these effects depend on the reduced form properties of the aggregate demand function that embodies the effect of changes in wealth and all asset yields and because these properties have to be imposed by assumption because of ambiguities.[20]

There is a further reason why aggregation of non-monetary assets is indicated and why the asumption that debt and capital are *relatively* close substitutes is not too unfounded. This arises from the B–M assumption that in the very long run debt and capital are perfect substitutes and, indeed, are actually fully aggregated in that run. Given that there is no theory as to the time path of substitution possibilities, one might as well start aggregating right away. I conclude therefore that for the issues at hand the disaggregated asset market model yields no significant insights and that the analysis could be fruitfully developed in terms of more aggregative concepts.

The second issue concerns the manner in which monetary and fiscal actions are translated into changes in prices and output. As should be obvious from section 2,

[19] The aggregation of non-monetary assets does obviously not assume that these assets are perfect substitutes; it only assumes that their relative yields are well behaved. For a further discussion, see Tobin (1961, 1969).

[20] See above, section 2.2.

these transmission channels are summarized in the reduced form aggregate demand function and derive from interest rate effects and wealth effects.[21] It is not entirely correct to argue that the adjustment of assets and output to policy changes is more pervasive than in Keynesian models, unless one wishes to take an unduly narrow view of the set of models that qualify as "Keynesian". Surely the "interest rate" is quite universally recognized as a channel of transmission, and wealth effects, too, are now enjoying broad use across schools of thought – from Metzler to Modigliani.[22] Since there are no further channels of transmission in the B–M model, I believe the claim to a more pervasive adjustment mechanism must be discounted. What this means, however, is that macroeconomic literature has to a considerable extent espoused a view that B–M, and a few "Keynesians", have advocated for more than a decade.

### *4.3. Monetarism?*

In this subsection, I propose to question to what extent the B–M model may qualify as "monetarist". B–M propose three features without which a theory does not qualify as "monetarist":[23]

(i) The long-run position to which the system moves is determined by stocks, particularly the stock of money, and not by flows.
(ii) The adjustment to a change in money involves substitution between money, other assets, and new production. Adjustment is not confined to a narrow range of assets, called bonds, or a single price, "the" interest rate.
(iii) The economic system is stable.

I have argued above that the development of the stability properties is not without problems and is inadequate as a basis for the inference that the economy is stable. An alternative interpretation of the stability issue, and one I believe closer to the B–M hypothesis, is that in a stochastic setting the money supply, via the behavior of the monetary authorities, is a source of variability in the aggregate rather than private behavior. While such a view may be perfectly justified, and in fact is an important question, it is a consideration altogether extraneous to the present model.

[21] There is no distinct role for "asset prices [to] join interest rates in the transmission of monetary changes"; asset prices affect aggregate demand either via asset yields or interest rates or else through a wealth effect.

[22] For a recent treatment, see Blinder and Solow (1974). See, too, Teigen (1970).

[23] See, too, Brunner (1970).

I have argued, too, that a proper interpretation of the concept of "the rate of interest" is perfectly consistent with a multiplicity of assets – in fact many more than three – and is therefore in no way inconsistent with a broad view of the adjustment process. I shall add here that the notion that money operates on a broad spectrum of assets and generates "a ripple throughout the economy" is in no manner particular to a monetarist approach but rather constitutes the common core of any general equilibrium approach to macroeconomics, although it should be recognized that the time structure of these ripples may differ quite drastically across models.[24]

The statement that is perhaps most controversial is the first proposition. The assertion that money plays a particular role in the analysis is in no way substantiated. Surely the stock of public debt outstanding plays at least as critical a role in the analysis. To show that point, consider the experiment of a helicopter increase in money under conditions where budgetary imbalance is entirely financed by money creation. The long-run effects of such a money increase are precisely zero – the increase in money causes transitorily an increase in output and prices that gives rise to a budget surplus and destruction of money until the initial stock of nominal balances is restored. In fact, the public debt plays a significantly more critical role since changes in public debt are not self-liquidating in the manner that monetary changes may be. There is another respect in which the public debt plays a special role in the analysis and one that accords poorly with one's conception of monetarism. As shown in section 2, the B–M model implies that an increase in public debt exerts an expansionary effect on aggregate demand and causes an increase in the price of capital. This is perhaps the exact opposite of what has been construed as a monetarist position where debt finance exerts a deflationary effect, if any.

I believe, in part, that B–M may have adopted their formulation out of a concern to ensure the stability of their model. In part the feature is due to the fact that the public debt is entirely undiscounted. As it stands, I believe the suggestion advanced by B–M that an increase in debt stimulates economic activity in the intermediate run and is inflationary must be considered the most controversial implication of their paper.

The departure from a narrow monetarist orthodoxy is obvious, too, in the analysis of an open market increase in the base and purchase of debt. Such a policy – if the budget is financed by money creation – will *lower* in the long run the price level, although it is expansionary in the short run. The departure from inherited thinking is largely, if not entirely, due to an explicit consideration of the budgetary process and the implied endogeneity of assets.

[24] See, for example, Tobin (1961), Modigliani (1971) and Cagan (1958).

## 5. Conclusion

The review and discussion of the B–M model has provided an opportunity to lay out the key elements of their approach. It has provided, too, an opportunity to question the extent to which their approach can be called "monetarist". It is appropriate now to ask what the significance of their model is. I believe it is correct to argue that their model is in the best tradition of eclectic macroeconomics. It embodies the Keynes–Metzler emphasis on portfolio balance, the Keynesian concern for aggregate demand as a determinant of output, the monetarist concern for the endogeneity of the price level, and a more novel concern with the role of the budget in macroeconomic dynamics. Were it not for their particular treatment of the effects of debt on the economy, one might wish to refer to the B–M model as a representation of the consensus view of macroeconomics, or of what one likes to think it should be.

## Bibliography


Blinder, A. and R. Solow, 1974, Analytical foundations of fiscal policy, in: The economics of finance (Brookings, Washington, D.C.).

Brunner, K., 1970, The monetarist revolution in monetary theory, Weltwirtschaftliches Archiv, no. 1.

Brunner, K., 1974, Inflation, money and the role of fiscal arrangements: An anayltical framework for the inflation problem, unpublished manuscript (University of Rochester, Rochester, N.Y.).

Brunner, K. and A. Meltzer, 1963, The role of financial intermediaries in the transmission of monetary policy, American Economic Review, May.

Brunner, K. and A. Meltzer, 1972, Money, debt and economic activity, Journal of Political Economy, Sept./Oct.

Brunner, K. and A. Meltzer, 1974, An aggregate theory for a closed economy, unpublished manuscript.

Cagan, P., Why do we use money in open market operations? Journal of Political Economy, Feb.

Foley, D. and M. Sidrauski, 1971, Monetary and fiscal policy in a growing economy (Macmillan, New York).

Marschak, J., 1965, Income, employment and the price level (Kelley, Clifton, N.Y.).

Modigliani, F., 1971, Monetary policy and consumption, in: Consumer spending and monetary policy: The linkages, FRBB Conference Series, no. 5 (Federal Reserve Band of Boston, Boston, Mass.).

Mussa, M., 1976, A study in macroeconomic dynamics (North-Holland, Amsterdam).

Teigen, R., 1970, The Keynesian-monetarist debate in the U.S.: A summary and evaluation, Statsøkonomisk Tidskrift, no. 1.

Tobin, J., 1961, Money, capital and other stores of value, American Economic Review, May.

Tobin, J., 1969, A general equilibrium approach to monetary theory, Journal of Money, Credit and Banking, Feb.

Tobin, J. and C. Hall, 1971, Income taxation, output and prices, in: J. Tobin, ed., Essays in macroeconomics, vol. 1 (North Holland, Amsterdam).

## 2. COMMENTS ON BRUNNER AND MELTZER

Robert H. RASCHE

This paper is one in a continuing series of (almost) the same model developed by Brunner and Meltzer (hereinafter called KM) which they view as a distinct alternative to the conventional model which has been developed over the past several decades. The first difference is the introduction of three distinct asset markets, money, bank credit (or bonds in the conventional terminology), and existing real capital. The third asset market originates under the assumptions: (a) that bank credit (bonds) and real capital are not perfect substitutes in portfolios, and (b) that transactions costs permit the existance of discrepancies between the price of existing capital and its reproduction cost. A second difference between the KM model and much of the conventional analysis is the explicit introduction of a government budget constraint and the emphasis on comparative static analysis of full stock–flow equilibria.

The first question which arises is: what is the nature of government bonds in the KM model? These play a fundamental role, through the government budget constraint, yet there seems to be some ambiguity throughout the paper as to their exact nature. The conventional approach has been to assume that the government issues fixed coupon rate consols, and thus the market value of the bonds, vary with the market interest rate [Christ (1973)]. KM seem to have this in mind, since they define $S$, the face value of the outstanding stock of government debt, and indicate that this will differ from the market value, $v(i,\tau)S$, as market interest rates vary relative to coupon rates. Under these conditions, unless the bonds are assumed to be consols, and the coupon rate is assumed to remain always the same, the stock of government debt will not remain homogeneous.

If the model is concerned with fixed price – variable rate securities – then it is probably most convenient to consider the government debt in the form of one-period loans, so that the entire debt must be refunded each period. Then the coupon rate can be adjusted so that it always equals the current market rate, and the market value of the debt will always equal the face value, that is $v(i, \tau) = 1$.

The ambiguities arise when the government budget constraint is introduced in equation (4). KM state that the value of government purchases of commodities, plus its wage bill, plus interest payments on the government debt *which are assumed sensitive to current market rates*, $I(i)S$, less taxes is equal to the change in base money plus the *change in the face value* of the stock of government debt. The constraint, written in this form holds only if the government is of the fixed price-variable rate form. If the assumption of a fixed coupon (with a coupon payment of $c$ per period), variable price security is retained, then the appropriate statement of the budget constraint is

$$pg + \bar{w}lg + cS - t(p, y, \bar{w}lg, \tau) \\ = \mathring{B} + \text{Proceeds of debt sale or retirement}, \tag{1}$$

where $c$ is the coupon rate on consoles, and

$$\text{Proceeds of debt sale or retirement} \\ = (1 - \mu)(pg + \bar{w}lg + cS - t) + v. \tag{2}$$

Under the alternative assumption of variable rate, fixed price securities, then the appropriate statement of the budget constraint is

$$pg + \bar{w}lg + iS - t(p, y, \bar{w}lg) \\ = \mathring{B} + \text{Proceeds of the debt sale or retirement}, \tag{1'}$$

where the proceeds of the debt sale or retirement are defined as in (2).

All of this would be relatively unimportant, except that it affects the behavior of the *bbe* curve (KM, figure 1) when alternative financing of deficits (or recouping of surpluses) is undertaken. KM analyze the behavior of the *bbe* curve in terms of upward or downward shifts at fixed real income levels as either base money is changed or government debt is changed. They conclude that an increase (decrease) in $B$ lowers (raises) the line, while an increase (decrease) in $S$ raises (lowers) the line. Sufficient conditions for this result to hold are that asset market equilbrium requires that interest rates increase in response to increases in $S$, and decrease in response to increase in $B$.

It is perhaps easier to get an intuitive idea of the response of the *bbe* curve by examining how it shifts to the right or left at given price levels in response to different financing choices. Under the respecification of (1), the equation for the *bbe* line is

$$pg + \bar{w}lg + cS - t(p, y, \bar{w}lg, \tau) = 0. \tag{3}$$

Note that now the left-hand side of the equation is a function only of $S$. As the stock of base money changes, the curve will not shift. As the stock of government debt increases (decreases) with fixed price, real income will have to rise (fall) to change tax revenues sufficiently to cover the changed debt service, and the *bbe* curve will shift to the right (left). This result requires no assumptions on the response of interest rates to assure asset market equilibrium when either government debt or base money are changed [this result is similar to that obtained by Christ (1973)].

This result can also be obtained by getting $\epsilon(I, i) = 0$ in the expression which KM derive for $\epsilon(P, B \mid bbe, g)$. Under this condition $\epsilon(p, B \mid bbe, g)$, which measures the upward or downward shift of the *bbe* curve in response to changes in the base money, is zero.

The behavior of the *bbe* line is crucial for comparison of intermediate-run equilibria which figure so prominently in the KM analysis. The intermediate-run equilibruim is one in which there is not only flow equilibrium, but also stock equilibrium in terms of the financial assets. Thus the government cannot be printing (destroying) base money or issuing (retiring) debt. Hence the equilibrium has to be a point on the *bbe* curve. The analysis of a displacement from an initial intermediate-run equilibrium at $p_0$, $y_0$, such that there is a flow equilibrium at $y_1$ less than $y_0$ with a budget deficit, suggests that with only consoles in the system, intermediate-run equilibrium would be restored at $p_0$, $y_0$ if the deficit is financed completely by printing base money ($\mu = 1$) and at some $p_2$, $y_2$, both greater than the respective initial stock-flow equilibrium values for any combination of debt and base money financing ($\mu < 1$), assuming that the system in fact converges to such an equilibrium. This contrasts with the KM result that printing mostly base money would result in an intermediate-run equilibrium at a price and real output combination less than $p_0$ and $y_0$, respectively.

Under the alternative assumption of one-period government bonds which are always sold at face value [which is equivalent to assuming that $\epsilon(I, i) = 1$], shifts of the *bbe* line analogous to those described by KM are obtained. A question which naturally arises is why restrict the analysis to two extreme positions of zero and one for $\epsilon(I, i)$. Allowing intermediate values of this parameter would require either introducing a mixture of the total stock of government debt between longs (consoles) and shorts (one-period bonds) or introducing bonds with $n$ period initial maturity ($1 < n < \infty$). It is tempting to argue that by allowing the value of $\epsilon(I, i)$ to vary, the effect of changing the maturity composition of the debt could be examined. Unfortunately, this does not seem to be an interesting experiment, since the model does not allow for substitution between these two types of securities or between either money or real capital and these two securities individually in portfolios of private economic units. With perfect substitution between long and short government debt in private portfolios, any potential impact of changing the maturity composition has been considerably emasculated.

The crucial question is whether the intermediate-run result differentiates the

KM model from the conventional wisdom? To answer this question it is necessary to compare the same types of equilibrium as are compared by KM. In constructing this comparison we shall assume all government debt is consoles, although an equally valid comparison could be constructed assuming one-period debt in both models. A very conventional model, though admittedly not the strict textbook *IS-LM* model that frequently is made the whipping boy of these discussions, is that of Modigliani (1963). This model is a two-asset model. Under the assumption that $W = W_0$, equations 4a, 5a, and 6 of table 1 in the Modigliani paper collapse to a $p - y$ relationship analygous to the KM $s$ curve. Equations 1, 2, 3, 7, 10, M.2, M.3, and M.4g of that model collapse to a $p - y$ relationship analogous to the KM $d + g$ curve, that is the locus of $p - y$ points which represent commodity market demand given that asset markets are in equilibrium. Finally, equation 8 of that model is similar to (1), though it fails to include debt service as part of the government budget. There is no reason why the *bbe* curve represented by (3) cannot be applied to this model also. Thus an initial stock-flow equilibrium in the Modigliani model could be represented by KM figure 1a. In the Modigliani model, a negative shock to the $d + g$ curve, which produced an inital flow equilibrium at $p_1, y_1$, would be accompanied by a government deficit which has to be covered by printing base money or issuing government debt. Printing money in the Modigliani model shifts the $d + g$ line to the right, and eventually stock-flow equilibrium is restored at $p_0, y_0$ just as in the KM model.

KM analyze the stock-flow equilibrium of their model when the government deficit is financed by selling government debt under the assumption that the sale of the debt will shift the $d + g$ curve to the right. The sufficient condition for this to arise is that the sum of the effect on aggregate demand through the change in non-human wealth as a result of the increased debt, plus the effect on aggregate demand through changes in the price of existing assets, more than offsets the effect on aggregate demand of the increased interest rates associated with the increased stock of government debt. In the conventional model, there is no market for existing assets, and it can be shown that a sufficient condition for Modigliani's $d + g$ curve to shift to the right in response to an increase in debt is that the wealth effect on aggregate demand coming through the consumption function exceeds the effect on aggregate demand through the interest rate increase which is necessary to maintain equilibrium in the money (and bond) market. Hence essentially the same restrictions will cause both models to behave in the same way in response to debt financing of the deficit. Without such restrictions, neither model would possess a stable stock–flow equilibrium under conditions of debt financing, since in both the *bbe* line would shift to the right from its position through $p_0$, $y_0$ in figure 1b, while the $d + g$ curve would shift to the left from its position through $p_1$, $y_1$. In both models, if the stock-flow equilibrium under debt financing is stable, the new equilibrium will lie to the right of $p_0$, $y_0$ along the $s$ curve. Thus in both, the stock–flow under financing by printing base money will correspond with the original pre-shock equilibrium. With debt financing in both models, the stock-flow equilibrium will be characterized by a higher price level and a higher level of real output than the original pre-shock stock–flow equilibrium.

In the light of these results, we should review the four principal conclusions that KM derive from their analysis of intermediate-run equilibrium. First, they conclude that the instantaneous adjustment of output to a budget deficit or surplus will be larger, the larger the proportion of it which is covered by changes in base money. This conclusion is hardly unique to the KM model; it is in fact the familiar result obtained by the usual analysis of strictly flow equilibrium of models such as that of Modigliani. Second, the total adjustment of output and prices, measured from the initial displacement to the intermediate-run stock–flow equilibrium, decreases as the proportion of financing covered by printing base money increases. We have shown this result to hold, even after the adjustment of the balanced budget condition to be consistent with console-type debt. However, we have shown that exactly the same type of outcomes also characterize the Modigliani model, analyzed under the same equilibrium assumptions. Third, any change in $\mu$ changes the position of the *bbe* line and affects the stock–flow equilibrium solution. This is true, but is solely dependent on the nature of the *bbe* line, and thus is not unique to the KM model either. Finally, their fourth principal conclusion that the maintenance of stock-flow equilibrium at constant prices requires a balanced budget and no open market operations, is not a conclusion from the model, but rather follows from the definition of a stock-flow equilibrium. It does not appear, therefore, that any of these qualitative conclusions are hypotheses which can discriminate between the KM model and the conventional literature once the stock–flow constraints are properly introduced into both models.

The *important contribution* of the Brunner–Meltzer analysis is the recognition that the stock–flow constraints imply certain *systematic adjustments* from the *initial flow equilibrium overtime.* In contrast while the Modigliani analysis goes beyond much of the conventional literature in recognizing the existance of the budget constraint, it does not develop the role of this stock–flow relationship for the adjustment of flow equilibria overtime.

The similarities discussed above, of course, do not say that the KM model is the same model as that of the conventional literature. Rather, they say that the two models cannot be discriminated on the basis of the *direction* of the change between equilibrium states in response to changes in various policy parameters. Neither can they be discriminated on the basis of statements about the relative size of the change in response to various policy actions. For example, the statement that "the speed of convergence to intermediate-run equilibrium and the equilibrium position depend on the value of $\mu$" or "the instantaneous rate of adjustment of output to a budget deficit or surplus increases with the value of $\mu$", are conclusions which are common to an analysis of the KM model and the model of the conventional literature.

The important alternative to statements such as the above, is to consider the effect on the instantaneous flow equilibrium, and the rate of adjustment from the instantaneous flow equilibrium to the intermediate-run equilibrium of the KM maintained hypothesis that certain parameters of the model are non-zero, against the alternative hypothesis of the conventional literature that they are zero.

As an illustration let us analyze the effect on these processes of setting the crucial parameters $\epsilon(L, P)$, $\epsilon(m, P)$ and $\epsilon(d, P)$ are equal to zero. In the KM model these parameters carry the weight of the monetarist allegation that "the adjustment to a change in money involves substitution between money, other assets, and new production".[1] If this monetarist assertion is of fundamental importance to the behavior of the economic system, then within the confines of the KM model we should be able to determine that the magnitude of a displacement from an initial stock–flow equilibrium, and the rate of return to a new stock–flow equilibrium will be systematically changed by the assumption that this substitution does not exist.

The assumptions of non-zero values for $\epsilon(L, P)$ and $\epsilon(d, P)$ are quite straightforward. The former is the representation of a broad range of substitution possibilities between money and fianancial assets (bank credit and government securities) and real capital, as contrasted with the conventional asumptions that money substitutes only for financial assets. The second arises because of the assumption that existing real capital can be traded, and in the less than long-run equilibrium states, the price of existing assets will differ from the reproduction cost because of information and transactions costs.

The attempt to discover the origins of the non-zero $\epsilon(m, P)$ and $\epsilon(a, P)$ parameters in the KM model suggests that there exists at least one additional ambiguity in the structure of the equations. In Brunner and Meltzer (1968), $a$ and $m$ are indicated to be functionally related to $k$, the currency demand deposit ratio; $r$, the weighted average required reserve ratio; $f$, the ratio of free reserves

[1] Note that if these three parameters are all assumed to be zero, then the KM model can be viewed as a block-recursive system of equations. The first block consists of the supply relationships, the commodity demand equation, the money demand and supply equations and the government budget constraint. These are sufficient to determine real output, the price of current production, the nominal interest rate, and the stock of money. The second block consists of the demand and supply equations for bank credit, and are sufficient to determine the price of existing real capital and the stock of bank credit. Under these restrictions, the first block of equations is essentially the conventional model.

to total deposits, which in turn is functionally related to the market rate of interest, $i$, and the discount rate $i_d$; $t$, the ratio of time deposits to publicly held demand deposits; and $d$, the ratio of Treasury deposits to publicly held demand deposits.

In Brunner and Meltzer (1972a), we are informed that the public's decisions on the distribution of money holdings between currency and demand deposits and between time deposits and demand deposits, as represented by the $k$ and $t$ in the earlier work, are now summarized by introducing market interest rates, $i$; time deposit rates, $i_t$; asset prices, $P$; wealth, $W_h$ and $W_n$: and the anticipated yield on real capital, $e$, into the $a$ and $m$ function.[2] Obviously this result is obtained by substituting demand functions for time deposits and currency of the general form,

$$C_p/D = k(i, i_t, P, W_h, W_n, e, p),$$

and/or

$$T/D = t(i, i_t, P, W_h, W_n, e, p),$$

into the bank credit and money multiplier relationships.[3] Throughout the KM work, money is consistently defined as demand deposits plus currency. Therefore, in KM (1968) we are faced with a world in which there are four means of holding gross wealth: money (including both currency and demand deposits), time deposits, government debt, and real capital. Implicit in the derivation of the $a$ and $m$ functions which appears in their later work (1972a, 1972b, 1974) is the assumption that money substitutes not only for government debt and real capital, but also for time deposits as indicated in the above equations. This can be inferred from the statement that "The stock of money is not identical to the stock of bank credit" [KM (1974, p. 8)]. Yet when we get to the means of holding wealth in the current KM analysis, the only other forms of holding wealth in addition to money and currency which are considered in discussing the $L$ (demand for cash balances) function, are government debt and real capital. (See also the statements "An intermediate position permitting adjustment of real capital, or claims to real capital, bonds and money seems to us more appropriate for aggregative analysis" [KM (1974, p. 2)], and "Money is a substitute for securities and real capital, not for securities alone" [KM (1974, p. 7)].) The model can be specified one way or the other, either time deposits can be considered an additional asset in the portfolios of the private sector, in which case $i_t$ should be explicitly introduced as an

[2] Brunner and Meltzer (1972, p. 45).

[3] An equation analogous to that given here for $T/D$ can be found as appendix II, equation A5 in Brunner and Meltzer (1968).

argument in both the $L$ function and the $\sigma$ function, or time deposits should be omitted from the analysis and the $i_t$ argument should be dropped from the $a$ and $m$ functions. In the former case, the analysis which KM have performed in their current work is incomplete, because they have considered only $n - 2$ of the $n$ markets. A complete static equilibrium analysis would require that a supply function of time deposits by banks be introduced and the equilibrium condition that the demand for time deposits equal the supply of time deposits must be added to the model. (Alternatively, the time deposit rate might be considered as being set exogenously by government interest rate ceiling policies such as Regulation Q.)

If we ignore the role of time deposits as an influence on $\epsilon(m, P)$, then the only way that the arguments $P$, $W_h$, $W_n$, and $e$ can get into the $a$ and $m$ functions is if it is assumed that the currency–deposit ratio is a function of these particular variables. If $\epsilon(k, P)$ is large, it implies that the degree of substitution between currency and government securities and real capital on the one hand differs from the degree of substitution between demand deposits and government securities and real capital as items in the portfolios of private sector economic units. This would seem to argue against the usefulness of an aggregate concept of money such as demand deposits plus currency. Since KM have been very consistent in both empirical and theoretical work in arguing for the validity of this aggregation, it seems safe to infer that they would regard the currency–deposit ratio as being very insensitive to either $i$, $P$, or $e$.[4] To minimize the complexity of the analysis below, we shall assume that $\epsilon(a, P)$, $\epsilon(a, e)$, $\epsilon(m, P)$ and $\epsilon(m, e)$ are sufficiently small so that they can be assumed to be zero.[5] Thus, there are two crucial parameters which distinguish the KM model from the conventional model: $\epsilon(d, P)$ and $\epsilon(L, P)$.

The first question which requires investigation is how far is a flow equilibrium displaced from an initial stock–flow equilibrium in response to some external shock, and how does this vary with the two parameters identified above. This requires determining the amount that the $d + g$ curve will shift in response to the assumed shock. For purposes of discussion, we shall assume that the external shock is a change in real government purchases of current production, $g$, unaccompanied by changes in taxes.

The vertical shift of the $d + g$ curve in response to such a policy action is

[4] In Brunner and Meltzer (1968, appendix II), we find a statement that "$k$ is dependent on a variety of costs and returns, as well as one wealth and other factors". They then immediately proceed to assume it given for purposes of that analysis.

[5] It does not follow from this discussion that $\epsilon(m, i)$ or $\epsilon(a, i)$ should be taken as zero. Brunner and Meltzer (1968) derive $m$ and $a$ as functions of the free reserve deposit ratio, which is responsive to $i$ as banks substitute between reserves and earning assets as returns change. The other elasticities disappear, because banks are assumed not to hold real capital in their asset portfolios.

measured by $\epsilon(p, g|d + g)$ (found in section 5 of KM). Thus the sensitivity of the displacement of flow equilibrium under fiscal shocks can be determined by

$$\frac{\partial\epsilon(p, g|d + g)}{\partial\bar{\epsilon}(d, P)} = [-\epsilon(P, p|AM)\epsilon(p, g|d + g)]$$
$$\times[\bar{\epsilon}(d, i)\epsilon(i, p|AM) + \bar{\epsilon}(d, P)\epsilon(P, p|AM) + \epsilon(d, p) + \epsilon(d, W_{\mathrm{h}})\,\epsilon(W_{\mathrm{h}}, p)]^{-1} < 0.$$

Thus, the larger $\bar{\epsilon}(d, P)$ the less sensitive will be the displacement of a flow equilibrium from an initial stock–flow equilibrium for a given percentage change in real government purchases.

The sensitivity of $\epsilon(p, g|d + g)$ to the degree of substitution between money and real assets, as measured by the size of $\epsilon(L, P)$, will be influenced by two factors, the degree of interest rate response, $\epsilon(i, p|AM)$, and the degree of response of existing asset prices, $\epsilon(P, p|AM)$, necessary to clear the asset markets. In KM appendix, part 3, both of these elasticities are shown to be functions of $\epsilon(MM, P)$, which in turn is shown to be a function of $\epsilon(L, P)$ in the appendix, part 1. Evaluating the relevant partial derivatives gives

$$\frac{\partial\epsilon(MM, P)}{\partial\epsilon(L, P)} = -1,$$

$$\frac{\partial\epsilon(P, p|AM)}{\partial\epsilon(L, P)} = \frac{-\epsilon(P, p|AM)}{\Delta}\epsilon(CM, i)\frac{\partial\epsilon(MM, P)}{\partial\epsilon(L, P)}$$
$$= \frac{\epsilon(P, p|AM)\epsilon(CM, i)}{\Delta},$$

where

$$\Delta = \epsilon(CM, i)\epsilon(MM, P) - \epsilon(MM, i)\epsilon(CM, P) < 0,$$

but

$$\epsilon(P, p|AM) < 0 \quad \text{and} \quad \epsilon(CM, i) > 0,$$

so

$$\frac{\partial\epsilon(P, p|AM)}{\partial\epsilon(L, P)} > 0.$$

Similarly,

$$\frac{\partial\epsilon(i, p|AM)}{\partial\epsilon(L, P)} = \frac{-\epsilon(CM, P)}{\Delta}\frac{\partial\epsilon(MM, P)}{\partial\epsilon(L, P)}$$

$$-\frac{\epsilon(i, p|AM)}{\Delta}\epsilon(CM, i)\frac{\partial\epsilon(MM, P)}{\partial\epsilon(L, P)}$$

$$= \frac{1}{\Delta}\left[\epsilon(CM, P) + \epsilon(i, p|AM)\epsilon(CM, i)\right] < 0.$$

Consequently the absolute values of both $\epsilon(P, p|AM)$ and $\epsilon(i, p|AM)$ decline as $\epsilon(L, P)$ gets larger.

But

$$\frac{\partial\epsilon(p, g|d + g)}{\partial\epsilon(L, P)} = \frac{\partial\epsilon(p, g|d + g)}{\partial\epsilon(i, p|AM)}\frac{\partial\epsilon(i, p|AM)}{\partial\epsilon(L, P)} + \frac{\partial\epsilon(p, g|d + g)}{\partial\epsilon(P, p|AM)}\frac{\partial\epsilon(P, p|AM)}{\partial\epsilon(L, P)},$$

and

$$\frac{\partial\epsilon(p, g|d + g)}{\partial\epsilon(i, p|AM)} = \left[-\epsilon(p, g|d + g)\,\bar{\epsilon}(d, i)\right] \times \left[\bar{\epsilon}(d, i)\epsilon(i, P|AM) + \bar{\epsilon}(d, P)\epsilon(P, p|AM) + \epsilon(d, p) + \epsilon(d, W_{\mathrm{h}})\epsilon(W_{\mathrm{h}}, p)\right]^{-1} < 0,$$

$$\frac{\partial\epsilon(p, g|d + g)}{\partial\epsilon(P, p|AM)} = \left[-\epsilon(p, g|d + g)\bar{\epsilon}(d, P)\right] \times \left[\bar{\epsilon}(d, i)\epsilon(i, P|AM) + \bar{\epsilon}(d, P)\epsilon(P, p|AM) + \epsilon(d, p) + \epsilon(d, W_{\mathrm{h}})\epsilon(W_{\mathrm{h}}, p)\right]^{-1} > 0.$$

So

$$\frac{\partial\epsilon(p, g|d + g)}{\partial\epsilon(L, P)} > 0.$$

Therefore, the stronger the degree of substitution between money and real capital, as measured by a larger $\epsilon(L, P)$, the larger the shift of the $d + g$ curve in response to a change in government purchases, and the farther the displacement of the instantaneous flow equilibrium from the initial stock–flow equilibrium.

An initial glance at this result might suggest that it is counter-intuitive. A closer consideration indicates that the model should be expected to behave this way. Any shock to the commodity market is going to affect the asset market equilibria. The greater the elasticity of substitution between money and real capital, or for that matter the elasticity of substitution between any two assets, the smaller will be the changes in asset prices that will restore equilibrium in the asset markets. However, these changes in asset prices have negative feedback effects on aggregate demand, and thus the smaller the changes in asset prices necessary to offset the impact of shocks in the asset markets, the larger the output effects which are necessary to equilibrate the commodity market.

The next question which should be addressed is what is the sensitivity of the initial rate of adjustment from an instantaneous flow equilibrium to a new stock–flow equilibrium to variations is the parameters $\bar{\epsilon}(d, P)$ and $\epsilon(L, P)$? Such an adjustment comes about because deficits (or surpluses) are financed by changes in base money or changes in the publicly held stock of government debt. KM have derived the relevant shift elasticities for the $d + g$ curve as $\epsilon(p, B|d + g)$ and $\epsilon(p, S|d + g)$. We shall consider only the response to printing base money here.

It is easily seen that

$$\frac{\partial\epsilon(p, B|d+g)}{\partial\bar{\epsilon}(d, P)} = \frac{-\epsilon(P, B|AM)}{\epsilon(d, p)} > 0,$$

so the more elastic current production is to changes in the price of existing capital, the faster will be the initial rate of adjustment from an instantaneous flow equilibrium toward an intermediate-run stock–flow equilibrium, when deficits (surpluses) are covered by changes in base money. To evaluate the sensitivity of $\epsilon(p, B|d + g)$ to $\epsilon(L, P)$ we must determine the sign of

$$\frac{\partial\epsilon(p, B|d+g)}{\partial\epsilon(L, P)} = \frac{-\bar{\epsilon}(d, i)}{\epsilon(d, p)}\frac{\partial\epsilon(i, B|AM)}{\partial\epsilon(L, P)} - \frac{\bar{\epsilon}(d, P)}{\epsilon(d, p)}\frac{\partial\epsilon(P, B|AM)}{\partial\epsilon(L, P)}.$$

But

$$\frac{\partial\epsilon(i, B|AM)}{\partial\epsilon(L, P)} = \frac{-1}{\Delta}\frac{\partial\epsilon(MM, P)}{\partial\epsilon(L, P)} - \frac{\epsilon(i, B|AM)}{\Delta}\frac{\partial\Delta}{\partial\epsilon(L, P)},$$

where $\epsilon(MM, P)$ and $\Delta$ are defined as above. Thus,

$$\frac{\partial\epsilon(i, B|AM)}{\partial\epsilon(L, P)} = \frac{1}{\Delta}[1 + \epsilon(i, B|AM)\epsilon(CM, i)],$$

$$\frac{\partial\epsilon(P, B|AM)}{\partial\epsilon(L, P)} = \frac{-\epsilon(P, B|AM)}{\Delta}\frac{\Delta}{\partial\epsilon(L, P)} = \frac{1}{\Delta}\epsilon(P, B|AM)\epsilon(CM, i) < 0.$$

Thus the shift of the $d + g$ curve which originates through changes in the price of existing assets as the stock of base money is changed, is unambiguously reduced as the degree of substitution between money and existing assests $\epsilon(L, P)$, is increased.

The effect through induced changes in interest rates is ambiguous. A sufficient condition for $\partial\epsilon(i, B|AM)/\partial\epsilon(L, P) < 0$ is $\epsilon(CM, i) < 1$, since

$$|\epsilon(i, B|AM)| = \left\{\frac{\epsilon(MM, P) - \epsilon(CM, P)}{[\epsilon(CM, i)/\epsilon(MM, i)]\epsilon(MM, P) - \epsilon(CM, P)}\right\}\epsilon(MM, i)$$

$$< \epsilon(MM, i) < \epsilon(CM, i),$$

by the order conditions given in KM appendix, part 1. But in this case we cannot determine the sign of $\partial\epsilon(p, B|d + g)/\partial\epsilon(L, P)$ and hence cannot substantiate the monetarist proposition that a broader range of portfolio substitution will imply stronger impacts of monetary shocks on the economy than does the interest rate only substitution conventionally assumed in the demand for money function.

On the other hand we can rewrite

$$|\epsilon(i, B|AM)| = \left\{\frac{\epsilon(MM, P) - \epsilon(CM, P)}{\epsilon(MM, P) - [\epsilon(MM, i)/\epsilon(CM, i)]\epsilon(CM, P)}\right\}\epsilon(CM, i)$$

$$> \epsilon(CM, i) > \epsilon(MM, i).$$

So, if $\epsilon(MM, i) = \epsilon(m, i) - \epsilon(L, i) > 1$, we have a sufficient condition for

$$\frac{\partial\epsilon(i, B|AM)}{\partial\epsilon(L, P)} > \frac{1}{\Delta}[1 - \epsilon(MM, i)^2] > 0.$$

In this case $\partial\epsilon(p, B|AM)/\partial\epsilon(L, P)$ is unambiguously negative, so the stronger the substitution between money and existing assets, the smaller will be the shift of the $d + g$ curve in response to changes in base money.

This would seem to be an extremely perverse view from a monetarist perspective. Fortunately for the monetarists, the weight of the empirical evidence seems to be against the proposition that $\epsilon(MM, i) > 1$. Unfortunately, the empirical work on demand for money functions has almost exclusively been conducted under the implicit restriction that $\epsilon(L, P) = 0$. Thus, the information that we have in the literature is not too informative on the question at hand. It appears, in the end, that the question of the broad versus narrow range of substitution for money and the dominance of monetary impulses, cannot be settled at this level of abstraction, but awaits further empirical tests.

KM proceed to analyze one additional equilibrium state, which they characterize as long-run. One feature of this long-run equilibrium is that money wages are not fixed. KM *assert* that the assumption of fixed money wages, characteristic of the intermediate-run equilibrium, is replaced with an assumption that the money wage rate responds positively to price changes. They also assert that the long-run equilibrium will occur at a full utilization of resources because of the dynamics of the labor market. Yet, nowhere in the analysis is there any indication of the nature of the demand and supply functions in the labor market, or any indication of the behavior of the economic units participating in this market which assures that the long-run demand and supply functions will intersect at full utilization of resources. Undoubtedly, the model can be extended to explicitly incorporate this behavior. At present, however, it seems fair to conclude that KM have not provided an explicit "price theoretic" bridge between their intermediate-run analysis and their long-run analysis. Consequently, at this point in the development of their model, it appears that they are also subject to the criticism that they have leveled at Friedman, namely compartmentalizing macro-economic analysis into two sets of problems, one in which the wage rate is fixed, and one in which it is flexible [Brunner and Meltzer (1927c)].

The second important characteristic of their long-run equilibrium is the assumption that everything is fully adjusted, in particular that $P = p$.[6] This implies the important restriction which KM acknowledge, that $i - \pi = e$, the anticipated rate of return to real capital. But this is nothing more than stating that in the long-run equilibrium the desired aggregate capital stock must be just equal to the actual capital stock, i.e., the long-run equilibrium is a stationary state with zero net investment. KM correctly note that this adds an additional equation to their model, but no additional endogenous variables, since they take $e$ as a parameter throughout the analysis. Hence, there is one less policy variable that can be determined exogenously if the capital stock is to remain at its initial long-run equilibrium value, and the system is to return to a new long-run equilibrium after some kind of exogenous shock. This however, is also true of the conventional macro-economic models when the stationary state assumption is applied. Again, the difference between KM and the "long-run" (i.e., completely flexible wage and price assumption) analysis of a model such as that of Modigliani is that the stationary-state stock restriction has not been applied to the analysis reported by Modigliani.

KM conduct their analysis of the long-run comparative equilibrium effects of monetary and fiscal policies under a different, but completely legitimate set of assumptions. They maintain the exogeneity of all of the policy instruments that are exogenous in the intermediate run. To close their system, they introduce the capital stock as an additional endogenous variable, and allow the actual capital stock to adjust to the new desired capital stock associated with long-run equilibrium (i.e., stationary state) after either a monetary or fiscal policy shock.

KM derive their long-run equilibrium conclusions by first investigating the nature of the stock–flow equilibrium under the assumptions of fixed capital stock,

[6] See Brunner and Meltzer (1974, p. 8 and p. 26).

but fully flexible wages. They conclude that after an open market purchase, this stock–flow equilibrium will be characterized by the same real output, lower $p$, higher $P$, and lower $i$, than the long-run equilibrium prior to the open market purchase.[7] They conclude that this cannot be a long-run equilibrium, since the constraint $i = (p/P)e + \pi$ cannot be satisfied under these circumstances, and therefore, in the long-run equilibrium there will be a larger capital stock.

Again it is useful to examine the conclusions that can be derived from the Modigliani model, when analyzing equilibria which are subject to an equivalent set of restrictions. Assuming fully flexible wages and prices, and a fixed capital stock, the stock-flow equilibrium after an open market purchase in that model will have the same level of real output and a lower price level and interest rate than the initial long-run equilibrium.[8] Since the marginal productivity of capital is larger than the interest rate, this cannot be a long-run equilibrium, and applying the same reasoning as KM, in the new long-run equilibrium there will be a larger capital stock. Again, there does not seem to be anything inherent in the nature of the KM model that produces qualitatively different conclusions from the conventional model, as long as care is taken to analyze both models under the same set of assumptions.

Two-questions seem to arise out of the above discussions: (1) is the KM theory really a monetarist theory, and (2) what is the relationship between the KM theory and the empirical monetarist models of the Andersen–Jordan type?

KM have provided three criteria by which to judge whether a theory is monetarist. First, "the long-run position to which the system moves is determined by stocks, particularly the stock of money, and not by flows".[9] At this point in time, this statement without the qualification regarding the stock of money, would appear relatively non-controversial. Certainly the KM model satisfies it, but so do other models, the proprietors of which may not particularly appreciate the title of monetarist. On the other hand, there does not seem to be anything in the KM

[7] Note that they assert that the qualitative nature of their conclusions does not depend on whether base money is added through standard open market operations, or distributed through airplanes. This may not hold up in the one case where money is distributed by airplanes, and then in adjusting to stock–flow equilibrium the cumulative surplus is liquidated totally by destroying base money. In this case, under the budget constraint specific to consoles [see (1) above], there would be no shift of the *bbe* curve, and the new intermediate stock–flow equilibrium would be restored at the original $p$ level.

[8] The distribution of money through an airplane, and the subsequent exclusive destruction of base money to cover the cumulative surplus incurred ($\mu = 1$), is an exception to this statement. Here the stock–flow equilibrium, assuming that government securities are consoles, will have the same price level and interest rate as the initial long-run equilibrium. Hence it will also be a long-run equilibrium. My suspicion is that the stock–flow equilibrium of the KM model, under these circumstances, is also a long-run equilibrium, but I have not attempted to rigorously prove it.

[9] Brunner and Meltzer (1974, p. 46).

model which would suggest that the stock of money (presumably base money) should be singled out above other stocks. Certainly the distribution of government securities by airplane and the recouping of the cumulative deficit exclusively in terms of such securities would also have an impact on the long-run equilibrium values of real income and prices under the KM specifications.

The second KM criterion is that "the adjustment to a change in money involves substitution between money, other assets, and new production".[10] KM certainly have allowed additional substitution possibilities among assets by relaxing the conventional assumptions. Unless one is prepared to acknowledge the wealth effects on new production as "substitution effects", it does not appear that they have encompassed the whole spectrum. If complete substitution between money and new production is to be allowed, then it almost seems imperative to carry the analysis all the way to a two-sector model such as that developed by Foley and Sidrauski (1971) or Park (1973). In these models, production in one sector is the increment to the stock of real assets, and direct substitution between real assets and money is allowed. The natural consequence of such an extension is that one becomes concerned with the allocation of total output among the two industries, and this would appear to violate the secondary "monetarist conjecture" that allocative detail is unimportant in considering aggregative stabilization issues.[11]

Further, it does not appear that the KM additions have produced qualitative results which differ from the traditional restricted model as long as the role of stock constraints is properly recognized. Obviously, the KM asset market specifications suggest that there could be serious specification problems with previous attempts to statistically estimate such functions, but that issue is beyond the scope of this discussion.

Third, KM claim that a monetarist specification will indicate that the economic system is stable. It is on this point that one might argue that their model is in danger for failing their own criteria. They have countered the Keynesian assertion on money wages with a counter assertion that though money wages do not adjust in the short run, in the long run they adjust in such a manner as to establish equilibrium at full utilization of resources. The justification for this counter assertion is labor market dynamics, but in a previous footnote, we are explicitly told "there is no labor market in our model". Thus, the assumption that the economic system adjusts in the long run to full utilization of resources is imposed exogeneously upon the KM model.

The second question is how do the Andersen–Jordan type models compare with the results derived by KM? It seems fair to conclude that if the KM model represents the true state of the world, then these so called reduced form models

[10] Brunner and Meltzer (1974, p. 46).
[11] Brunner and Meltzer (1974, p. 49).

are seriously misspecified. The KM model suggests that an important omitted variable in such regressions is the stock of government debt. The Andersen–Jordan model omits completely any consideration of changes in the stock of government debt. Second, the KM model suggests that the intermediate-run impacts of open market operations, on both prices and real output, are smaller than the short-run impacts. The reduced form models consistently indicate that the impact of changes in the money stock on nominal income increase over the short periods of time in which the long-run impact is assumed to be realized. Finally, it does not suggest that the intermediate-or long-run effects of fiscal policy actions are zero, either on real output or prices.

In conclusion, the KM analysis suggests that more attention should be given to the exact nature of the equilibrium states that are compared in the usual comparative static model of analysis of macroeconomic analysis. However, it also strongly suggests that the issues separating monetarists from non-monetarists are probably considerably less important than they are made out to be at this level of abstraction. This suggests that it may be possible, with a concerted effort at communication in a common language, to develop a general theoretical construct within which particular monetarist and non-monetarist propositions can be formulated as restrictions on specific parameters. If this can be achieved, then we shall be in a position to determine whether or not the data generated by historical experiences are sufficiently rich to reject one set of propositions in favor of the other.

## Bibliography


Brunner, K. and A. H. Meltzer, 1968, Liquidity traps for money, bank credit and interest rates, Journal of Political Economy 16, pp. 1–37.

Brunner, K. and A. H. Meltzer, 1972a, A monetarist framework for aggregative analysis, Proceedings of the First Konstanz Seminar on Monetary Theory and Monetary Policy, Kredit und Kapital 5, pp. 31–88.

Brunner, K. and A. H. Meltzer, 1972b, Money, debt and economic activity, Journal of Political Economy 80, pp. 951–977.

Brunner, K. and A. H. Meltzer, 1972c, Friedman's monetary theory, Journal of Political Economy 80, pp. 837–851.

Brunner, K. and A. H. Meltzer, 1974, An aggregate theory for a closed economy, this volume.

Christ, C., 1973, Dynamic macroeconomic policy effects on income and prices under government budget restraint, Working Papers in Economics 6, mimeo. (Department of Political Economy, The Johns Hopkins University, Balimore, Md.).

Foley, D. and D. Sidrauski, 1971, Monetary and fiscal policy in a growing economy (Macmillan, New York).

Modigliani, F., 1963, The monetary mechanism and its interaction with real phenomena, Review of Economics and Statistics 45, Suppl., Feb., pp. 79–107.

Park, Y. C., 1973, The transmission process and the relative effectiveness of monetary and fiscal policy in a two-sector neoclassical model, Journal of Money, Credit and Banking 5, pp. 595–622.

## 3. COMMENTS ON BRUNNER AND MELTZER

Thomas MAYER*

### 1. Introduction

The Brunner–Meltzer model presented here and in previous papers is an important contribution to macroeconomics. Previous criticisms of the reigning neo-Keynesian synthesis have usually taken two forms. On the one hand, there is the rather abstract Patinkin model using the real balance effect as its analytic tool, and centering around the invariance proposition. On the other hand, there is the Friedmanian challenge with its argument that the historical evidence shows changes in the money stock to have a dominating effect on money income. On an analytic level discussions of Friedman's model at one time focused on the interest elasticity of the demand for money, and nowadays focus (or should focus) instead on the snap-back of interest rates when the money stock changes.

Brunner and Meltzer, however, advocate a third approach. In their model the real balance effect does not play an important role, and the invariance proposition is denied. At the same time, they accept a significant interest elasticity of demand for money, and do not rely on the Friedmanian snap-back of interest rates. Rather than look at flow effects as both Keynesians and Friedmanians tend to do, they focus on relative price effects and on stock effects. Their analysis is therefore not a quantity theory model in the sense of Friedman's, though it is a quantity theory approach in the sense that changes in the quantity of money dominate income. It is an original contribution to macroeconomics which employs different mechanisms than those used in the standard Keynesian-quantity theory debates.

### 2. The Analytic Horizon

One way in which the Brunner–Meltzer model differs from both the standard Keynesian and quantity theory models is that Brunner and Meltzer focus on

*I am indebted to Karl Brunner for many helpful comments on an earlier draft. Obviously, he is not responsible for any remaining errors.

relatively long-run equilibriums, ones with a much longer time horizon than those used both by Keynesians and Friedmanians. In the Brunner–Meltzer model there is a flow equilibrium, but that is superseded by a long-run equilibrium in which stocks have advanced. This long-run equilibrium is generally ignored by Keynesians. A good example of this is furnished by the fact that one of the main mechanisms used by Brunner and Meltzer, the impact of a deficit on the outstanding stock of government bonds, and hence on expenditures, had already been discovered more than 25 years ago by Abba Lerner (1948), who, however, did not attach much importance to it, presumably because he was interested in a shorter-run equilibrium. And although this Lerner effect has been (independently) rediscovered from time to time by other Keynesian economists, it has not really been integrated into the standard Keynesian model.

More significantly, the basic quantity theory conclusion, that a rise in the money stock leads *eventually* to a proportional rise in the price level, far from contradicting Keynesian theory, fits well into it. Keynes pointed out that the quantity theory is valid if two conditions are met. One is full employment, the other is that velocity is constant. Suppose that the quantity of money is increased at a time when the economy is not at full employment. Neither a Keynesian nor a quantity theorist would then claim that prices will rise proportionately in the short run. But eventually, when some exogenous factor causes the economy to hit its full employment ceiling in any case, perhaps in the following expansion, perhaps only an expansion several cycles into the future, then the previous increase in the quantity of money will raise prices rather than output. And the effect of the price rise is to reduce the real stock of money, and hence to raise the interest rate back to its initial level, so that velocity is no longer depressed by a lower interest rate. Despite this, Keynesians reject the quantity theory because it was precisely in connection with regard to the validity of the quantity theory that Keynes (1923) wrote: "In the long run we are all dead."

Hence, one issue in Brunner–Meltzer's debate with Keynesians relates to the proper length of the analytic horizon. Are Keynesians justified in ignoring long-run stock effects, or do these have to be introduced even if one is interested only in the current business cycle?

But a warning is in order here. The disagreement about the appropriate analytic horizon is only part of the dispute. Brunner and Meltzer's analysis disagrees also with the Keynesian analysis of flow effects. Thus, in their model, newly created money is spent directly on all assets, not just on bonds, and the relative price of capital goods and of current output plays an important role. It is, of course, true that the Friedmanian model also allows money to be spent directly on goods rather than just on bonds, but Brunner and Meltzer develop this point in considerably more detail than Friedman does by distinguishing between the money market and the credit market. Thus, while some economists have argued that

Friedman's discussion of the transmission process is essentially the same as Keynes's,[1] this cannot be said about the Brunner–Meltzer transmission process.

### 3. Isolating the Strategic Variables

The above may suggest that the Brunner–Meltzer model is clearly superior to the Keynesian one. Not only does it provide a long-run analysis (which includes some factors ignored by the growth model extensions of the Keynesian paradigm), but also, even for the short run, it adds factors ignored by Keynesians. But this does not necessarily make it superior since the Brunner–Meltzer model excludes certain factors stressed by Keynesians. And while on a *formal* level these factors could be added to the Brunner–Meltzer model they are contrary to the *empirical* hypotheses to which Brunner and Meltzer adhere.

The Keynesian factors which Brunner and Meltzer ignore are major Keynesian determinants of expenditures. The Keynesian model focuses on what motiviates spenders, and therefore provides a rich discussion of the variables underlying the marginal efficiency of investment and the propensity to consume. In the Keynesian model the *MEI* is highly unstable, and hence the factors underlying it need comprehensive analysis. (And to a limited extent, the same is true for the *LP* schedule.) This view of the world emerges very clearly in the Keynesian research strategy used to build econometric models. Here, the estimate of income is built up by adding up expenditures in various sectors, though, of course, interrelations are also considered. By contrast, a monetarist model works from the top down by deducing aggregate expenditures from the stock of money without worrying about shifts in expenditure incentives. These are assumed essentially stable, except insofar as they are affected by changes in the money stock. A clear example of the Keynesian's emphasis on changing expenditure motives as the essence of the macroeconomic problem can be seen in Paul Samuelson's classic introductory text.[2] Students are given a picture of an economy in which aggregate demand would attain its right level only by accident, since it depends upon shifting incentives to invest.

On the other hand, Brunner and Meltzer accept as their underlying *empirical* hypothesis, the proposition that expenditure incentives are stable, in the sense that the private sector, if not disturbed by government policy, is stable. Hence, in their macroeconomics, most of the determinants of the *MEI* can be ignored.

[1] Cf. Okun (1963).

[2] Elementary textbooks are a good source for determining what a paradigm is all about, because the author is forced to state his doctrine simply, and without the usual qualifications that are added to journal articles only to ward off criticism, without really changing what the author is driving at.

To a Keynesian, this is a wrong judgment, one that invalidates their model, in the sense that, while their analysis may be formally correct in tracing out those interrelations they do consider, they leave out the important factors. Thus, a Keynesian may accept Brunner and Meltzer's analysis as showing that the economy *tends* towards a particular long-run equilibrium, and yet he can argue that their model does not provide much insight into the functioning of the economy; that it is Hamlet without the Prince of Denmark. Long before the economy approaches anywhere near its Brunner–Meltzer equilibrium, this equilibrium is changed by shifts of the *MEI*. Now this sort of criticism of equilibrium analysis is old hat, and certainly applies also to the microeconomic analysis we all accept, but the extent to which it should be treated seriously depends upon how important these shifts are. This is an empirical issue and since Brunner and Meltzer are concerned only with analytic issues in this paper they do not deal with it here.

## 4. The Interpretation of Stability

The stability of the private sector therefore emerges as a central issue. Unfortunately, Brunner and Meltzer interpret the Keynesian proposition that the private sector is stable in a very questionable way. They interpret stability to mean that when shocked the system tends to move back toward a full employment, stable price equilibrium. But when Keynesians talk of the instability of the private sector, and of the need for government stabilization policies, they usually do not deny that the system is stable in the Brunner–Meltzer sense. Rather, they mean either, or both, of two things. One is that exogenous shocks cause frequent and wide departures of income from its previous equilibrium level, departures which can be cyclical in nature. The second is that it takes the equilibrating factors a long time to return the economy to equilibrium, and that the suffering caused on the way should not be tolerated.

Thus, those Keynesians who believe in the existence of cost-push inflation do *not* assume as Brunner and Meltzer imply that "prices or wages move independently of . . . the values of financial variables". Surely, just about any economist believes that a sufficiently strong monetary policy could break any inflation. The real issue is whether a cost-push inflation can be broken by moneary policy at an acceptable cost in terms of unemployment. Similarly, most economists would agree that continuous substantial inflation requires a continuous growth in the money stock. Those who do not talk about the monetary expansion involved in inflation refrain from doing so because they accept – as "given" – a monetary policy that, to a greater or lesser extent, finances inflation generated by other factors.

Similarly, Brunner and Meltzer's statement that "maintained fiscal changes do not induce steady inflation or deflation whether financed entirely by debt or by base money", is also acceptable to Keynesians. Any modern Keynesian setting up a halfway elaborate model would look at the effects on stocks if he were concerned with the long run. Rather, what Keynesians are unwilling to accept is that a maintained deficit is not expansionary over a short time horizon such as the one used in the St. Louis model.

## 5. Does the Brunner–Meltzer Model Support Monetarism?

In what ways does the Brunner–Meltzer analysis support the heart of monetarism, which is that changes in money income are primarily explainable by changes in the money stock? One obvious way is that it rejects the Tobin (1947) paradigm by which the effect of changes in the money stock depends only on the slopes of the *LP* and *MEI* curves. If one uses empirically plausible values for these two slopes one gets a result which, while intermediate between the two theories, give more support to the Keynesian theory than the quantity theory.[3] Brunner and Meltzer have now shown that this sort of exercise is invalid; relative price and stock effects may validate monetarism regardless of the slopes of the *MEI* and *LP* functions. In this way their work supports monetarism.

In addition, it also supports a number of other monetarist propositions, such as the monetarist model of the transmission process, belief in the inherent stability of the private sector, the irrelevance of allocative detail in explaining changes in money income, etc.[4] However, it is important to note that such "support" consists only of developing an analytic framework in which all of these results find a home. In their paper Brunner and Meltzer have not tried to present empirical evidence validating these propositions; presumably this task is left for subsequent papers. But until they do, a Keynesian could reject their analysis as being a logical exercise which provides little insight into how the economy functions, and one which ignores the most strategic factor, the variability of the *MEI*.

In this connection it is worth noting that, although the standard Keynesian model has no relative price effects, it does allow for some wealth effects. Thus, the essentially Keynesian FMP model has a substantial wealth effect running from interest rates to security values, and hence to household wealth and consumption. And Tobin (1972) too has stressed the significance of a wealth term in the consumption function, though, admittedly many Keynesian econometric

[3] See Mayer (1964) and Tucker (1965).

[4] Elsewhere I have set out the twelve propositions that form monetarism and discussed their interconnections [Mayer (1967)].

models do not have these wealth effects. Yet the standard Keynesian model is certainly poorer in terms of wealth effects than is the Brunner–Meltzer model. This is no accident. Someone who thinks that erratic shifts in the expenditure functions are important will focus on the determinants of these shifts, rather than on wealth effects. But to someone who believes that the private sector is inherentely stable, long-run wealth effects are worthy of more attention. Hence it is not surprising that Brunner and Meltzer place wealth effects in the front center of the stage while Keynesians *usually* treat them as supporting actors.

So far I have focused in large part on stock effects. But Brunner and Meltzer also introduce a relative price effect, and attach more importance to it than they do to stock effects. By introducing this effect Brunner and Meltzer link macroeconomics with modern price theory which stresses adjustment lags and disequilibrium positions. Keynesians have largely ignored relative price effects.[5] This too can be explained as a result of the Keynesian's hypothesis that expenditure motives are highly volatile. If demand and supply curves shift a great deal, then movements along these curves are less important than if these curves are stable.

Apart from its introduction of relative price and wealth effects the Brunner–Meltzer analysis is also monetarist in the sense that they allow money holders to buy real capital and consumption goods as well as bonds. Thus in the substitution effects part of their transmission mechanism, the money–interest rates–investment route is not the only one. How important is this? Keynes talked only about the substitution of money and bonds. But since he treated bonds and capital as perfect substitutes it is not clear that it matters that he did not allow money holders to buy capital directly. Keynes' denial that excess money balances are used to buy consumer goods seems more serious. He eliminated this possibility by making the assumptions – on rather questionable grounds – that the interest elasticity of consumption is zero. This allowed him to dichotomize household decisions into those relating to the allocation of income flows, and those relating to asset composition. But surely, this assumption of zero interest elasticity of consumption is not a critical part of Keynesian theory, and could easily be abandoned.[6] And the magnitude of the error introduced by this assumption is, of course, again an empirical issue on which the Brunner–Meltzer model so far is silent.

Another point that Brunner and Meltzer make is that their analysis supports the monetarist position because it shows the dominance of stocks over flows. But, in a

[5] A partial, but notable exception is Tobin.

[6] Unfortunately, it is hard to see from the Brunner–Meltzer model how much difference this assumption of the interest inelasticity of consumption makes standing on its own. I *may* therefore be wrong in treating it as minor.

long-run context, such a dominance is surely not distinctively monetarist, but is a necessary condition of any valid analysis. In no proper theory are flow market fully in equilibrium unless asset markets are too. In this respect the dispute between the Brunner–Meltzer model and the Keynesian model involves either a disagreement about the proper time horizon of economic analysis, or a disagreement about the speed with which significant stock effects occur. By showing that there are numerous stock effects which should be taken into account Brunner and Meltzer show that the assumption that asset markets disequilibrium can be ignored in short- and medium-term forecasts is more risky than it previously seemed. But while this is suggestive evidence it is far from conclusive evidence.

## 6. Conclusion

Thus the Brunner–Meltzer analysis has opened a new chapter in the dispute about the Keynesian model. They have gone completely beyond the issue of the slope of the *LP* schedule, which we now know to be an irrelevant issue, and also beyond the still very much alive issue of the interest rate snap-back. Instead of dealing with such essentially empirical issues they have raised much more basic theoretical ones by introducing stock and relative price effects which are omitted in the Keynesian model. In turn, they have omitted the Keynesian emphasis on certain factors which change the *MEI*.

On a theoretical level the issue is now set out: are the Keynesian factors which shift expenditure functions, and are omitted by Brunner and Meltzer, more or less important than the relative price and stock effects they have introduced? Obviously, this issue can only be settled by empirical tests. But, I suspect that it will prove inordinately difficult to do so. Yet the considerations raised by Brunner and Meltzer cannot simply be ignored on the grounds that they are difficult to test. Since their model stands in sharp contradiction to the standard Keynesian model we teach in our introductory courses, to reject their model because we just do not know whether it is right, requires us also to reject the standard Keynesian model for the same reason. When we, or our textbooks, tell our students that the private sector is inherently unstable are we not really relying on our students lacking the gumption to demand that we provide evidence? This is the rather embarassing issue raised by the Brunner–Meltzer analysis.

## Bibliography

Keynes, J. M., 1923, A tract on monetary reform (Macmillan, London) p. 80.

Lerner, A., 1948, The burden of the national debt, in: L. Meltzer et al., Income, employment, and public policy (Norton, New York) p. 265.

Mayer, T., 1964, Multiplier and velocity analysis: An evaluation, Journal of Political Economy LXXII, Dec., pp. 563–574.

Mayer, T., 1975, The structure of monetarism, Kredit und Kapital, nos. 2 and 3.

Okun, A., 1963, Comments on Friedman and Schwartz's "Money and business cycles", Review of Economics and Statistics, Feb., p. 74.

Tobin, J., 1947, Liquidity preference and monetary policy, Review of Economics and Statistics XXIX, May, pp. 124–131.

Tobin, J., 1972, Wealth, liquidity and the propensity to consume, in: B. Strumpel et al., eds., Human behavior in economic affairs (Jassey–Bass, San Francisco, Calif.).

Tucker, D., 1965, Mayer's test of Keynesianism: A correction, Journal of Political Economy LXXIII, Aug., pp. 394–395.

## REPLY

## Monetarism: The Principal Issues, Areas of Agreement and the Work Remaining

Karl BRUNNER and Allan H. MELTZER*

The most surprising difference revealed to us by the Brown University Conference on Monetarism came in the descriptions of the central issue. Franco Modigliani and Albert Ando devote most of their paper to demonstrating that fiscal policy has a temporary effect on real income and a lasting effect on the price level. For them "the main significant area of remaining disagreement seems to be over the short- and medium-run impact of macrofiscal actions on aggregate money income". Jerome Stein defines monetarism as "a set of propositions in direct opposition to Keynesian fiscal policy". James Tobin writes: "A characteristic monetarist proposition is that pure fiscal policy does not matter for aggregate real demand, nominal income and price level".

We describe the central issues under discussion in a very different way. For us, there are three main issues that have been discussed at various levels – theory, evidence, policy – and that have spawned a number of partly related issues such as research strategy. The principal issues, for us, are the nature of the transmission mechanism expressed by the interpretation and the relevance of the *IS–LM* model, the nature of the relation between allocative adjustments and aggregative behaviour, and the nature of the processes generating economic fluctuations or persistent inflation. The last issue is occasionally divided into two parts. One concerns the internal stability of the private sector and the other the nature of the impulse force driving an economy.

The central issues cover a wide range of policy viewpoints that differ in emphasis and content. They also subsume a wide range of conflicting propositions about the (short- and long-run, main and side) effects of various policies – monetary as well as fiscal. We do not know how or when the issues about money and

* We appreciate the continued financial support of the National Science Foundation.

monetary policy were settled. We continue to read policy statements in which market interest rates are used as the indicator of monetary policy, or statements linking the high level of market rates observed recently with correspondingly high real rates of interest. We also note statements denying the effect of money on prices during periods in which resources are idle or asserting the "autonomy of the wage unit". Other statements attribute to Western societies a "built-in inflationary bias" independent of past patterns of government policies, or emphasize the private sector's "inherently weak adjustment mechanisms" that are apparently incapable of eliminating persistent unemployment. We find, no less frequently, statements that have no meaning unless *IS* and *LM* curves are approximately independent as in the usual statement of the standard model and the discussion of the (internal or external) assignment problem.

As the examples illustrate, the issues in the discussion have covered a wide range of theoretical and empirical topics. Does everyone agree about the non-fiscal issues? Has the Radcliffe view been rejected? Do all economists recognize that money and credit are not "the same" and that it is useful and important to distinguish between them? Do all agree that it is useful to distinguish between real and (non-money) financial assets? Or, does the disagreement extend beyond the effect of fiscal policy to embrace these narrower and broader issues, as we believe?

We are unable to reconcile the apparent consensus on the principal issue, as described in the other papers in this volume, with the protracted dispute over theory, evidence and policy. Moreover, we find substantial disagreement in the papers, once we pass beyond some general and formal statements. For Modigliani and Ando, the main issues are empirical. Tobin's paper is entirely non-empirical. Although he discusses the steps required to convert standard *IS–LM* analysis into a full analysis of the interaction of stocks and flows, his analysis remains rigidly Keynesian.

There are different versions of Keynesian theory. In Tobin's version Keynesian analysis means that (1) prices remain constant as long as output remains below "full employment" output; (2) debt and capital are perfect substitutes, as in Metzler's interpretation of Keynes; (3) "wealth effects" are relevant only, if at all, in the long run; and (4) no distinction is made between real rates and market rates of interest. This last point is a consequence of (1) and is simply introduced for emphasis. We accept a reinterpretation of proposition (2) for the long run, and the others not at all. Our analysis of fiscal policy differs as a consequence. A major difference is that real yields on financial and real assets are not equal in the short and intermediate run of our analysis. Further, we find that the principal effect of fiscal policy results from the adjustment of financial stocks. We note also that, in contrast to traditional macro-theory, real effects of public debt do not depend on the public's perception of government debt as net wealth. Lastly, we believe that the long-run effects of fiscal policy on capital stock, prices and output have been neglected.

For us, the propositions now loosely connected under the name "monetarism" began as a set of empirical observations. As examples, we cite: (1) comparison of the relative effectiveness of monetary and pure fiscal policies in controlling early post-war inflation; (2) comparison of the relative effectiveness of fiscal and monetary policies in producing the inflation of the last ten years; (3) the observed positive relation between money, interest rates, output and prices during the cyclical expansions and contractions; (4) the finding, since replicated many times, that the multiplier of a balanced budget is less than unity; (5) the accumulated evidence showing that the observed correlations between money and measures of economic activity are independent of the nature of the money-supply process; and (6) evidence that long-run movements of output and employment are independent of the level of money stock and the rate of monetary growth.

Some of these empirical propositions are inconsistent with the Hicks version of *IS–LM* theory that dominates most policy discussions. Other propositions can be made consistent with this standard theory only by postulating that the standard *LM* curve is vertical, contrary to empirical evidence that we and others have provided. The above propositions are, therefore, propositions in search of a revised, extended or alternative, theory. For us, one main issue in the discussion has been the content of the alternative theory.[1]

Stein's paper shows that he shares at least part of our view. Although his description of the principal issue is restrictive, his paper develops and tests an analytic framework that extends beyond the Hicks and Metzler versions of standard macroeconomic theory. Stein recognizes that the empirical issue cannot be decided by measuring the interest elasticity of the demand for money. He disagrees with both Tobin and Modigliani and Ando about the way to resolve *their* central issue.

The discussants of our papers do not fully agree on the central issue, our contribution or the state of the debate. Rudiger Dornbusch describes our work as "in the best tradition of eclectic macroeconomics". Thomas Mayer recognizes that the central issues are empirical, but he tends occassionally to formulate them in a potentially misleading way, as a conflict between Keynesian analysis and the

[1] For examples of our earlier statements of the same point see Meltzer (1965), Brunner (1968) and our criticism (1973, p. 838) of Friedman's theoretical framework on the grounds that they do not generate "the empirical regularities that support 'monetarism'". Stein's paper in this volume moves beyond the *IS–LM* framework suggesting that he shares our contention that the issue (or issues) cannot be resolved within that framework. As his paper shows, the relative slope of standard *IS* and *LM* curves are neither necessary nor sufficient for demonstrating the relative "effectiveness" of pure fiscal or monetary policy.

quantity theory. Dornbusch rejects our use of the Marshallian notion of runs, argues that the state variables are "*jointly* endogeneous . . . capital accumulation, wage revisions, and budget financing are con-current processes. This implies (sic.) that in terms of comparative statics we can only study the impact effect of a disturbance and the steady state but not the intermediate and long run".[2] Robert Rasche discovers ambiguities and emphasizes that the qualitative results coincide with (a properly extended and modified) Modigliani system, vintage 1963.

We believe that in these and other comments our able discussants failed to distinguish between some important issues. They fail to distinguish between old and new issues on one side and between "theoretical" and empirical issues on the other. These distinctions, or more properly failures to distinguish, help to explain why economists can meet, agree in principle and on principles, then disagree about appropriate policy.[3]

Insufficient distinction between the "analytic eclecticism" expressed by a formal model on the one side and a class of empirical hypotheses on the other obliterates some crucial differences. The term "eclectic" requires clarification. The use of the word obscures the relation between economic theory and empirical evidence. "Theory" as used by economists most often refers to an analytic framework with some broad constraints on admissible interpretations. An example most relevant to one set of comments on our paper is the use of supplementary constraints on the interest elasticity of the demand for money and the adjustment of money wages to distinguish "Keynesian" and "quantity theory" versions of the standard framework. The standard framework can be described as "eclectic", i.e., capable of accepting either set of empirical constraints. "Analytical eclecticism" of this kind can be exploited to clarify differences and relations between empirical hypotheses. But it should also be noted that "analytic eclecticism" yields little information. It forms a first stage in the construction of hypotheses and requires supplementary statements to produce informative hypotheses.

Some major conjectures constituting "monetarism" are not statements about

[2] Dornbusch goes on to suggest that a complete dynamic model of the "entire equilibrium path of the system" is the appropriate way to investigate the system. We regard this as a peculiar statement. First, we do not understand why Dornbusch restricts the dynamics to the equilibrium path. Second, economists are so far from developing, estimating and comparing nonlinear dynamic models that the statement denies the usefulness of economics for most contemporary macro policy *issues*. Third, we have information about *relative* speeds of adjustment and means of obtaining such information, so we can resolve some issues about intermediate-run effects. On this point we agree with Modigliani and Ando and Tobin's interpretation of Walter Heller's statement. Later, Dornbusch also recognizes that the main unresolved issues are empirical.

[3] An alternative interpretation is that the policy differences are the result of differences in values. There are important differences of this kind, but as long-term participants in the discussion, we find no basis for the denial of all cognitive, intellectual and substantive differences that contribute to differences in policy statements and in the expected or predicted effects of policies.

our formal model. They are statements about the world we inhabit and they occur as supplementary propositions attached to the "analytically eclectic" framework. The section of our paper called "Monetarist Implications and Conjectures" misled at least one of our discussants. He read our statements about monetarist conjectures as propositions whose truth follows directly from our basic analytic framework. We have difficulty reconciling this interpretation with our many statements about conditions that must be met for the statements to be true and our frequent references to necessary evidence in the very same paragraphs. To remove any remaining doubt, we wish to make clear that the principal monetarist propositions are empirical propositions to be tested against alternatives using a model or theory capable of discriminating between them.

A related distinction is relevant to the comment of a discussant who objects that our particular impulse and stability hypotheses cannot be exhibited as a logical implication of the basic framework.[4] Logical implication cannot widen empirical content. Both impulse and stability hypothesis are supplementary specifications to move the basic framework beyond a very general level to a class of empirical hypotheses.[5] The supplementary hypotheses and the basic framework jointly produce the "monetarist" propositions to be applied in any discussion of policy.

Our analysis also distinguishes between the initial impulse and the transmission of the impulse. A distinguishing characteristic of "monetarism" is the importance,

[4] Rasche comments in the following manner "there does not seem to be anything in the KM model which would suggest that the stock of money . . . should be singled out above other stocks". He emphasizes that distributing government securities would also affect the long-run equilibrium under our specification. Indeed it would, and so would the miraculous creation of real assets by government fiat, large autonomous variations in money wages or the anticipated net yield on real capital. The basic framework is designed to clarify issues such as the nature of the transmission mechanism. We have emphasized for many years the importance of moving beyond the basic analytic framework to incorporate hypotheses about impulse, stability and the relation between allocative detail and aggregative behavior. We note, in contrast that Dornbusch finds our "empirical judgments" implicit in our modelling. This involves two aspects: (1) a tighter formulation of the basic framework to yield propositions more useful than a forest of Jacobians, and (2) an adjustment of the basic formulation by introducing supplementary conjectures.

[5] Another example may be drawn from Rasche to demonstrate that crucial differences in propositions disappear when suitably disregarded. We refer to Rasche's discussion of an increase in the stock of government debt. He compares our analysis with (a modified and extended) Modigliani (1963) and concludes "... essentially the same restrictions will cause both models to behave the same way in response to debt financing of the deficit". Rasche argues that both models imply that an increase in $S$ pushes the $(d + g)$ line to the right. In the Modigliani model, this is accomplished by a direct wealth effect on consumption sufficiently large to overcome the interest effect. Our model assigns a very low value to the direct wealth effect and emphasizes the crucial role of relative changes in real yields on financial and real assets. The Metzler form of the Modigliani model cannot incorporate our mechanism. The two models determine entirely different and logically inconsistent sufficiency condition for the proposition about the response of the $(d + g)$ line. It is difficult to see any point in describing such inconsistent conditions as essentially "the same restrictions".

emphasis and attention given to the growth rate of money. Accelerations and decelerations of money are said to have a dominant influence on real output; the growth rate of money is said to be the principal determinant of the rate of inflation. These propositions are empirically testable statements about the principal *impulses* affecting aggregates. They also involve, implicitly, propositions about the nature of the transmission mechanism.[6] The statements are not intended, by us, as assertions that fiscal policy, anticipations, resources, tastes and a host of other forces do not have *any* effect on relative prices and output. Nor are the statements intended as a denial of any effect of fiscal policy on the price level. On the contrary, we are able to reconcile the propositions that monetary growth dominates the rate of inflation and fiscal policy determines the long-run price level.

The most prevalent alternative to monetarism is "(empirical) eclecticism". "Eclectic economists" assert that monopoly power, anticipations, wage push and a host of other forces – including pure (debt financed) fiscal policies – act as impulses initiating changes in aggregate output and the price level. The quantitative effect of these impulses is regarded as no less important than the effect of monetary impulses. Many of these statements, in our judgment, fail to recognize the nature of the monetary impulse and the transmission of the initial monetary impulse to wages and anticipations. "Wage-push" theories exemplify this failure. Other statements seem to be based on confusion between monopoly power and changes in monopoly power. Lastly, some "eclectic positions" involve an implicit refusal to advance testable hypotheses. A monetarist analysis accepts the "analytic eclecticism" described above but rejects the prevalent "eclectic agnosticism" addressed to the propagation of economic fluctuations and inflations.[7]

In the Hicksian framework, the role of interest rates in the transmission mech-

[6] Growth and acceleration of output are observable approximations to the analytic partition of monetary growth on a systematic (or anticipated) component and an unanticipated deviation.

[7] There exists a disposition to obscure important and substantial differences between alternative hypotheses. One frequently encounters assertions to the effect that nobody means really this or that. Mayer contends for instance that adherents of a cost push theory do not assume wage-price movements to occur independently relative to market conditions. We contend on the contrary that such assertions are frequently made. If the assertions do not mean what they say, then language is used in a singularly disinformative manner. When Abba Lerner insists on the "autonomy of the wage unit" relative to the history of excess supplies on the labor market we understand him precisely to mean what he says. Mayer also emphasizes (in the spirit of a remark made by Tobin) that Keynesians would (of course) look at the effect of stocks "if they were concerned with the long run". But the very fact that this enters as an afterthought into Keynesian analysis, and without assigning any role to the credit market, reveals the comparatively low level of importance attached to this element. What is the relative frequency of textbooks on macro-theory, cast in the Keynesian mold, which actually incorporate this aspect? How many teachers do actually explore it in their classes, and how many econometric models do recognize it? The record does not seem to show that teachers are generally aware of it and will move to discuss the matter when the "really basic" short-run problems have been discussed.

anism and the effect of pure fiscal policy become related issues. The reason is that acceptance of the Keynesian dichotomy implies that *IS* and *LM* are independent. As Thomas Mayer recognizes "wealth effects" are referred to frequently but dismissed universally as slow, small and unimportant for short- and medium-run adjustment and for policy discussions. Evidence showing non-zero interest elasticities of expenditure function and demand function for money is interpreted as evidence about the transmission mechanism and as evidence in favor of "eclecticism", non-monetarism or anti-monetarism.

The Hicksian interpretation requires that *IS* and *LM* remain fixed and independent once fiscal and monetary policy have been specified.[8] In our analysis, the two curves move interdependently and the interpretation of their slopes differs from the traditional interpretation.[9] A zero interest elasticity of the demand for money is neither necessary nor sufficient for any "monetarist" proposition, and monetarism does not impose any restriction on the absolute value of the interest elasticity of the demand for money. A zero interest elasticity of the demand for money combined with a zero interest elasticity of aggregate expenditure eliminates any effect of debt financing on prices and output.[10] An effect of both fiscal and monetary policy on output and prices remains.

The issues in the monetarist controversy are not limited to the comparatively narrow question of whether fiscal policies have a temporary effect on real output. Nor can the issues continue to be discussed usefully as a conflict between quantity theory and Keynesian theory. The propositions subsumed by the term "quantity theory" differ substantially from monetarist propositions bearing on the central issues described above. As in any fruitful discussion, participants adjust their

[8] Friedman's (1966) argument that the interest elasticity of the demand for money has no consequence for the long-run comparative statics solutions is a restatement of a point made by Modigliani (1944). For those who accept the Hicksian *IS–LM* framework, the proposition that the demand function for money has a non-zero interest elasticity and the proposition that fiscal policy affects income (positively) are logically equivalent statements.

[9] The difference can be seen as follows: The slope of the *IS* line derived from our model is represented by the elasticity

$$\epsilon(i, y|IS) = \frac{1 - (1 - \nu)\,\epsilon(d, y)}{\bar{\epsilon}(d, i) + \epsilon(d, P)\cdot\epsilon(P, i|CM)} < 0,$$

where $\epsilon(P, i|LM)$ is the response of $P$ to $i$ defined by the *CM* equation. The slope of the *LM* line appears as

$$\epsilon(i, y|LM) = \frac{\epsilon(m, y) - \bar{\epsilon}(L, y)}{[\epsilon(m, i) - \epsilon(L, i)] + [\epsilon(m, P) - \epsilon(L, P)]\cdot\epsilon(P, i|CM)} > 0.$$

Note that *IS* and *LM* have slopes that are neither vertical nor horizontal even if $\epsilon(d, i) = \epsilon(L, i) = 0$.

[10] The restrictions make $\epsilon(d, i)$ and $\epsilon(P, S|AM)$ approximately zero and therefore make $\bar{\epsilon}(p, S|0, AM)$ and $\bar{\epsilon}(y, S|0, AM)$ approximately zero. See equations in section 3.2 and the appendix of our paper.

positions overtime; the issues change, and the theory changes. A point by point commentary and refutations of the discussants comments would hide rather than highlight the progress that we believe has been made and the issues that remain.

The accumulation of theoretical and empirical work resulting from the monetarist controversy has eliminated the Hicksian model as a relevant basis for policy statements. The model applies only to an instantaneous adjustment of flow markets. Many economists appear to accept, in principle, that the Hicksian framework is deficient for policy, but they ignore these deficiencies when making policy statements. These positions would be reconciled provided the departures from the Hicksian framework are of minor economic importance, even if statistically significant. That is why we have stated the central issues as empirical issues, not estoric questions about the logical structure of "theories" to be answered with elegantly neat formal exercises.

In the remaining sections of our paper we discuss some of the more important differences between our analysis and the *IS–LM* analysis of the Hicks or Metzler type. Many of the differences addressed in our discussion arise in the treatment of fiscal policy and the credit market. Some may be small, others large. Those are empirical judgments to be resolved only after they are fomulated as testable statements.

We turn, first, to the budget equation and point out some implications for the analysis of fiscal policies. Then, we discuss the distinction between credit and money, the related issue of intermediation and disintermediation, and the role of the credit market in the transmission of policy. In a final section, we reconsider some implications of monetarism for fluctuations in prices and output.

## 1. Fiscal Policy, the Government Sector and the Government Debt

In Hicks' version of *IS–LM*, the distribution of expenditure between the government and the private sector is irrelevant. Government is as efficient and productive as any private firm. Changes in government expenditure, at less than full employment, change real output but have no effect on prices because the price level is fixed. The same results would have been achieved by private investment, if private investors were willing to spend. In the Metzler version, real output is fixed. The long-run effects of a change in government spending (or taxes) is shown as a change in the price level. The problem is analyzed as a change in the ownership of a fixed capital stock or, more accurately, the right to income produced by the capital stock. For debt and capital to remain perfect substitutes, increases in debt must displace an equivalent amount of private investment.

In the Hicks and Metzler models, government is treated as a convenient device without significance for the working of the model and without substance for the principal conclusions. The role of government in models of closed economies, is, we believe, fully described by the equilibrium condition,[11]

$$G - T = SA - IN.$$

Whether written in real or nominal terms, the equation assures that when the government budget is balanced, the left-hand side must be zero, so private investment $IN$ equals private savings $SA$. And, conversely, when the private sector is in equilibrium, the government's budget is balanced. Further, the system is equilibrated by mutual adjustments of the four magnitudes. The nature of the adjustment reflects the specific constraints imposed on the process. Under one set of (Keynesian) restrictions an expansion of $G$ increases mainly $T$ and $SA$. Under an alternative set (of non-Keynesian constraints) the expansion of $G$ mainly lowers $IN$.

The government hires no labor in this analysis and pays no interest on outstanding bonds. The effect of the government budget is identified with the position of the $IS$ line. Financing and links via the asset markets from $G - T$ to $SA - IN$ are disregarded. An exploration of these links reveals important effects of fiscal policy on private investment usually dismissed by "traditional theory".[12]

The Keynesian procedure of treating the response to changes in government spending and to autonomous private investment as equivalent neglects any shorter-run effect of issuing debt. Once we include a properly specified budget equation, this procedure is misleading and invalid. The change in government spending must be financed, and any debt issued or withdrawn exerts an effect over time that must be considered when determining the size of the response to fiscal policy.[13]

[11] $IN$ = private investment; $SA$ = private saving; $G$ = government spending; $T$ = tax collections.

[12] Some comments on our discussants are relevant here. Dornbusch, in his section 3, explicitly takes the position that investment and government expenditure are perfect substitutes.

Mayer considers our analysis as a type of quantity theory. We can only guess how a "quantity theorist" would discuss government expenditure and its financing. Would output be total output or private sector output? Would the stock of debt appear in the velocity function?

Rasche points out that Modigliani (1963, pp. 93–97) disaggregated government purchases into consumption, investment and labor services. We agree with Rasche that Modigliani *discusses* some of the short- and long-term consequences of fiscal policy more thoroughly and completely than others had done or now do. His *analysis*, however does not show some main effects of financing fiscal policy. Debt and capital remain perfect substitutes in portfolios. The only asset demand in the model is the demand for money. There are no interest payments on the debt and therefore a long-run analysis, if provided, would be incomplete. Prices are fixed at less than full employment. There is no government budget equation. The only equation added to the model in the section discussing the budget is a tax equation.

[13] A revival of vulgar Keynesianism in form of the "Neo-Cambridge theory" uses the relation $G - T = SA - IN +$ current account deficit, supplemented with a Kaldor–Kalecki assertion that $SA = IN$ to establish that the manner of financing the budget deficit really does not matter.

In our analysis government purchases of output – whether for consumption or investment – have a larger and longer-lasting effect on the budget position (expressed by the *bbe* line) than on the output market (expressed by the $d + g$ line). If the effect on the budget position were not larger, the initial response of output and the price level would be reversed after it occurs. Increased government purchases of goods would reduce the deficit or produce a budget surplus when resources are unemployed. The direct effect on the output market is a one-time change. Once the output market reaches short-run equilibrium, any further effect of fiscal policy is a consequence of budget financing. This effect continues until the budget is balanced, and the size of the effect depends on how the budget is financed.

As an example, assume full employment and flexible money wages instead of the rigid wages used in most of our present paper.[14] An increase in taxes lowers the price level, but with flexible wages output is unchanged. The Metzler-type *IS–LM* analysis ends here. In our analysis, as in Christ's (1969), there is no reason for the budget to be balanced at the price level that clears the output market. The financing of the budget affects relative prices and the short-run position of the asset and output markets.

The size and direction of the effect on output and prices of issuing or withdrawing government debt are empirical issues. Evidence may show that changes in debt have little or no effect on output or the price level. Or, the effect of debt finance on prices and output may be negative. In these cases, the effect on expenditure of a pure fiscal change – fiscal change with constant monetary base – is less than or exactly equal to the effect resulting from the fiscal change. In the next subsections, we compare the short-run effects of a change in real government expenditure implied by our model to the effects implied by the Hicks–Keynes model. We show that, even at this level, there are differences in implication. We proceed then to discuss the effects of separating bonds and real capital and the role of the budget equation.

### *1.1. Conventional Fiscal Policy in the Short Run*

Under the extreme Keynesian assumption of completely rigid money wages and moneyprices, the impact effect of a change in the real value of government

[14] Our assumption of fixed money wages and capital stocks (for any given moment of time) is intended to bring the analysis as close as possible to Keynes' discussion. This permits differences in results to be more clearly related to the separation of debt and private capital and the role of the budget equation. A more general analysis includes wage adjustments and capital accumulations. See Brunner (1974b).

expenditure ($g$) on real output ($y$) depends on $\gamma$, the ratio of $g/y$,[15]

$$\epsilon(y, g|d + g) = \gamma/\{1 - (1 - \gamma)\,[\bar{\epsilon}(d, i)\,\epsilon(i, y|AM) + \bar{\epsilon}(d, P)\,\epsilon(P, y|AM) + \epsilon(d, W_{\mathrm{h}})\,\epsilon(W_{\mathrm{h}}, y) + \epsilon(d, e)\,\epsilon(e, y)]\}.$$

In the more conventional terms of "the" multiplier of government purchases,

$$y_g = 1/\{1 - [d_i i_y + d_p P_y + d_{W_{\mathrm{h}}} W_{\mathrm{h}_y} + d_e e_y]\},$$

where the subscripted variables are derivatives.

For "the" multiplier to exceed unity or for the elasticity to exceed $\gamma$, the bracketed expression in the denominators must be positive, and this condition is likely to be met. In the notation of our paper, the bracketed elasticity is $\bar{\epsilon}(d, y)$, and the conditions for a negative value are discussed (section 3) and found to be remote. It follows, therefore, that changes in $g$ change private output by a multiple; "the" Keynesian multiplier is greater than unity in the short run with prices and money wages constant.

The stability of the short-run multiplier depends on the responses of the anticipated return to real capital. If this response is as erratic and unpredictable as Keynes alleged – if waves of optimism or pessimism or unpredictable "animal spirits" change businessmen's anticipations markedly – the multiplier of government expenditure is erratic also. An optimistic response to an increase in $g$ raises $e_y$ and raises "the multiplier" (and via the asset market responses also raises $P_y$); a pessimistic response lowers the multiplier. Unpredictable anticipations that fluctuate over a wide range make the government expenditure multiplier, and other multipliers, unpredictable from one episode to another.

In the conventional Hicksian analysis the analogue of $d_i$ determines the slope of *IS*, and the slope of *IS*, in turn, determines at a first step, the effectiveness of *monetary* policy. The effectiveness of *fiscal* policy depends on the slope of the demand function for money. Numerous papers have made these points, and it is a main point of the Tobin and Buiter paper in this volume.

Our analysis reaches different conclusions. The relative responses of the demand for money, $L$, and asset supply, $\sigma$, to variations in the anticipated net yield, $e$, on real capital affect the size of the responses to fiscal and monetary changes. A very large numerical value of the interest elasticity of private expenditure combined with a response of $\sigma$ to $e$ at least as large numerically as the response of $L$ to $e$ *lowers* the response to fiscal policy and raises the response to

[15] All symbols are defined in our paper elsewhere in this volume. We use standard symbols where possible. $P$ is the price level of real capital, discussed more fully below. For the derivation of several of the elasticities and their signs, see the appendix to our paper in this volume. Note that the response of $y$ is equal under the "Keynesian conditions" to the horizontal shift elasticity of $d + g$.

monetary policy. A small elasticity $\epsilon(d,i)$ raises the value of the fiscal multiplier under these circumstances. A value of $\sigma_e$ [or $\epsilon(\sigma, e)$] sufficiently smaller than $L_e$ [or $\epsilon(L, e)$] reverses the relation between the multiplier and $d_i$ [or $\epsilon(d, i)$]. The response $\epsilon(y, g|d + g)$ increases in this case as $\epsilon(d, i)$ increases numerically, whereas the monetary effect declines. To the extent that the increase in output raises interest rates and reduces private expenditure, there is short-run substitution between private and government expenditure. Substitution of this kind is at times referred to as "real crowding out". It is obvious that "crowding out" of this kind cannot reduce the short-run multiplier of real expenditure to zero. A potent form of real short-run crowding out appears to require offsetting changes in the anticipated return to private capital or rapid adjustments in money wages.[16]

Our discussion of the real effect of government expenditure has been restricted to the Hicks–Keynes case of fixed prices and wages. We can extend this analysis [Brunner and Meltzer (1973)], in a more or less conventional way. In the output market, aggregate real expenditure, $E$, equals output,

$$E(r, y, M/p, g) = y.$$

Invoking Walras' law leaves the money market as the relevant asset market.

$$M/p = L(i, y),$$

with $r$ and $i$ real and market rates of interest, respectively.

Their relation is

$$i = r + \pi,$$

where $\pi$ is the anticipated rate of inflation and, in the long run,

$$\pi = dp/p,$$

the actual rate of inflation. A Phillips-type relation determines the rate of price change,

$$dp/p = h(y - y_0, \pi),$$

with $h(0,\pi) = \pi$, and

$$\text{sign } dp/p = \text{sign } (y - y_0),$$

for $\pi = 0$.

Clearly, in this analysis the value of the multiplier depends on the slope of the demand function for money and, as in our analysis, on what happens to prices.

[16] The closest analogue to the slope of the demand for money in our analysis is $\epsilon(P, y|AM)$ (or $P_y$ in "the multiplier"). The sign of $P_y$ is ambiguous, as shown in our appendix. Zero responses of both $P$ and $i$ to $y$ on the asset markets probably raise the value of the fiscal response.

If prices change, the conventional *IS* curve shifts. Increased prices lower private spending, and lower prices increase spending. The adjustment of prices reduces the response of total real expenditure to real government expenditure.

The simple model can be completed to solve for the principal variables of interest. With $g$, $y_0$ and $M$ taken as given and anticipations $\pi$ determined by past monetary growth we can compute the price level from knowledge of the past. The system then determines $y$, $p$, $dp/p$, $i$, and $r$.

A similar conclusion is reached using our formulation. If we relax the assumed constancy of money prices and money wages, we find an additional reason for fluctuations in the value of the output multiplier for real government expenditure. The proportions in which the response of nominal output to a change in government spending is distributed between prices and real output depends on the slope of the aggregate supply curve and the response of money wages. Low rates of utilization reduce the response of prices and wages and leave the value of the real multiplier close to the Keynesian presumption. A rapid adjustment of money wages raises the price level and lowers the response of real output toward zero.

The effectiveness of government expenditure in expanding or slowing the economy depends in our analysis on the speed with which money wages respond to the change in expenditure induced by policy.[17] If wage earners learn to anticipate policy changes, the real effect of the policy declines and the short-run price reponse increases. The effect of policy, and anticipations of policy, on the anticipations of private producers and consumers is, here and elsewhere, a much neglected aspect of policy analysis. [See Lucas (1975).]

To this point in our discussion of a change in government expenditure, we have ignored the government budget and the financing of the budget. This permits our analysis to remain comparable to the standard analysis and to generate similar implications about the short-run effects of government expenditure. Even at this level there are some differences, however. In our representation of the Hicks–Keynes analysis, the movement from short- to long-run equilibrium depends on interest rate anticipations. The crucial comparison is between the market rate of interest, the anticipated rate of inflation, and the actual rate of inflation proximately determined by the current position of the economy and the slope of the Phillips-type curve. It is not surprising, though it is unnecessary, that even sophisticated Keynesians have often emphasized the role of interest rates as borrowing costs, not their role as relative prices.

In the monetarist, or relative price model, the crucial comparison is between money wages and real wages. Anticipations can be introduced into our model to supplement the role of relative prices in adjusting to long-run equilibrium. And

[17] The analysis underlying this point is developed in greater detail in section 3.3 of our paper in this volume and also in Brunner's (1974b) analysis of longer-run aspects.

money wages can be brought into the Hicks–Keynes model by adding a supply curve of output. The two adjustments can be made comparable in every detail by making the models identical.

Of course, the policy implications change as the models change. Once prices are permitted to respond to fiscal policy, the standard *IS–LM* implications either vanish or become trivial. The slope of *LM plus* the shift of *IS* induced by price changes determines the response to fiscal policy. In the relative price or monetarist model, the analogue to the slope of *LM* has an ambiguous effect on the response. The speed and size of the response of money wages are the important determinants of the real effects of fiscal policy.

### *1.2. The Budget and the Role of Debt Finance*

The government budget equation introduces an additional dimension. Without the budget equation, it may be useful for some purpose to describe investment and government expenditure as perfect substitutes. It makes little sense to describe short-term changes in debt, issued or withdrawn in the financing of the budget, as equivalent to changes in the capital stock. The latter may have no short-term effect. If prices are fixed, as in short-run Keynesian analysis of less than full employment, changes in debt change real *private* wealth. Discounting of future tax liabilities may offset part of the change. It remains to be shown that consumers, though incapable of forecasting the effects of fiscal policy on prices, can forecast the true value of future tax liabilities in a multiple tax system. The two assumptions of Keynesian analysis seem to us inconsistent.

If there is no effect of debt finance on expenditure or prices, there are but three possibilities to explore. Either the budget is balanced at every short-run price and output combination following a fiscal change, or debt issues and retirements have no effect on interest rates and asset prices, or the effects on interest rates and asset prices cancel.

The first alternative is both implausible and inconsistent without hypothesis. It is implausible that tax rates can be set so that every change in government expenditure changes prices and output in the short run by the amount required to balance the budget. In a world of this kind, maintaining full use of resources without inflation would be a matter of finding the full employment $g$. Our analysis shows that a one-percent change in $g$ has a much greater effect on the budget position than on prices and output, so the budget moves toward deficit following fiscal expansion and toward surplus following fiscal contraction. Following a pure fiscal policy, the budget is unbalanced, and the stock of debt changes in the short and intermediate run.

The second alternative is no less implausible. Debt issues and retirements have no effect on prices, output or interest rates. Interest payments rise and fall with issues and retirements, so any surplus or deficit achieved by pure fiscal policy grows continuously and at an accelerating rate. The absence of any effect of debt issues on prices and output is, again, inconsistent with our hypothesis.

Lastly, the response of prices and output to government debt is zero or negative, if

$$-\epsilon(d, i)\,\epsilon(i, S|AM) \geqq \epsilon(d, P)\,\epsilon(P, S|AM) + \epsilon(d, W_n)\,vS/W_n.$$

Ignoring wealth effects and other small terms, the expression reduces to the following approximate inequality,

$$-\epsilon(d, i)/\epsilon(d, P) \geqq -\epsilon(L, i)/\epsilon(L, P)$$

Again, the interest elasticities "behind the slopes" of both the *IS* and *LM* curves of standard analysis are among the determinants of the response to this fiscal action, but these elasticities are not sufficient to determine the response. Our postulate, that the right side of the inequality above exceeds the left, is consistent with most empirical evidence on the interest elasticities of money and expenditure, but of course, the relative size of the two denominators can reverse the inequality.[18]

Is expenditure on new production a closer substitute for existing assets than for money holding? We believe new houses are closer substitutes for old houses, new cars for used cars, new machines for old machines than any of these assets are for money. If so, our postulate is on firm ground. Increases in debt stimulate (mildly) the economy in the short run, and the system converges to a stock–flow equilibrium following a pure fiscal policy.[19]

[18] Note that the denominators of the inequality require information in addition to the slopes of *IS* and *LM*.

[19] One discussant, Dornbusch, recasts part of our argument in terms of real rates and market rates of interest and argues that our position is implausible. Asset prices in our analysis are the price of real assets, not just the prices of claims to real assets. The two are not identical. We have long maintained – Brunner–Meltzer (1963) – that in positions other than long-run equilibrium, it is useful to distinguish three kinds of real assets held by the public. One type has organized markets for claims and current output but not existing stocks; one has organized markets only for new production. Moreover, even on Dornbusch's narrow interpretation of asset prices, our analysis does not imply that an increase in debt lowers the real rate of return. His implication is a partial equilibrium result, as he recognizes, and is obtained by holding output prices constant. It is true that real income streams would be more valuable if debt issues raise asset prices without changing current or anticipated output prices. This is avoided in our analysis. Even in the short run, changes in asset prices induce changes in output prices through the interaction of asset and output markets. Real rates are defined as the ratio $r = pe/P$ in our analysis. For real rates to fall, with constant anticipations of the return to real capital, $p/P$ must fall. Our analysis shows $\epsilon(P, S) > 0$. The sign depends on the (negative) interest elasticity of the demand for money. Our postulate, discussed at length, makes $\epsilon(p, S) > 0$, so the effect on real rates depends on relative orders of magnitude.

We cannot be absolutely sure that the model is stable or that the world is stable. Therefore, we cannot be sure that increasing debt raises output and prices so that pure fiscal policy is stabilizing. Investigation of the stability of pure fiscal policy and of the magnitude of fiscal effects in a stock–flow analysis is another empirical issue on which useful knowledge has not been accumulated. Discussion and evidence have remained in the *IS–LM* tradition, and progress has been restricted.

We would not belabor the point about debt finance were it not for the recent arguments made by Modigliani and Ando (section 3) claiming to have proof that the demand for money is (1) independent of wealth, and (2) depends only on short-term interest rates and the volume of transactions. Their argument is based on an appendix by Ando and Shell included as part of an earlier paper by Ando and Modigliani (1974). The authors claim to offer an analytic justification for the Hicksian interpretation of the transmission mechanism.

The proof consists of a demonstration that in (1) a two-period world, where (2) first-period consumption is determined independently of portfolio choice, (3) there is no yield, pecuniary or otherwise on money, (4) money is determined by the monetary authority and (5) real consumption is not equal to the volume of transactions, the short-term rate of interest is independent of wealth and the yield on real assets.

Is it surprising that individuals optimizating over a single period consider only a one-period rate when setting money balances? The result does not hold as soon as the individual's horizon extends many periods ahead or individuals consider their wealth position when allocating deposits between time and demand accounts. Proper optimization in the two-period model initially introduced by the authors implies the very opposite of the authors' conclusion. The demand for money depends separately on yields on financial and real assets and on wealth. The justification for the Hicksian interpretation vanishes.

On the basis of assumptions removing any relevant portfolio adjustments, Modigliani and Ando eliminate any effect of debt issues on interest rates. However, the effect of debt on asset prices would remain in our analysis, and the positive response of output and prices to debt is on firmer ground. It would remain true, even on their assumptions, that government debt and private capital cannot be combined as perfect substitutes in the short and intermediate run.[20]

[20] Modigliani and Ando refer to some regressions in a paper by Goldfeld (1973) as evidence to support their position. We fail to see the relevance of this evidence for their position. The regressions (table 14) of the money on measured change in wealth is obtained holding lagged money constant. The coefficient on lagged $M$ is close to unity, so the regression can be interpreted as evidence that the change in money is positively related to change in wealth. Any interpretation of these data must be accepted or rejected cautiously. Quarterly data on wealth appear to have been computed from the relatively unreliable estimates of the flow of funds financial accounts and

To bring out the differences between our analysis of substitution and the Keynes–Hicks–Metzler analysis, we strip the details of the asset markets down to three equations, of which two are independent. There are no banks and wealth is defined at its market value. All partial derivatives shown differ from zero and express our view of the substitution relations governing balance sheet positions and the nature of the transmission mechanism,

$$
\begin{aligned}
&B + vS + PK &&= W_{\mathrm{n}} &&[\text{wealth at market value}],\\
&B(\overset{-}{i}, \overset{+}{P}, \overset{+}{p} \,..\, \overset{-}{e}) &&= B &&[\text{currency}],\\
&S(i - \overset{+}{\pi}, \overset{+}{P}, \overset{-}{p} \,..\, \overset{-}{e}) &&= vS &&[\text{bonds}],\\
&K(i - \overset{-}{\pi}, P, \overset{+}{p} \,..\, \overset{-}{e}) &&= PK &&[\text{capital}].
\end{aligned}
$$

The constraint on asset exchanges, usually called "Walras law", makes one of the three-asset market equations redundant. We remove the capital equation. This decision reflects considerations of research strategy and involves no issue of analysis.

Modigliani and Ando take a Hicksian approach. "Infinite transaction costs" are implicitly used to remove the real asset market from the substitution relations, and Walras law removes the bond market. Under the circumstances there is no market for real assets. It follows that the derivatives of $B$ and $S$ with respect to $P$ and $e$ necessarily vanish. The "interest mechanism", understood in a narrow sense as the yield on financial assets, conveys all monetary impulses, and the slope conditions of *IS–LM* contain all relevant information about the transmission of policy.

The Metzler version of Keynesian analysis differs from the Hicksian version, and the difference changes the interpretation of interest rates. The markets for bonds and capital are aggregated into a single market for non-money assets. We obtain again a two-asset model along the lines urged by Mayer, Dornbusch, or Rasche reinterpreting Modgliani (1963). The reduction to one-asset market can be justified with one of two distinct arguments. The first asserts that financial and real assets are much closer substitutes than money and financial assets. An assumption of "perfect substitutability" between financial and real assets is taken

*Footnote 20 continued*
capital gains, but the data are not described. Also the two-period model of Ando and Shell implies that the demand for money is independent of the anticipated rate of inflation, but neither Goldfeld nor his regressions (table 11) provide support for this interpretation. Furthermore, Goldfeld recognizes (1973, p. 613) that any reasonable interpretation of "transactions" should include portfolio shifts related to existing wealth and the accumulation of wealth. All in all, we find little empirical support for the Modigliani–Ando position in the evidence they cite. A recent paper by Khan (1974) reaches the opposite conclusion about the effects of long-run and short-term rates.

as a simplifying approximation to the real world. The second argument treats money and financial assets as closer substitutes than financial and real assets but emphasizes that aggregating $S$ and $K$ into a single non-money asset is a useful approximation for small changes in $S$ and $K$ relative to the observed variation in $B$. Both arguments yield the proposition that monetary impulses are conveyed by the "interest mechanism" and that all relevant information is conveyed by the slopes of the *IS* and *LM* curves.

The interpretation of the slopes and the meaning of "the interest rate" differs in the Hicks and Metzler versions. The difference is clearly revealed by empirical studies of the effect of monetary policies. The investigations by Hitch and Hall before World War II and the more recent studies by Warren Smith for the Joint Economic Committee or by Irwin Friend et alia for the Department of Commerce rely on a Hicksian interpretation of the transmission mechanism. They are incomplete relative to Metzler's interpretation, or ours. Attempts to interpret the "interest" elasticity of aggregate demand for output in terms of relative borrowing costs depend also on a Hicksian interpretation. Such statements have no meaning in a model of the Metzler type.

Our analysis is much closer to Metzler's interpretation than to Hicks'. We accept the second argument justifying aggregation of bonds and capital provided aggregation is applied within a limited range in which variations in relative real yields of financial and real assets are small compared to the magnitude of the anticipated inflation rate. Aggregation of $S$ and $K$ beyond this range obscures important problems, particularly the basic difference with the Hicksian analysis about substitution between financial assets and money and the difference in the meaning attached to the term "the rate of interest".

In our analysis changes in relative real yields on financial and real assets are an important part of short- and intermediate-run adjustments. Relative variations in $S$ and $K$ are reflected in the short to intermediate run by changes in relative yields. Moreover, changes in $S$ modify the position of the budget line, whereas changes in $K$ affect the value of long-run output.[21]

[21] In his analysis of the steady state, Dornbusch, uses the postulate of perfect substitutability between financial and real assets to remove the credit market and present the money market as the only portfolio description required. Our steady state analysis imposes the conditions, $i - \pi = e$ and $P = p$. These conditions neither imply nor require removal of the credit market. They neither require nor imply "perfect substitutability" of financial and real assets. They state only that in the steady state yields on financial and real asset and prices of new and existing assets adjust to equality. It follows that the composition and magnitude of wealth is completely endogenized in full adjustment. The partition of $D$ (i.e., the cumulative deficit) into $S$ and $B$ represented by $\mu$, is endogenous.

*1.3. The Budget and the Fiscal Multiplier*

Traditional Keynesian theory identifies the effect of fiscal policy with the effect on flow equilibrium. Adjustment of assets and the response to the adjustment is neglected. Introduction of the budget equation brings the financing of fiscal policy into greater prominence. The total effect of fiscal policy, in our work, is the sum of the pure fiscal effect, holding financial stocks constant, and the effect of changes in asset stocks. The pure fiscal effect is represented by the shift of expenditure ($d + g$) along the supply curve of output. The total effect is given by the shift of the balanced budget equation, or *bbe* line. The size of the relative shifts of $d + g$ and *bbe* show the relative magnitudes. The difference between the total effect and the pure fiscal effect is the financial effect – the effect of issuing financial assets, base money and bonds.

Tobin and Buiter's long-run system is a four-equation model. The budget equation determines the income multiplier. The size of the multiplier depends only on the marginal tax rate, so the effect of fiscal policy appears to be independent of financial stocks. This result depends on the treatment of total government expenditure on output, labor, and interest as exogenous and on the postulate that taxes depend only on income.[22]

A problem arises in the interpretation of the results. The dynamic adjustment imposed by the budget process implies that the size of the budget deficit or surplus determines the adjustment of financial assets. The output and asset markets jointly determine the response of output to variations in outstanding stocks. The multiplier in the Tobin–Buiter long-run analysis, therefore, has a substantially different interpretation than the traditional Keynesian multiplier. Despite the representation of the multiplier as the reciprocal of the marginal tax rate, the Tobin–Buiter multiplier summarizes the adjustment on asset and output markets and the total effect of fiscal policy.

The point becomes clearer if we combine the budget equation used by Tobin and Buiter with the most simple, naive quantity theory,

$$MV = Y,$$

$$G' - \phi Y = \mathring{M}.$$

Total government expenditures, $G'$, have no effect on the output market. Yet, the multiplier is the reciprocal of the marginal tax rate, $\phi^{-1}$. The reason is that the multiplier still expresses the adjustment of the money stock imposed by the budget equation.

[22] A complete analysis would distinguish between taxes on human and non-human wealth.

*1.4. The Role of Government Employment*

Our reservations about the Keynesian assumption that government spending and private spending are perfect substitutes increase when the budget equation is properly specified by including the government's wage bill. Increases in government employment at constant money wages reduce long-run private output in proportion to the number of workers drawn from private employment. This is a matter of arithmetic and accounting. In addition, there are direct and indirect effects on money wages and prices when the government changes the demand for labor. The "direct" effects operate via output and labor markets, the "indirect effects" via adjustments of financial stocks induced by budget disequilibria.

We assume that the government pays the prevailing money wage rate, a rate that is equal to the value of the marginal product in the private sector. Workers in the government sector may produce more or less than workers in the private sector. There is no market mechanism to maintain equality between marginal productivity and real wages in public employment, and published measures of output do not include independent estimates of the product of public employees.

A change in public employment, $lg$, changes output in the private sector according to,

$$\epsilon(y, lg) = \frac{\epsilon(d, W_h)\,\epsilon(W_h, lg)}{1 - (1 - \gamma)\,\bar{\epsilon}(d, y)} + \frac{\epsilon(d, i)\,\epsilon(i, lg|AM) + \epsilon(d, P)\,\epsilon(P, lg|AM)}{1 - (1 - \gamma)\,\bar{\epsilon}(d, y)}$$

$$+ \frac{[\epsilon(d, W_h)\,\epsilon(W_h, w) + \epsilon(d, p)\,\epsilon(p, w) + \bar{\epsilon}(d, w)]}{1 - (1 - \gamma)\,\bar{\epsilon}(d, y)}\,\epsilon(w, lg),$$

where

$$\bar{\epsilon}(d, w) = \epsilon(d, i)\,\epsilon(i, w|AM) + \epsilon(d, P)\,\epsilon(P, w|AM) < 0.$$

Government absorption of labor raises human wealth and expenditure. The first term of $\epsilon(y, lg)$ shows this response. To the extent that the numerator is less than $\gamma$, the first term is less than the response to $g$. The second term introduces the feedback from the asset markets (holding $w$ constant). This term is negative and shows that adjustments in interest rate, $i$, and asset price, $P$, offset the first term, at least in part. The combined effect of the two terms is almost certainly less than $\epsilon(y, g)$. Moreover, if there is any adjustment in output price, $p$, to variations in output (capacity utilization effect) at constant efficiency wages, the response of $y$ to $lg$ declines. The reason is that in the denominator, $\bar{\epsilon}(d, y)$, the total elasticity of $d$ with respect to $y$ (containing the underlying feedback effects from the asset markets) includes the negative component $\epsilon(d, p)$.

An assumption of fixed money wages is difficult to justify for problems involving large reallocation of labor between private and government sector. Any change in money wages resulting from the change in government hiring shifts both the $(d + g)$ and the $s$ curve. An increase in money wages reduces private production but has two offsetting influences on $d + g$. One, via $W_h$, raises $d + g$; the other, via $i$ and $P$, lowers $d + g$. The net effect of the shifts due to an increase in money wages probably raises price and lowers output in the short run.

The last terms of the expression defining $\epsilon(y, lg)$ describe the contribution made by the wage adjustments. The first component in the numerator reflects the direct effect via $W_h$ and the last component the indirect effect via the asset markets. The middle component shows the effect of changes in supply.

We expect that, except at times of major recession, the principal effect of a change in $lg$ is on prices and not on output. Empirical work on the effects of government policies in labor markets would fill an important gap in our knowledge of the effects of fiscal policies and the government budget on the economy.

### *1.5. Interest Payments*

The role of interest payments (net of taxes) on government debt is explored in our paper. The short-run effect on the budget position of changes in interest payments induced by variations in interest rates depends on the maturity of the outstanding debt. A relatively short average maturity exposes the government budget to pro-cyclical fluctuations in interest payments.

The longer-term effect of recognizing interest payments in the budget equation is that all but the most trivial monetary policies are non-neutral. Our analysis shows that following a change in the base the economy reaches long-run equilibrium with a changed composition of real wealth. This result occurs because all changes in money generate a budget surplus or deficit and, in general, induce changes in debt, interest payments, prices or output to restore budget balance at the new level of interest payments.

The only exception to this proposition occurs if money is distributed by helicopter and then withdrawn by budget finance. This case, $\mu = 1$, is trivial because it establishes only that, with $g$ fixed by policy, a stable equilibrium can be restored by restoring identical conditions. It is true that our result depends on "sufficient progressivity" of the tax revenue function with respect to nominal values. Tax revenue functions homogeneous of first degree with respect to price level $p$ and money wages $w$ are however consistent with our results, provided nominal government expenditures, $pg$, on goods is a policy variable. Our analysis however cannot produce Dornbusch's proposition (section 3) that "an open market purchase of money and sale of debt would have no long-run effects if the budget was entirely financed by money creation". An open market operation changes debt and disturbs neutrality in our analysis, as in the Metzler analysis. Moreover, the change in base money to finance the budget changes relative stocks of assets, relative prices and the long-run equilibrium.

### *1.6. Some Remaining Fiscal Issues*

Two additional fiscal policy issues require attention. One is the effect of a balanced budget change in taxes and government spending. The other is the role of tax anticipations and budget anticipations.

In Keynesian theory, increases in the level of the budget have an expansive effect on output in the short run. The reason is that even in complex Keynesian models, changes in expenditure initially change spending dollar for dollar while changes in taxes change both saving and spending. Evidence from econometric studies often fails to support this conclusion. Tax changes are found to have a larger effect, per dollar, than changes in expenditure.

Our analysis of taxes and spending differs from the standard treatment, so our analysis of the balanced budget multiplier differs also. The short-run effect of a change in the level of a balanced budget depends on a variety of factors including the type of expenditure change. Changes in government employment or government wage payments induce smaller short-run changes in private expenditure than equal changes in government spending on output. From the budget equation,

$$pg + wlg - t(p, y, wlg; \tau) + I(i)S = 0,$$

we can find the change in government spending that balances a change in tax rates ($\tau$) on income from labor or capital

$$dg = \frac{t_y y_\tau + t_\tau}{p - t_y y_g} d\tau,$$

or

$$\frac{dg}{g} = \frac{\epsilon(t, y)\,\epsilon(y, \tau) + \epsilon(t, \tau)}{(pg/t) - \epsilon(t, y)\,\epsilon(y, g)} \frac{d\tau}{\tau}.$$

Prices and money wages are kept constant, as in the usual Keynesian short run, and the effects on interest payments are neglected to simplify. Subscripted variables are partial derivatives.

The balanced budget change induces a change in real output, per unit $d\tau$, that may be positive or negative. The change in output, for any given $d\tau/\tau$ depends on the elasticities $\epsilon(y, g)$ and $\epsilon(y, \tau)$ and the change, $dg/g$, that balances the budget,

$$\epsilon(y, g)\frac{dg}{g} + \epsilon(y, \tau)\frac{d\tau}{\tau}$$

$$= \frac{\gamma}{1 - (1 - \gamma)\,\bar{\epsilon}(d, y)}\left[\frac{\epsilon(t, y)\,\epsilon(y, \tau) + \epsilon(t, \tau)}{(pg/t) - \epsilon(t, y)\,\epsilon(y, g)} + \frac{1 - \gamma}{\gamma}\bar{\epsilon}(d, \tau)\right]\frac{d\tau}{\tau},$$

$$\bar{\epsilon}(d, y) = \epsilon(d, i)\,\epsilon(i, y|AM) + \epsilon(d, P)\,\epsilon(P, y|AM) + \epsilon(d, W_h)\,\epsilon(W_h, y) + \epsilon(d, e)\,\epsilon(e, y) > 0,$$

where

$$\bar{\epsilon}(d, \tau) = \epsilon(d, i)\,\epsilon(i, \tau|AM) + \epsilon(d, P)\,\epsilon(P, \tau|AM) + \epsilon(d, W_h)\,\epsilon(W_h, \tau) + \epsilon(d, e)\,\epsilon(e, \tau) < 0.$$

The sign depends on a comparison of $\bar{\epsilon}(d, \tau)$ and the first term in the bracketed expression. The first term shows the amount by which government expenditure changes to equal a unit change in $d\tau/\tau$. The sign of the first term depends on the relative magnitude of two components in the numerator, the positive direct response $\epsilon(t, \tau)$ of tax revenues to changes in tax rates and the negative indirect effect $\epsilon(t, y)\,\epsilon(y, \tau)$. A sufficiently small direct effect reinforced by a marginal tax rate $\epsilon(t, y)$ and a response $\epsilon(y, \tau)$ sufficiently large, i.e.,

$$-\epsilon(y, \tau) > \epsilon(t, \tau)/\epsilon(t, y) > 0,$$

assures a negative first term in the numerator. Moreover, with $pg/t$ sufficiently large relative to $\epsilon(t, y)\,\epsilon(y, g)$ the bracketed expression is necessarily negative. The balanced budget multiplier is then negative. A necessary and sufficient condition for a positive balanced budget multiplier is the following inequality,

$$\gamma[\epsilon(t, y)\,\epsilon(y, \tau) + \epsilon(t, \tau)] > -(1 - \gamma)\,\bar{\epsilon}(d, \tau)\,[(pg/t) - \epsilon(t, y)\,\epsilon(y, g)].$$

The inequality is a constraint on the tax arrangements. Our analysis determines that the sign and magnitude of the balanced budget multiplier depends sensitively on the nature of the tax system. The results extend to balanced changes in $lg$ and $\tau$. With $\gamma_{lg} < \gamma_g$ the $(lg, \tau)$ balanced budget multiplier is numerically smaller than the $(g, \tau)$ balanced budget multiplier.

Another issue to be discussed in connection with the budget is the long-term effect of progressive taxation in a growing economy. It is well-known that an expanding output raises the budget surplus whenever tax rates are sufficiently progressive. Inflation increases the tax burden on the private sector. A progressive tax rate schedule brings a persistent increase in the tax parameters $\tau$ as output and prices rise. The increase in $\tau$ lowers the long-run levels of human and real capital and lowers the private sector's long-run output.

Do rational individuals anticipate that tax rates will fall in the future? Or, do they anticipate additional increases in the share of output absorbed by government or allocated by government? Do consumers anticipate future tax payments to pay the losses on government guarantees of risk securities? Answers to these questions must enter the calculation of long-term investors in market economies. Anticipated tax rates affect the yield on private capital, the choice of labor or leisure and the type of training and investment in skills. The size of the budget, in our model, affects the price level. Aggregative analysis has completely neglected the government sector's production process that absorbs as inputs portions of private sector output and labor. The process yields a mixed output of income transfers, consumables, capital goods or (intermediate) inputs for the private sector. The net effect of this operation on private demand and the long-run stock of human and real capital affects efficiency and the taxes paid. On most of these long-run questions and issues, as on the short-run fiscal issues we have discussed at greater length, empirical knowledge is either tenuous or absent. These issues, not the slope of the *LM* curve, are for us the outstanding issues about the effects of fiscal policy in the short, intermediate and long run.

## 2. Credit, Money and Intermediation

An important difference between economies with three distinct assets and economies in which two of the assets are assumed to be "perfect substitutes" occurs during the early stage of the adjustment from one full equilibrium to the next. Intermediation and disintermediation are the names now commonly used to describe a highly visible part of the adjustment of asset positions, the shift into or out of time and saving deposits.

The difference between the outstanding stocks of bank credit and money, at any point in time, measures the extent of intermediation or disintermediation.[23]

[23] Thomas Mayer (section 2) is the only discussant who recognizes this point. His attempt to discuss our analysis in the context of Keynesian versus quantity theories causes him (section 5) to dismiss the distinction between debt and real capital as not of critical importance for the analysis of capital acquisition or investment. Robert Rasche discusses parallels between our analysis and Modigliani (1963). Modigliani introduces a demand for bonds, but it enters his model solely as an afterthought, and he notes (p. 81) that "it is permissible to treat this market as the redundant one and we shall find it convenient to do so". For Modigliani, "the two components of the money supply and hence their sum *M* is exogenously determined by the government ..." (p. 81). Later in his paper, Modigliani has a perceptive, early statement of the budget equation, as we noted above. While showing how the model can be adjusted to admit the government budget equation, Modigliani

This is a matter of arithmetic that follows from the consolidated balance sheet of the banking system and the definition of money as the sum of currency and demand deposits of the public. In our notation,

$$a(\ \ )B - m(\ \ )B = (a - m)B = T - B,$$

or

$$T = (1 + a - m)B,$$

where $T$ is the total stock of commercial bank time deposits. The way in which time deposits change and the consequences of such changes is part of monetary analysis. In our model, the simultaneous adjustment of the asset markets – the markets for money and credit – determines the size of outstanding time deposits and the distribution of the existing stock of government securities between banks and non-banks. In this section, we discuss some of these relations, then turn to a related topic, the transmission of monetary policy.

Behind the simplified, consolidated balance sheet of the banking system and the relation of credit to money lie the interest rate and asset pricing mechanisms. In a closed economy with government debt outstanding, the stock of bank credit is the sum of loans ($L_b$) and government securities held by banks ($S_b$). This sum is equal to the supply of earning assets to banks ($\sigma$); $v$ is the value per dollar of debt, and $v$ depends on interest rates and tax rates,

$$a(\ \ )B = L_b + S_b = L_p + v(S - S_p) = \sigma.$$

Equilibrium on the bank credit market determines the distribution of government debt between banks and non-banks (the public). The public owns money ($M$), time deposits ($T$), government debt ($vS_p$), and

$$M + T + vS_p + PK = L_p + N \quad \text{(with } N = W_\text{n} \text{ in our analysis)},$$

capital ($PK$). On the liabilities side, the public has loans ($L_p$) and net worth ($N$). The equations make clear that intermediation and disintermediation involve changes in time deposits relative to $B$ and $M$ brought about by changes in the asset multiplier ($a$) relative to the monetary multiplier ($m$). In the public's wealth statement, intermediation appears as either a complementary change in $T$ and $L_p$ or more frequently as offsetting changes in $T$ and $S_p$.

*Footnote 23 continued*
(p. 93) eliminates all bank deposits. Nowhere in his paper is there recognition of the adjustment process called intermediation. Our third discussant, Dornbusch, believes that aggregation using a single rate of interest is sufficient (section 4.2). If the statement means that portfolio adjustment has no effect on relative interest rates and asset yields or that changes in debt relative to real capital have no effect on portfolio composition, we believe he is wrong. The issue can be resolved by evidence.

In our formal model of the money and credit market (1968), the ratio of commercial bank time deposits to demand deposits is a determinant of the asset and money multipliers. The ratio depends on the interest rate paid on time deposits, $i_t$, and on market rates. Changes in relative interest rates induce changes in intermediation mainly by changing the multipliers. For this reason, we have disregarded the effect of $i_t$ on $L$ and $\sigma$.[24]

If all interest rates adjusted at the same rate to new information, rates on time deposits would rise and fall with interest rates on open market assets. The redistribution of existing stocks of bonds between banks and non-banks would be eliminated, or reduced in magnitude. Controls on rates paid on time and demand deposits contribute to a loss in efficiency by requiring adjustment of asset portfolios instead of changes in rates. Constraints, information and adjustment costs are the essential condition for the variability in relative interest rates causing the phenomenon known as intermediation.

The asset market equations permit us to describe the operation of monetary policy and the associated intermediation processes as an integral part of the transmission mechanism through which monetary (and fiscal) policy affects prices and output in our analysis. An acceleration of the base induces banks to expand earning assets and lowers market interest rates. The initial decline in market rates induces the public to sell securities to banks and, at given interest rates on time deposits, to reallocate assets from bonds to time deposits. Banks adjust the interest rates offered on time deposits in response to market rates and according to the competitive state of their liability business. The lowering of $i_t$ modifies the response of time deposits.

The net effect of this process on intermediation depends on the relative variability of $i_t$ and $i$ determined by the degree of competitiveness of bank liability business and the relative substitutability of demand deposits, time deposits and real assets. The result is shown in figure 1. The vertical axis represents the market

[24] Rasche comments on the role of time deposits and interest on time deposits. He notes that "the only other forms of holding wealth in addition to money are government debt and real capital". This statement confuses the wealth statement (i.e., the description of the public's net worth) and the public's balance sheet or description of asset positions. The equations in this section make clear that time deposits have an important part in our analysis of the interaction between money and credit markets. The interest rate $i_t$ on time deposits has not been introduced as an argument of $L$ and $\sigma$. The reason is that, we believe, the effect is small relative to the effect on the multipliers. The response of $L$ and $\sigma$ to $i_t$ can be included by reinterpreting the elasticities of $L$ and $\sigma$ with respect to $i$ as total elasticities,

$$\bar{\epsilon}(L, i) = \epsilon(\overset{-}{L}, i) + \epsilon(\overset{-}{L}, i_t) \cdot \epsilon(\overset{+}{i_t}, i) < \epsilon(L, i) < 0,$$

and

$$\bar{\epsilon}(\sigma, i) = \epsilon(\overset{-}{\sigma}, i) + \epsilon(\overset{+}{\sigma}, i_t) \cdot \epsilon(\overset{+}{i_t}, i) > \epsilon(\sigma, i) < 0.$$

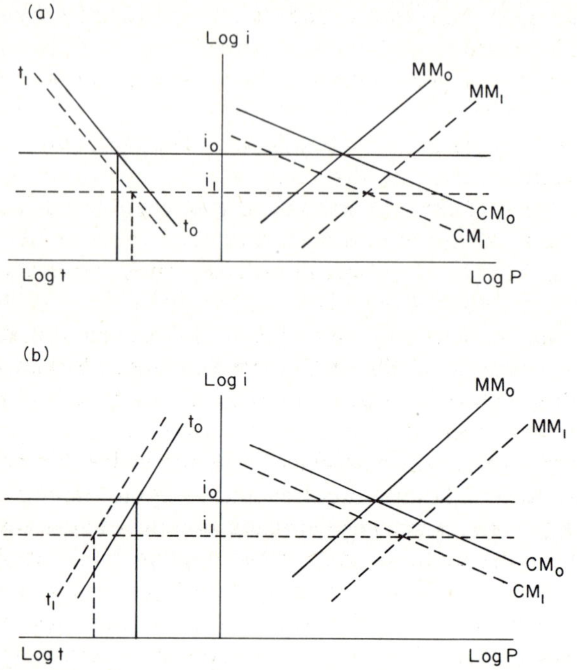


FIGURE 1

rate $i$ and the horizontal axis on the right shows the asset price level $P$. The horizontal axis on the left measures the time deposit ratio $t$ and reflects the degree of intermediation and changes in this degree. The quadrant on the right contains a downward sloping *CM* curve and and upward sloping *MM* curve. The *CM* curve is the locus of $(i, P)$ combinations satisfying the credit market equation for given values of other variables. Similarly, the *MM* curve represents the locus of $(i, P)$ combinations satisfying the money market equation. The sign of the slopes is easily derived from our analysis of asset market interaction. The intersection of the two lines determines the market rate, $i$, and the asset price level. The slopes of both lines reflect implicitly the dependence on $i_t$. The denominator of both slope expressions involves the total elasticity of $L$ and $\sigma$ with respect to $i$, including a small component to reflect dependence on $i_t$. The quadrant on the left shows the time deposit ratio as a function of $i$. The slope of the $t$ line measures the total elasticity,

$$\overline{\epsilon}(t, i) = \epsilon(t, i) + \epsilon(t, i_t)\, \epsilon(i_t, i),$$

where $\epsilon(t, i)$ and $\epsilon(t, i_t)$ are partial elasticities and $\epsilon(i_t, i)$ expresses the responsiveness of $i_t$ to given market conditions.

The elasticity $\epsilon(i_t, i)$ describes the banks supply of time deposits as a price setting function. The elasticity $\epsilon(i_t, i)$ is confined to the closed unit interval and rises with the competitiveness of bank liability business. The total interest elasticity $\epsilon(t, i)$ assumes the negative sign of its first component whenever competitiveness of time deposit business is sufficiently low or $i_t$ moves close to a ceiling rate. In the absence of a relevant ceiling rate and with a highly competitive deposit business the positive second component prevails and the $t$ line in figure 1 slopes to the northwest.

Two distinct states are examined in figure 1. Figure 1a describes a relatively competitive bank liability business; in figure 1b there is either little competition or an effective ceiling on $i_t$. In both cases, an increase in the base lowers both *CM* and *MM* and, under the order constraints in our analysis, the intersection moves down and to the right. The horizontal interest line describing the prevailing market rate moves down and in case of pronounced deposit competition (and absence of ceilings) the value of $t$ slides to the right along the $t$ line of figure 1a. The resulting reduction in $t$ and consequent disintermediation is moderated by the effect of a higher $P$ on $t$ [i.e., $\epsilon(t, P) > 0$] pushing the $t$ line slightly to the left. The net amount of disintermediation depends, therefore, on the magnitude of the decline in $i$, the relative competitiveness of time deposit business expressed by the relative steepness of the $t$ line and the responsiveness of $t$ to $P$. In figure 1b, the expansion of the base raises the level of intermediation. The positive response of the intermediation level reaches a maximum when deposit competition vanishes and $t$ is extremely responsive to $P$.

A corresponding pair of figures can be used to show the effect of changes in the anticipated net yield, $e$, on real capital and in real income, $y$. An increase in $y$ or $e$ pushes the intersection in the right quadrant up and to the right, in a northeasterly direction. Under competitive conditions, intermediation increases. A reduction in $y$ or $e$ lowers the intermediation level. The effects are reversed in sign and moderated in magnitude (by the response to $P$) under weak deposit competition. These patterns of intermediation cannot by analyzed using traditional *IS–LM* analysis.

### 3. Monetarism Once Again

A central problem in macroeconomics for more than a century has been to explain why fluctuations occur. The problem can be separated into two parts: the initiating impulse and the adjustment process by which the impulse is transmitted from market to market and from short- to long-run equilibrium. Both topics have been disputed, hotly, at times.

Recent discussion attended extensively to the transmission or adjustment process. Implications of alternative hypotheses about adjustment processes fill the literature, including most of this paper and the other papers in this volume. Yet, there are very few issues remaining in dispute about the adjustment process. The remaining issues are important, however, and not as esoteric as they may appear. Their resolution conditions the choice of stabilization policies.

The major issue discussed at length, is whether it is useful to retain *IS* and *LM* as a basic paradigm. In our framework, the shifts in the curves are at least as important as their slopes. There is no lack of empirical evidence on this question. One of the most prominent features of post-war fluctuation in developed economies is that changes in interest rates and the prices of claims to real capital are large relative to changes in output and employment. Similar observations are available for the mild cycles that have occurred in many countries. The experience of the last thirty years includes a number of episodes during which the growth rate of output declined, interest rates and asset prices declined and real output rose.

Output, or the growth rate of output, interest rates, and money stocks rise and fall together during mild cycles. We believe that there is no consistent way to explain these observations that does not introduce systematic shifts in conventional *IS* and *LM* curves as part of the transmission of monetary policy. If output price levels adjust slowly, as most evidence suggests, the usual real balance effect cannot explain the observed movements in prices, output and market interest rates. Broadening the concept of interest rates from the old-style Keynesian identification with borrowing costs to include stock prices is a step in the right direction, but much too small a step.[25]

The emphasis given by monetarists to a broader range of substitutes for money is expressed by the proposition that asset prices join interest rates in the transmission of monetary and fiscal policies. The core of this issue is the role of changes in relative prices in the adjustment or transmission process.

[25] Thomas Mayer (section 5) refers to the problem of the forecaster who uses a Keynesian model and cites the "substanted wealth effect" in the FMP model. The FMP model certainly does not hew to the old Keynesian position on this issue. Short-run shifts in consumption expenditure have a prominent role. These shifts are to a considerable extent the result of short-term fluctuations in the prices of common stocks. The identification of the relative price change with a "wealth" effect is certainly acceptable. The problem comes in the identification of the wealth effect with the changes in the market value of securities instead of the change in the prices of existing assets, of which common stocks are one part. We expect that the use of common stock prices as a measure of asset prices caused the FMP model to predict a much larger decline in consumption expenditure during 1974 than occurred just as it misled James Tobin in his forecasts of investment spending. See Tobin (1974).

An alternative way to bring some empirical content to this issue is to compare explanations of fluctuations in market interest rates. The extended Hicksian model, written above, describes market rates as the sum of two components, real rates, $r$, and anticipated inflation, $\pi$,

$$i = r + \pi.$$

Broadly speaking, Keynesians treat prices and anticipated prices as constant in the short run. Their explanations emphasize changes in the marginal efficiency of investment brought about by changes in optimism of businessmen and possibly consumers. The "wealth adjustment" to stock market prices is one channel by which changes in optimism can affect interest rates. Fisherians or quantity theorists hold real rates constant, or approximately so and, following Fisher, emphasize the dominance of changes in anticipations.

We believe that a more complete statement of the interest equation and of the reason for fluctuation in economic activity, interest rates and prices, requires a redefinition of $r$ to reflect relative price changes on a broad range of assets. The expected return to real capital, $e$, need not be constant, but we believe it is not a dominant (antonomous) factor in cycles. Changes in interest rates during mild cycles have been largely the result of changes in relative prices of assets and output. In the years of the gold standard, cyclical changes in anticipated long-term inflation were small and had very little cyclical effect on long-term rates. In the past forty years, fluctuations in price anticipations have been larger and have contributed not only to the time trend in rates but to cyclical changes as well. Indeed, we have difficulty finding a suitable rationale for the strong Keynesian position that emphasizes (or emphasized) the effect of anticipations on interest rates through $e$ or $r$ while denying or minimizing the effect of price anticipations and price changes on output, employment and interest rates.

A second monetarist proposition – the relative stability of the private and public sectors – became explicit in the discussion of interest rate changes. Monetarists attribute fluctuation in economic activity and prices to government policies. Monetary changes resulting from longer-run fiscal developments deserve particular attention. The monetarist hypothesis emphasizes the relative stability of the private sector. Keynesians traditionally emphaisze the instability of private expenditures as a cause of fluctuations that is independent of the economic policies pursued by government. This issue has been recognized by Tobin in a paper circulated subsequent to the Conference at Brown University. Tobin (1975) contends that Keynesian analysis should be less concerned with the existence of an "underemployment equilibrium" and more concerned about adjustment mechanisms of the economy that are "too weak to eliminate persistent unemployment" with stable policies and flexible prices and wages. We note however, that most econometric models developed within the general Keynesian framework fail to show evidence of explosive oscillations or deflationary drift. The private sector described by these models appears to be stable [Hickman (1972), Brunner (1973)].

The failure of econometric models to produce evidence of short-term explosive oscillations or unstable dynamics is contrary to two main alternatives to the monetarist conjecture. One is the Keynes–Wicksell proposition that centers attention on the instability of expectations. The other is a proposition that we identify with the eclecticism of Wesley Mitchell and Arthur Burns at the National Bureau. Their work attributes fluctuations to the unstable, internal dynamics of real economic activity or the pervasive effects of cumulated, serially and contemporaneously correlated random disturbances. Large, econometric models and recent attempts to specify a National Bureau model fail to support these propositions.[26]

Two of our discussants misinterpret our views on stability. One writes that *exogenous shocks* may "cause frequent and wide departures of income from its previous equilibrium" (Mayer, section 5). Another argues that our model can be unstable if there are pure fiscal policies (Dornbusch, section 4.2).[27] We cannot understand how their statements bear on our interpretation of stability. To us stability of the private sector means that in the absence of impulses in the form of government policies the system moves to equilibrium. Our version of monetarism does not deny that if exogenous shocks take the form of government policies, including fiscal policies, the system may oscillate or even explode into inflation or cumulative deflation. Our proposition asserts that cyclical instability is mainly the product of government policies that are imposed on a stabilizing private sector. This view is in contrast to the views of leading eclectics.

Furthermore, our analysis implies that, subject to some qualifications of little empirical importance, the private sector absorbs the shock of impulses emanating from the government sector. This is not intended as a statement about any properties of the model other than its truth value and ability to generate true statements about the causes of observed fluctuations in output and prices.

Our third monetarist proposition emphasizes the dominant role of stocks. Fiscal policy determines the financial stocks and exerts an important influence on the longer-run evolution of an economy. The discussants generally accept this point and find no conflict with the Keynesian position. We disagree. The proposition is in conflict with the standard analysis of Metzler. The standard analysis

[26] See the paper by Gregory Chow and Geoffrey Moore in Hickman (1973). The instability was explicitly reaffirmed by Arthur Burns (1973) in a letter addressed to Senator Proxmire in October 1973.

[27] Dornbusch's overlooks our discussion of stability in section 3.2 and footnotes 9 and 13 of our paper earlier in this volume.

implies that, in a stationary closed economy, real capital is fixed and does not change with changes in policy. Our analysis implies that any change in the stocks of money or debt changes the stock of capital, the level of real output and the price level. Fiscal expansions lower the long-run stock of real capital and the private sector's output. Monetary expansion raises long-run real output and the stock of capital.

The organization of our analysis into a sequence of runs from short-run flow equilibrium to full stock–flow equilibrium with wage adjustment permits us to work out implications of fiscal and monetary changes in an orderly way. By distinguishing "runs", we are able to show that fiscal policy has a substantial long-run influence on the composition of assets, the long-run level of output produced by the private sector and on the price level. Monetary policy has greater importance for short- and intermediate-run fluctuations and for inflation. In the absence of a substantive, general dynamic model subsuming all runs into one continuous process, it seems useful to generate testable propositions of this kind by exploiting information about differences in speed of adjustment of variables.

Our last issue is the importance or lack of importance of allocative detail for aggregate analysis. Modigliani and Ando argue that structural detail is important. The mass of allocative detail in large scale econometric models seems to us irrelevant for aggregative analysis. We assert that a small number of explicitly stated allocative patterns have observable aggregative consequences. The structure of bank earning assets or the division of output between consumption and investment yields comparatively little information about short-run movements of economic aggregates. Although our analysis implies that the effects of different sources of monetary growth vary in principle, the differences are of small order relative to the magnitude of most phenomena to be explained. Similarly, the forces determining the relative position of individual price changes within the total frequency distribution of price changes have a negligible influence on the position of the distribution. Correspondingly, the factors shifting the distribution have little systematic effect on the relative position of individual items.

Our conjectures are brought forward to bring out fundamental empirical issues about the nature of the economic process. Differences about these issues determine differences in research strategy that separate monetarists from Keynesians or eclectics. Our approach looks beyond quarterly changes in a mass of variables to seek explanations about the major contours of inflation, unemployment, prices and real income.

We have developed a number of testable implications and conjectures bearing on the relative importance of various impulses, the transmission of changes, the role of the government budget, and other implications of a three asset model with a government budget equation. These implications go beyond the question other participants considered to be the remaining issue in the monetarist dispute. Deciding whether the implications are correct is the only way we know to decide whether the three-asset models represent an advance in our understanding of the world or a minor adjustment of *IS–LM*.

## Bibliography


Ando A, and F. Modigliani, 1975, Some reflections on describing structures of financial sectors, in: The Brookings model: Perspective and development (North-Holland, Amsterdam).

Brunner, K., 1968, The role of money and monetary policy, Review Federal Reserve Bank of St. Louis 50, July.

Brunner, K., 1974a, Book review of: B. G. Hickman, ed., Econometric models of cyclical behavior, Journal of Economic Literature 12.

Brunner, K., 1974b, Inflation, money and the role of fiscal arrangements: An analytic framework for the inflation problem, presented at the International Conference on The New Inflation, Milano, June, to be published.

Brunner, K. and A. Meltzer, 1963, The place of financial intermediaries in the transmission mechanism, Proceedings of the American Economic Association 53, May.

Brunner, K. and A. Meltzer, 1968, Liquidity traps for money, bank credit and interest rate, Journal of Political Economy 76, Jan./Feb.

Brunner, K. and A. Meltzer, 1973, Mr. Hicks and the monetarists, Economica, Feb.

Burns, A. F., 1973, Letter from Chairman Burns to Senator Proxmire, Federal Reserve Bank of New York Monthly Review 55, Nov.

Christ, C., 1969, A model of monetary and fiscal policy effects on the money stock, price level and real output, Journal of Money, Credit and Banking 1.

Friedman, M., 1966, Interest rates and the demand for money, Journal of Law and Economics IX, Oct.

Goldfeld, S., 1973, The demand for money revisited, Brookings Papers on Economic Activity 3.

Hickman, B. G., 1973, Econometric models of cyclical behavior (Columbia University Press, New York).

Khan, M., 1974, The stability of the demand-for-money function in the U.S. 1909–1965, Journal of Political Economy 82, Nov.

Lucas, R., 1975, Econometric policy evaluation: A critique, Carnegie-Rochester Conference Series (North-Holland, Amsterdam).

Meltzer, A. H., 1965, Monetary theory and monetary history, Schweizerische Zeitschrift für Volkswirtschaft und Statistik 101, Dec.

Modigliani, F., 1944, Liquidity preference and the theory of interest and money, Econometrica 12.

Modigliani, F., 1963, The monetary mechanism and its interaction with real phenomena, The Review of Economics and Statistics 45, Suppl., Feb.

Tobin, J., 1974, Monetary policy in 1974, Brookings Papers on Economic Activity 4.

Tobin, J., 1975, Keynesian models of recession and depression, Proceedings of the American Economic Association 65, May.

Chapter 3

# INSIDE THE MONETARIST BLACK BOX

Jerome L. STEIN*

## 1. Introduction

Monetarism is a set of propositions in direct opposition of Keynesian fiscal policy. Neither monetarists nor Keynesians constitute monolithic groups, but the former accept a common set of propositions which the latter group denies. There are three key monetarist propositions.

(M-1) ... fiscal actions in the absence of accommodative monetary actions exert little net influence on total spending and therefore have little influence on output and the price level. [Andersen and Carlson (1970, p. 8)]

Changes in high employment expenditures, with the money stock held constant, first have a positive influence on total spending, but the influence becomes significantly negative after three quarters. Fiscal actions, unaccompanied by changes in money, have little net effect on GNP over five quarters.

For short periods, and for extended periods in which the rate of change of Federal expenditures is either accelerating or decelerating, fiscal effects are significant. The estimated coefficients for changes in money and changes in Federal expenditures are in general agreement with the monetarist view of the response of total spending to these two variables. [ibid., p. 11]

The inference is that only monetary policy, not fiscal policy, can be used to control the level of aggregate demand for a period longer than a year.

* Versions of my AER 1974 paper, and early versions of this development, where tried out at: MIT, Chicago, Queens University, Rochester, Federal Reserve Bank of St. Louis, University of Connecticut, Board of Governors of the Federal Reserve System, Wharton and Yale. I am indebted to the participants at those workshops, and to Costas Azariadis and George Borts, for their perceptive and helpful criticisms.

(M-2) ... onsets of downswings or upswings occurred at very different levels of monetary growth.... Changes in the pace of economic activity are not associated with any particular money growth and occur independently of the *level* of monetary growth. They only depend on the previous *changes* in monetary growth, whatever its inherited level. [Brunner (1970, p. 14)]

Maintenance of a utilization rate of resources beyond the longer-run equilibrium level determined essentially by nonmonetary cost and yield factors thus requires a *continued* and *uninterrupted* acceleration of the money stock and consequently a *continued increase* in the actual rate of inflation. [ibid., p. 25]

(M-3) There is a consistent though not precise relation between the rate of growth of the quantity of money and the rate of growth of nominal income.... If the quantity of money grows rapidly, so will nominal income; and conversely. [Friedman (1970, p. 22)]

Accelerations or decelerations in the rate of monetary expansion can affect the unemployment rate; but when the rate of monetary expansion converges to a constant, there will be no relation between the unemployment rate and the constant rate of monetary expansion. The latter will be the main determinant of the longrun growth of nominal, but not real, income.

There is a prevasive view that the monetarists have a "black box" and have not explained the causal mechanism which could imply propositions (M-1) – (M-3). For example, Rasche wrote:

> On the one hand, we are left without a clearly specified analytical framework for the monetarist approach which can be contrasted with the well-developed static income determination model. On the other hand, and even more importantly, there is no general model which can produce the post-Keynesian model as a particular case, and the monetarist and classical models as alternative cases. Such a framework is useful in order to discriminate between alternative hypotheses and to construct empirical tests which have the potential to refute one, or both, positions. [Rasche (1973, p. 15)]

Some monetarists would take issue with this statement. Nevertheless, Blinder and Solow (1973) who developed the work of Silber (1970), Laidler (1973), Rasche (1973), Scadding (1972), the author (1974) and Tobin (1972), in addition to the participants at this conference, have found it intellectually challenging to explore the analytic foundations of monetarism. The present paper develops my earlier model in a way which "can produce the post-Keynesian model as a particular case, and the monetarist and classical models as alternative cases". Then an empirical test is proposed and undertaken to determine which empirical specification is inconsistent with the data.

## 2. The Behavioral Equations[1]

My model is characterized by wage and price flexibility and an endogenously determined unemployment rate. This is a short-run rather than a growth model, insofar as the *ratio* of effective labor *supplied* per unit of capital is assumed to be relatively constant during the period considered. If the equation for the growth of capital is explicitly included, a growth model would be obtained.

Table 1 is derived from an explicit analysis of: the labor market, the assets markets for capital and bonds, the excess demand for goods, two price change equations and a government budget balance equation.

TABLE 1
Summary of the macro-economic model.

| | | |
|---|---|---|
| (3a) | $Dw/w = \alpha + \pi^* - \pi + h(U)$ | Real wage change |
| (5) | $U = F[w/A(t), G_1]$ | Unemployment rate |
| (15) | $\rho = g(U, \pi^*, m, \theta)$ | Bond market |
| (16b) | $G - T = [D\theta + (1 + \theta)\mu]m$ | Government budget balance |
| (17) | $Dm/m = \mu - n - \pi$ | Change in real balances/capital |
| (21a) | $\pi = P(U, \pi^*, m, G, \theta)$ | Price change |
| (22) | $D\pi^* = b(\pi - \pi^*)$ | Adaptive expectations |

*Endogenous variables are:* the unemployment rate ($U$), the rate of price change ($\pi$), the expected rate of price change ($\pi^*$), the real wage ($w$), real balances per unit of capital ($m$), the nominal rate of interest ($\rho$), and the ratio of government interest bearing debt to the money supply ($\theta$).

*Control variables are:* the rate of monetary expansion ($\mu$), real government purchases of goods and services per unit of capital ($G$), real government purchases of labor services per unit of capital ($G_1 \leq G$), and real taxes per unit of capital ($T$).

[1] This section summarizes my 1974 model. A glossary of mathematical symbols is contained at the end of this paper.

*Exogenous variables are*: the rate of labor augmenting technical change ($\alpha$), the growth of effective labor ($n$), and the relatively constant ratio of effective labor supplied per unit of capital ($x_s$).

No one of these equations represent a departure from the current "oral tradition" of macro-economics; but the "gestalt" yields interesting and novel results.

### *2.1. The Labor Market and Unemployment Equation*

Instead of taking the nominal wage as exogenous or as an algebraic function of the current unemployment rate, a Walrasian labor market equation (1) states that: the proportionate rate of change of the nominal wage $W$ is a linear combination of several elements. The first is the expected long-term rate of Harrod neutral technical progress $\alpha$ plus the expected rate of price change $\pi^*$. No dichotomy is made between expectations of employers and employees in this single-sector macro-economic model. Variable $\pi^*$ reflects both the expected change in the price of output and the price of goods purchased by consumers. It is assumed that there is no money illusion and that the coefficient of the price expectations term is unity. When both employers and employees expect the prices of goods sold and purchased to rise by one percentage point, there is no opposition to raise the nominal wage by one percentage point.

The second element is a function of the excess demand for labor $(N_d - N_s)/N_s$, where $N_d$ and $N_s$ refer to the quantities demanded or supplied, respectively. Define $x_i \equiv AN_i/K$ ($i$ = d, s) as the ratio of effective labor demanded or supplied per unit of capital. Variable $A(t)$ grows at rate $\alpha$. Operator $D \equiv \mathrm{d}/\mathrm{d}t$.

$$\frac{DW}{W} = \alpha + \pi^* + \lambda_w \left(\frac{N_d - N_s}{N_s}\right) = \alpha + \pi^* + \lambda_w \left(\frac{x_d - x_s}{x_s}\right); \qquad (1)$$

$$\lambda_w' > 0.$$

Although the excess demand for labor per unit of capital is not directly observable, equation (2) states that the measured unemployment rate $U$ is negatively related to the excess demand for labor. Both positive and negative excess demands for labor are associated with a positive unemployment rate; and it does not require that either firms be on their demand curves for labor or that households be on their supply curves. This equation is sufficiently general to be consistent with a wide variety of micro-economic theories of labor markets,

$$U = H\left(\frac{x_d - x_s}{x_s}\right); \qquad H' < 0, \quad 1 \geqq U \geqq 0. \qquad (2)$$

The inverse function is

$$\frac{x_d - x_s}{x_s} = H^{-1}(U). \tag{2a}$$

Substitute (2a) into (1) and derive the frequently used wage change equation

$$DW/W = \alpha + \pi^* + h(U); \qquad h \equiv \lambda_w \circ H^{-1}, \quad h' < 0. \tag{3}$$

The $h$ function is a macro-economic relation which reflects the distribution of employment and unemployment among the various sectors of the economy. It is quite possible that the $h$ function is related to the dispersion of the unemployment or to the composition of the labor force which, in turn, is related to the actual rate of price change $\pi \equiv Dp/p$ (where $p$ is the price level), even though the coefficient of the expected rate of price change $\pi^*$ in equation (1) is unity. Therefore, the $h$ function may be $h(U, \pi)$ instead of $h(U)$. These possibilities must be borne in mind in interpreting the empirical results in section 4.

The real wage $w \equiv W/p$ grows at rate $DW/W$ less $\pi$. By subtracting the rate of price change $\pi$ from both sides of (3), the following equation for the growth of the real wage is derived,

$$Dw/w = \alpha + \pi^* - \pi + h(U), \tag{3a}$$

which is entered in table 1.

The excess demand for labor per unit of total capital requires some explanation. The demand for labor services arises from both the private sector and the government sector. In the former, the ratio of effective labor demanded per unit of capital $x'_d$ is negatively related to the real wage $w$, deflated by the level of productivity $A(t)$ which grows at rate $\alpha$. This is just marginal productivity theory. The government also purchases the services of labor directly; and is not a profit maximizer in the usual sense. The government demand for labor services per unit of total capital is $G_1$. Then the total quantity of labor demanded per unit of capital is $x_d \equiv x'_d + G_1$. Equation (4) describes the excess demand for labor,

$$\frac{x_d - x_s}{x_s} = f\left(\frac{w}{A(t)}, G_1\right); \qquad f_1 < 0, \quad f_2 > 0. \tag{4}$$

Substitute (4) into (2) and derive an equation for the unemployment rate, where $U$ is positively related to the adjusted real wage $w/A(t)$, and is negatively related to the level of labor services demanded by the government per unit of capital,

$$U = F\left(\frac{w}{A(t)}, G_1\right); \qquad F \equiv H \circ f, \quad F_1 > 0, \quad F_2 < 0,$$

$$\beta_1 \equiv F_1(w/A), \qquad \beta_2 \equiv -F_2. \tag{5}$$

which is entered in table 1.

This formulation does not imply that fiscal policy, reflected by variations in $G_1$, can affect the unemployment rate over any sustained period of time. What happens to $U$ as a result of variations in $G_1$ will depend upon the repercussions upon the adjusted real wage $w/A(t)$. Consider equations (3a) and (5). The level of $U$ will affect the growth of the nominal wage, and the latter will react back upon the level of $U$. Models which assume that the nominal wage is either exogenous or algebraically related to the unemployment rate[2] tend to overemphasize the effects of fiscal policy relative to the models which contain (3a) and (5).

## 2.2. *The Assets Markets*[3]

### 2.2.1. *The market for existing capital and the investment demand equation*

Capital goods consist of all durable goods which produce a flow of goods and services, regardless of whether they are owned by firms or by households. Some of the goods will be sold in competitive markets at prices equal to their capital values. Others may not be actively traded, but their implicit prices to their owners will be their capital values.

Let the desired rate of change of the ratio of physical capital ($K$) to output ($Y$) be positively related to the ratio of the market price of existing capital to the price of a unit of currently produced output. Denote this ratio by $q$. If $q$ exceeds unity, it is profitable to purchase a unit of current output and use it as a capital good. This constitutes a demand for investment. If $q$ were less than unity, it is cheaper to buy an existing capital asset than to purchase a unit of newly produced output; and investment is discouraged. A general theory of investment [Keynes (1930, vol. I, pp. 200–209), Tobin (1969)] is described by

$$D \ln K/Y = \phi(q - 1); \qquad \phi' > 0. \tag{6}$$

The market price of an existing asset is its present value. Let the quasi-rents expected at $t$ units of time from the present be $P^*(t)\ r^*(t)$. Assume that: (i) the price level $p^*(t)$ expected to prevail is $p(0)e^{\pi^* t}$; (ii) the expected real rent is $r(0)e^{-\delta t}$, where $r(0)$ is the current rent and $\delta$ is the depreciation rate; and (iii) the average interest rate which is expected to prevail during the life of the asset is equal to the current rate $\rho(0)$. Then the ratio $q$, of the market price of capital to the

[2] See Blinder and Solow and a critique of their paper by Ando.

[3] The analysis in this section is quite compatible with Tobin's (1969) analysis of portfolio equilibrium.

price of current output is described by

$$q = \int_0^\infty \frac{p^*(t)}{p(0)} r^*(t)\, e^{-\rho t}\, dt = \frac{r}{\rho + \delta - \pi^*}. \tag{7}$$

Output per unit of capital $y$ and the rent per unit of capital $r$ are assumed to be smooth concave functions of the ratio of effective labor employed per unit capital, denoted by $x$ without a subscript. Equation (8) is a definition of $x$:

$$x \equiv (1 - U)x_s. \tag{8}$$

It follows that $y$ and $r$ are negatively related to $U$,

$$y = y(x) = y(U); \qquad y' < 0. \tag{9}$$

$$r = r(x) = R(U); \qquad R' < 0. \tag{10}$$

Economic units assume that output will grow at long-run rate $n$, the growth of effective labor. The desired gross growth of capital, derived from (6), (7) and (10), is given by (11) – it is the investment demand equation,

$$I/K = n + \delta + \phi(q - 1) = n + \delta + I[R(U) + \pi^* - \rho - \delta]; \qquad I' > 0. \tag{11}$$

Variable $I$ is real investment demand.

In long-run equilibrium,[4] when the desired growth of capital $DK/K$ is equal to the growth of output $n$, the marginal efficiency of investment $R(U) - \delta$ will be equal to the real rate of interest $\rho - \pi^*$, i.e., $q$ will equal unity.

### *2.2.2. The bond market*[5]

The nominal rate of interest on bonds ($\rho$) equilibrates the bond market. By the wealth constraint, the excess supply of real balances would then be equal to the stock excess demand for capital. Since the monetarist controversy relies heavily upon the "crowding-out" effect, a discussion of equilibrium in the financial markets is required.

Firms generally wish to supply a stock of bonds and households generally provide a stock demand for bonds. Let $d$ represent the real stock excess demand for

[4] See the author (1971, ch. 5) for an analysis of a growing economy and the resulting long-run steady state.

[5] I measure the rent per unit of capital in terms of reproduction cost $R(U)$, whereas the Yale approach focuses upon $R/q$, the rent in terms of the market price of capital. As I read Tobin (1969, p. 25), I do not think that this is any substantive differences between his approach and the one taken here.

bonds by the private sector. Quantity $d$ is related: (i) negatively to the rent per unit of capital $R(U)$; (ii) negatively to the expected rate of price change $\pi^*$; (iii) positively to the nominal rate of interest; (iv) positively with the quantity of real balances $M/p$; and (v) positively with the real value of capital $K$ valued at replacement cost. Then,

$$d = d[R(U), \rho, \pi^*, M/p, K]; \qquad d_1 < 0, \quad d_2 > 0, \quad d_3 < 0, \quad d_4 > 0, \quad d_5 > 0,$$

is the private stock excess demand for real bonds. Assume that the real private stock excess demand for bonds is a function which is homogeneous of degree one in real balances and real capital. Then the real private stock excess demand for bonds per unit of capital, denoted by $B = d/K$, can be written as

$$B = d/K = B(U, \rho, \pi^*, m); \qquad B_1 > 0, \quad B_2 > 0, \quad B_3 < 0, \quad B_4 > 0, \quad B_2 + B_3 > 0, \tag{12}$$

where $m \equiv M/pK$ denotes real balances per unit of capital. What is the rationale for these inequalities?

A rise in $U$ will lower the rent per unit of capital which, in turn, will increase the attractiveness of bonds relative to real capital. In this manner, the real private stock excess demand for bonds per unit of capital will be positively related to the unemployment rate, $B_1 > 0$. A rise in the expected rate of price change $\pi^*$ will decrease the attractiveness of holding money and bonds relative to real capital, so $B_3 < 0$. If the nominal rate of interest $\rho$ and the expected rate of price change both rose by the same amount, there will be no substitution effect between bonds and real capital. However, the yield on money declines relative to the yields on bonds and real capital. As a result of the substitution of bonds for money, the excess demand for bonds will rise, $B_2 + B_3 > 0$.

Real balances and real bonds are complementary assets in portfolios. Given the vector of yields, as real balances per unit of capital ($m$) rise, investors want to hold more bonds per unit of capital and firms are less inclined to go into debt,[6] $B_4 > 0$.

Private and government bonds are assumed to be perfect substitutes in portfolios. Equilibrium in the bond market requires that: the real stock excess demand for bonds by the private sector be equal to the real stock of government bonds. If the real stock of government interest bearing debt per unit of capital is $z \equiv Z/pK$, where $Z$ is the nominal stock, bond market equilibrium implies that[7]

[6] Suppose $d = d[R(U), \rho, \pi^*]\,(M/P + K)$ were the real private excess demand for bonds. Then, $B = d/K = d(\cdot)(1 + m)$ and $\partial B/\partial m = d(\cdot) \equiv B_4 > 0$.

[7] I could have included $z$ as an argument in the $B(\cdot)$ function with no change in results.

$$z = B(U, \rho, \pi^*, m). \tag{13}$$

Define $\theta$ as the ratio of the stock of government bonds to the stock of money,

$$\theta \equiv Z/M \equiv z/m. \tag{14}$$

Solve (13) for the equilibrium nominal rate of interest, and use (14) to write $z \equiv \theta m$; equation (15) is derived and entered in Table 1. Partial $g_3$ assumes that $z$ is given, and partial $g_4$ assumes that $m$ is given,

$$\rho = g(U, \pi^*, m, \theta); \qquad g_1 < 0, \quad 1 > g_2 > 0, \quad g_3 < 0, \quad g_4 > 0. \tag{15}$$

Two crucuial results should be noted: (a) A rise in the expected rate of price change raises the nominal rate of interest by a smaller amount, and (b) a rise in the debt–money ratio $\theta$ raises the nominal rate of interest.

### 2.3. *The Government Budget Constraint*

The government budget constraint must be kept in mind throughout the analysis.[8] Government purchases of goods and services ($GpK$) minus taxes less transfer payments ($TpK$) must be equal to the flow of government bonds $DZ$ plus the issuance of new highpowered money $DM$. Variable $T$ refers to real net taxes less transfer payments per unit of capital and $G$ refers to real government purchases of good and services per unit of capital. The government budget constraint is

$$G - T = (DZ + DM)/pK. \tag{16a}$$

The money supply is assumed to consist entirely of high-powered money which grows at rate $\mu$, so $DM/M \equiv \mu$. Variable $\theta \equiv Z/M$ and $m \equiv M/pK$. Equation (16a) can be written as

$$G - T = [D\theta + (1 + \theta)\mu]m, \tag{16b}$$

and is entered into table 1.

Equations (16a) or (16b) must always be satisfied. It follows that we need only consider three out of four variables ($G$, $T$, $\mu$, $\theta$), and the fourth will be determined from the budget constraint. I generally focus upon $G - T$ and $\mu$ as control variables, and $\theta$ is endogenous; but other choices are equally valid.

Real balances per unit of capital grow in the manner described by (17) which is entered in table 1. Since it was assumed that the ratio of effective labor supplied per unit of capital is relatively constant, capital grows at approximately rate $n$,

$$Dm/m = \mu - n - \pi. \tag{17}$$

[8] Carl Christ has emphasized this condition in his writings on macro-economics.

*2.4. The Rate of Price Change*

The rate of price change $\pi \equiv Dp/p$ is assumed to be the sum of two elements: a demand pull and a cost push effect. Instead of assuming that the goods market is always in equilibrium, I assume that the rate of price change is described by (18), which is analogous to wage change equation (1). The cost push effect is $DW/W - \alpha$, the growth of the nominal wage in excess of the rate of Harrod neutral technical change. The demand pull effect is a function of the real excess demand for goods per unit of capital, denoted by $E$.

Coefficient $\lambda_p$ is finite speed of response. The price change equation is

$$\pi = (DW/W - \alpha) + \lambda_p E(\cdot). \tag{18}$$

The real excess demand for goods per unit of capital is the sum of real planned investment per unit of capital $I/K$ [equation (11)] plus real planned consumption per unit of capital $C/K$ plus real government purchases per unit of capital $G$ less $y$, output per unit of capital,[9]

$$E = C/K + I/K + G - y. \tag{18a}$$

Consumption is assumed to depend upon wealth, though any reasonable consumption function can be used in this model. There are two components of wealth: capitalized output and some combination of real balances and government debt. It is convenient to deflate the variables by the stock of capital, so that consumption per unit of capital is positively related to: output per unit of capital capitalized at the real return to capital $Y(U)/R(U)$, real balances per unit of capital $m$, and real government debt per unit of capital $z \equiv \theta m$. It is assumed that $Y(U)/R(U)$ is negatively to the unemployment rate, so that $C_1$ in equation (19) is negative,

$$\frac{C}{K} = C(U, m, \theta); \qquad C_1 < 0, \quad C_2 > 0, \quad C_3 > 0. \tag{19}$$

Since it is not clear whether real debt is regarded as much a part of wealth as is real balances, each component of private wealth is treated separately.

Consumption demand has been considered a function of wealth rather than of disposable income. Nevertheless equation (19) can be written explicitly in terms of the budget deficit or surplus. From the government budget balance equation (16b) solve for $m$, and substitute the derived value of $m$ into the consumption

[9] I could have used the quantity of output supplied, rather than the actual quantity produced, and still derive equation (20). In each case the supply will depend upon the unemployment rate. When the government also hires labor directly ($G_1 > 0$) then total output of goods and services per unit of capital is $y + G_1$.

function. Then the consumption function can be written as

$$\frac{C}{K} = C\left[U, \frac{G - T}{D\theta + (1 + \theta)\mu}, \theta\right], \tag{19a}$$

provided that the budget is not in balance. If the debt–money ratio $\theta$ is constant, then consumption will be positively related to the government deficit,

$$\frac{\partial(C/K)}{\partial G} = \frac{-\partial(C/K)}{\partial T} = \frac{C_2}{(1 + \theta)\mu} > 0. \tag{19b}$$

The effects of Keynesian fiscal policy will affect consumption in this model through its effects upon wealth.

Substitute (9), (11) and (19) into (18a) and derive an expression for the real excess demand for goods per unit of capital:

$$\begin{aligned} E &= C(U, m, \theta) + n + \delta + I[R(U) + \pi^* - \rho - \delta] + G - y(U) \\ &= E(U, \pi^*, m, \rho, G, \theta). \end{aligned} \tag{20}$$

The nominal rate of interest, determined in the bond market, is described by (15). Substitute (20), (15) and (3) into (18) to derive the rate of price change. The price change equation, entered in table 1, is

$$\pi = \pi^* + h(U) + \lambda_p E[U, \pi^*, m, g(U, \pi^*, m, \theta), G, \theta], \tag{21}$$

or

$$\pi = P(U, \pi^*, m, G, \theta); \qquad P_3^* \equiv mP_3. \tag{21a}$$

This equation contains the essence of the difference between the monetarists and the fiscalists, as I will show in section 3 below.

Coefficient $P_5$ which is crucial to the entire analysis subsumes two countervailing effects. It is defined as

$$P_5 = \lambda_p \left[\frac{\partial E}{\partial \rho}\frac{\partial \rho}{\partial \theta} + \frac{\partial E}{\partial \theta}\right] = \lambda_p \left[\frac{\partial I}{\partial \rho}\frac{\partial \rho}{\partial \theta} + \frac{\partial C}{\partial \theta}\right]. \tag{21b}$$

Given real balances per unit of capital, a rise in $\theta$ signifies an increase in the quantity of interest bearing debt. For example, a reduction in taxes which is financed by a greater growth in the interest bearing debt will raise $\theta$. One effect of the resulting increase in private wealth will be to raise consumption demand – $\partial C/\partial\theta > 0$; and there will be a rise in excess aggregate demand. The second effect is connected with portfolio balance. To induce people to hold a larger quantity of bonds in their portfolios, they must be offered a higher rate of interest; $\partial\rho/\partial\theta$ is positive in bond market equilibrium equation (15). However, a higher nominal rate of interest exerts a depressing effect upon excess aggregate demand;

$\partial I/\partial \rho$ is negative. Coefficient $P_5$ is the sum of the two effects – the stimulating $\partial C/\partial \theta$ effect and the inhibiting $\partial I/\partial \rho \; \partial \rho/\partial \theta$ effect. Within the context of this model, the entire monetarist–fiscalist (neo-Keynesian) controversy hinges upon the sign of $P_5$. In no way must monetarists assume that there is no substitution between money and bonds (i.e., an interest inelastic demand for money). Quite the contrary, for $\partial \rho/\partial \theta$ is positive in the bond market equilibrium equation. These points will be discussed in detail in section 3 below.

Finally, for want of anything better, the adaptive expectations equation is used for the formation of expectations,

$$D\pi^* = b(\pi - \pi^*), \tag{22}$$

and it is entered in table 1.

Price change equation (21) [or (21a)] and its components are consistent with the monetarist view of the transmission mechanism. Friedman has described this mechanism as follows:

> An increased rate of monetary growth, whether produced through open-market operations or in other ways, raises the amount of cash that people and businesses have relative to other assets. The holders of the now excess cash will try to adjust their portfolios by buying other assets. . . . However, as people *attempt* to change their cash balances, the effect spreads from one asset to another. This tends to raise the prices of assets and to reduce interest rates, which encourages spending to produce new assets and also encourages spending on current services rather than on purchasing existing assets. That is how the initial effect on balance-sheets gets translated into an effect on income and spending. The difference in this area between the monetarists and the Keynesians is not on the nature of the process, but on the range of assets considered. . . . The monetarists . . . give importance to such assets as durable and even semi-durable consumer goods, structures and other real property . . . they regard market interest rates stressed by the Keynesians as only a small part of the total spectrum of rates that are relevant. [Friedman (1970, pp. 24–25).]

## 3. An Analytical Derivation of Monetarist or Fiscalist Conclusions

The model described in table 1 is inherently dynamic as a result of the wage change (3a) and budget balance (16b) equations, even if the adaptive price expectations equation is replaced with an algebraic equation. Monetarists and fiscalists disagree on the trajectories that the economy will follow as a consequence of changes in fiscal policy. The logical basis of this disagreement will be explained on the basis of table 1. Monetarist proposition (M-2) was discussed in my earlier (1974) paper, and will not be examined here.

Section 3.1 examines the steady-state characteristics of the model, and relates it to the standard *IS–LM* paradigm. Section 3.2 is exclusively concerned with the dynamic adjustment to fiscal policies.

### 3.1. *The Steady State Viewed through the IS–LM Paradigm*

Define the steady state as a situation where the unemployment rate ($U_e$), the actual ($\pi_e$) and the expected ($\pi_e^*$) rates of price change are constant, when the rate of monetary expansion ($\mu$) and real government purchases per unit of capital ($G$) are constant.[10] Subscript "e" denotes an equilibrium value. What are the implications of these conditions for the equations in table 1?

Equation (5) implies that, when $U$ and $G$ are constant the adjusted real wage $w/A(t)$ is constant so that the real wage grows at rate $\alpha$. Equation (22) implies that, when $\pi^*$ is constant, the actual and expected rates of price change are equal. Combining these two conditions, equation (3a) states that the equilibrium unemployment rate is determined by

$$h(U_e) = 0, \tag{23}$$

and just depends upon the $h$ function. At $U_e$, the nominal wage grows at rate $DW/W = \alpha + \pi$. When $U$ and $\pi^* = \pi$ are constant, equation (21a) implies that the equilibrium rate of price change is equal to the growth of the money supply less the growth of effective labor plus $P_5/P_3$ times the change in the debt–money ratio. When $\pi_e = \pi_e^*$, $U_e$ and $G$ are constant, differentiation of (21a) with respect to time implies that

$$(m\partial P/\partial m)(\mu - n - \pi) + \frac{\partial P}{\partial \theta} D\theta = 0.$$

Let $P_3^* \equiv m\partial P/\partial m$ and $P_5 \equiv \partial P/\partial \theta$. Then we derive the equilibrium rate of price change,

$$\pi_e = \mu - n + \frac{P_5}{P_3^*} D\theta. \tag{24}$$

Equation (18) or (21) implies that, when $\pi^* - \pi = h(U_e) = 0$, the market for goods is cleared – the real excess demand for goods per unit of capital is zero,

$$E(U_e, \pi_e, m, \rho, G, \theta) = 0. \tag{25}$$

[10] Assume that $G_1$ is a constant fraction of $G$.

The nominal rate of interest $\rho$ is given by

$$\rho = g(U_e, \pi_e, m, \theta). \tag{26}$$

Now we have two equations which resemble the familiar *IS–LM* model. Equation (25) is the set of interest rates and real balances per unit of capital that clear the market for goods. Call it the *IS* curve.[11] Equation (26) is the set of $(\rho, m)$ which is consistent with equilibrium in the bond market. Call it the *BB'* curve.[12] Both curves are evaluated at given values of $U_e$ and $\pi_e$; and that is why the *IS–LM* model is a partial analysis.

The *IS* curve drawn in figure 1 is upward sloping. A rise in real balances per unit of capital will raise excess aggregate demand. To equilibrate the goods market, the nominal rate of interest must rise.

The *BB'* curve is negatively sloped. A rise in real balances induces a rise in the demand for bonds. A decline in interest rates occurs to equilibrate the bond market.

Suppose that $\theta$ were initially constant, so that money and debt grow at rate $\mu$. Equilibrium will be at $S_1 = (m_1, \rho_1)$. Suppose that the government reduced taxes and financed the deficit with the sale of bonds. What would happen? Only an analysis of the dynamical system can tell the full story, because the $U$, $\pi$ and $\pi^*$ variables will begin to change. An examination of equations (25)–(26) or figure 1 discloses what are the crucial variables[13] in the dynamic analysis.

When the government runs a larger deficit (as a result of the tax reduction) which is financed through bond sales, $D\theta$ becomes positive. From (16b), it follows that

$$D\theta = \frac{G - T}{m} - (1 + \theta)\mu > 0. \tag{27}$$

Both the *IS* and *BB'* curves shift upwards steadily as a result of the rise in $\theta$. The upward shift of the *IS* curve, *per unit of time*, is given by

$$D\rho \bigg|_{m}^{IS} = \frac{E_\theta}{-E_\rho} D\theta, \tag{28a}$$

which is derived from (25) above. The reason for the shift is that the deficit raises private wealth; and consumption demand is stimulated by $E_\theta D\theta$. Only if the

[11] Strictly speaking the *IS* curve is the set of nominal interest rates $\rho$ and nominal income py which clear the goods market. But $y = y(U)$ and $U_e$ is given. Therefore, we can consider the *IS* curve as the set of $\rho$ and $M/pK$ which equilibrate the goods market.

[12] I focus upon the equilibrium in the bond market (*BB'* curve) rather than upon the condition whereby the quantity of money demanded is equal to the stock in existence (*LM* curve).

[13] See Silber (1970) and then Blinder and Solow.

nominal rate of interest rises by enough to crowd out an equal amount of private investment will the goods market be cleared at the given $m$.

Since the deficit raises the ratio of bonds to money, the bond market can only remain in equilibrium at the given m if the nominal rate of interest rises by $g_4 D\theta$. This is derived from equation (26). Then, people will be induced to hold the larger bond–money ratio. This means that the $BB'$ curve keeps shifting upwards at rate

$$D\rho \Big|_{m}^{BB'} = g_4 D\theta. \tag{28b}$$

The vertical shift of the $IS$ curve less the shift of the $BB'$ curve per unit of time is

$$(D\rho^{IS} - D\rho^{BB'}) \Big|_{m} = \frac{E_\theta + g_4 E_\rho}{-E_\rho} \equiv \frac{P_5}{(-E_\rho)}, \tag{28c}$$

where $P_5$ is the partial derivative in the price change equation (21a), and $(-E_\rho)$ is positive.

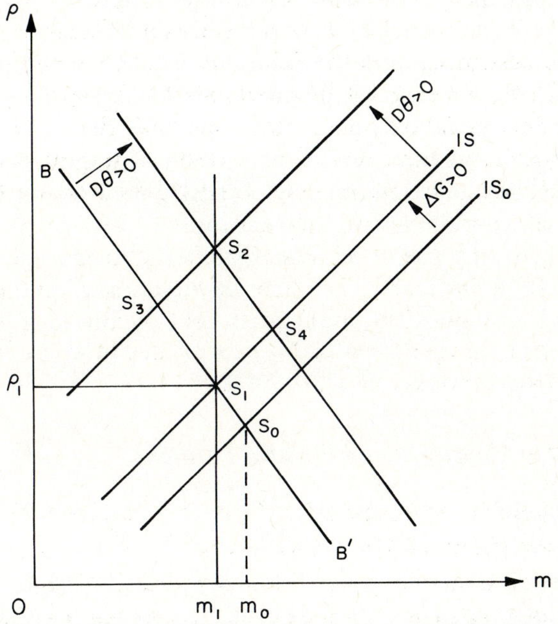


FIGURE 1. The rise in the level of government purchases from $G$ to $G + \Delta G$ raises the $IS$ curve from $IS_0$ to $IS$. The growth of the interest bearing debt at rate $D\theta$ (given the rate of monetary expansion) shifts both the $IS$ and $BB'$ curves upwards per unit of time. Monetarists claim that the locus of intersection is in the northerly ($S_1 S_2$) or north-easterly direction ($S_1 S_4$), whereas fiscalists claim it is in the north-westerly direction ($S_1 S_3$).

A heuristic account of the monetarist position can be given using figure 1; and a rigorous analysis is contained in section 3.2. The starting point is that the supply of debt and the debt–money ratio are rising. To derive *monetarist* results, assume that $P_5$ is non-positive: the *IS* curve shifts upwards by *no more than* the $BB'$ curve. Suppose $P_5$ were zero so that both curves rose by the same amount per unit of time. The economy would be moving along line $S_1 S_2$. The interest rate would rise by just enough to crowd out enough investment so that (given $M/K$, i.e., if $\mu = n$) the goods market could remain in equilibrium at the same price level. Real balances per unit of capital could remain at $m_1$. This means that the real wage could remain unchanged, and the tax cut per se would not reduce the unemployment rate.

If $P_5$ were negative, then the $BB'$ curve would be rising relative to the *IS* curve. The economy would be travelling in a north-east direction such as $S_1 S_4$. To be sure the interest rate would be rising; but the market for goods could only remain in equilibrium if real balances per unit of capital were higher. This means that (given $M/K$) the price level would have to fall. As a consequence, the real wage would rise; and the unemployment rate would rise temporarily.

A *fiscalist* result would be obtained if $P_5$ were positive. The *IS* curve would be shifting up relative to the $BB'$ curve; and the economy would be moving in the north-west direction $S_1 S_3$. Equilibrium in the goods market could only prevail if real balances per unit of capital declined. The price level rises and reduces the value of $m$. But the rise in the price level reduces the real wage and tends to reduce the level of unemployment temporarily. Fiscal policy would then be temporarily effective in reducing the unemployment rate.

The *IS–LM* framework is only useful on a heuristic level, because too many variables are taken as given: in particular, the unemployment rate and the rate of price change. Section 3.2 examines the monetarist controversy in a rigorous manner.

### *3.2. Dynamic Analysis of the Monetarist and Fiscalist Positions*

#### *3.2.1. The dynamic equations*

Table 2 contains the explicit dynamic model implied by table 1. Equation (29) is the unemployment change equation. It is derived by differentiating (5) with respect to time and then substituting (3a). Coefficient $\beta_1 \equiv F_1 w/A$ is the change in the unemployment rate resulting from a percentage point change in the adjusted real wage $w/A$; and $\beta_2 \equiv -F_2$ which reflects the government purchases of services.

Equation (26) is the differential equation for the rate of price change. It is

TABLE 2
The dynamic macro-economic model.

| | | |
|---|---|---|
| (29) | $DU$ | $= \beta_1 h(U) - \beta_1 \pi + \beta_1 \pi^* - \beta_2 DG_1$ |
| (30) | $D\pi$ | $= \beta_1 P_1 h(U) - (P_1\beta_1 + P_3^* - P_2 b)\pi + (P_1\beta_1 - P_2 b)\pi^* + P_3^*(\mu - n)$ $+ P_4 DG - P_1\beta_2 DG_1 + P_5 D\theta$ |
| (22) | $D\pi^*$ | $= b\pi - b\pi^*$ |

derived by differentiating (21a) with respect to time, and then substituting (29), (22) and (17) in the resulting expression. Coefficient $P_3^* \equiv m\partial P/\partial m$ is a pure number: the change in the rate of price change resulting from a unit percentage change in real balances per unit of capital. Equation (22) is unchanged from table 1.

A simplification of table 2 will be sufficient to explain the analytic differences between the monetarists and the fiscalists. Assume that: (i) the government only purchases goods, not services, so that $G_1 = 0$; (ii) the net impact of price changes is upon real balances per unit of capital, i.e., that $P_1\beta_1 - P_3 b$ is approximately zero. What does that mean? A rise in the rate of price change will raise the expected rate of price change by "$b$" units; and the resulting effect upon the rate of inflation will be $P_2 b$. This is a destabilizing element. On the other hand, a unit rise in the rate of price change lowers the adjusted real wage $w/A$ by one percentage point; and employment is increased by $\beta_1$ units. It is assumed that savings rise by more than investment (i.e., the marginal propensity to save exceeds the marginal propensity to invest); and the rate of price change is reduced by $P_1\beta_1$ units. To simplify the analytic exposition assume that the two effects cancel each other, and only the real balance effect $P_3^*$ remains (iii) linearize $h(U)$ around $h(U_e) = 0$. Define $x_1 \equiv U - U_e$, the deviation of $U$ from its equilibrium value and derive $h(U) = -h'x_1$, where $h' = -h'(U_e) > 0$. Table 3, based upon table 2, will facilitate a graphic analysis of the model summarized in table 1.

If the expected rate of price change were exogenous, rather than described by (22), then the dynamical system would be stable if

$$-(\beta_1 h' + P_3^*) < 0,$$
$$\beta_1 h'(P_3^* - P_1\beta_1) > 0.$$

TABLE 3
A simplified version of the dynamic model.

| | | |
|---|---|---|
| (31) | $Dx_1$ | $= -\beta_1 h' x_1 - \beta_1 \pi + \beta_1 \pi^*$ |
| (32) | $D\pi$ | $= -\beta_1 h' P_1 x_1 - P_3^* \pi + P_3^*(\mu - n) + P_4 DG + P_5 D\theta$ |
| (22) | $D\pi^*$ | $= b\pi - b\pi^*$ |

These conditions will be used in construction of a phase diagram.

Define the $UU'$ curve as the set of $(x_1, \pi)$ associated with a constant unemployment rate ($Dx_1 = 0$). This curve is derived from (31) and is described by

$$\pi = -h'x_1 + \pi^*, \tag{34}$$

$$\partial Dx_1/\partial x_1 = -\beta_1 h' < 0. \tag{34a}$$

The $UU'$ curve drawn in figure 2 is negatively sloped for the following reason. Suppose that the unemployment rate rose to $x_1^*$. What must happen to the rate of price change $\pi$ so that the unemployment rate would remain there? As a result of the rise in the unemployment rate, the growth of the nominal wage would change by $-h'x_1^*$ units. If the rate of price change were constant, the adjusted real wage $w/A(t)$ would decline; and firms would be induced to hire more labor.

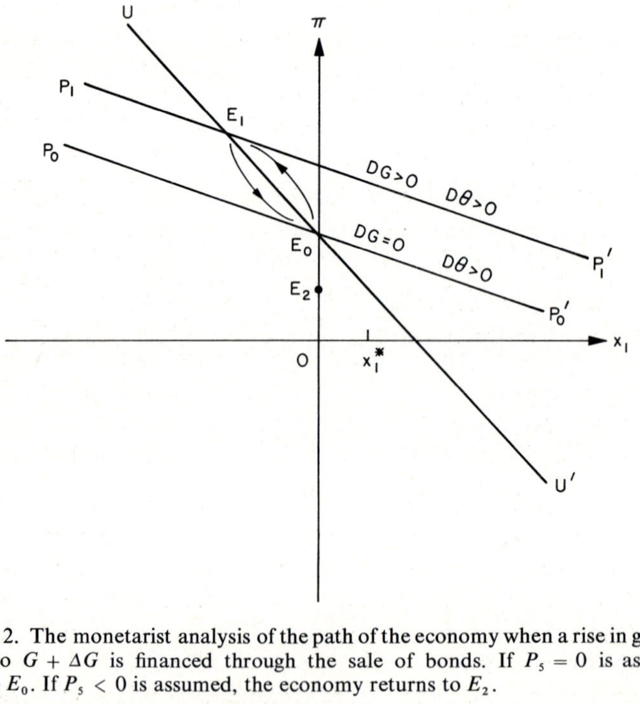


FIGURE 2. The monetarist analysis of the path of the economy when a rise in government purchases from $G$ to $G + \Delta G$ is financed through the sale of bonds. If $P_5 = 0$ is assumed, the economy returns to $E_0$. If $P_5 < 0$ is assumed, the economy returns to $E_2$.

$$UU' = [(x_1, \pi) \mid \pi = -h'x_1 + \pi^*]$$

$$PP' = \left[(x_1, \pi) \mid \pi = \frac{-\beta_1 h' P_1}{P_3^*} x_1 + (\mu - n) + \frac{1}{P_3^*}(P_4 DG + P_5 D\theta)\right].$$

Thereby, the unemployment rate could not remain at $x_1^*$. Only if the rate of price change declined by $h'x_1^*$ units would there by no change in the adjusted real wage so that $x_1$ would remain at $x_1^*$. This argument establishes the negatively sloped $UU'$ curve and inequality (34a). Given the rate of price change, the economy moves horizontally to the $UU'$ curve. Both monetarists and fiscalists could accept the $UU'$ curve; but fiscalists could claim that the rate at which the economy converges to the equilibrium rate of unemployment is too slow to be socially acceptable.

When the actual and expected rates of price change are equal, as must occur in the steady state, the $UU'$ curve will coincide with the ordinate $x_1 = 0$.

Define the $PP'$ curve as the set of $(x_1, \pi)$ associated with a constant rate of price change ($D\pi = 0$). It is derived from (32) by setting $D\pi = 0$; and it is described by

$$\pi = \frac{-\beta_1 h' P_1}{P_3^*} x_1 + (\mu - n) + \frac{1}{P_3^*}[P_4 DG + P_5 D\theta], \tag{35}$$

$$\partial D\pi / \partial\pi = -P_3^* < 0. \tag{35a}$$

The rate of price change tends to move towards the $PP'$ curve in a vertical direction. Why? If the economy were displaced above the $PP'$ curve, the rate of price change would reduce real balances per unit of capital (when $DG = D\theta = 0$). The net effect is to reduce excess aggregate demand; and the rate of price change will be reduced.

The $PP'$ curve could be either positively or negatively sloped, depending upon whether the marginal propensity to save were greater than or less than the marginal propensity to invest. However, the slope of the $PP'$ curve must exceed algebraically the slope of the $UU'$ curve, if stability condition (33b) is to be satisfied.

### *3.2.2. Bond-financed fiscal policy: a monetarist view*

Suppose that: (i) money and debt were initially growing at rate $\mu$, and (ii) then the level of government purchases of goods (*not* services $G_1$) per unit of capital rose smoothly from $G$ to $G + \Delta G = G'$ and remained at the higher level. (iii) Insofar as the higher government expenditures are financed through the sale of bonds, the ratio of interest bearing debt to money must grow steadily. What will be the trajectory of the endogenous variables resulting from the deficit financing?

Monetarist results will be obtained if it is assumed that $P_5$ is non-positive. (iv) Suppose that $P_5$ is zero. When real government purchases per unit of capital are rising ($DG > 0$), the $PP'$ curve will shift upwards from $P_0P_0'$ to $P_1P_1'$, because the intercept term rises from $(\mu - n)$ to $(\mu - n) + (P_4/P_3^*)DG$. At the initial level of unemployment, there is a rise in the excess demand for goods. The rate of price change will rise above $\mu - n$; and the adjusted real wage will consequently decline. As the economy travels along trajectory $E_0E_1$, the unemployment rate declines and the rate of price change rises.

When real government purchases of goods stabilize at the higher level, the $PP'$ curve shifts back to $P_0P_0'$ because the intercept term is again just $\mu - n$. At unemployment rate $x_1 = 0$, a rate of price change in excess of $\mu - n$ would imply a reduction in real balances per unit of capital. Excess aggregate demand would decline and bring the rate of price change back to $\mu - n$. The downward shift of the $PP'$ curve that occurs when $G$ stabilizes induces the economy to follow trajectory $E_1E_0$ back to the original equilibrium $E_0$. The rate of price change will return to $\mu - n$, the adjusted real wage would return to its original level and the unemployment rate will return to $x_1 = 0$ (i.e., $U = U_e$).

What has happened in terms of the $IS$–$BB'$ curves? Equilibrium was initially at $S_0$ with an unemployment rate of $U_e$. The rise in $G$ to $G' = G + \Delta G$ shifts the $IS$ curve from $IS_0$ to $IS$. Real balances per unit of capital decline[14] to $m_1$ and the nominal rate of interest increases. This is the initial effect of a change in the flow demand for goods resulting from a rise in $G$ to $G'$. There is also a wealth effect. When $P_5 = 0$, the government deficits (which imply $D\theta > 0$) shift the $IS$ and $BB'$ curves upwards along $S_1S_2$ at rate,

$$D_\rho = (E_\theta / -E_\rho)D\theta = g_4 D\theta. \tag{36}$$

Nominal interest rates rise at this rate to crowd out an amount of private investment equal to the rise in private consumption, induced by the increase in private wealth. Not change occurs in either the unemployment rate $U_e$ or the equilibrium rate of price change $\pi_e = \mu - n$ (when $P_5 = 0$).

Monetarists have focused upon nominal income $Y_N \equiv pyK = py(U)K$, whereas I have viewed the dynamic process in terms of the unemployment rate and rate of price change. A simple transition can be made from the dynamic analysis (figure 2) to the trajectory of the growth of nominal income (figure 3).

The proportionate rate of change of nominal income $Y_N$ is described by equation (37a) where capital is assumed to be growing at rate $n$, the growth of effective

[14] At the equilibrium $U_e$ and $\pi_e$,

$$\pi_e = \pi_e^* + h(U_e) + \lambda_p E[U_e, \pi_e^*, m, g(U_e, \pi_e^*, m, \theta), G, \theta] = P(U_e, \pi_e^*, m, G, \theta).$$

When $P_5 = 0$, then

$$dm/dG = -P_G/P_m = -E_G/(E_m + E_p g_m) < 0.$$

This describes the movement from $S_0$ to $S_1$ in figure 1.

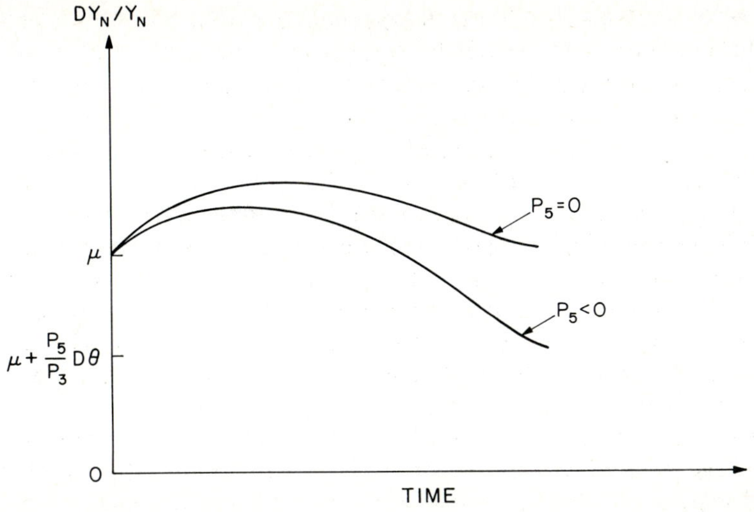


FIGURE 3. The monetarist view of the growth in nominal income, when a rise in government expenditures from $G$ to $G + \Delta G$ is financed through the sale of bonds. When $P_5 = 0$, the growth of nominal income returns to $\mu$. When $P_5 < 0$, the growth of nominal income will be less than $\mu$ (in the steady state).

labor. The phase diagram (figure 2) describes the movement of components $U$ and $\pi$.

$$Y_N \equiv pKy(U), \tag{37}$$

$$\frac{DY_N}{Y_N} = \pi + n + \frac{y'(U)}{y(U)} Dx_1; \qquad y' < 0. \tag{37a}$$

In equilibrium (when $P_5 = 0$), the growth of nominal income will be equal to the rate of monetary expansion $\mu$. Substitute (24) into (37a), and let $Dx_1 = 0$, to derive

$$(DY_N/Y_N)_e = \mu, \quad \text{when} \quad P_5 = 0. \tag{37b}$$

Along trajectory $E_0E_1$ (figure 2), the rate of price change exceeds $\mu - n$ and the unemployment rate is declining. During this phase, nominal income will be rising at a faster rate than $\mu$, the equilibrium rate. When the level of real government purchases of goods per unit of capital stabilizes, then the economy follows trajectory $E_1E_0$ to the original equilibrium. A reverse movement occurs in the growth of nominal income. The rate of price change declines to $\mu - n$; and the unemployment rate rises. At the new equilibrium, nominal income will again grow at rate $\mu$. Figure 3, based upon the phase diagram figure 2, describes the monetarist course of events.

If $P_5$ were negative then, when $G$ levels off, the $PP'$ curve would lie below the $P_0P_0'$ curve drawn in figure 2. The reason is that the new intercept, which is the equilibrium rate of price change, will be

$$\pi_e = \mu - n + \frac{P_5}{P_3^*} D\theta < \mu - n, \quad \text{when} \quad P_5 < 0. \tag{38a}$$

The economy will settle down at an equilibrium point $E_2$. Since the unemployment rate will return to $x_1 = 0$, the equilibrium growth of nominal income is given by

$$(DY_N/Y_N)_e = \mu + \frac{P_5}{P_3^*} D\theta < \mu, \quad \text{when} \quad P_5 < 0. \tag{38b}$$

The trajectory of nominal income is described in figure 3. It starts at $\mu$, rises to a peak when $DG > 0$, and then declines to $\mu + (P_5/P_3^*)D\theta$ when $G$ levels off but the deficits raise $\theta$ steadily.

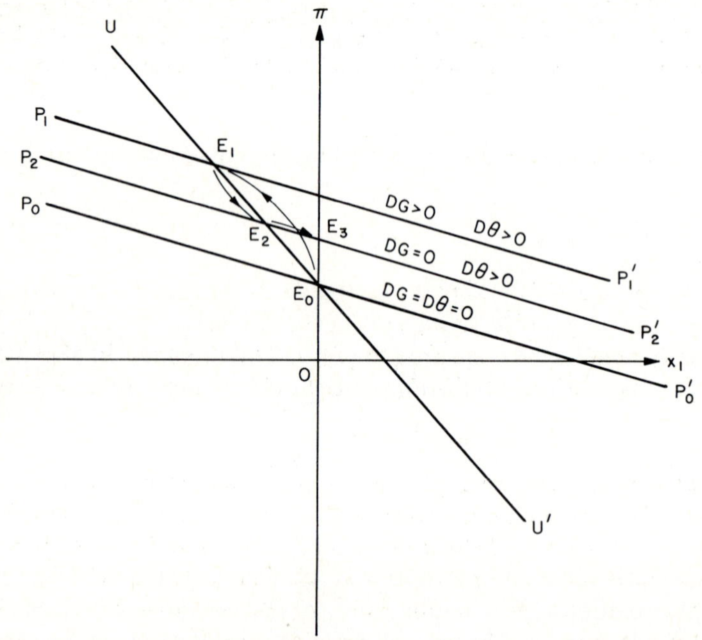


FIGURE 4. The fiscalist (neo-Keynesian) analysis assumes that $P_5 > 0$. The rise in government purchases from $G$ to $G + \Delta G$, financed through the sale of bonds, will drive the economy from $E_0$ to $E_1$ and then to $E_2$ where it will remain until expectations change. The final equilibrium will be at $E_3$.

Monetarist propositions (M-l) have thereby been generated without assuming that the demand for real balances is interest inelastic or that employers and employees have different price perceptions.

### *3.2.3. The Fiscalist Viewpoint*

A fiscalist (i.e., the neo-Keynesian) would make a different forecast of the effects of a higher level of government expenditures which are financed through bond sales. Figures 4 and 5 describe a fiscalist position. In terms of my model, the fiscalist must claim that $P_5$ is positive.

When real government purchases of goods per unit of capital rise ($DG > 0$), and are financed through the sale of bonds, the $PP'$ curve shifts upwards to $P_1P_1'$ from $P_0P_0'$ (figure 4). The intercept rises from $\mu - n$ to $(\mu - n) + (1/P_3^*)(P_4DG + P_5D\theta)$; and the economy follows trajectory $E_0E_1$. The story is the same as was told in connection with the monetarist analysis.

What happens when $G$ levels off, but the debt-money ratio continues to rise? Here the accounts differ significantly. The $PP'$ curve shifts down to $P_2P_2'$ because the intercept term declines to $\mu - n + (P_5/P_3^*)D\theta > \mu - n$; but it lies above the original $P_0P_0'$ curve. The economy follows trajectory $E_1E_2$. The rate of price

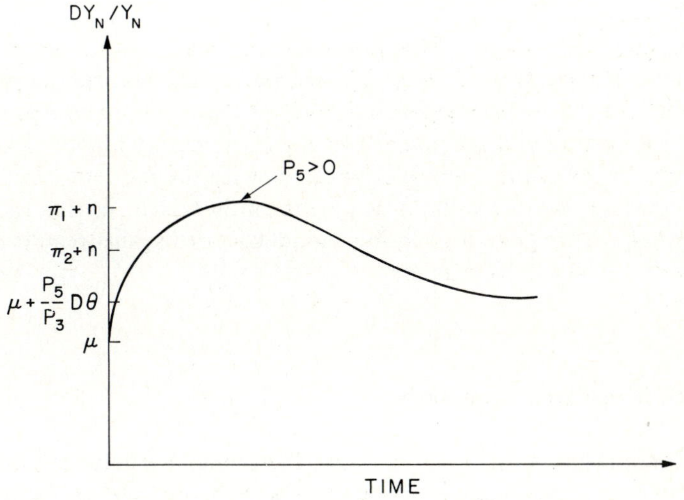


FIGURE 5. The fiscalist (neo-Keynesian) view of the growth in nominal income, when a rise in government expenditures from $G$ to $G + \Delta G$ is financed through the sale of bonds. When the expected rate of price change catches up to the actual, the equilibrium growth of nominal income will exceed the rate of monetary expansion. Since it is assumed that $P_5 > 0$, the growth of nominal income will be permanently raised.

change recedes from its peak (at $E_1$ where $\pi = \pi_1$); and the unemployment rate rises. Eventually, the unemployment rate will return to $x_1 = 0$, when the expected rate of price change $\pi^*$ catches up to $\pi$; and the economy will follow trajectory $E_2E_3$. However, this convergence will take a long time. Insofar as the short run is concerned (say, two to three years), trajectory $E_0E_1E_2$ is relevant. The rise in real government purchases of goods is associated with a decline in the unemployment rate and a rise in the rate of price change.

Fiscalists maintain that a rise in real government purchases of goods will lead to a higher growth of nominal income, even if the expenditures are financed through the sale of bonds. This result is obtained in the following manner. The equilibrium growth of nominal income is (39), using (24) and (37a). At $E_0$, nominal income will grow at rate $\mu$; but at $E_3$ it will grow at rate $\mu + (P_5/P_3^*)D\theta > \mu$.

$$(DY_N/Y_N)_e = \{\mu - n + (P_5/P_3^*)D\theta\} + n = \mu + (P_5/P_3^*)D\theta > \mu. \tag{39}$$

The growth of nominal income is described in figure 5, based upon figure 4 and (39). The maximum growth of nominal income occurs as the economy travels along trajectory $E_0E_1$, where the rate of price change rises to a maximum and unemployment is declining. A long time may be spent near $E_2$ (where $\pi = \pi_2$) along trajectory $E_1E_2$, if expectations change slowly. Nominal income will grow at rate $\pi_2 + n$ in the neighborhood of $E_2$.

The fiscalist conclusion is that: a rise in the level of real government purchases of goods per unit of capital, from $G$ to $G'$, will permanently raise the growth of nominal income from its initial level $\mu$ to $\mu + (P_5/P_3^*)D\theta$. There will be an intervening period where nominal income grows at a significantly higher rate, during the $E_0E_1$ stretch, for example. This is at variance with the monetarist claim that the growth of nominal income will not be permanently raised. Within the framework of my model, I have generated either monetarist or fiscalist results depending upon the value of the $P_5$ coefficient.

## 4. A Test of the Monetarist Hypothesis

In the two preceding parts I have argued that the crucial monetarist proposition is that $P_5 \leqq 0$: a rise in the growth of the interest bearing debt will shift the *IS* curve up by no more than it shifts the $BB'$ curve upwards. The next question is one of fact: is this crucial monetarist proposition consistent with the data? A test of the monetarist hypothesis is formulated in section 4.1; and the evidence is evaluated in the remaining sections.

### *4.1. Formulation of a Statistical Hypothesis*

The dynamical system described by table 2 can be written as a vector-matrix differential equation (40). Vector $X$ refers to the state variables $x_1, \pi, \pi^*$, and vector $C$ refers to the controls $DG_1$, $DG$, $\mu$, $D\theta$,

$$DX(t) = AX(t) + BC(t). \tag{40}$$

My ultimate objective is to estimate matrices $A$ and $B$, so that optimal controls could be formulated.[15] Unfortunately, the results of such an estimation were not clear cut,[16] so I had to work with the solution of the system – equation (41). Time $t - \delta$ is an arbitrary earlier time period, where $\delta$ is an arbitrary constant. I selected an interval $\delta$ of three quarters so that I am sufficiently distant from the date of prediction so as to make it challenging.

$$X(t) = \mathrm{e}^{A\delta} X(t - \delta) + \int_{t-\delta}^{t} \mathrm{e}^{A(t-T)} BC(T)\mathrm{d}T. \tag{41}$$

The state $X(t)$ depends upon its value at $t - \delta$ and the entire pattern of control inputs that were applied from that date until the present.[17]

State variables $U(t)$, $\pi(t)$ refer to a given quarter and $U(t - 3)$, $\pi(t - 3)$ refer to their respective values three quarters earlier. The rate of price change $\pi(t)$ refers to the percentage change of the *GNP* deflator between the current quarter and the same quarter in the previous year. All changes refer to corresponding quarters. This method of measurement gives a much smoother series than would be derived from using consecutive quarters with seasonally adjusted data. A dynamical system such as (40) will generally exhibit smooth movements in the state variable (e.g., room temperature) even though there are erratic movements in the control variable (e.g., thermostat settings). Equation (41) should make this point clear. During the 16 quarters from 1967.I through 1970.IV, the mean rate of price change was 4.35 percent per year between corresponding quarters with a standard deviation of 0.76. If consecutive quarters are used (all data are seasonally adjusted), the mean rate of price change was 4.37 percent per year, but the standard deviation was 0.87 percent. In this example, the use of consecutive quarters increased the standard deviation by 14 percent. These results led me to use price changes between corresponding quarters for $\pi$, $DG$, $\mu$ and $DZ/Z$.

[15] See the author and Infante (1973) for a derivation of control laws when there are no explicit costs of control.

[16] The coefficients had the correct signs, but several crucial ones were not significant. It is easier to estimate the coefficients of an integral [in equation (41)] than the coefficients of derivatives [in equation (40)].

[17] This is the theoretical meaning of a lag structure.

Private spending decisions are described by the consumption and investment functions. Therefore, the government sector must contain all three levels of government. Variable $G$ refers to real federal, state and local purchases of goods and services (in 1958 prices) in a given quarter, divided by the civilian labor force for the entire year. The civilian labor force was used to adjust for growth because appropriate measurements of capital are not available. To calculate $DG$, the change in $G$ between corresponding quarters was used.

Variable $\mu$ refers to the percentage change in currency plus demand deposits between corresponding quarters. Money includes both highpowered money and inside money. This departure from the assumption made in the model, that all money is highpowered, will make the empirical work vulnerable to the well-known criticism that control $\mu$ may not be independent of the state variable $X(t - \delta)$. I see no way to resolve this criticism: what is exogenous and what is endogenous? This caveat should be kept in mind in interpreting the statistical results.

Let the growth of the interest bearing debt of the federal government held by private investors $DZ/Z$ (exclude the debt held by government accounts and the federal reserve banks) be denoted by $\gamma$. Variable $\gamma$ replaces $D\theta$, but they are linked by the identity

$$D\theta/\theta \equiv DZ/Z - DM/M \equiv \gamma - \mu.$$

Variable $\gamma$ refers to the percentage change between corresponding quarters.

Suppose that the values of the controls change at $\ldots T, T + \delta, T + 2\delta, \ldots$ and are constant during the open interval $(t - \delta, t)$. Denote the value of the control input during this interval by $C(t - \delta)$. Suppose that observations of the state variables are taken at $\ldots T, T + \delta, T + 2\delta, \ldots$ Then a linear sampled data system is derived, whose solution is given by (42). Let matrix $A^*$ refer to $e^{A\delta}$ and matrix $B^*$ refer to the term in brackets. Since the sample period of length $\delta$ is given and matrices $A$ and $B$ are assumed to be constant, matrices $A^*$ and $B^*$ will be constant. Equation (43) is derived.

$$X(t) = e^{A\delta}\ X(t - \delta) + \left(\int_{t-\delta}^{t} e^{A(t-T)}\, B\, dT\right) C(t - \delta), \tag{42}$$

$$X(t) = A^*\, X(t - \delta) + B^*\, C(t - \delta). \tag{43}$$

The assumption in (42) was that the control variable $C(t - \delta)$ was constant during the interval from $t - \delta$ to $t$. For this reason, I used moving averages of the control inputs during the preceding $\delta = 3$ quarters rather than three observations per control variable. I defined vector

$$C(t - \delta) \equiv \tfrac{1}{3}[C(t - 1) + C(t - 2) + C(t - 3)]$$

as the relatively constant control input. In other words, I want to say that the average rate of monetary expansion $\mu(t - \delta)$, the average rate of change of the interest bearing debt $\gamma(t - \delta)$ and the average change in real government purchases of goods and services per member of the civilian labor force $DG(t - \delta)$ during the previous three quarters are the relevant policy inputs into the system.

Assume that $G_1$ is a relatively fixed fraction of $G$, so that the distinction between the government's purchases of goods and its purchases of services can be eliminated.

Any method of deriving the expected rate of price change is arbitrary and $\pi^*(t)$ will be highly correlated with $\pi(t)$. A serious multicollinearity problem will arise. I dropped $\pi^*(t)$ as a state variable in my estimation procedure. My state variables in (43) are $U$ and $\pi$, and my control variables are $DG(t - \delta)$, $\mu(t - \delta)$, $\gamma(t - \delta)$.

The unemployment and price change equations implied by (43) are equations (44) and (45), respectively. $R_{10}$ and $R_{20}$ are constants; and $j_1(t)$, $j_2(t)$ are expected to be autocorrelated disturbance terms. The $j_i(t)$ terms reflect the real disturbances impinging upon an economic system which do not stem directly from fiscal or monetary policy; and these disturbances would be serially correlated. The international sector has been neglected. Disturbances in the export demand or import supply, arising from exchange rate variations or from foreign price level movements, which are not directly correlated with the control $C(t - \delta)$, will be autocorrelated components of $j(t)$.

$$U(t) = R_{10} + R_{11}\, U(t - 3) + R_{12}\, \pi(t - 3) + S_{11} DG(t - \delta) + S_{12}\, \mu(t - \delta) + S_{13}\, \gamma(t - \delta) + j_1(t), \tag{44}$$

$$\pi(t) = R_{20} + R_{21}\, U(t - 3) + R_{22}\, \pi(t - 3) + S_{21} DG(t - \delta) + S_{22}\, \mu(t - \delta) + S_{23}\, \gamma(t - \delta) + j_2(t). \tag{45}$$

The monetarist hypothesis is that the growth of the interest bearing debt shifts up the $BB'$ curve by at least as much as it shifts the $IS$ curve upwards, so that this policy is *not* expansive. In terms of figure 2, a rise in $\gamma$ (i.e., $D\theta$) will either lower the $PP'$ curve or keep it constant. Therefore, the unemployment rate will not decline and rate of price change will not rise.

The empirical counterparts of $P_5 \leqq 0$ are

$$\partial U(t)/\partial \gamma(t - \delta) = S_{13} \geqq 0, \tag{46a}$$

$$\partial \pi(t)/\partial \gamma(t - \delta) = S_{23} \leqq 0. \tag{46b}$$

Is this monetarist hypothesis consistent with the data? What is the best way to test the hypothesis that $P_5$ is non-positive is a difficult econometric problem. To what extent are $C(t-3)$ and $\{U(t-3), \pi(t-3)\}$ independent of each other? The money supply is not truly exogenous, but I treat $\mu(t)$ as if it were independent of the earlier unemployment and inflation rates. My econometric procedure contains many flaws and is amenable to the severe criticism that I just raised. Moreover, the expected rate of price change remains elusive. I hope it will stimulate others to develop better estimates. Nevertheless, can we agree that: the fiscalists (neo-Keynesians) claim that $S_{13} < 0$, $S_{23} > 0$ and the monetarists claim that $S_{13} \geqq 0$, $S_{23} \leqq 0$?

This is my response to James Tobin's (1972) intellectual challenge:

> If the monetarists and neo-Keynesians could agree as to which values of which parameters in which behavior relations imply which policy conclusions, then they could concentrate on the evidence regarding the values of those parameters.

With many caveats in mind, let us look at the data.

### *4.2. The Effects of the Control Variables upon the State Variables*

Table 4 contains the parameter estimates of the unemployment rate equation (44), and table 5 refers to the price change equation (45). The fiscalist hypothesis is that: (a) the unemployment rate is negatively related to the growth of the debt, and (b) the rate of price change is positively related to the growth of the debt. Monetarists reject this hypothesis.

Each table refers to the entire period 1960.IV–1973.IV and to a subperiod.[18] There is a significant amount of autocorrelation of the residuals from the regression equations based upon the original data, so that the standard errors do not have their usual meanings. For this reason, the variables (denoted generically by) $Y(t)$ were transformed to $Y(t) - \rho Y(t-1)$, where $\rho$ is the relevant autocorrelation coefficient; and the parameters were re-estimated. The "$t$" statistics are given in parentheses.

The equations based upon the original and transformed variables yield relatively similar results insofar as the hypothesis is concerned. In each case, the monetarist hypothesis (46a), (46b) is not inconsistent with the data. If taxes are reduced and the resulting deficit is financed through the sale of bonds, the rate of price change will not be increased and the unemployment rate will not be decreased. Were the deficit to be financed by a rise in the rate of monetary expan-

[18] These regressions were used to predict outside the sample period and also give us an idea of how things changed during the "stagflation" period.

TABLE 4
The unemployment rate equation (44).

| | 1960.IV–1970.IV | | | | 1960.IV–1973.IV | | | |
|---|---|---|---|---|---|---|---|---|
| $U(t)$ on: | Original (1) | | Transformed (2) | | Original (3) | | Transformed (4) | |
| Constant $R_{10}$ | 4.8 | (6.0) | 5.5 | (6.0) | 3.4 | (5.3) | 4.1 | (5.8) |
| $U(t-3)$ $R_{11}$ | 0.27 | (2.4) | 0.16 | (1.2) | 0.48 | (5.1) | 0.34 | (3.3) |
| $\pi(t-3)$ $R_{12}$ | 0.095 | (1.2) | −0.06 | (−0.6) | 0.16 | (2.6) | 0.05 | (0.6) |
| $DG(t-\delta)$ $S_{11}$ | −0.005 | (−5.0) | −0.005 | (−3.8) | −0.005 | (−5.3) | −0.004 | (−3.3) |
| $\mu(t-\delta)$ $S_{12}$ | −0.39 | (−9.0) | −0.32 | (−6.0) | −0.3 | (−7.6) | −0.24 | (−5.2) |
| $\gamma(t-\delta)$ $S_{13}$ | 0.11 | (2.5) | 0.05 | (1.0) | 0.15 | (3.4) | 0.09 | (2.1) |
| Stand. error | 0.34 | | 0.23 | | 0.36 | | 0.23 | |
| $R^2$ | 0.91 | | 0.71 | | 0.89 | | 0.6 | |
| Durbin–Watson | 0.62 | | 1.2 | | 0.5 | | 1.0 | |

*Source:* See appendix for data.

TABLE 5
The rate of price change equation (45).

| | 1960.IV–1970.IV | | | | 1960.IV–1973.IV | | | |
|---|---|---|---|---|---|---|---|---|
| $\pi(t)$ on: | Original | | Transformed | | Original | | Transformed | |
| Constant $R_{20}$ | 1.9 | (2.8) | 2.0 | (2.3) | 3.3 | (2.6) | 1.0 | (−0.5) |
| $U(t-3)$ $R_{21}$ | −0.29 | (−3.1) | −0.3 | (−2.4) | −0.49 | (−2.6) | −0.34 | (−1.8) |
| $\pi(t-3)$ $R_{22}$ | 0.73 | (10.7) | 0.64 | (6.9) | 0.48 | (4.0) | 0.16 | (0.8) |
| $DG(t-3)$ $S_{21}$ | 0.00 | (0.0) | −0.00 | (−0.3) | −0.003 | (−1.6) | −0.003 | (−1.2) |
| $\mu(t-\delta)$ $S_{22}$ | 0.13 | (3.6) | 0.17 | (3.5) | 0.2 | (2.6) | 0.04 | (0.5) |
| $\gamma(t-\delta)$ $S_{23}$ | −0.06 | (−1.6) | −0.09 | (−1.9) | −0.013 | (−0.15) | −0.16 | (−2.1) |
| Stand. error | 0.28 | | 0.23 | | 0.71 | | 0.38 | |
| $R^2$ | 0.97 | | 0.9 | | 0.82 | | 0.26 | |
| Durbin–Watson | 0.87 | | 1.6 | | 0.37 | | 1.5 | |

*Source:* See appendix for data.

sion, then the rate of price change would increase and the unemployment rate would decline. This effect is highly significant statistically.

According to table 4, the unemployment rate $U$ is negatively related to: (i) the average change in real government purchases of goods and services per member of the civilian labor force $DG(t-\delta)$, and (ii) the average rate of monetary expansion $\mu(t - \delta)$. These results are implied by the model described in table 2, where the government's demand for labor services affects the unemployment rate directly.[19] (iii) The unemployment rate is not negatively related to the growth of the debt.

In table 5, the rate of price change $\pi$ is positively related to the average rate of monetary expansion $\mu(t - \delta)$. However, it is not positively related to $DG(t - \delta)$ or to the average growth of the debt $\gamma(t - \delta)$. In fact, it appears that the growth of the debt raises the $BB'$ curve by more than it raises the $IS$ curve, and thereby exerts a contractionary influence upon the economy. This is seen in both tables 4 and table 5. To be sure, the Durbin–Watson statistics are quite low. Nevertheless, it seems that the monetarist position should be taken seriously. A rise in the growth of the debt does not seem to be expansionary.

A monetarist position that $P_5 = 0$ (but not that $P_5 < 0$) implies that the $\gamma(t - \delta)$ term could be dropped from the regression. Tables 6 and 7 contain the results of the regressions during the periods 1962.IV–1970.IV and 1960.IV–1970.IV, when the growth of the debt term is dropped, i.e., $P_5$ is assumed to be zero. These regressions will be used for predictions outside the sample period and for a closer look at some of the controversies concerning the effects of fiscal policy.

Column 1 in each table exhibits a high degree of autocorrelation of errors from the regression. These variables are then transformed using the relevant autocorrelation coefficient; and the parameter estimates, based upon the transformed variables are given in column 2 of each table. The "$t$" statistics are in

TABLE 6
The unemployment rate equation ($P_5 = 0$).

| | 1962.IV–1970.IV | | | | 1960.IV–1970.IV | |
|---|---|---|---|---|---|---|
| $U(t)$ on: | Original (1) | | Transformed (2) | | Original (3) | |
| Constant | 0.9 | (0.7) | 3.0 | (2.8) | 3.9 | (5.3) |
| $U(t-3)$ | 0.84 | (4.5) | 0.46 | (2.7) | 0.41 | (3.9) |
| $\pi(t-3)$ | 0.35 | (3.1) | 0.15 | (1.5) | 0.12 | (1.3) |
| $DG(t-\delta)$ | −0.002 | (−2.1) | −0.004 | (−3.6) | −0.005 | (1.3) |
| $\mu(t-\delta)$ | −0.24 | (−5.6) | −0.21 | (−4.7) | −0.33 | (−8.8) |
| Stand. error | 0.295 | | 0.185 | | 0.36 | |
| $R^2$ | 0.89 | | 0.79 | | 0.9 | |
| Durbin–Watson | 0.65 | | 1.6 | | 0.5 | |

[19]This result is explained analytically, in connection with the "stagflation" phenomenon, in my 1974 paper and will not be repeated here.

TABLE 7
The price change equation ($P_5 = 0$).

| | 1962.IV–1970.IV | | | | 1960.IV–1970.IV | |
|---|---|---|---|---|---|---|
| $\pi(t)$ on: | Original (1) | | Transformed (2) | | Original (3) | |
| Constant | 2.7 | (2.5) | 2.7 | (2.3) | 2.4 | (4.0) |
| $U(t-3)$ | −0.42 | (−2.6) | −0.42 | (−2.3) | −0.37 | (−4.4) |
| $\pi(t-3)$ | 0.73 | (7.4) | 0.66 | (6.0) | 0.72 | (10.0) |
| $DG(t-\delta)$ | 0.000 | (0.0) | −0.000 | (−0.0) | −0.000 | (−0.6) |
| $\mu(t-\delta)$ | 0.07 | (1.8) | 0.10 | (2.1) | 0.097 | (3.3) |
| Stand. error | 0.258 | | 0.199 | | 0.29 | |
| $R^2$ | 0.97 | | 0.88 | | 0.96 | |
| Durbin–Watson | 0.73 | | 1.65 | | 0.9 | |

parentheses. Column 3 contains the results for the period 1960.IV–1970.IV based upon the original data. These results are similar to those in column 2.

The results are similar to those derived in tables 4 and 5: (a) The unemployment rate is negatively related to the three-quarter moving averages of the control variables $DG(t-\delta)$ and $\mu(t-\delta)$. However, (b) the only control variable which directly affects the rate of price change is $\mu(t-\delta)$, the moving average of the rate of monetary expansion.

### 4.3. *Qualifications, Implications and Reservations Concerning the Quantitative Estimates*

Apparently, the regression coefficients in tables 4–7 are not inconsistent with the monetarist hypothesis, whereas they are inconsistent with the fiscalist hypothesis. How much confidence should be placed in these quantitative estimates? Two criteria are adduced. First, the steady-state solutions implied by tables 4 and 5 are compared with the implications of the model described in table 1. Second, the predictive accuracy of the regression equations is examined outside the sample period.

#### 4.3.1. *Steady-state solutions*

The regression equations (44), (45) and the coefficient estimates cited in tables 4–7 imply the equilibrium rate of unemployment ($U_e$) and rate of price change ($\pi_e$).

There are several different ways to define the equilibrium situation. First, set

$$U(t) = U(t-3) = U_e, \qquad \pi(t) = \pi(t-3) = \pi_e,$$
$$DG(t-\delta) = \gamma(t-\delta) = 0, \qquad \mu(t-\delta) = \mu.$$

This means that the nominal debt and real government purchases per member of the civilian labor force are assumed to be constant. Second, set

$$U(t) = U(t-\delta) = U_e, \qquad \pi(t) = \pi(t-\delta) = \pi_e,$$
$$DG(t-\delta) = 0, \qquad \mu(t-\delta) = \gamma(t-\delta) = \mu.$$

Money and government debt are assumed to be growing at the same rate $\mu$, but real government purchases per member of the civilian labor force are assumed to be constant.

According to the model $h(U_e) = 0$. If $h$ is linearized as $h(U) = h_0 - h_1 U$, then $U_e = h_0/h_1$. The equilibrium rate of price change is described by equation (24),

$$\pi_e = \mu - n + \frac{P_5}{P_3^*} D\theta.$$

Since $D\theta/\theta \equiv \gamma - \mu$, the equilibrium rate of price change can be written as

$$\pi_e = \left(1 - \frac{P_5\theta}{P_3^*}\right)\mu + \left(\frac{P_5\theta}{P_3^*}\gamma - n\right). \tag{47}$$

If $\gamma = 0$, then

$$\pi_e = \left(1 - \frac{P_5\theta}{P_3^*}\right)\mu - n, \tag{47a}$$

whereas if $\gamma = \mu$, then $D\theta = 0$ and

$$\pi_e = \mu - n. \tag{47b}$$

Are these theoretical results consistent with those derived from tables 4 and 5?

Several crucial questions arise. (1) Does the steady-state solution for $U_e$ imply that the equilibrium rate of unemployment is independent of the rate of monetary expansion? (2) Does the derived equilibrium rate of price change ($\pi_e$) satisfy steady-state equation (24)? During the period 1960–1973, real *GNP* grew at 4.2 percent per year. Was

$$\pi_e = \left(1 - \frac{P_5\theta}{P_3^*}\right)\mu + \left(\frac{P_5\theta}{P_3^*}\gamma - 4.2\right)?$$

Since the estimates of $P_5$ are negative, is the coefficient of $\mu$ greater than unity; and is the constant term in parentheses greater than 4.2? (3) What is the relation between the "short-term" impact of changes in the rate of monetary expansion (i.e., $S_{12} \equiv \partial U(t)/\partial\mu(t-\delta)$ and $S_{22} \equiv \partial\pi(t)/\partial\mu(t-\delta)$ when $\gamma = 0$) and the long-run impacts (i.e., $dU_e/d\mu$ and $d\pi_e/d\mu$)? Recall that $\mu(t-\delta)$ is a three quarter moving average of rates of monetary expansion, so that the phrase "short-run" refers to three quarters.

Table 8 summarizes the relevant information and it is based upon tables 4 and 5. Row 1, table 8 is based upon the original data: the regression coefficients contained in column 1 of tables 4 and 5. Row 2, table 8 is based upon the transformed variables: the regression coefficients contained in column 2 of tables 4 and 5.

Each pair of these monetarist equations implies that: (a) there is *no unique* equilibrium rate of unemployment which is independent of monetary and debt management policy. (b) There *need not* be a trade-off between the steady-state rate of unemployment $U_e$ and steady-state rate of price change $\pi_e$. These points can be made in several ways. The equations in table 8 can be written as

$$\begin{bmatrix} U_e - 6 \\ \pi_e \end{bmatrix} = \begin{bmatrix} -0.4 & 0.1 \\ 0.8 & -0.3 \end{bmatrix} \begin{bmatrix} \mu \\ \gamma \end{bmatrix} \tag{48}$$

To be sure, the unemployment rate is negatively related to the growth of the money supply; but it is positively related to the growth of the debt (a strong monetarist result). Since the matrix is of rank 2, it is *mathematically*[20] possible to achieve any $(U_e, \pi_e)$ with the two instruments $\mu$ and $\gamma$. For example, to achieve a five percent equilibrium rate of unemployment with no inflation in the steady-state set $(U_e, \pi_e)$ equal to (5, 0) and solve for the required rate of monetary expansion and growth of the debt. It turns out that the required rate of monetary expansion is 7.7 percent per year; but the interest bearing debt must grow at a phenomenal rate of 21 percent per year. This result taxes my credulity and arises because $P_5$ is negative: the growth of the debt *per se* is deflationary.

The deflationary aspect of the federal debt can be seen by comparing columns 2 and 4 in table 8. If $\mu = 4.8$ percent per year (the rate between 1960 and 1973), but the debt is constant, the steady-state inflation rate is 4.18 percent per year. On the other hand, if both money and debt grow at 4.8 percent per year, the steady-state inflation rate is only 2.74 percent per year. (The rate of inflation between 1960 and 1973 was 3.1 percent per year; and the average unemployment rate was 4.9 percent.)

The results cited in table 8 are consistent with another monetarist proposition: concerning the timing of price and output changes. Milton Friedman wrote:

> If the rate of monetary growth is reduced then about six to nine months later, the rate of growth of nominal income and also of physical output will decline. However, the rate of price rise will be affected very little. . .

[20] The values of the elements in the matrix may not be independent of the values of the control variables $\mu$ and $\gamma$. What is "mathematically" possible may not be economically feasible.

TABLE 8
The steady-state and half-life implications.

| Steady-state equations (1) | $\mu = 4.8$; $\gamma = 0$ (2) | Ratio of short-run to long-run effect $\gamma = 0$; $\frac{S_{12}}{dU_e/d\mu}, \frac{S_{22}}{d\pi_e/d\mu}$ (3) | $\mu = \gamma = 4.8$ (4) | Ratio of short-run to long-run effect $\gamma = \mu$; $\frac{S_{12} + S_{13}}{dU_e/d\mu}, \frac{S_{22} + S_{23}}{d\pi_e/d\mu}$ (5) | Half-life $\gamma = 0$ (6) |
|---|---|---|---|---|---|
| (1) Col. 1, tables 4, 5 | | | | | |
| (a) $U_e = 6.43 - 0.43\mu + 0.09\gamma$ | 4.37 | 0.91 | 4.8 | 0.65 | |
| (b) $\pi_e = 0.87\mu - 0.3\gamma$ | 4.18 | 0.15 | 2.74 | 0.08 | |
| (2) Col. 2, tables 4, 5 | | | | | |
| (a) $U_e = 6.64 - 0.46\mu + 0.11\gamma$ | 4.43 | 0.7 | 4.96 | 0.8 | 1.7 qtrs. ~ 2 qtrs. |
| (b) $\pi_e = 0.86\mu - 0.36\gamma$ | 4.13 | 0.2 | 2.4 | 0.14 | 9.9 qtrs. ~ 10 qtrs. |

*Note:* Col. (1) contains the steady-state equations. Col. (2) contains $U_e$ and $\pi_e$ associated with a constant debt $\gamma = 0$ but a rate of monetary expansion of 4.8 percent per year. Col. (4) contains $U_e$ and $\pi_e$ when $\gamma = \mu = 4.8$ percent per year. Col. (3) contains the ratio of the short-run (3 qtrs.) to the long-run effect of a change in the rate of monetary expansion upon the unemployment rate and rate of price change respectively, when the debt is constant. Col. (5) does the same thing when money and debt are growing at the same rate. Col. (6) contains the half-life of the effect of a change in $\mu$ upon the unemployment rate and rate of price change.

On the average, the effect on prices comes about six to nine months after the effect on income and output, so the total delay between a change in monetary growth and a change in the rate of inflation averages something like 12–18 months. That is why it is a long road to hoe to stop an inflation that has been allowed to start. It cannot be stopped overnight.

Even after allowance for the delay in the effect of monetary growth, the relation is far from perfect. [Friedman (1970, p. 23)]

The short-run effect of a change in the rate of monetary expansion upon the unemployment rate is $S_{12}$ and upon the rate of price change is $S_{22}$, when the debt is constant; and the long-run effect is $\mathrm{d}U_e/\mathrm{d}\mu$ and $\mathrm{d}\pi_e/\mathrm{d}\mu$ upon the unemployment rate and rate of price change respectively. Friedman claimed that the ratio of the short-run effect to the long-run effect is greater for the unemployment rate than for the rate of price change. In terms of my model, Friedman's position is that, when the debt is constant, inequality (49a) is satisfied; when money and debt are growing at the same rate, inequality (49b) is satisfied,

$$\frac{S_{12}}{\mathrm{d}U_e/\mathrm{d}\mu} > \frac{S_{22}}{\mathrm{d}\pi_e/\mathrm{d}\mu}, \tag{49a}$$

$$\frac{S_{12} + S_{13}}{\mathrm{d}U_e/\mathrm{d}\mu} > \frac{S_{22} + S_{23}}{\mathrm{d}\pi_e/\mathrm{d}\mu}. \tag{49b}$$

According to column 3 in table 8, inequality (49a) is satisfied: 0.91 exceeds 0.15 or 0.7 exceeds 0.2. Similarly, according to column 5 in table 8, inequality (49b) is satisfied: 0.65 exceeds 0.08 or 0.8 exceeds 0.14.

There is another way to compare the speeds of response of the unemployment rate and rate of price change to changes in the rate of monetary expansion. Let $X(t)$ be a variable and $X_e$ its steady-state value. If the convergence to equilibrium is exponential, then

$$X(t)/X_e = 1 - \mathrm{e}^{-at}. \tag{50}$$

Under these conditions, we can estimate the speed of response "$a$" and its implied half-life from the data in table 8. Consider the estimates in rows 2a, 2b (based upon the transformed variables) in column 3 when the debt is constant. Then, the unemployment rate equation is

$$U(3)/U_e = 1 - \mathrm{e}^{-3a} = 0.7, \tag{51a}$$

where time is measured in quarters (and $\mu$ was a moving three quarter average). The implied value of "$a$" is 0.4. The half-life $T$ is determined by solving

$$0.5 = \mathrm{e}^{-0.4T}, \tag{51b}$$

and

$$T = 1.73 \text{ quarters or } 5.2 \text{ months.} \tag{51c}$$

The price change equation is

$$\pi(3)/\pi_e = 1 - e^{-3a} = 0.2. \tag{52a}$$

The implied value of "$a$" is 0.07. The half-life $T$ is determined by solving

$$0.5 = e^{-0.07T}, \tag{52b}$$

and

$$T = 9.9 \text{ quarters or } 29.7 \text{ months.} \tag{52c}$$

The half-life for the effect of a change in $\mu$ (rounding) is 2 quarters for the unemployment rate and 10 quarters for the rate of price change. These are not very different from Friedman's results.

A serious source of doubt concerning the validity of the quantitative results concerns the equilibrium rate of price change equation. In no case (row 1b or 2b in table 8) do we get equation (47a) or (47b). The coefficient of $\mu$ (row 1b or 2b) is somewhat below unity, which suggests that $P_5$ is positive! Moreover, the constant term is essentially zero; and that should not occur. These are most troublesome points which lead me to suspend judgment concerning the quantitative estimates.

### *4.3.2. Predictions outside the sample period*

How well can the monetarist equations in table 6 and 7 [which do not contain $\gamma(t - \delta)$ as a variable and hence assume that $P_5 = 0$, such that bond financing shifts the $BB'$ curve vertically by as much as it shifts the $IS$ curve] predict the course of events outside the sample period? Table 9 describes how accurately the unemployment rate was predicted during a span of time 1971.I–1973.IV which lies outside the sample period 1962.IV–1970.IV.

The root mean square error (RMSE) summarized the accuracy of prediction. Two standards of comparison are used. (i) A naive forecast completely disregards the control inputs, and assumes that the state variable is equal to its value three quarters earlier. (ii) The prediction from a regression, using data from the entire period and considering all the control inputs, is the second standard of comparison. Obviously, the prediction within the sample period (col. 5) yields the lowest RMSE, 0.26, which is 46 percent of the RMSE derived from a naive forecast (col. 2) that $U(t) = U(t - 3)$. Columns 3 and 4 contain predictions outside the sample period. They are based upon the regressions in table 6, columns 1 and 2,

TABLE 9
Prediction of the unemployment rate 1971.I–1973.IV.

| | Actual $U(t)$ | Naive $U(t) = U(t-3)$ | Predicted: Original data | Predicted: Transformed variables | Within sample period | $DG(t-\delta)$ | $\mu(t-\delta)$ |
|---|---|---|---|---|---|---|---|
| | (1) | (2) | (3) | (4) | (5) | (6) | (7) |
| 1971.I | 5.97% | 4.83 | 6.13 | 5.75 | 6.16 | −151 | 4.29% p.a. |
| II | 5.97 | 5.24 | 6.16 | 5.67 | 6.15 | −135 | 5.05 |
| III | 6. | 5.8 | 6.42 | 5.64 | 6.14 | −105 | 5.93 |
| IV | 5.93 | 5.97 | 6.23 | 5.37 | 5.95 | −68.3 | 6.81 |
| 1972.I | 5.9 | 5.97 | 6.08 | 5.15 | 5.88 | −31 | 7.11 |
| II | 5.7 | 6 | 5.73 | 4.83 | 5.67 | −1.33 | 7.92 |
| III | 5.6 | 5.93 | 5.09 | 4.41 | 5.25 | 27 | 8.3 |
| IV | 5.3 | 5.9 | 4.88 | 4.24 | 4.92 | 29 | 9.02 |
| 1973.I | 5 | 5.7 | 4.33 | 3.98 | 4.49 | 12 | 9.58 |
| II | 4.9 | 5.6 | 4.33 | 4.05 | 4.5 | −6.33 | 9.4 |
| III | 4.7 | 5.3 | 4.34 | 4.09 | 4.62 | −15.7 | 9.09 |
| IV | 4.7 | 5 | 4.42 | 4.2 | 4.7 | −8.33 | 7.81 |
| RMSE | | 0.57 | 0.39 | 0.75 | 0.26 | | |
| RMSE ÷ RMSE col. 2 | | (1.00) | (0.68) | (1.32) | (0.46) | | |

*Note:* The prediction in col. 3 is based upon table 6, col. 1. The prediction in col. 4 is based upon table 6, col. 2. col. 5 is based upon table 4, col. 3 which contains the 1971.I–1973.IV period and takes account of $y(t-\delta)$. Col. 6 and col. 7 are the control inputs. The root mean square error error (RMSE) is $\left(\frac{1}{n}\sum_{i=1}^{n} e_i^2\right)^{1/2}$; and the figure in parentheses is the ratio of the RMSE to that derived from a naive forecast.

respectively, where the sample period is 1962.IV–1970.IV. When the original data are used to estimate the regression coefficients, then the RMSE is 0.39, which is 68 percent of the error resulting from a naive forecast. When the transformed variables are used to estimate the regression coefficients, the RMSE (0.75) exceeds that resulting from the naive forecast (0.37).

The predicted decline in the unemployment rate during this period, from 6 percent to 4.4 percent is quite accurate; and it is attributed to the rise in real government purchases per member of the civilian labor force and to the rise in the rate of monetary expansion. Both monetary policy and the path of real government purchases were expansionary.

TABLE 10
Prediction of the rate of price change 1971.I–1973.IV based upon regression equation (45).

| | Actual $\pi(t)$ (1) | Naive $\pi(t) = \pi(t-3)$ (2) | Predicted Original data (3) | Predicted Transformed variables (4) | Predicted Within period (5) | $\mu(t-\delta)$ (6) |
|---|---|---|---|---|---|---|
| 1971.I | 5.17% p.a. | 5.31 | 4.83 | 4.66 | 4.79 | 4.29 |
| II | 5.18 | 5.06 | 4.52 | 4.4 | 4.56 | 5.05 |
| III | 4.89 | 5.26 | 4.49 | 4.39 | 4.47 | 5.93 |
| IV | 3.65 | 5.17 | 4.41 | 4.34 | 4.39 | 6.81 |
| 1972.I | 3.66 | 5.18 | 4.44 | 4.38 | 4.33 | 7.11 |
| II | 2.84 | 4.89 | 4.27 | 4.26 | 4.23 | 7.92 |
| III | 2.83 | 3.65 | 3.42 | 3.51 | 3.65 | 8.3 |
| IV | 3.3 | 3.66 | 3.48 | 3.6 | 3.82 | 9.02 |
| 1973.I | 3.4 | 2.84 | 3 | 3.2 | 3.69 | 9.58 |
| II | 4.8 | 2.83 | 3.03 | 3.22 | 3.76 | 9.4 |
| III | 5.9 | 3.3 | 3.48 | 3.62 | 4.09 | 9.1 |
| IV | 7.1 | 3.4 | 3.59 | 3.68 | 4.02 | 7.8 |
| RMSE | | 1.69 (1.0) | 1.47 (0.87) | 1.41 (0.83) | 1.24 (0.73) | |

*Note:* Prediction in col. 3 is based upon the regression in table 7, col. 1; prediction in col. 4 is based upon the regression in table 7, col. 2. The prediction in col. 5 is based upon the regression in table 5, col. 3 which covers the entire period and uses all the control variables. RMSE is described in the note to table 9.

Table 10, which predicts the rate of price change outside the sample period, is similar to table 9; and it is based upon table 7, cols. 1–3. There is no doubt that it was difficult to predict the rate or price change during the periods of the administered price freeze, the subsequent administered thaws and the freeing of the exchange rate. The high RMSE in table 10, relative to those in table 9, demonstrate this point.

Arthur Burns invoked five ad hoc factors to account for the upsurge of the price level:

> The extraordinary upsurge of the price level this year reflects a variety of special influences. First, there has been a world-wide economic boom superimposed on the boom in the United States. Second, we have encountered critical shortages of basic materials. . . . Third, farm product prices escalated strongly as a result of crop failures in many countries last year. Fourth, fuel

prices spurted upwards. . . . And fifth, the depreciation of the dollar in foreign exchange markets has served to boost prices of imported goods and to add to the demands pressing on our productive resources. [Burns (1973, p. 21)]

On scientific grounds, ad hoc reasons are to be deprecated but the predictions in table 10 based upon regression equation (45) are unsatisfactory. The reason for this failure may not lie in the ad hoc reasons cited above. The source of the trouble is that: the underprediction of the inflation at the end of 1973 resulted because the $\pi(t-3)$ terms in the prediction equation (45) reflect the administered control situation during 1972 rather than free market conditions. Errors of prediction occurred because we were forced to use incorrect data for the initial conditions.

A more sensible method of prediction would be as follows. First, determine what would have been the steady-state rate of price change $\pi_e$ had there been no administrative controls. Second, we have an estimate of the speed of convergence of the rate of price change to its steady-state value. Third, use initial conditions prevailing prior to the price freeze. In this manner, we can predict the rate of price change and the price level. This method in general is inferior to regression equation (45) because it ignores $U(t-3)$, $\pi(t-3)$, $DG(t-\delta)$; however, it is essential to avoid using fictitious values for $\pi(t-3)$.

Table 8 (col. 1; rows 1b and 2b) indicates that the steady-state derivative $d\pi_e/d\mu$ ranges from 0.5 to 0.9, depending on whether $\gamma = \mu$ or $\gamma$ is independent of $\mu$. Suppose that we use a midpoint estimate of 0.7. Then

$$d\pi_e = 0.7\ d\mu \tag{53a}$$

is used to track the steady-state rate of price change.

This means that

$$\pi_e(t_1) = \pi_e(t_0) + 0.7\,[\mu(t_1) - \mu(t_0)], \tag{53b}$$

where $\pi_e(t)$ is the steady-state corresponding to $\mu(t)$. We do not know $\pi_e$, because I do not believe that the constant term in table 8, col. 1, rows 1b and 2b, is zero. Instead, I shall assume that the rate of price change in 1960, denoted by $\pi(60) = 1.5\%$ p.a., was a steady-state rate corresponding to the actual rate of monetary expansion $\mu(60 = 0.6\%$ p.a. Then the equilibrium rate of price change at any time $\pi_e(t)$ corresponding to the observed rate of monetary expansion is

$$\pi_e(t) = \pi_e(60) + 0.7\,[\mu(t) - \mu(60)] = 1.5 + 0.7\,[\mu(t) - 0.6]. \tag{53c}$$

Table 11 refers to year-to-year changes in the *GNP* deflator and the money supply for the period 1961–1973. In column 2, the steady-state rate of price change $\pi_e(t)$ is calculated corresponding to the value of $\mu(t)$. For example, the money

TABLE 11
Prediction of the inflation rate and *GNP* price deflator, 1961–1973.

| | Rate of monetary expansion $\mu$ (1) | Implied steady-state inflation $\pi_e$ (2) | Predicted rate of inflation $\pi'$ (3) | Official rate of inflation $\pi$ (4) | Predicted price level $p'$ (5) | Official price level $p$ (6) |
|---|---|---|---|---|---|---|
| 1961 | 3.1% p.a. | 3.25% p.a. | | 1.3% p.a. | | 104.62 |
| 1962 | 1.5 | 2.13 | 1.5 | 1.1 | 106.2 | 105.8 |
| 1963 | 3.7 | 3.67 | 1.7 | 1.3 | 108 | 107.2 |
| 1964 | 4.6 | 4.3 | 2.0 | 1.6 | 110.2 | 108.9 |
| 1965 | 4.6 | 4.3 | 2.3 | 1.8 | 112.7 | 110.9 |
| 1966 | 2.4 | 2.76 | 2.0 | 2.8 | 114.9 | 113.9 |
| 1967 | 6.6 | 5.7 | 3.5 | 3.2 | 119 | 117.6 |
| 1968 | 7.8 | 6.54 | 4.0 | 4.0 | 123.7 | 122.3 |
| 1969 | 3.5 | 3.53 | 3.9 | 4.8 | 128.6 | 128.2 |
| 1970 | 6 | 5.28 | 4.9 | 5.5 | 134.9 | 135.2 |
| 1971 | 6.3 | 5.49 | 5.5 | 4.7 | 142.3 | 141.6 |
| 1972 | 8.7 | 7.17 | 5.9 | 3.2 | 150.7 | 146.1 |
| 1973 | 5.7 | 5.07 | 5.7 | 5.3 | 159.3 | 153.9 |

*Note:* Data were taken from the 1974 Report of the Council of Economic Advisers. Col. 2 is $\pi_e(t) = 1.5 + 0.7\,[\mu(t) - 0.6]$. Col. 3 is $\pi'(t_1) = \pi(t_0) + 0.244\,[\pi_e(t_1) - \pi(t_0)]$ for 1961–1971, and $\pi'(t_0) + 0.244\,[\pi_e(t_1) - \pi'(t_0)]$ for 1972 and 1973. Col. 5 is $p'(t_1) = p'(t_0)[1 + \pi'(t_1)]$.

supply grew by 8.7 percent from 1971 to 1972. Hence,

$$\pi_e(72) = 1.5 + 0.7\,(8.7 - 0.6) = 7.17\%\ \text{p.a.}$$

Use the estimated speed of response $a = 0.07$ derived in equation (52a). Then during a period of one year (four quarters), the initial rate of price change will have traversed 24.4% ($= 1 - e^{-0.07t}$, where $t = 4$ quarters) of the gap to the new steady state. For example, the rate of price change in 1966 was 2.8% p.a. The 1967 steady-state rate was 5.7% p.a. The predicted 1967 rate of price change, denoted by $\pi'$, is

$$\pi'(t_1) = \pi(t_0) + 0.244\,[\pi_e(t_1) - \pi(t_0)], \tag{53d}$$

$$\pi'(67) = 2.8 + 0.244\,(5.67 - 2.8) = 3.5\%\ \text{p.a.}$$

These predicted values assume that the official rates of price change $\pi(t_0)$ are free market rates of price change. Prices were frozen from August 15, 1971; therefore, for 1972 and 1973, I use the previously predicted rate of price change $\pi'(t_0)$ instead of the actual rate $\pi(t_0)$. For example, the predicted 1972 rate of price change was $\pi'(72) = 5.9\%$, whereas the officially reported rate of price change was 3.2% p.a. To predict the 1973 rate of inflation, I used

$$\begin{aligned}\pi'(73) &= \pi'(72) + 0.244\left[\pi_e(73) - \pi'(72)\right] = 5.9 + 0.244(5.07 - 5.9)\\ &= 5.9 + 0.244\,(5.07 - 5.9) = 5.7. \end{aligned} \tag{53e}$$

The predicted inflation rate for 1973 was 5.7% p.a. and the actual rate was 5.3% p.a. Column 3 contains the predicted rate of inflation; and column 4 of table 11 contains the official rate of inflation. Column 5 contains the predicted price level $p'(t_1)$, where

$$p'(t_1) = p'(t_0)\left[1 + \pi'(t_1)\right]. \tag{53f}$$

For example, the price level (*GNP* deflator) in 1961 was 104.62 and the predicted inflation rate for 1962 was 1.5 percent. Consequently, the predicted 1962 price level is 104.62 (1 + 0.015) = 106.19. The predicted price level for 1963 is 106.19 (1 + 0.017) = 108, etc. Column 6 contains the actual price level.

The Council of Economic Advisers wrote in their 1974 Report on p. 65:

> There is no simple explanation for the price behavior which was the most extraordinary in almost a generation and which confounded the Council and most economists.

Table 11 suggests that this statement is not justified; and there may well be some explanatory power to the simple model presented above. The predicted rate of inflation in 1973 was quite close to the actual rate. However, an upsurge in inflation is expected to bring the official price level up to the predicted price level. In 1972 the price index was 146.1 and the predicted price index was 159.3. A nine percent rate of inflation was required to correct for the controls during the previous few years and to take account of the 1973 rate of monetary expansion. My conclusion is that the acceleration of the inflation at the end of 1973 was a reflection of the gap between the official price index and the one that would be generated by a free market economy.

If the 1974 rate of monetary expansion is 7% p.a., then the predicted price index for 1974 is 168.49, and the observed inflation rate should be 9.5 per cent. The derivation is as follows:

$$\pi_e(74) = 1.5 + 0.7\,(7 - 0.6) = 5.98 \tag{54a}$$

is the steady-state rate of price change corresponding to a 7% p.a. rate of monetary expansion. The predicted *free market* rate of inflation is

$$\begin{aligned}\pi'(74) &= \pi'(73) + 0.244\left[5.98 - \pi'(73)\right]\\ &= 5.7 + 0.244\,(5.98 - 5.7) = 5.77. \end{aligned} \tag{54b}$$

Therefore, the predicted *GNP* deflator is

$$p'(74) = p'(73)\left[1 + \pi'(74)\right]$$
$$= 159.3\,(1 + 0.057) = 168.49. \tag{54c}$$

The *official* 1973 price level is 153.9. If there are no controls, the price level will rise to the predicted level of 168.49; and the *observed* rate of inflation in 1974 should be 9.5 percent. No ad hoc reasons were adduced in making this prediction.

### 4.4. *Conclusions: The Efficacy of the 1964 Tax Reduction*

This essay has been concerned with several issues. (1) Can a general but simple model be formulated which could imply either monetarist or fiscalist results? (2) What are the crucial parameters which distinguish between the two models? (3) What inferences can be drawn from the data concerning the values of these parameters, and how accurately can the unemployment rate and inflation rate be predicted? An analysis of the controversy between Arthur Okun and Milton Friedman, concerning the efficacy of the 1964 tax cut, will effectively summarize the contributions in this essay.

Okun wrote:

> The stimulus of tax reduction dominated the economic scene in 1964 and the first half of 1965. The unemployment rate which had been fluctuating aimlessly in the range between $5\frac{1}{2}$ and 6 percent all during 1962 and 1963, fell to five percent during the course of 1964 and declined further to 4.7 percent during the Spring of 1965. [Okun (1970, p. 47)]
>
> The heavy reliance on tax cuts, rather than expenditure increases, in providing fiscal stimulus was a particularly interesting feature of the period. [ibid., p. 52]

Friedman was unconvinced that fiscal policy, in the form of a bond-financed tax reduction, was responsible for the economic expansion:

> . . . So far as I know, there has been no empirical demonstration that the tax cut had any effect on the flow of income in the U.S. There has been no demonstration that if monetary policies had been maintained unchanged . . . the tax cut would have been really expansionary on nominal income. [Friedman (1969, p. 55)]

Okun replied that Friedman confused cause and effect: his reply crystallized the difference between their points of view:

> Both preceding and following the enactment of the tax cut, monetary strategy was geared to provide the reserves needed to stabilized interest rates and the availability of credit. [Okun (1970, p. 56)]
>
> ... An accommodative or rate-oriented monetary policy fixes the interest rate and makes the LM curve horizontal in the relevant range. There is no dispute among economists that a permanent tax cut ... shifts the *IS* curve. Given a horizontal *LM* curve, a shift in the *IS* curve necessarily changes the level of income. [ibid., p. 57, note 30]

Table 12 describes what was going on, during the 1963.IV–1965.IV period, in terms of the unemployment rate $U(t)$ and my control variables: the three quarters moving average change in real (federal, state and local) government purchases of goods, and services per number of the civilian labor force $DG(t-\delta)$, the three quarter moving average rate of monetary expansion $\mu(t-\delta)$ and the ratio of the federal interest bearing debt held by private investors to the money supply $\theta$. Column 2 contains the predicted unemployment rate based upon the parameters in table 6, column 1; and column 3 is based upon the parameters in table 4, column 1.

TABLE 12
Determinants and predictions of the unemployment rate, 1963.III–1965.IV.

| | Unemployment (1) | Predicted (2) | Unemployment (3) | $DG(t-\delta)$ (4) | $\mu(t-\delta)$ (5) | $\theta$ (6) |
|---|---|---|---|---|---|---|
| 1963.III | 5.57% | 5.5 | 5.73 | 27.3 | 2.14% p.a. | 1.428 |
| 1963.IV | 5.65 | 5.29 | 5.46 | 16.7 | 2.86 | 1.423 |
| 1964.I | 5.45 | 5.38 | 5.23 | 5.67 | 3.61 | 1.428 |
| 1964.II | 5.29 | 5.16 | 5.07 | −5.33 | 3.96 | 1.409 |
| 1964.III | 5.08 | 5.34 | 5.16 | −4.67 | 3.76 | 1.387 |
| 1964.IV | 5.03 | 5.19 | 5.19 | −13.7 | 3.72 | 1.389 |
| 1965.I | 4.85 | 5.1 | 5.17 | −14.7 | 3.8 | 1.389 |
| 1965.II | 4.72 | 4.95 | 5.15 | −27.3 | 3.94 | 1.353 |
| 1965.III | 4.46 | 4.85 | 5.11 | −30.7 | 3.96 | 1.316 |
| 1965.IV | 4.2 | 4.63 | 4.84 | −7.33 | 3.89 | 1.315 |

*Note:* See text above for definitions of variables.

The dispute between Okun and Friedman concerns the following question: did the tax reduction *per se*, as distinct from the rise in the rate of monetary expansion, produce the subsequent decline in the rate of unemployment?

Within the framework of my model, a monetarist should reply to Okun as follows. To be sure, a permanent tax cut which produces a steady deficit will raise wealth steadily; and, as a result, the *IS* curve [equation (25)] will shift upwards steadily. What Okun failed to realize was that the *BB′* (or "*LM*") curve, which describes the equilibrium condition in the bond market, will also shift upwards as a result of a bond-financed deficit. Only if nominal interest rates rise will the public absorb a larger ratio of debt to money $\theta$ in their portfolios. In no way need the monetarists (who claim that the unemployment rate will not be affected by a bond-financed tax reduction) assume that the demand for money is interest inelastic, i.e., that the *BB′* (or "*LM*") curve is vertical. Okun's reference to the empirical work on the subject of the interest elasticity of the demand for money is irrelevant to the controversy. A monetarist should claim that the *BB′* curve shifts upwards by at least as much as does the *IS* curve (see figure 1). This means that $P_5 \leqq 0$ in equation (21a). No greater excess demand for goods would result from the bond-financed tax cut. Consequently, there would be no upward shift in the *PP′* curve in the phase diagram (figure 2); and the unemployment rate would not decline.

Okun's position would have to be that $P_5 > 0$: the *IS* curve would shift upwards relative to the *BB′* curve (figure 1). The price level would rise, real balances per unit of capital $m$ would decline; and the adjusted real wage would be lowered. In terms of my phase diagram, figure 4, the *PP′* curve would shift upwards; and the unemployment rate would decline. To be sure, the accommodative monetary policy which monetized debt to keep the long-term interest rate steady strengthened the expansionary effect by also increasing the rate of monetary expansion. Nevertheless, there would have been a decline in the unemployment rate, albeit a smaller decline, had there been no increase in the rate of monetary expansion.

A monetarist response would be that the policy of pegging the interest rate forced the monetary authorities to increase the rate of monetary expansion. Had there been no increase in $\mu$, a bond-financed tax cut would have led to *no rise* in the excess demand for goods. The price level would not have risen and there would have been no decline in the unemployment rate. On the other hand, within the framework of my model, when $P_5 = 0$, a bond-financed rise in real government purchases would lead to a rise in the price level and a rise in the level of nominal income. This phenomenon was described in figure 1 as the movement from $S_0$ to $S_1$ to $S_2$, etc. However, there would be no change in the long-run growth of nominal income; but nominal income will grow asymptotically at the rate of monetary expansion (figure 3).

The regression equations (tables 4 and 6) yielded statistically significant estimates consistent with the monetarist position that $P_5 \leqq 0$. These equations led me to predict that the unemployment rate would decline by 0.9 points from 1963.III to 1965.IV, whereas the actual unemployment rate declined by 1.4 points. Three forces were operative during that period. First, fiscal variable $DG(t - \delta)$ was declining, and thereby tended to raise the unemployment rate. Second, the moving average rate of monetary expansion $\mu(t - \delta)$ was rising from 2.1 to 3.9 percent per annum; and this tended to reduce the unemployment rate about from 0.6 to 0.8 points. Third, the debt–money ratio was declining from 1.4 to 1.3. The monetary authorities were monetizing enough debt to raise the ratio of money to debt by 7 percent.

The rise in the rate of monetary expansion and the decline in the debt–money ratio $\theta$ raised the intercept of the $PP'$ curve relative to that of the $UU'$ curve (figure 2). As a result, the economy moved along a trajectory like $E_0E_1$ to a lower rate of unemployment. According to this monetarist explanation, which is based upon the empirical work above, it was not the tax cut *per se* that drove the economy "onward and upward". It was the rise in the rate of monetary expansion and the decline in the debt–money ratio.

This summarizes my answers to the questions posed at the beginning of this section. On theoretical grounds, where do the monetarists and neo-Keynesians disagree? What inferences can be drawn from the data concerning the crucial parameter $P_5$, which distinguishes between these two groups? Although I am not convinced beyond a reasonable doubt that $P_5$ has the non-positive sign that monetarists must claim (within the framework of my model), it seems unlikely that the fiscalist view of history (e.g., as described by Okun) is consistent with the evidence. If my theoretical explanation is accepted, then much more research must be invested to determine the sign of the crucial parameter $P_5$ beyond a reasonable doubt.

## Appendix 1. Basic Data

| | $U(t)$ (1) | $\pi(t)$ (2) | $DG(t - \delta)$ (3) | $\mu(t - \delta)$ (4) | $\gamma(t - \delta)$ (5) |
|---|---|---|---|---|---|
| 1973.IV | 4.7% | 7.1% p.a. | \$−8.33 | 7.81% p.a. | 4.8% p.a. |
| 1973.III | 4.7 | 5.9 | −15.7 | 9.09 | 5.8 |
| 1973.II | 4.9 | 4.8 | −6.33 | 9.4 | 5.4 |
| 1973.I | 5 | 3.4 | 12 | 9.58 | 6 |
| 1972.IV | 5.3 | 3.3 | 29 | 9.02 | 6.87 |

| | $U(t)$ (1) | $\pi(t)$ (2) | $DG(t-\delta)$ (3) | $\mu(t-\delta)$ (4) | $\gamma(t-\delta)$ (5) |
|---|---|---|---|---|---|
| 1972.III | 5.6 | 2.83 | 27 | 8.3 | 7.47 |
| 1972.II | 5.7 | 2.84 | −1.33 | 7.92 | 7.07 |
| 1972.I | 5.9 | 3.66 | −31 | 7.11 | 5.63 |
| 1971.IV | 5.93 | 3.65 | −68.3 | 6.81 | 4.23 |
| 1971.III | 6 | 4.89 | −105 | 5.93 | 2.93 |
| 1971.II | 5.97 | 5.18 | −135 | 5.05 | 2.23 |
| 1971.I | 5.97 | 5.17 | −151 | 4.29 | 1.27 |
| 1970.IV | 5.8 | 5.26 | −146 | 3.71 | −0.1 |
| 1970.III | 5.24 | 5.06 | −124 | 3.98 | −1.57 |
| 1970.II | 4.83 | 5.31 | −92 | 4.92 | −2.2 |
| 1970.I | 4.15 | 5.48 | −67.3 | 6.52 | −1.8 |
| 1969.IV | 3.58 | 5.05 | −40 | 7.68 | −0.83 |
| 1969.III | 3.63 | 4.94 | 4 | 7.88 | 1 |
| 1969.II | 3.43 | 4.58 | 45 | 7.45 | 2.73 |
| 1969.I | 3.36 | 4.39 | 72.3 | 6.95 | 4.07 |
| 1968.IV | 3.4 | 4 | 74.7 | 7.08 | 4.13 |
| 1968.III | 3.6 | 4.1 | 84.7 | 6.9 | 3.4 |
| 1968.II | 3.59 | 4.1 | 99 | 6.18 | 2.13 |
| 1968.I | 3.66 | 3.7 | 128 | 4.48 | 0.6 |
| 1967.IV | 3.93 | 3.2 | 153 | 2.87 | −0.333 |
| 1967.III | 3.91 | 3.1 | 166 | 2.06 | −0.867 |
| 1967.II | 3.85 | 2.9 | 160 | 2.73 | −0.767 |
| 1967.I | 3.71 | 3.3 | 144 | 4.2 | −0.967 |
| 1966.IV | 3.69 | 3.2 | 129 | 5.13 | −0.9 |
| 1966.III | 3.81 | 2.9 | 103 | 5.16 | −0.933 |
| 1966.II | 3.86 | 2.4 | 68.7 | 4.48 | −1.07 |
| 1966.I | 3.81 | 2.1 | 21 | 4.05 | −0.9 |
| 1965.IV | 4.2 | 1.7 | −7.33 | 3.89 | −0.167 |
| 1965.III | 4.46 | 1.7 | −30.7 | 3.96 | 0.8 |
| 1965.II | 4.72 | 1.9 | −27.3 | 3.94 | 1.1 |
| 1965.I | 4.85 | 1.7 | −14.7 | 3.8 | 0.9 |
| 1964.IV | 5.03 | 1.8 | −13.7 | 3.72 | 0.6 |
| 1964.III | 5.08 | 1.9 | −4.67 | 3.76 | 0.4 |
| 1964.II | 5.29 | 1.9 | −5.33 | 3.96 | 0.6 |
| 1964.I | 5.45 | 1.7 | 5.67 | 3.61 | 0.967 |
| 1963.IV | 5.65 | 1.7 | 16.7 | 2.86 | 1.57 |
| 1963.III | 5.57 | 1.5 | 27.3 | 2.14 | 1.93 |
| 1963.II | 5.75 | 1.5 | 58.7 | 1.98 | 2 |
| 1963.I | 5.57 | 1.3 | 81 | 2.24 | 2.37 |

| | $U(t)$ (1) | $\pi(t)$ (2) | $DG(t-\delta)$ (3) | $\mu(t-\delta)$ (4) | $\gamma(t-\delta)$ (5) |
|---|---|---|---|---|---|
| 1962.IV | 5.67 | 1.1 | 98.7 | 2.7 | 2.6 |
| 1962.III | 5.66 | 1 | 107 | 2.88 | 2.77 |
| 1962.II | 5.52 | 0.9 | 88.3 | 2.56 | 2.3 |
| 1962.I | 5.55 | 1 | 68.7 | 1.98 | 1.23 |
| 1961.IV | 6.22 | 1.2 | 48.7 | 0.868 | 0.033 |
| 1961.III | 6.75 | 1.5 | 40.3 | −0.241 | −1 |
| 1961.II | 7.01 | 1.4 | 22.7 | −0.813 | −1.2 |
| 1961.I | 6.97 | 1.7 | −1.67 | −0.506 | −1.13 |
| 1960.IV | 6.4 | 1.5 | −24 | 0.621 | 0.233 |
| 1960.III | 5.7 | 1.5 | | | |
| 1960.II | 5.2 | 1.6 | | | |
| 1960.I | 5.2 | 1.6 | | | |

*Note*: All data are taken from annual reports of the Council of Economic Advisers. Col. (1) is the reported unemployment rate as a percentage of the civilian labor force. Col. (2) is the percentage change in the implicit *GNP* deflator between corresponding quarters: e.g., 1974 IV and 1973 IV. Col. (3) is a three-quarter moving average of the change in real (federal, state and local) purchases of goods and services per number of the civilian labor force between corresponding quarters. If $G(t)$ is real (1958 prices) government purchases of goods and services per member of the civilian labor force then $DG(t) = G(t) - G(t-4)$, where time $t$ is measured in quarters. $DG(t-\delta) \equiv \frac{1}{3}[DG(t-1) + DG(t-2) + DG(t-3)]$. Col. (4) is a three-quarter moving average of the percentage change in the $M_1$ money supply between corresponding quarters. If $\mu(t)$ is $[M_1(t) - M_1(t-4)] \times [M_1(t-4)]^{-1}$, then $\mu(t-\delta) = \frac{1}{3}[\mu(t-1) + \mu(t-2) + \mu(t-3)]$. Col. (5) is a three-quarter moving average of the percentage change in the total public debt securities between corresponding quarters; and is calculated in the same manner as was done in col. (4).

## Appendix 2. Glossary of Symbols

| *Symbol* | | *Equation* |
|---|---|---|
| $\alpha \equiv DA/A$ | Rate of labor augmenting technical change | 1 |
| $A$ | Level of technology | 1 |
| $b$ | Speed of response of expectations | 22 |
| $\beta_1$ | The change in the unemployment rate resulting from a percentage point change in the adjusted real wage | 5 |
| $\beta_2$ | The change in the employment rate resulting from a change in real government purchases per unit of capital | 5 |

| *Symbol* | | *Equation* |
|---|---|---|
| $B$ | Real private stock excess demand for bonds per unit of capital; and the mapping into this variable | 12 |
| $\gamma \equiv DZ/Z$ | Rate of growth of the interest-bearing debt | 16 |
| $C$ | Real consumption; and the mapping into consumption per unit of capital | 19 |
| $\delta$ | Depreciation rate | 7 |
| $D$ | Operator d/d$t$ | 7 |
| $d$ | Real private stock excess demand for bonds | 12 |
| $E$ | Real excess demand for goods per unit of capital | 18a |
| $F \equiv H \circ f$ | A mapping into the unemployment rate | 5 |
| $f$ | A mapping into the excess demand for labor | 4 |
| $g$ | A mapping into the nominal rate of interest | 15 |
| $G_1$ | Real government purchases of labor services per unit of capital | |
| $G$ | Real government purchases of goods and services per unit of capital | 18a |
| $H$ | A mapping into the unemployment rate | 2 |
| $h \equiv \lambda_w \circ H^{-1}$ | A mapping from the unemployment rate into the rate of change of the nominal wage | 3 |
| $I$ | Real investment; also a mapping into desired real investment per unit of capital. This is similar to $\phi$ | 11 |
| $K$ | Real capital stock | 11 |
| $\lambda_p, \lambda_w$ | Speeds of response in the product and labor markets | 1,18 |
| $M$ | Stock of money | |
| $m \equiv M/pK$ | Real balances per unit of capital | 12 |
| $\mu \equiv DM/M$ | Rate of monetary expansion | 17 |
| $n$ | Growth of the supply of effective labor; also growth of capital | 17 |
| $N_d, N_s$ | Quantity of labor demanded or supplied | 1 |
| $p$ | price level of output | |
| $p^*$ | Expected price level | |
| $P(\cdot)$ | A mapping into the rate of price change | 21 |
| $\pi \equiv Dp/p$ | Rate of price change | 3a |
| $\pi^*$ | Expected rate of price change | 1 |
| $q$ | Ratio of the capital value of an asset to its supply price | 6 |
| $\rho$ | Nominal rate of interest | 7 |

| *Symbol* | | *Equation* |
|---|---|---|
| $r^*$ | Expected rent per unit of capital | 7 |
| $R$ | A mapping from the unemployment rate to the rent per unit of capital | |
| $R_{ij}$ | Coefficients in regression equations (44), (45); see tables 4 and 5 | |
| $S_{ij}$ | Coefficients in regression equations (44), (45); see tables 4 and 5 | |
| $\theta \equiv Z/M \equiv z/m$ | Ratio of federal interest-bearing debt to the stock of money | 14 |
| $T$ | Real taxes less transfers per unit of capital | 16 |
| $U$ | Unemployment rate | 2 |
| $W$ | Nominal wage | 1 |
| $w$ | Real wage | 4 |
| $x_d, x_s$ | Ratio of effective labor demanded, supplied, per unit of capital | 7 |
| $x \equiv (1 - U)x_s$ | Employment per unit of capital | 8 |
| $y$ | Output per unit of capital; also mapping from $U$ to $y$ | 9 |
| $Y$ | Output | 9 |
| $Z$ | Value of interest-bearing debt | 14 |
| $z$ | Real value of interest-bearing debt per unit of capital | 13 |

## Bibliography


Andersen, L. and K. Carlson, 1970, A monetarist model for economic stabilization, Federal Reserve Bank of St. Louis Review 52, no. 4, April.

Ando, A., 1974, Some aspects of stabilization policies, the monetarist controversy, and the MPS model, International Economic Review 15, no. 2.

Blinder, A. and R. Solow, 1973, Does fiscal policy matter?, Journal of Public Economics 2.

Brunner, K., 1970, The 'monetarist revolution' in monetary theory, Weltwirtschaftliches Archiv 105, no. 1.

Burns, A., 1973, Letter on monetary policy. Federal Reserve Bank of St. Louis Review 55, no. 11, Nov.

Christ, C., 1968, A simple macro-economic model with a government budget restraint, Journal of Political Economy 76, Jan./Feb.

Friedman, M., 1970, The counter-revolution in monetary theory (Institute for Economic Affairs, London).

Friedman, M. and W. Heller, 1969, Monetary vs. fiscal policy (W. W. Norton, New York).

Keynes, J., 1930, A treatise on money, I (Macmillan, London).

Laidler, D., 1973, The influence of money on real income and inflation, Manchester School, Dec.

Okun, A., 1970, The political economy of prosperity (W. W. Norton, New York).
Rasche, R., 1973, A comparative static analysis of some monetarist propositions, Federal Reserve Bank of St. Louis Review 55, no. 12, Dec.
Scadding, J., 1973, The relationship between the stock of money and changes in output and prices: 1954–1969 (Prices and Incomes Commission, Ottawa).
Silber, W., 1970, Fiscal policy in IS–LM analysis: A correction, Journal of Money, Credit and Banking II, no. 4, Nov.
Stein, J., 1971, Money and capacity growth (Columbia University Press, New York).
Stein, J., 1974, Unemployment, inflation and monetarism, American Economic Review LXIV, Dec.
Stein, J. and Infante, 1973, Optimal stabilization policies, Journal of Money, Credit and Banking V, no. 1, part II, Feb.
Tobin, J., 1969, A general equilibrium approach to monetary theory, Journal of Money, Credit and Banking I, no. 1, Feb.
Tobin, J., 1972, Friedman's theoretical framework, Journal of Political Economy 80, no. 5, Sept.

# 1. COMMENTS ON STEIN

Carl F. CHRIST

## 1. Introduction

Professor Stein has given us an original and thought-provoking paper. I have spend many interesting and pleasant hours studying it. It reports a serious effort to meet the challenge that has been put by Professor Tobin and others to construct a model that would reflect the fundamental differences between schools of thought on the issues we are confronting here today.

My discussion will be organized in three parts, dealing with the theoretical model, the econometric specifications, and the estimates obtained.

## 2. The Theoretical Model

The theoretical model is an ingenious one, incorporating in a simple way many of the phenomena that must be analyzed in order to achieve Stein's aim, which is to decide whether the monetarist or the non-monetarist position is more nearly correct. His model has seven equations, reproduced here (using his equation-numbers in square brackets):

| | | |
|---|---|---|
| $Dw/w = \alpha + \pi^* - \pi + h(U)$ | Real wage adjustment | [3a] |
| $U = F(w/A, G_1)$ | Unemployment | [5] |
| $\rho = g(U, \pi^*, m, \theta)$ | Nominal bond interest | [15] |
| $G - T = [D\theta + (1 - \theta)\mu]m$ | Government budget | [16b] |
| $Dm/m = \mu - n - \pi$ | Growth of real balances/capital | [17] |
| $\pi = P(U, \pi^*, m, G, \theta)$ | Price adjustment | [21a] |
| $D\pi^* = (\pi - \pi^*)b$ | Adaptive price expectations | [22] |

There is a real wage adjustment equation depending upon the unemployment rate, productivity change, and expected inflation. There is an unemployment rate equation depending upon unit labor cost (and on government employment which is dropped later). There is a price adjustment equation depending upon the unemployment rate, expected inflation, and the per-unit-of-physical-capital quantities of money, government bonds privately held, and government purchases. There is an adaptive price expectations equation. There is an equation defining the growth rate of real balances per unit of capital as the growth rate of the money stock minus the growth rate of physical capital (assumed to be equal to the exogenous growth rate of the labor force) minus the inflation rate. There is an equation for the bond yield, derived from asset market equilibrium, and depending upon the unemployment rate, expected inflation, and the stocks of money and bonds per unit of real capital. There is a government budget restraint requiring that the government deficit be financed by some combination of issuing money and bonds.

The price adjustment equation is derived from the excess of desired expenditure (for consumption plus investment plus government purchases) over total output. Consumption is assumed to depend on physical capital, money, bonds, and the unemployment rate, but not on income. Gross investment is assumed to depend on the capital stock, the real rental price of capital goods, the real bond yield, depreciation rates, and the growth rate of the labor force.

Stein proceeds to reduce the number of equations from 7 to 2 in order to obtain a more manageable system. Consider just now a reduction from 7 to 5.

First, note that the bond yield $\rho$ appears in only one of the seven equations, namely the bond yield equation. Therefore we can drop both that variable and that equation, leaving six equations and six variables. By doing so, we lose none of the content of Stein's theory, because the substantive content of the bond yield equation has already been incorporated via the investment function into the price adjustment equation.

Second, note that the tax variable $T$ appears in only one equation of the system, namely the government budget restraint. Stein eventually regards $T$ as endogenous. Therefore we can drop both that variable and that equation, leaving five equations and five endogenous variables. Unlike the bond yield equation mentioned just above, however, the government budget restraint has not been incorporated into any of the other equations. Therefore this procedure of dropping it and the tax variable $T$ means that the remaining five-equation model ignores the government budget restraint and ignores taxes. This is because the consumption expenditure function, which as noted above underlies the price adjustment equation, does not provide for any dependence of consumption upon taxes. I believe this is a serious flaw in Stein's model. Dornbusch makes the same comment about the Brunner–Meltzer paper.

Three other points should be made with respect to Stein's government budget restraint. First, the foreign sector is neglected, so that the government in this model does not have the option of financing part of its deficit by reducing its holdings of gold and foreign exchange. Second, the interest rate does not appear in the budget restraint, presumably because all bonds in this model are assumed to be short-term so that there are no capital gains or losses experienced by bond holders. Third, the Federal government budget should be treated separately from state and local government budgets, because only the Federal government can create high-powered money.

There are several ways in which a promonetarist bias may be thought to be built into the model that Stein uses. First, as noted earlier, consumption is assumed to depend on the unemployment rate, physical capital, money, and bonds. Thus fiscal policy can affect consumption only indirectly by changing unemployment, or by changing physical capital or the total or composition of financial wealth. Most economists would prefer to allow for the possibility that changes in taxes affect consumption directly through changing disposable income. Second, in the wage adjustment equation, the coefficient of the expected rate of inflation is specified to be unity, rather than being specified as a parameter to be estimated. Third, money illusion and wage rigidity are assumed away in the wage adjustment equation, even in the short run.

Two additional points: the model provides for no effect of interest rates upon consumption, at given levels of wealth. And the labor demand function underlying the unemployment equation provides that the quantity of labor demanded depends upon the real wage of labor, but neglects any influence of the return to capital upon the demand for labor; similarly, the investment demand underlying the price adjustment equation does not respond to the real wage.

Stein refers to a steady state in which unemployment, the efficiency wage, the rate of inflation, and the expected rate of inflation are all constant, but in which his variable $\theta$, defined as the ratio of bonds to money held by the private sector, may be changing. I would prefer not to regard such a situation as a steady state, for when the ratio of bonds to money changes, the interest rate will change, and then the rates of growth of capital and output will change. I would prefer to reserve the term "steady state" for a situation in which any budget deficit or surplus is accommodated by identical rates of change in the private sector's holdings of bonds and of money, so that the ratio of bonds to money remains constant, and the interest rate can then remain constant.

Stein's view is that the monetarist controversy reduces to the question of the algebraic sign of the quantity $P_5$, which is the partial derivative of the price adjustment equation with respect to the ratio of bonds to money held by the private sector. In his model, this derivative is expressed as

$$P_5 \equiv \frac{\partial P}{\partial \theta} \equiv \frac{\partial \pi}{\partial \theta} = \frac{\partial \pi}{\partial E}\left[\frac{\partial C}{\partial \theta} + \frac{\partial \rho}{\partial \theta}\frac{\partial I}{\partial \rho}\right], \tag{1}$$

where $d\pi/dE$ is the response of the rate of inflation $\pi$ to the size of excess aggregate demand $E$ (a positive quantity); $dC/d\theta$ is the response of consumption $C$ to a change in the ratio $\theta$ of bonds to money (a positive quantity); $d\rho/d\theta$ is the response of the interest rate $\rho$ to an increase in the ratio of bonds to money (a positive quantity); and $dI/d\rho$ is the response of investment $I$ to an increase in the interest rate (a negative quantity). Thus Stein is saying that the monetarist controversy reduces to the question of whether the expression in square brackets above is positive, zero, or negative. He concludes that if it is zero or negative, the monetarists are correct, and if it is positive, the non-monetarists are correct.

This says that if the response of consumption to an increase in the ratio of bonds to money is sufficiently small, relative to the response of the interest rate to a change in the same ratio, and relative to the absolute value of the response of investment to a change in interest, then the monetarist position is correct; and if the opposite holds, the non-monetarist position is correct.

It is clear that Stein has tried to respond to the challenge to discover the parameters about which monetarists and non-monetarists disagree, so that we may try to measure them and throw light on the controversy. However, I am not persuaded that the monetarist controversy is reducible simply to the sign of $P_5$.

## 3. The Econometric Specifications

I turn now to the econometric specifications that Stein uses for his empirical estimation. These econometric specifications are obtained from his theoretical model by the following set of steps.

First, as noted earlier, drop the interest rate variable $\rho$ and the bond yield equation (recall that the substance of the bond yield equation is incorporated in other equations of the model).

Second, as noted earlier, let the tax variable $T$ be endogenous, and drop the government budget restraint from the model.

Third, take the time derivatives of the unemployment equation and the price adjustment equation. This removes the levels of all variables except the unemployment rate $U$, which is still present because of the wage adjustment equation. In particular, the model is such that this differentiation with respect to time *removes the levels of the money stock, the bond stock, and the level of government purchases.* Note that the tax variable $T$ has already disappeared.

Fourth, linearize the resulting unemployment and price adjustment equations.

Fifth, drop the expected rate of inflation $\pi^*$ and the equation generating it. This is done in two stages, first dropping the equation and regarding the expected inflation rate $\pi^*$ as exogenous, and ultimately dropping the variable altogether on the questionable ground that it is so highly correlated with the actual inflation rate as to be empirically intractable.

Sixth, assume that $P_1 \beta_1 - P_2 b$ is equal to 0, where $P_1$ and $P_2$ are the partial derivatives of the price adjustment equation with respect to the unemployment rate and the expected inflation rate, $\beta_1$ is the efficiency wage times the partial derivative of the unemployment function with respect to the efficiency wage, and $b$ is the rate at which price expectations change in response to an excess of the actual rate of inflation over the expected rate. This assumption retains little practical consequence once it has been assumed that the expected rate of inflation plays no role in the model.

The resulting econometric specification is as follows:

$$\begin{pmatrix} \dot{U} \\ \dot{\pi} \end{pmatrix} = A \begin{pmatrix} U \\ \pi \end{pmatrix} + B \begin{pmatrix} \dot{G} \\ \mu \\ \gamma \end{pmatrix}, \tag{2}$$

where $U$ and $\pi$ are the unemployment rate and the inflation rate, respectively, $A$ and $B$ are $2 \times 2$ and $2 \times 3$ matrices of coefficients, $\dot{G}$ is the rate change of government purchases per unit of capital, $\mu$ is the rate of growth of the money stock, and $\gamma$ is the rate of growth of the privately held stock of government bonds.

Stein says that the results of attempting to estimate these equations were "not clear cut", so that it was necessary for him to integrate them over an arbitrary interval of time, which he chose to be three calender quarters, and obtain the following equivalent pair of equations:

$$\begin{pmatrix} U \\ \pi \end{pmatrix} = R \begin{pmatrix} U_{-3} \\ \pi_{-3} \end{pmatrix} + S \begin{pmatrix} \dot{G}_{\mathrm{av}} \\ \mu_{\mathrm{av}} \\ \gamma_{\mathrm{av}} \end{pmatrix} + \begin{pmatrix} R_{10} \\ R_{20} \end{pmatrix}, \tag{3}$$

where $R$ and $S$ are $2 \times 2$ and $2 \times 3$ matrices of coefficients, $R_{10}$ and $R_{20}$ are constants of integration related to the initial conditions, $\dot{G}_{\mathrm{av}}$, $\mu_{\mathrm{av}}$ and $\gamma_{\mathrm{av}}$ are the average values of $\dot{G}$, $\mu$, and $\gamma$ over the preceding three quarters, and a subscript "$-3$" indicates the value of a variable three quarters earlier.

This econometric specification has the virtue that it contains only two equations, and two endogenous variables, the unemployment rate and the inflation rate. Notice however, that it has been constructed in such a way that it cannot study empirically any of the following issues:

First, it cannot study the determination of the equilibrium *level* of prices. If we know what the price level was at some time in the past, we can find out by following the inflation rate what it turns out to be at some time later. But we never find out from this model what determines the price level itself.

Second, this model cannot study the effect of a balanced-budget step increase in both government purchases and taxation. The model simply assumes that the effect of such a fiscal policy change upon both the level of unemployment and the rate of inflation must be zero. If we make such a step change, then afterward $\dot{G}$ will be zero again as it was before. $\mu$ and $\gamma$ are the rates of growth of money and bonds, and they will be unaffected by the step change. Hence this specification says that there cannot be any steady state effect of government balanced budget multiplier policy upon the unemployment rate or the inflation rate. This is one of the things that we would like to know empirically, and Stein's model settles the question by fiat before we ever get to making the estimates.

Third, this model cannot study the effect of step changes in private holdings of bonds and money brought about by an open market purchase or open market sale of bonds by the Federal Reserve. The model assumes that the effect of this upon the equilibrium values of the unemployment rate and the inflation rate must be zero, since the *stocks* of money and bonds play no role.

Fourth, the model cannot study the effect of past interest rates upon unemployment and inflation. We have here reduced form difference equations of the first order for the unemployment rate and the inflation rate, which depend only upon their own values three quarters earlier and the average values of three policy variables during the preceding interval of three quarters. (If there were other lagged endogenous variables appearing in the reduced form equations for unemployment and inflation, one could of course eliminate those other variables by expressing their influence in terms of values of unemployment and inflation with longer lags, but then the resulting system would not be a first-order difference equation system.)

Fifth, the model cannot study the role of expectations in shaping the response of the economy to monetary and fiscal policies.

Expressing these relationships in linearized form may be an overly stringent procedure in this case.

In my view it is unrealistic to choose the tax variable $T$ as endogenous, although the simplicity of this procedure provides a temptation to which I must confess to having yielded on one occasion. It would be much more in keeping with American economic policy institutions to assume that government purchases, tax and transfer rates, and the privately held stock of government bonds are exogenous, while the level of tax and transfer payments and the high powered money stock are determined endogenously by the interaction of the economy with these policy variables.

Stein's choice of the length of the time over which to integrate his differential equations is arbitrary. The integrated equations (3) are formally correct with any value of the interval $\delta$, from zero to infinity. Hence one could choose an interval longer than three quarters, or shorter. It is not clear how such a change would affect the empirical results, but neither is it clear that the results would be invariant to a change in the length of this interval.

## 4. The Estimates

I turn now to the estimates obtained by Stein for the two equations in (3).

I would be interested to know what the results were like when Stein attempted to estimate equation (2), results which he said were not clear cut. Also, what results would be obtained with different intervals of time in the integrated version (3) of those equations? Further, what happens if the equations are estimated using the rate of growth of the high-powered money stock rather than of the conventional money stock?

It is interesting to note that the estimated coefficients obtained by Stein all imply that the dynamic process for unemployment and inflation is stable. In addition, most of them imply complex roots of the characteristic equation of the system, which means cyclical motion when the system is disturbed from equilibrium. The only two exceptions are the estimates for the period 1960 to 1970 when the value of the parameter $P_5$ is estimated rather than being set equal to zero a priori.

Stein presents several predictions based upon his two estimated equations.

The post-sample predictions from the unemployment equation are quite good. The root mean square of the prediction error runs about four thirds as large as the standard error of the residuals during the sample period, where the predictions extend from one quarter ahead to twelve quarters ahead.

The post-sample predictions for the rate of inflation equation are rather poor: it failed to predict the rise in the rate of inflation which took place since 1971. Stein presents an alternative prediction mechanism for the rate of inflation, which predicts much better than his model. It is equivalent to a modified version of the quantity theory of money, follows:

$$P_e = M^{0.7} e^{\alpha + \beta t}, \tag{4}$$

$$\begin{aligned} \therefore \ln P_e &= 0.7 \ln M + \alpha + \beta t, \\ &= 0.7 \ln M + \alpha + (\pi_0 - 0.7\mu_0)t, \end{aligned} \tag{5}$$

$$\therefore \mathrm{d} \ln P_e/\mathrm{d}t = \dot{P}_e/P_e = \pi_e = 0.7\mu + \pi_0 - 0.7\mu_0, \tag{6}$$

where $P_e$ is the equilibrium price level, $M$ is the money stock, $t$ is time, and $\alpha$ and $\beta$ are parameters, $\beta$ being equal to Stein's $\pi_0 - 0.7\mu_0$, where $\pi_0$ and $\mu_0$ are base period rates of inflation and money stock growth, respectively. It would be interesting to know what kind of predictions of the price level and the rate of inflation would result from a choice of an exponent of $M$ different from 0.7, and different initial values of $\pi_0$ and $\mu_0$.

Stein presents within-sample predictions of the unemployment rate from 1963 to 1965 in connection with his discussion of the tax cut of 1964. They are rather good, but of course within-sample predictions don't provide a very revealing test: they are always rather good because the estimation procedure insures that residuals during the sample period will be small.

Stein notes that his matrix of coefficients in equation (3), namely the matrix $R$, is non-singular. Hence he says correctly that it is possible to get arbitrary equilibrium rates of unemployment and inflation by suitable choices of the rates of growth of the money stock and the stock of bonds, $\mu$ and $\gamma$. However, the matrix $R$ as estimated is not very far from singular, and therefore it is quite possible that this model describes a situation where arbitrary equilibrium rates of unemployment and inflation are not possible, but where instead the equilibrium unemployment rate must be a linear function of the equilibrium inflation rate.

Stein refers to the steady state of his two-equation system. I would urge that it not be regarded as a steady state unless the rates of growth of money and bonds are equal, so that the ratio of money to bonds is constant and the interest rate can be expected to remain constant.

Some of the empirical results obtained by Stein lend support to the monetarist view, as he notes in his paper. In particular, increases in the rate of growth in the money stock have large effects, usually statistically significant, creating decreases in unemployment and increases in the rate of inflation, whereas increases in the rate of growth of the stock of bonds have small effects, though often statistically significant, leading to increases in unemployment and decreases in the rate of inflation.

However, some of Stein's results lend support to the non-monetarist view. Consider the long-run steady-state equilibrium obtained from Stein's two estimated equations by setting the growth rates of money and bonds equal to each other and constant. Then consider different equilibria obtained by choosing different constant rates of growth for money and bonds. They generate a long-run Phillips curve, which from Stein's table 8 is either $U_e = 6.43 - 0.60\pi_e$ (based on original 1960–1970 data) or $U_e = 6.64 - 0.70\pi_e$ (based on transformed 1960–1970 data). The slopes of Stein's estimated coefficients, and their $t$ ratios, are such that his results would be extremely unlikely in case the long-run Phillips curve were actually vertical.

I would like to conclude by thanking Professor Stein for a provocative and inspiring paper, and at the same time by expressing reservations about his empirical conclusions because of the simplifications that he has introduced in obtaining them.

## 2. COMMENTS ON STEIN

Jürg NIEHANS

This is an interesting, in many respects original, and ingenious paper. It also is not easy reading. My comments should be taken less as a criticism of Stein's particular paper, than as a (minor) contribution, stimulated by this paper, to the debate about monetarism.

It is Stein's main proposition that the whole complex issue can be reduced to the sign of a single coefficient. Economic "isms" have rarely been so sharply defined. "Classicism", "marginalism", "neoclassicism", "Keynesianism", etc. forever remained rather vague bodies of beliefs, analytical tools and paradigms, defying persistent attempts to spell out exactly what they were all about and being themselves continually modified in the process. Even the Physiocrats, perhaps the most precisely defined school in the history of economic analysis, had as their article of faith the whole "Tableau Economique" and not just a single parameter. My comments will be mostly on the ways and means by which Stein achieves such a remarkable concentration of the issues.

While much of the potential richness of Stein's model lies in its dynamic implications, the taxonomic argument depends only on its steady-state properties. It should be realized, however, that Stein's "steady state" still allows for continuous changes in the debt–money ratio ($\theta$) and in government expenditures ($G$), presumably implying continuous changes in real interest rates [see equation (35)]. It might have been clearer to reserve the term "steady state" to the case where interest rates remain constant and thus $D\theta = DG = 0$. In terms of such a narrower definition, a once-over increase in $\theta$ or $g$ would be reflected not in the steady-state rate of inflation, but in the *price level* at any given moment in the steady state. Stein's steady state is also decidedly Keynesian in the sense that it does not allow for the addition of investment to the capital stock, which, in effect, is regarded as fixed. Alternatively, $K$ could have been treated as variable, like money and bonds. The dynamics of the model would then have determined the full adjustment path from one stock–flow equilibrium to another.

In Stein's view, the crucial question is whether bonds "dropped from helicopters" (that is, used to finance transfer payments or tax reductions) raise or

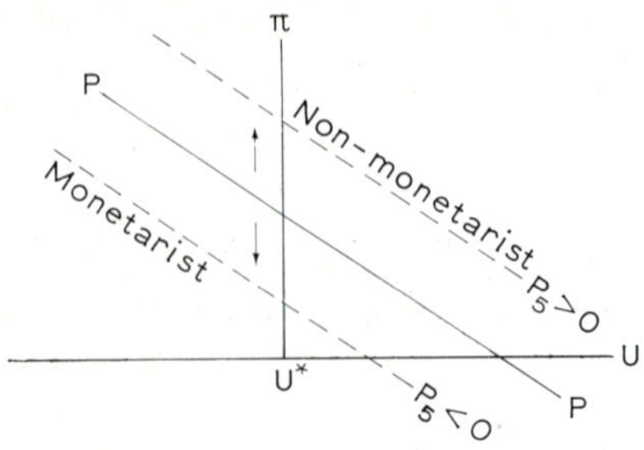


FIGURE 1

lower what he defines as the steady-state rate on inflation. In the steady state, actual inflation equals expected inflation. For a given rate of monetary expansion, a given change in the debt ratio, and a given increase in government purchases, the rate of inflation ($\pi$) can then be expressed as a function of unemployment ($U$), as depicted in figure 1. But we also know that in the steady state actual unemployment equals normal unemployment ($U^*$). In terms of the graph, the effect of give-away bonds on steady-state inflation is thus expressed by the movement of the *PP* curve up or down along the vertical axis, its direction depending on the sign of Stein's $P_5$. Monetarists, so Stein tells us, would expect this sign to be negative, while their opponents would expect it to be positive. I shall now contrast this characterization of monetarism with the one which emerged from the debate over recent years. It seems to me that debate was about three propositions.

(1) *Monetary policies are considerably more effective in influencing nominal income than non-monetary ("fiscal") macro-policies.*

This first proposition is about the relative size of certain *reduced-form* coefficients in macro-economic models, relating the change in national income to the underlying changes in certain policy variables. Its meaning can be made more precise in terms of a government/central bank budget constraint (for a closed economy), $G - T = DM + DB$ (see table 1).[1] Monetary policies consist in increasing the money supply to finance expenditures (symbolically, $DM/G$), to lower taxes or increase transfers ($DM/-T$), or to reduce debt ($DM/-DB$).

[1] It is not quite clear what type of bonds is represented by Stein's $B$. Since their real value is measured by $B$ and not something like $B/\rho$, they seem to be some interest-bearing deposits which can be withdrawn daily at face value. However, such deposits would be very close substitutes for money. Since one of the issues in the debate is exactly the significance of the difference between money and bonds, it would have been better to make bonds clearly different from money.

TABLE 1

| Monetary policies | Non-monetary policies |
|---|---|
| Expenditure money (*DM*/*G*) | Balanced-budget expansion (*G*/*T*) |
| Transfer money (*DM*/ $-T$) | Debt-financed expenditures (*G*/*DB*) |
| Open market operations (*DM*/ $-DB$) | Transfer bonds (*DB*/ $-T$) |

Non-monetary ("fiscal") policies can be defined as financing expenditures by taxes (*G*/*T*), financing expenditures by new debt (*G*/*DB*) or going into debt to lower taxes (*DB*/ $-T$). Three of the six policies can be chosen independently. If we decide to work in terms of the three monetary policies, any two of them imply one of the non-monetary policies as indicated by the connecting lines. A monetarist would, I think, tend to argue that the monetary policies are, dollar for dollar, considerably more effective than the non-monetary policies. For an extreme monetarist, the non-monetary policies would have virtually no influence on money national income, which implies that the three monetary policies all have the same effect. What matters, then, is only the quantity of the money supplied and not the way it is created. For the non-monetarist, on the other hand, it makes a considerable difference which way money is created, which implies that at least some of the non-monetary policies are quite effective.

(2) *Historically, fluctuations in money national income were largely caused by monetary policies (and not by non-monetary policies or disturbances in the private sector).*

This proposition is, of course, related to the first inasmuch as high reduced-form coefficients help to strengthen the influence of monetary policies. In addition, however, its validity depends on the *actual variations* in the policy variables. Even if monetary policy is highly effective dollar for dollar, it may still have had little influence on historical developments because it did not fluctuate much, and vice versa.

(3) *The effect of monetary policy is transmitted to national income not only through the bond yield, but also through other channels.*

This proposition, often not fully articulated and thus slightly mysterious, seems to relate to some of the *structural coefficients* of the underlying model. In particular, a monetarist would assign critical importance to the demand function for money, including its sensitivity to different interest rates, to expected inflation and to real income. He may also be interested in the speed with which actual cash balances adjust to desired cash balances. In addition, the elasticities of the demands for other assets, including investment goods, with respect to the different interest rates would be regarded as important. These structural coefficients would be expected to be such that an increase in the money supply results in an expansion in nominal income, though probably with a lag. Since the bond yield is not the only "transmission mechanism", monetary policy may be effective even in the presence of "liquidity traps", and the bond yield may not be a reliable indicator of the effect of monetary policy.

How is Stein's characterization of monetarism related to the much broader characterization embodied in these propositions? On the *monetary interpretation of history* it remains silent. One may thus be a monetarist in Stein's sense and still assign no significant influence to monetary factors in the explanation of economic fluctuations (and vice versa).

With respect to the *reduced-form* properties, Stein's criterion focuses exclusively on the policy of dropping bonds from airplanes (that is, $DB/-T$) and, more specifically, on the *sign* of its effect on money income. The empirical results on this point, while suggestive, are not clear-cut, and thus the main issue appears to remain in doubt. However, I believe Stein makes it unduly difficult, in this respect, for the monetarists to prove their point. I am not aware that a major protagonist of monetarism has argued that inflation could indeed be dampened by dropping bonds from airplanes. In fact, I am not aware that the sign of this effect has been a serious issue. I also believe it can be rigorously shown that in the very long run, when even the capital stock has had time to adjust, transfer bonds will not lower prices.

The debate has actually been about the *relative size* of the effects of $(DB/-T)$, $(DM/-T)$ and $(G/T)$. With respect to the pairwise comparison between $(DB/-T)$ $(DM/-T)$, a monetarist could well admit the possibility that $(DB/-T)$, taken by itself, may be somewhat expansionary, as long as this effect remained "small" relative to $(DM/-T)$. To put it another way around, a monetarist does not have to argue that open market purchases are more inflationary than issuing new money through transfer payments; it is good enough for him to find that it is not much less inflationary. In this respect, Stein's empirical results about three-period effects are clear-cut: The coefficients of $\mu$, the rate of monetary expansion, in tables 4 and 5 have the right sign, are significant, and absolutely much larger than the coefficients of $\gamma$, whatever the latters' sign.[2] In the light of these results, there really does not seem to be much difference between open market purchases

[2] For the purpose of theoretical analysis, Stein measures debt by the debt–money ratio. In the empirical part of the paper he measures it by the rate of expansion of debt. I think the exposition would have gained if the same variable had been used throughout, preferably the rate of expansion, since it permits symmetrical treatment of money and debt.

and dropping money from airplanes. What matters is indeed the money, and not the way it is created.

However, this is only one part of the question. The other part is about the relative effect of transfer money ($DM/-T$) and expenditure money ($DM/G$). A monetarist would tend to argue that the two effects are not very different, while a fiscalist would probably expect stronger effects from expenditure money. In Stein's model this issue takes the (equivalent) form of the question whether the effect of a balanced-budget expansion on prices and/or output is clearly positive and rather "large" or ambiguous in sign and "small". The results in table 4 suggest a significant short-run effect of tax-financed expenditures on employment, but in view of the difference in dimensions it is difficult to decide whether the effect is "large" or "small" relative to the effect of money-financed transfer payments. Still, these results lend support to the non-monetarist view that budget policies have significant employment effects in the short run, even if they are not associated with a monetary expansion. Table 5 reveals no significant effect of expenditures on prices. In view of the inertia of prices within three quarters, this should surprise neither monetarists nor non-monetarists. The marked difference in adjustment speeds for $\mu$ and $\pi$ also cannot be attributed to specific monetarist properties of the model.

In interpreting these results, we have to keep in mind that public expenditures appear in Stein's theoretical model only as a direct component of aggregate demand. Strangely, neither expenditures nor taxes are allowed to influence private demand for consumption, investment, and bonds.[3] Most of the more familiar links between fiscal policy and private demand are thus suppressed. Specifically, the balanced-budget multiplier of Keynesian macro-economics is based on the assumption that an increase in taxes reduces private saving at a given income and thus the private demand for assets. It would also be interesting to go beyond Keynesian theory by allowing for the effect of specific government expenditures on private demand. This effect would probably be quite different for different types of expenditures. Thus public construction activity may either stimulate or reduce private investment demand and tax-financed public schools may reduce private school expenditures by just about the same amount, leaving saving unchanged.

So far, my comments related to the steady-state and the three-period effects of various policies in Stein's model. However, it may be argued that the main differences between monetarists and nonmonetarists do not, in fact, relate to either of these, but to the speed with which the steady state is approached.

[3] Alternatively, it could be assumed that the effects of expenditures and taxes are exactly symmetrical in each demand function.

Specifically, both sides might possibly agree that the steady-state effects of tax-financed expenditures and of debt-financed tax reductions (and thus of debt-financed expenditures) are both quite small. In terms of Stein's model, this would imply a value of $P_5$ close to zero. However, non-monetarists would expect that there would initially be a strong expansionary effect, lasting for many quarters, while the monetarists would expect even this temporary effect to be weak and short-lived. Correspondingly, non-monetarists would expect that money paid out for transfers would have a much stronger expansionary effect than open market purchases for a considerable period of time (though not forever), while monetarists would expect roughly the same effect after, say, about a year. So far, Stein has made relatively little use of the time-profile of the adjustment path. It would be interesting to know the adjustment paths of the major variables implied in the model, perhaps based on simulations with plausible initial conditions and structural coefficients.[4]

My next comment relates to the identification of "important" *structural coefficients*. We notice at once that the demand for money does not appear explicitly in Stein's model. Instead, the demand for additional money balances is treated as a residual which can be obtained, if desired, by subtracting the demand for additional bonds from the difference between saving and investment. The implied elasticities of the demand for money with respect to interest rates, real income, inflation, and the like, are not worked out. Stein's model must thus be classified as extremely non-monetarist in the sense that it treats the structural coefficients of the demand for money as particularly unimportant. I think the analysis would have been more lucid if it had been conducted in terms of three stock demand functions for, respectively, capital goods, bonds and money.

There are three structural coefficients which are of decisive importance in Stein's model [equation (21b)]. These relate, respectively, to the interest elasticity of investment [equation (11)], the interest elasticity of the demand for bonds [equation (12)], and the effect of give-away bonds on consumption demand [equation (19)]. A monetarist, in Stein's world, would have to argue that the interest elasticity of investment is (absolutely) "large", that the interest elasticity of bond demand is "small", and that the bond effect on consumption is also "small". The opposite assumption would lead to non-monetarist results. It thus turns out that the bond yield is again of crucial importance, while no other interest elasticities seem to play a role. In this respect, Stein's model has a decidedly Keynesian flavor. It is true, as Stein notes in section 2.4, that a monetarist is not

[4] Typically, these adjustment paths will exhibit oscillations (as, indeed, they do in Stein's figures 3 and 5). As a consequence, it does not make much sense to measure the speed of adjustment by the ratio of the three-quarter effect to the steady-state effect (cf. table 8). The assumption of an exponential convergence to equilibrium [equation (50)] is inconsistent with the properties of the model.

forced to assume that there is no substitution between money and bonds, but it is also true that perfect substitution (that is, the "liquidity trap") would yield non-monetarist conclusions, while the result becomes more monetarist in proportion as the substitutability between money and bonds is lowered.

The dominating position of the bond yield in Stein's model is probably due to the fact that the rate of return on capital is rigidly tied to the unemployment rate and thus cannot vary once unemployment is at the natural rate, and also to the assumption that saving is assumed to be independent of the two interest rates. This does not leave much scope for monetarist transmission mechanisms. I would conjecture that less restrictive models would show the monetarist notions in a different light. I might be forgiven for referring to a macro-model I recently used to analyze the effects of the money supply on prices, output and employment.[5] It turned out that a low-enough level of the cross-interest elasticities of the various asset demands would indeed validate the monetarist view about the transmission mechanism and would push the effect of transfer bonds on nominal income to zero. At the same time, the bond yield would become an extremely unreliable indicator of monetary policy, the transmission operating through other channels.

This concludes my discussion of Stein's characterization of monetarism. It is true that I cannot yet convince myself that "$P_5$ positive" and "$P_5$ negative" should really be the battle cries in the debate about monetarism. I also believe that once an issue is reduced to such simple terms, it will usually have lost most of its vitality. But be this as it may, Stein has made an important contribution to the debate.

[5] J. Niehans, Monetary policy with full stock adjustment, *Zeitschrift für Wirtschafts- und Sozialwissenschaften*, vol. 1, no. 1, 1974.

## 3. COMMENTS ON STEIN

Robert M. SOLOW

I agree that Professor Stein has zeroed in on what now appears to be the critical issue as between monetarists and eclectic Keynesians: what are the consequences of bond-financed government spending or tax reduction? (I say "now" only because Professor Friedman seemed to deny that this was the issue. And I say "seemed" because he did not give a *Yes* or *No* answer to the question: Do you believe the effects of fiscal policy "certain to be temporary and likely to be minor"?)

To conduct a critical experiment on the central issue, one must embed it in a model of the macro-economy, and that is where the trouble begins. Monetarism is a syndrome as well as a doctrine. There is Little Monetarism and there is Great Monetarism. The great-monetarist syndrome extends from the narrow proposition here under discussion through convictions about the reality of a natural rate of unemployment and the utility of the hypothesis of rational expectations, and all the way to beliefs like *laissez-faire* and political conservatism, which certainly have no strict logical connection with Little Monetarism. (I have been struck by the fact that monetarism has no left wing, no parallels to Paul McCracken and Henry Wallich, whom I would classify as right-wing eclectic Keynesians. Perhaps *they* are also left-wing monetarists? That would be interesting, but I doubt it. In any case, it is an interesting topic for a historian of contemporary economic thought.) It seems to me that Stein has embedded his test in a model that is, in other respects, definitely Great-Monetarist. There are several places *en route* to the final test where I would not casually accept the specification of the surrounding model really matters when it comes to the "crucial experiment", as I will try to explain later. So while I admire the paper for its clear-sightedness and its ingenuity, I think it is very far from settling the question.

Here are my reservations about the model in which Professor Stein embeds his test. I am not asserting, in each instance, that Stein is wrong; only that he has made a choice on which a reasonable person might disagree.

(1) I am not prepared to buy equations (1) or (3), in which unemployment (in units of *effective* labor, by the way) drives the *real* wage, on assumptions that yield a natural rate of unemployment. It would take a conference by itself to debate the issues here; Stein's assumptions would not be mine.

(2) Equation (4) contains the implicit assumption that the supply of labor is a function of the real wage per unit of effective labor. Stein comments that models which take the money wage as exogenous or relate it to the unemployment rate "overemphasize fiscal policy relative to such models as this". That turn of phrase rather prejudges the issue! By now the real wage has been falling for over a year; money wages have been rising, of course, but they have been outstripped by consumer prices. Ask yourself if the same reduction in real wages could have been brought about, *in fact* in the contemporary U.S. economy, by a reduction in money wages with the price level stationary. To my eye, certainly not; or at least not without strikes, protests, and general *Geschrei*. That does not suggest the real wage as the appropriate argument for a labor-supply function. It is all very reminiscent of Keynes's once-mysterious discussion of involuntary unemployment in *The General Theory*.

(3) I query whether the model insures that (9) and (10) will satisfy the identity $wx = y - r$.

(4) The model is constructed as if the interest-bearing government debt were instantaneously refundable, i.e., consists of securities redeemable at any time at their face value, bearing interest at the current market rate. I note that these interest payments appear to be omitted from (16a); they can not be tucked into transfer payments, because then the total of transfers would be a function of the interest rate. This choice may make a little trouble for the empirical work, because the debt is not in fact instantaneously refundable.

(5) In (18), the price level is made equal to a mark-up times the money wage per unit of effective labor, where the *rate of change* of the mark-up factor is proportional to excess demand in the market for good and services. That is at least questionable; other models make the *level* of the mark-up depend on excess demand.

(6) Consumption is made to depend only on wealth, and the definition of wealth excludes the present value of future labor income. This seems dubious to me, to say the least; though for all I know it may be the *dernier cri* in consumption functions and I am just showing how old-fashioned I am.

(7) The most transparent version of the model is in Stein's table 3. Here is a model in which, so long as the expected rate of inflation equals the actual rate, the unemployment rate moves monotonically toward the natural rate of unemployment, regardless of whatever else is happening. I can not believe that.

(8) I have not been able to figure out why $D\theta$ does not go to zero in some of these models as tax revenues rise.

So much for the model itself. Now this structure is used to provide a test on the sign of the key coefficient $P_5$. This is certainly an improvement on the reduced-form models of Friedman–Meiselman and Anderson–Jordan, which, I am convinced, are simply incapable of throwing any light on *anything*. Stein's model has a good deal more structure and carries much more intellectual conviction. Nevertheless I fear it can't get us very far toward that crucial experiment, and I want to explain why.

When you think about what actually *happens* in the empirical part of the paper, you find that (44) and (45) are estimated from time series, and everything turns on the signs of the regression coefficients $S_{13}$ and $S_{23}$. Now when would you expect $\gamma$ to take on large values, i.e., when would you expect the federal interest-bearing debt to be growing rapidly? Presumably when the budget deficit is unusually large, so generally when the unemployment rate is high (and, more tenuously, perhaps when the rate of inflation is low). There are lags to be taken into account here, but they probably do not change the normal presumption. Therefore the zero-order correlation between $\gamma$ and the dependent variables will likely be positive in (44) and negative in (45). That is to say, they will be "monetarist" in appearance, though this says absolutely nothing about the causal significance. The value of the test thus depends *entirely* on the ability of (44) and (45) to capture all the other influences on unemployment and inflation and capture them correctly.

Since $U_{t-3}$ and $\pi_{t-3}$ appear in the equations for $U_t$ and $\pi_t$, it is presumably the transformed equations we should look at, and even these will probably overestimate the explanatory power of the model. I think it might be better, from this narrow point of view, to estimate the equations in first-difference form and look at $R^2$. But in any case the transformed fits are not terribly good. It is hard to believe that $S_{13}$ and $S_{23}$ are purified of the misleading reverse correlation between unemployment rate and budget deficit. That is why I think that Professor Stein's test may well be sensitive to the particular assumptions he has built into the rest of the model, and why I am skeptical about the possibility of getting a conclusive test of the basic hypothesis in a small-scale model.

I would not want to be read as believing that the big models can deliver an answer. I am skeptical about them too, for related but slightly different reasons. This is not the time to go into that. For now, I think we have to proceed along both lines, and to bring theory to bear as well, but more in the spirit of building up a weight of evidence than in the hope of finding a single crucial experiment.

## 4. COMMENTS ON STEIN

John L. SCADDING

I think it was Jerry Stein who, during the course of the discussion, called for repeated testing of our models before we place much confidence in them. This note is in the spirit of that appeal. Two years ago I had estimated a model remarkably similar to Stein's using quarterly Canadian data for 1954–1969. The purpose of this note is to summarize briefly the results of that replication.

The model I used is almost identical to Stein's: three differential equations to explain the rate of inflation, the expected rate of inflation and the rate of growth of real output (expressed as the deviation from the postwar trend rate of growth). Stein of course used the unemployment rate rather than the output rate. The difference is not substantive, however. My output equation is constructed from an analysis of labor market behavior and could easily be recast in terms of the unemployment rate. In fact, in the paper I translated some of the empirical results for the output equation into equivalent results for the unemployment rate.

The testing of the model was somewhat different. Some of those differences are in effect replies to criticisms of Stein's test procedures. The results I obtained suggest those criticisms are not important: my results are not qualitatively different from Stein's.

I did not smooth the data, although I did use seasonal dummies for the output equation because output growth rates computed from seasonally adjusted levels of real *GNP* still showed pronounced seasonal variation. Like Stein, I found that the equations gave more satisfactory results when estimated in integral rather than difference equation form. The latter gave improbably long estimates of the average lags, probably because of the bias inherent in using lagged endogenous variables when the errors are serially correlated.

Unlike Stein, I did not integrate out the impulse and forcing functions; instead, I approximated the solution integrals as distributed lags of the contemporaneous and past policy variables. Nor did I fix the average lag. Instead, I used the restrictions on the distributed lag functions implied by the structure of the model to select the average lag. For example, the neutrality hypothesis built into the model implied that the weights on money in the output equation should sum to zero. A large number of lag lengths was tested and the one whose sum of weights was closest to zero was chosen as the correct one. That lag length incidentally also produced the highest $R^2$ – a value larger than the Modigliani magic number of 0.50.

The test results were broadly the same as Stein's. A change in the money growth rate had its maximum effect on output growth 3 to 6 quarters later, depending on whether the change was permanent or transitory. It took two to four times longer for all effects to disappear: 12 quarters after the money growth rate changed, the output growth rate returned to its trend value.

Like Stein, I found the results for the inflation rate equation to be much less satisfactory. For the Canadian data at least, I think the source of the problem is the sharp peak in the inflation rate observed at the tail-end of every postwar business cycle. Those peaks may be an indication of some sort of catching-up or overshooting phenomenon. Whatever their explanation, they spell trouble for the low-order polynomial lags typically used in econometric models. Such lag structures are incapable of capturing such sharp cycles – or rather they attempt to capture them by overestimating the average lag.

## REPLY*
### A Keynesian Can Be a Monetarist

Jerome L. STEIN

My discussants have explicated the issues brilliantly, and we are all in their debt. On the basis of their criticisms, how should my paper have been rewritten? I shall confine my reply to four topics: what are the issues, what is the relation between my $P_5$ and asset substitution effects, what interpretation should be given to the empirical tests, and what produced the recession of 1974–1975?

### 1. What are the Issues that Divide us?

Repeatedly, there were questions concerning the differences between monetarists and non-monetarists. I should have oriented my paper around Milton Friedman's position concerning the *necessary and sufficient* conditions for sustained inflation and the growth of nominal income. He wrote:

> There is a consistent though not precise relationship between the rate of growth of the quantity of money and the rate of growth of nominal income and conversely. [Friedman (1973, p. 27)]

Inflation is exclusively a monetary phenomenon, according to the monetarists. A restrictive fiscal policy combined with an expansionary monetary policy cannot curb inflation. Again, I quote Friedman:

> It follows from the propositions I have so far stated that *inflation is always and everywhere a monetary phenomenon* in the sense that it is and can be produced only by a more rapid increase in the quantity of money than in output. However,

*The references refer to the bibliography in my article. Equations, figures and tables in this reply are prefixed by R, to distinguish between them and those in the original article. I am deeply indebted to J. Niehans and R. M. Solow for their helpful criticisms of an earlier draft.

the reason for the rapid increase in the quantity of money may be very different under different circumstances. [Friedman (1973, p. 28)]

Let $Y_N$ be nominal income, $M$ the money stock, $P$ the price index, $n$ is the growth of effective labor, and $D$ the operator d/d$t$. Monetarism is the view that, as the period under consideration lengthens,

$$D \ln Y_N \Longleftrightarrow D \ln M \Longleftrightarrow D \ln P + n, \qquad \text{(R-1)}$$

so that the middle term is the necessary and sufficient condition for the right- and left-hand terms.

Unlike the Federal Reserve Bank of St. Louis, Friedman did not claim that the level of nominal income $Y_N$ cannot be affected by fiscal policy. His focus was not upon levels, but on rates of change over a sustained period as described in equation (R-1) above. If the Civil War or the World Wars were financed through the sale of bonds to citizens, but without a rise in the rate of monetary expansion, then there would have been no sustained inflation. There would have been a temporary rise in the growth of nominal income and the rate of inflation as government purchases were accelerated. When the latter settle down at the higher level, both the growth of nominal income and the rate of inflation would return to their former equilibrium values. Nevertheless, both the absolute price level $P(t)$ and the level of nominal income $Y_N(t)$ will be permanently higher as a result of the higher level of real government purchases of goods.

This can be seen in figures 1–3 in my paper. Suppose that $P_5$ were approximately zero. As a result of a rise in real government purchases per unit of capital from $G$ to $G + \Delta G$, the equilibrium level of real balances per unit of capital declines from $m_0$ to $m_1$ in figure 1. This means that the absolute price level is permanently raised; but its rate of growth will return to $\mu - n$ as described in figure 2.

Figure 3 describes what will happen to the level of nominal income, if the wars were financed through the sale of bonds. The logarithm of nominal income is the integral $\int^t D \ln Y_N(\tau)\mathrm{d}\tau$, which is the area under the curve $P_5 = 0$ in that figure. As a result of the rise in the level of real government purchases per unit of capital, the level of nominal income would be permanently raised by the segment of the curve above $D \ln Y_N = \mu$. The rate of growth of nominal income, which is the integrand, will return to the rate of monetary expansion $\mu$ when the economy returns to $E_0$ in figure 2. However, $\ln Y_N(t)$ will be on a higher trend line which has the same slope $\mu$ as before. This view states that what matters for the rate of inflation or growth of nominal income, over a decade or more, is the actual rate of monetary expansion, not the way it is brought about. Jürg Niehans explicated this point in his usual lucid manner.

Moreover, the second basic monetarist proposition is that, accelerations or decelerations in the rate of monetary expansion lead to short-run fluctuations in the unemployment rate. The level of the unemployment rate, however, is independent of the rate of monetary expansion. [See Brunner (1970, p. 14), Friedman (1970, p. 23).]

My paper was designed to explore the conditions whereby these monetarist results could be generated within the framework of a model whose structure could be acceptable to neo-Keynesians, and which does not assume that the *LM* curve is vertical or that the *IS* curve is horizontal. Moreover, the unemployment rate and the price level must be state variables if the model is to have any relevance for the monetarist controversy or as an explanation of empirical phenomena. Unfortunately, many articles critical of monetarism rely upon the standard *IS–LM* models where either the price level or the unemployment rate is fixed. If we can agree on the general structure of the model, then, the dispute would be narrowed down to empirical questions concerning the magnitude of certain coefficients.

## 2. The Relation between $P_5$ and Inter-Asset Substitution Effects

Suppose that the level of real government purchases of goods per unit of capital were raised from $G$ to $G + \Delta G$. Let this be associated with a permanent deficit which is financed exclusively through the sale of bonds. The growth of the interest-bearing debt is permanently raised without any change in the rate of monetary expansion. What would be the effects of this policy upon the growth of nominal income and the rate of inflation? I proved that monetarist results are derived if $P_5$ were non-positive. The rise in $G$ to $G + \Delta G$ would lead to a temporary rise in the growth of nominal income. When $P_5 = 0$, the *growth* of nominal income $D \ln Y_N$ is described in figure 3; and it will return to its long-run equilibrium value equal to the rate of monetary expansion. The *level* of nominal income $Y_N(t)$ will be permanently higher as a result of the rise in real government purchases of goods per unit of capital. On the other hand, fiscalist results would occur if $P_5$ were positive, as described in figure 5. The rise in the growth of the interest-bearing debt would lead to a rise in the equilibrium growth of nominal income, without a corresponding rise in the rate of monetary expansion.

My $P_5$ effect seemed esoteric and Jürg Niehans questioned whether its sign should be the battle cry in the debate about monetarism. If I were rewriting my paper in light of my discussants' analysis, I would relate the sign of $P_5$ to the familiar discussion of the substitutability among assets: money, bonds and capital. Consider a spectrum of interest yielding government securities: Treasury bills with short maturities and government bonds with long maturities. In the fiscalist case, the financing of government expenditures is done with securities which are closer substitutes for money than they are for capital. In the monetarist case, the financing is done with securities which are closer substitutes for capital than they are for money. I show that $P_5$ is positive in the first case and it is negative in the second case. The empirical question concerning the sign of $P_5$ is the same as the empirical question concerning the substitutability among assets. How does the sign of $P_5$ vary with the maturity of the debt? Specifically, a major issue that divides us is whether $P_5$ is negative when the debt is financed with long-term securities.

### *2.1. Bonds and Capital as Perfect Substitutes Imply ($P_5 < 0$) Strong Monetarist Results*

If bonds and capital are perfect substitutes, then their yields must be equal when there are positive quantities of each in existence. The nominal rate of interest on bonds $\rho$ must equal the yield on capital: $r(U) + \pi^*$, the rent plus the expected rate of price change. If this were not the case, there would be an excess supply of, or demand for, bonds; and the nominal rate of interest would adjust instantly to equal $r(U) + \pi^*$.

To show that $P_5 < 0$ when bonds and capital are perfect substitutes, and $P_5 > 0$ when bonds and money are perfect substitutes, it is more convenient to work with the demand for money than with the demand for bonds, in describing portfolio equilibrium.[1] Let the demand for money relative to the sum of bonds and capital (which are assumed to be perfect substitutes) be negatively related to the yield on the latter. Define $m \equiv M/pK$ as real balances per unit of capital, and $z \equiv Z/pK$ as real bonds per unit of capital. Then the demand for real balances per unit of capital is

$$m_{\mathrm{d}} = L[r(U) + \pi^*](1 + z); \qquad L' < 0, \tag{R-2}$$

where $m_{\mathrm{d}}$ denotes the quantity demanded.[2]

Suppose that the rate of price change were described by equation (R-3). The rate of price change is equal to the expected rate of price change $\pi^*$ plus some function of the excess supply of real balances per unit of capital $\lambda_m(m - m_{\mathrm{d}})$.

[1] In my book, *Money and capacity growth* (1971), I worked explicitly with the demand for money; and the demand for bonds was implicit. On the basis of Walras' Law for stocks, it does not make any difference which equation is explicit: it is a question of analytical convenience. The orientation of this section of my reply follows that of chapter 5 in my book.

[2] Recall that the nominal rate of interest must adjust instantaneously to equal the yield on capital.

Then

$$\pi = \pi^* + \lambda_m[m - L(\cdot)(1 + z)]. \tag{R-3}$$

It is clear that $P_5$ is negative because

$$P_5 = \partial\pi/\partial z = -\lambda_m L(\cdot) < 0. \tag{R-3a}$$

Recall that $z \equiv \theta m$, so that $P_5$ just considers a variation in $z$ given $m$.

An intuitive explanation can be given for the negative $P_5$ effect. What would happen if transfer payments to the public were made with bonds? Since bonds and capital are perfect substitutes, it is equivalent to making transfer payments in the form of capital. An excess demand for money results from the rise in the other component of the portfolio: bonds plus capital. People will offer bonds–capital in exchange for money. The price level of goods will decline and the stock of real balances in existence will rise. In this manner, the system will return to equilibrium. An excess demand for money relative to capital is deflationary: $P_5$ is negative. Monetarist results will be obtained by assuming that the bonds used to finance the deficit are closer substitutes for capital than they are for money.

### 2.2. *Bonds and Money as Perfect Substitutes Imply ($P_5 > 0$) Fiscalist Results*

If money and bonds are perfect substitutes, in the sense that the marginal rate of substitution between them is independent of relative quantities, then the nominal rate of interest on bonds must equal to marginal non-pecuniary yield on money. The portfolio demand equation could be viewed as equation (R-4). The ratio of money plus bonds demanded per dollar of capital $(m + z)_d$ depends negatively upon the yield earned by capital,

$$(m + z)_d = L[r(U) + \pi^*]; \qquad L' < 0. \tag{R-4}$$

Let the price change equation (3) be modified to equation (R-5) the rate of price change $\pi$ is equal to the expected rate of price change $\pi^*$ plus some function of the excess supply of the financial assets $m + z$ which are perfect substitutes,

$$\pi = \pi^* + \lambda_m[m + z - L(\cdot)]. \tag{R-5}$$

It is clear that $P_5$ is positive because

$$P_5 = \partial\pi/\partial z = \lambda_m > 0. \tag{R-5a}$$

Fiscalist results are obtained in this case, where the bonds used to finance the deficit and money are perfect substitutes. If transfer payments are made with such bonds, the ratio of financial assets to capital rises. An excess demand for capital results and the price level of goods rises.

The conclusion is that monetarist results will be obtained unless the government deficit is financed with securities which are close substitutes for money ($P_5 > 0$). The empirical question is: what maturity of the debt, denoted by "$s$", implies that $P_5 = 0$? Say that this critical maturity is $s^*$ years: $P_5(s^*) = 0$. Then if the government expenditures are financed with securities having a maturity of less than $s^*$ years, the standard neo-Keynesian results will occur. Were the expenditures to be financed with securities having a maturity of $s^*$ years or more, then monetarist results would occur. As the maturity of the debt increases, the results tend to be more monetarist; and as the maturity of the debt decreases, the results tend to be more neo-Keynesian. This means that $P_5'(s) < 0$. I am even more convinced now than I was that the sign of $P_5(s)$ is the essence of the difference between the monetarists and the neo-Keynesians. Research should be directed to the question: what is the crucial maturity $s^*$ such that $P_5(s^*) = 0$? Viewed in this manner, I believe that the substantive differences among us are empirical rather than theoretical.

## 3. The Interpretation of the Empirical Data

### 3.1. *Is There an Obvious Monetarist Bias?*

The empirical test of the hypothesis that $P_5 \leqq 0$, i.e., that bonds are closer substitutes for capital than they are for money, revolved assumed the signs of $\partial U/\partial \gamma$ and $\partial \pi/\partial \gamma$ in equations (44) and (45), where $\gamma$ was a three-quarter moving average of the growth of the total public debt between corresponding quarters. My test of the monetarist hypothesis refers to the historical financing of government deficits. On the basis of the discussion in section 2 above, I should have considered the short-term and long-term debt separately; but this will have to be the subject of further research. The monetarist hypothesis implied that $\partial U(t)/\partial \gamma(t - \delta) \geqq 0$ and $\partial \pi(t)/\partial \gamma(t - \delta) \leqq 0$. A tax reduction which was financed through bond sales would not reduce the unemployment rate.

Bob Solow raised an interesting and sensible criticism of that test. He wrote:

> Now when would you expect $\gamma$ to take on large values, i.e., when could you expect the federal interest-bearing debt to be growing rapidly? Presumably when the budget deficit is unusually large, so generally when the unemployment rate is high (and, more tenuously, perhaps when the rate of inflation is low).... Therefore, the zero-order correlation between $\gamma$ and the dependent variables

> will be likely to be positive in (44) $[\partial U(t)/\partial \gamma\,(t-\delta)]$ and negative in (45) $[\partial \pi(t)/\partial \gamma(t-\delta)]$. That is to say, they will be 'monetarist' in appearance, though this says absolutely nothing about causal significance.

To my surprise, his conjecture was not correct. I examined the zero-order correlation between $U(t)$ and $\gamma(t-\delta)$ for the period 1960.IV–1970.IV. There was absolutely no relation between these variables, as is shown in regression equation (R-6) below. The "$t$" values are in parentheses. The coefficient of $\gamma(t-\delta)$ was not significantly different from zero, and had the wrong sign,

$$\underset{(26.7)}{U(t) = 4.83} - \underset{(-0.7)}{0.0695}\gamma(t-\delta). \tag{R-6}$$

A more detailed chronological examination of this result, that there is no zero-order relation between these variables, is interesting. The mean unemployment rate during this period was 4.78 percent; and the mean growth of the debt was 0.58 percent per year. Table R-1 categorizes $U(t)$ and $\gamma(t-\delta)$ relative to their mean values. Solow's conjecture was that the entries would lie in the boxes along the principal diagonal: when $U(t)$ was above (below) the mean then the three-quarter moving average growth of the debt $\gamma(t-\delta)$ would also be above (below) its mean.

It is clear that there is no interaction between the rows and the columns. The actual frequencies were practically the same as the expected frequencies: chi-square is 1.1 with one degree of freedom. There was a high growth of the debt $\gamma(t-\delta)$ both during the early Kennedy–Johnson years when the unemployment rate was high, and during the height of the Vietnam War when the unemployment rate was low. Criticism of the monetarist hypothesis must be made on other grounds than that both $U(t)$ and $\gamma(t-\delta)$ are both correlated with the business cycle.

### *3.2. Does the Consumption Function Bias the Results?*

Carl Christ raised several highly significant questions concerning the role of taxes in the consumption function.

> ... the consumption function, which ... underlies the price adjustment equation, does not provide for any dependence of consumption upon taxes. I believe this is a serious flaw in Stein's model. ... this model cannot study the effect of a balanced-budget step increase in both government purchases and taxation. The model simply assumes that the effect of such a fiscal policy change upon both the level of unemployment and the rate of inflation must be zero.

TABLE R-1
The relation between the unemployment rate $U(t)$ and the three-quarter moving average growth of the interest-bearing debt 1960 IV–1970 IV.

| | Growth of debt | | | | |
|---|---|---|---|---|---|
| | $\gamma(t-\delta) > 0.58\%$ p.a. | | $\gamma(t-\delta) < 0.58\%$ p.a. | | Frequency |
| Unemployment | 1970.III | 1962.IV | 1970.IV | | |
| | 1965.I | III | II | | |
| | 1964.IV | II | 1964.III | | |
| | II | I | 1961.IV | | |
| $U(t) > 4.78\%$ | I | | III | | |
| | 1963.IV | | II | | |
| | III | | I | | |
| | II | | 1960.IV | | |
| | I | | | | |
| | Actual 13 | | Actual 8 | | |
| | Expected 11.3 | | Expected 9.7 | | 21 |
| | 1969.III | 1965.III | 1970.I | 1966.IV | |
| | II | II | 1969.IV | III | |
| $U(t) < 4.78\%$ | I | | 1967.IV | II | |
| | 1968.IV | | III | I | |
| | III | | II | 1965.IV | |
| | II | | I | | |
| | I | | | | |
| | Actual 9 | | Actual 11 | | |
| | Expected 10.7 | | Expected 9.3 | | 20 |
| Frequency | | 22 | | 19 | 41 |

Another objection was that the interest payments on the debt were tucked into the taxes less transfer payments category, whereas they should be viewed as a function of the interest rate.

Were I rewriting the paper, I would indicate more clearly that my estimating equations do account for step changes in government purchases of goods and services, the money stock and the quantity of government bonds. The $DG(t-\delta)$ variable is defined as a three-quarter moving average, where $G(t)$ is the real value of government purchases in a given quarter,

$$DG(t - \delta) \equiv \tfrac{1}{3} \sum_{i=1}^{3} [G(t - i) - G(t - i - 4)]$$

$$\equiv \tfrac{1}{3}[G(t - 1) + G(t - 2) + G(t - 3) - G(t - 5) - G(t - 6) - G(t - 7)].$$

A step rise in $G(t)$ to a permanently higher level would make $DG(t - \delta)$ positive for six subsequent quarters. It is the acceleration or deceleration of $G$ which affects the unemployment rate. When $DG(t - \delta)$ returns to zero at $t + 7$, the effect upon the unemployment rate emanating directly from the control variable disappears; but it will take a much longer time for the unemployment rate to reach its equilibrium level, due to the inertia in the system.

The price level $p(t)$ is affected by the level of $G$ as described in figure 1 and equation (25). A rise in $G$ to $G + \Delta G$ will lower the steady-state level of real balances; hence, it must raise the absolute price level. I apologize for not being clear on these important points.

My estimating equations do account for the effects of step changes in the control variables because I work with integrals [in equations (41) or (42)] and not with derivatives. My procedure copes with the Dirac delta function.

My specification of the consumption function seemed to bias the results against fiscal policy because it did not explicitly include taxes and transfer payments, including interest on the debt. It was a function of wealth and not of disposable income. I should have been more explicit in showing why my econometric procedure does not produce such a bias.

Equation (R-7) is my consumption function, where $y(U)$ is output per unit of capital, $m \equiv M/pK$ is real balances per unit of capital and $z \equiv \theta m \equiv Z/pK$ is real government debt per unit of capital,[3]

$$C/K = C[y(U), m, z]. \tag{R-7}$$

Traditionally, consumption per unit of capital is assumed to depend upon real disposable income per unit of capital $y_d$. The latter is defined as output per unit of capital less real taxes plus transfers per unit of capital $T$. Interest payments on the debt are subsumed under $T$.

$$y_d = y(U) - T. \tag{R-8}$$

[3]The logic of this consumption function is that consumption depends upon capitalized output $y(U)/R(U)$ and real financial wealth $m$, $z$. Since $y(U) = wx + R$, where $w$ is the real wage and $x$ is the ratio of employment per unit of capital, capitalized output is

$$y(U)/R(U) = \frac{w}{R(U)}(1 - U)x_s + 1.$$

The government budget constraint is (R-9), assuming that all money is outside money. Define $DM/M = \mu$ and $DZ/Z \equiv \gamma$. Then,

$$G - T = DM/pK + DZ/pK = \mu m + \gamma z \tag{R-9}$$

is the budget constraint. A convenient feature of this formulation of the budget constraint is that a tax rate schedule need not be built into the consumption function, nor must account be taken of interest payments on the debt. Just focus upon the growth of the non-interest-bearing debt $\mu$ and the growth of the interest-bearing debt $\gamma$ to detect the efficacy of a tax cut or variations in transfer payments.

Substitute (R-9) into (R-8) to derive real disposable income. Then, the usual fiscalist consumption function is

$$C/K = C_{\mathrm{F}}(y_{\mathrm{d}}) = C_{\mathrm{F}}[y(U) - G + \mu m + \gamma z]. \tag{R-10}$$

Equation (R-10) is similar in many respects to my consumption function (R-7). The efficacy of a tax cut upon spending and hence upon total employment would be seen by examining $\partial U(t)/\partial\gamma(t-\delta)$ and $\partial\pi(t)/\partial\gamma(t-\delta)$ in reduced form equations (44) and (45). There is no need to decide whether the consumption function is (R-7) or (R-10). In this respect, my econometric procedure does not bias the results against the fiscalists.

To be sure, there are fundamental differences between the two formulations. In (R-10), a tax reduction has an immediate impact upon consumption, so the economy can be controlled quickly. In (R-7), a tax reduction will affect consumption only insofar as it affects $m$ or $z$. Moreover, if debt is not considered part of wealth then a deficit financed with bonds would not lead to a rise in consumption.

If there is a permanent step increase in both taxes and government expenditures, then $G$ will rise and $DG(t-\delta)$ will be positive for six quarters. The deficit $\mu m + \gamma z$ will not change. According to my equation (44), there will be a temporary decline in the unemployment rate below its equilibrium level. In this manner, my formulation explains the effect of a step increase in both government purchases and taxes. I do not think that the formulation contains a serious monetarist bias.

My model and orientation is Keynesian. In particular, I do not allow labor to determine its real wage $w$ because the change in the real wage is [eq. (3a)]

$$Dw/w = \alpha + \pi^* - \pi + h(U).$$

Labor cannot determine the actual rate of price change $\pi$, therefore, it cannot determine $Dw/w$. The absolute value of $h'(U)$ can be expected to be smaller when nominal wages tend to decline than when they tend to rise. This modification would make my $UU'$ curve piecewise linear; and my formulation would be consistent with Keynes' observation (cited by Solow), that labor reacts differently to a rise in prices than it does to an attempted cut in nominal wages. When money wages tend to decline, the convergence to the steady state would be too slow to be socially acceptable. The existence of an equilibrium rate of unemployment $U_e$ is not relevant to the short-run counter-cyclical problems, and it does not negate the desirability of an intelligent stabilization policy. A Keynesian can be a monetarist.

### *3.3. The Robustness of the Empirical Tests*

Carl Christ correctly indicated that my choice of the time interval over which to integrate the differential equations is arbitrary: they can be integrated over any time interval. Nevertheless, he noted: "It is not clear how such a change [in the time interval] would affect the empirical results, but neither is it clear that the results would be invariant to a change in the length of this interval."

Very recently, Michael J. Hamburger and Rutbert D. Reisch applied my model to an open economy.[4] In the course of their analysis, they used a different estimation procedure. (a) Observations on the dependent variables were spaced four quarters apart rather than every quarter. Serial correlation was thereby reduced. (b) The control variable began to influence the state variable in the current period, rather than with a one quarter lag. (c) The control variables were then measured as annual averages, rather than as three-quarter moving averages. This was an important simplification for countries other than the U.S. (d) The data were fitted to the period 1954.IV to 1970.IV rather than to 1960.IV to 1970.IV. Their purpose was to determine the combined effects of change in the estimation procedure and the lengthening of the sample period. Their conclusions were as follows:

> The results shown on the right-hand sides of Tables 3 and 4 are generally quite similar to Stein's which are reproduced on the left-hand sides of the tables. The main differences introduced as a result of our modifications are a substantial drop in the serial correlations in the residuals and a decline in the significance of money ($\mu$) in the price change equation. However, given the similarity in the parameter estimates and the much smaller number of degrees of freedom in our sample as compared to Stein's (12 versus 36), this finding may not be very surprising or disturbing.

On the basis of the Hamburger–Reisch study, the empirical results seem to be relatively robust to different methods of estimation.

[4] M. J. Hamburger and R. D. Reisch, Inflation, unemployment and macro-economic policy in open economies: An empirical analysis, Carnegie-Mellon/University of Rochester Conference on Public Policy, April 1975. This will appear in a book published by North-Holland Publishing Co.

## 4. Stagflation and the Recession of 1974–1975

Bob Solow posed an important question: "If the model says that the 1974 inflation is fully accounted for by monetary policy, to what does it attribute the recession of 1974–1975?" A macro-economic theory worthy of its name must be able to answer Solow's question in a non-tautological manner and without adducing ad hoc factors extraneous to the model.

### *4.1. A Revised Model*[5]

Shortly after presenting my paper, I addressed myself to the question: "How can the recent rounds of stagflation be explained within the context of the "Black Box" model?" It became clear to me that an alteration in the wage change equation would permit me to explain this phenomenon and to answer Solow's question. The resulting product has a high degree of predictive power.

Suppose that there is an excess demand for goods and services. Firms bid up nominal wages in their quest for additional labor to produce the increase in goods and services demanded. Within each industry, labor thinks that a rise in the nominal wage signifies a rise in the purchasing power of the wage over consumer goods; and additional employment in offered at the higher nominal wage. A decline occurs in the unemployment rate as firms demand, and labor offers, more employment. Since the excess demand for goods and services is pervasive, the prices of wage goods rise by more than labor anticipated. Firms forecast the rise in the prices of their products more accurately than labor forecasts the rise in the consumer price index. This is to be expected because the latter refers to an index number which is remote from people's direct experience, whereas the former is part of the firm's day-to-day experience.

Labor discovers that it is working at a lower than anticipated real wage: the quantity supplied is below the long-run supply of labor, during the phase of unanticipated inflation. Suppose that the demand for and supply of labor functions are linear in the real wage $w$, where

$$\text{(a)}\ w_s = ax$$

$$\text{(b)}\ w_d = b - cx$$

are the supply and demand prices for labor per unit of capital ($x$), respectively.

[5] The model and empirical results presented here are based upon my paper: *The paradox of stagflation*, presented at the Miami University Conference on Inflation, 15–16 May 1975, Oxford, Ohio. The proceedings of this conference will be published in book form.

Simply for convenience, assume that firms are always on the demand curves for labor. Then, the difference between the supply price and the actual real wage is

(c) $w_s - w_d = (a + c)x - b.$

Employment per unit of capital is defined as

(d) $x \equiv (1 - U)x_s,$

where $x_s$ is the civilian labor force per unit of capital. The equilibrium rate of unemployment $U_e$, or of employment per unit of capital $x_e$, is given by the condition $w_s = w_d$,

(e) $x_s(1 - U_e) = x_e = b/(a + c).$

Consequently, the difference between the supply price and demand price for labor is

(f) $w_s - w_d = (a + c)x_s(U_e - U) = -\lambda_1 x_1,$

where $x_1 \equiv U - U_e$ and $\lambda_1 \equiv (a + c)x_s$.

Define $g(t)$ as the present value of the real wages lost (or gained) because the unanticipated inflation (or deflation) resulted in a situation where labor is not operating on its long-run supply curve. It is given by

$$g(t) = -\lambda_1 \int^t x_1(t - \tau)e^{-\rho(t-\tau)}d\tau, \tag{R-11}$$

$$Dg(t) = -\lambda_1 x_1(t) \equiv -\lambda_1[U(t) - U_e]. \tag{R-12}$$

My revised wage change equation becomes (R-13) instead of (3). The new element reflects the view that the recent path of the unemployment rate is a crucial variable in affecting the growth of the nominal wage. It concerns the ability of labor which is currently employed to make us for previously unanticipated declines in the real wage.

$$DW/W = \alpha + \pi^* + h(U) + g(t). \tag{R-13}$$

Labor will tend to succeed in its wage demands,

$$\frac{\partial DW/W}{\partial g(t)} > 0,$$

because profits will have risen during the period when the real wage was below the long-run supply of labor. Employers would be hard pressed to explain why they cannot compensate labor, out of their windfall profits, for the unanticipated losses in the real wage suffered by labor which is currently employed.

TABLE R-2
The basic equations in the revised model.

| | |
|---|---|
| (R-14) | $DU = \beta(\pi^* + h(U) + g - \pi)$ |
| (R-15) | $Dg = -\lambda_1 (U - U_e)$ |
| (R-16) | $\pi = P(U, \pi^*, m, g; \theta, G)$ |
| (R-17) | $Dm/m = \mu - n - \pi$ |
| (R-18) | $D\pi^* = b(\pi - \pi^*)$ |

*Key:* $U$ is the unemployment rate, $\pi$ is the rate of price change; $\pi^*$ is the expected rate of price change; $m$ are real balances per unit of capital; $g$ is the present value of the difference between the supply price and the demand price for labor, integrated over past unemployment rates; $D \equiv d/dt$.

With the substitution of (R-13) for (3), and the addition of (R-12), the dynamic model is described in table R-2. The other equations are unchanged. Although the steady-state properties are the same as before, it is now a fourth-order dynamical system. The overshooting of the equilibrium and the stagflation phenomenon are inherent in the $g(t)$ term, which reflects the attempt of labor to be compensated for the losses in the real wage during the previous period of unanticipated inflation.

A virtue of this revised model is that the recent periods of stagflation and the 1974–1975 recession need not be accounted for on the basis of "expectations", exogenous factors or business cum union monopolies. The popular expectations argument, at best, is "meaningless" in the sense that it does not rest upon a refutable hypothesis. Moreover, if expectations did indeed generate the stagflation then the imposition of a wage–price freeze was a brilliant démarche: it provided a cooling-off period. Were the overshooting of price expectations the culprit in the stagflation process, a vigilant policeman in the form of a Prices and Incomes Commission would be all that is needed for as long a period as expectations outran the reality. As far as I know, no scientific evidence has ever been presented to recommend that cure.

### *4.2. A Theoretical Explanation of Stagflation and the Recent Recession*

A phase diagram can be constructed from the equations in table R-2. The $UU'$ curve is the locus of $x_1 \equiv U - U_e$ and $\pi$ such that there is no tendency for the unemployment rate to change. Its intercept is $\pi^*(t) + g(t)$. The $PP'$ curve is the locus of $x_1$ and $\pi$ such that there is no tendency for the rate of price change to accelerate or decelerate.

Suppose that the economy were in equilibrium at point $E_0$ in figure R-1. The unemployment rate has been in equilibrium for some time $x_1 = g = 0$; and the actual and expected rates of price change are equal to the rate of monetary expansion per unit of capital $\pi = \pi^* = \mu - n$. Then the rate of monetary expansion rises significantly to $\mu_1 > \mu_0$. What will happen?

Formally the $PP'$ curve shifts upwards to $P_1P_1'$. Real money balances rise. Firms and households use the unexpectedly larger real balances to demand more goods and financial assets, thereby raising their prices. Capital formation and the production of consumer goods are stimulated. Firms bid up nominal wages in their quest for additional labor to produce the increased demand for goods and services. The economy heads along trajectory $E_0 A$ in figure R-1. The excess demand for goods raises the rate of price change; and the unemployment rate decreases since labor does not fully anticipate the inflation.

For the reasons adduced earlier, labor finds itself selling its services at a price below the long-run supply of labor. Variable $g(t)$, which represents the present value of the difference between the supply price and the demand price for labor becomes positive. Stage two of the stagflation process concerns the attempt of labor to make up for previous cumulative losses of the real wage by raising the growth of the nominal wage. Moreover, the inflationary expectations will be adjusted more closely to the rate of monetary expansion per unit of capital $\mu_1 - n$. Formally, the $UU'$ curve will shift upwards to $U_1U_1'$ with an intercept of $g(t) + \pi^*(t)$. Since $g(t)$ is positive, the intercept of the $U_1U_1'$ curve exceeds the intercept $\pi^*(t)$ of the $P_1P_1'$ curve. Figure R-2 describes this situation whereby the economy follows trajectory $A'AA''B$. What does this mean in economic terms?

Current wage negotiations attempt to rectify the cumulative real wage losses resulting from the previously unanticipated inflation and to protect labor from the more accurately perceived future inflation $\mu_1 - n$. At the same time that labor costs are rising, real balances per unit of capital are declining due to the accelerating inflation. Firms and households attempt to build up their depleted real balances by decreasing the growth of their real purchases of goods and services relative to the growth rate of capital. Costs per unit of output accelerate just as the demand for goods and services decelerate. Prices may even accelerate just when excess capacity begins to develop. To be sure, if the demand for goods had not declined the inflation would have been even more severe. If the unemployment rate had not risen as a result of the cost–price squeeze, the nominal wage would have risen by more than it did. During stage two, which is stagflation, the economy moves along trajectory $A'AA''B$ (figure R-2). Unemployment, the growth of unit labor costs and inflation rise. Even when the rate of inflation declines, unemployment continue to rise (segment $A''B$).

In stage three, the monetary authorities reduce the rate of monetary expansion at an inopportune time – when labor costs are rising due to the $g(t)$ catch up factor, and real balances per unit of capital are declining due to the inflation. This

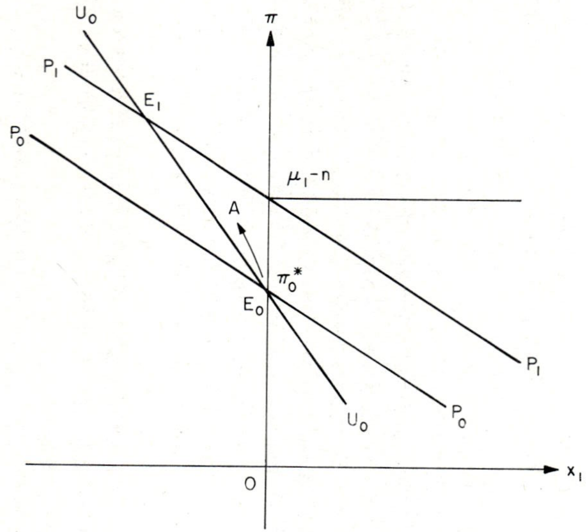


FIGURE R-1. When the rate of monetary expansion rises to $\mu_1$, the economy follows trajectory $E_0A$. The unemployment rate declines and the inflation rate rises.

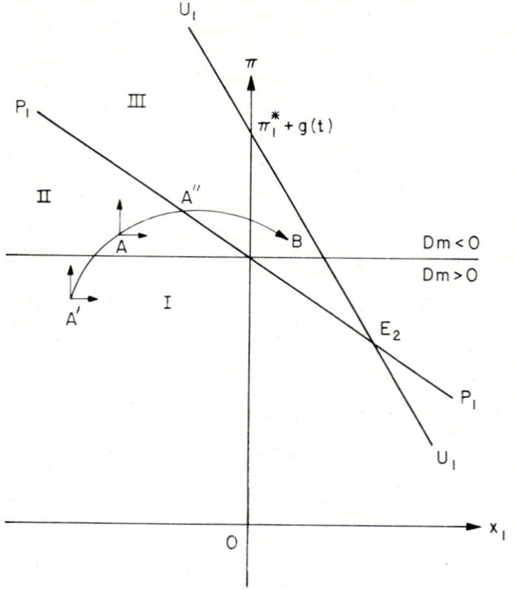


FIGURE R-2. When labor attempts to recoup its real wage losses from the previously unanticipated inflation, the economy follows trajectory $A'AA''B$ and stagflation is generated.

monetary deceleration, described by a downward shift of the $PP'$ curve (not drawn here), aggravates the decline in real balances per unit of capital. A "hard landing" is produced, which is just what a rapid deceleration means.

Firms and households attempt to rebuild their real balances per unit of capital by scaling down the growth in their demand for goods, services and financial assets. As a result of the decline in the growth in the demand and the rise in labor costs, the unemployment rate rises drastically. At this stage, the shock is so severe that the rate of inflation declines.

This is my theoretical answer to Bob Solow's question: The recession of 1974–1975 was produced in Washington, D.C.

### *4.3. Empirical Evidence in Support of the Theory*

The theory developed above was tested in the following way. Estimating equations (R-19) and (R-20) are from column 1 of tables 6 and 7 in the "black box" paper. They were based upon a sample period 1962.IV–1970.IV. Only the constant term in (R-19) is not significantly different from zero.

$$U(t) = 0.9 + 0.84U(t-3) + 0.35\pi(t-3) - 0.002DG(t-\delta) - 0.24\mu(t-\delta); \quad \text{S.E.} = 0.3, \qquad \text{(R-19)}$$

$$\pi(t) = 2.7 - 0.42U(t-3) + 0.73\pi(t-3) + 0.07\mu(t-\delta); \quad \text{S.E.} = 0.26. \qquad \text{(R-20)}$$

A necessary but not sufficient condition for the acceptance of a model is its ability to predict outside the sample period. Table R-3 is an update of table 9, column 3. It shows how my relatively simple dynamic model is able to predict the unemployment rate outside the sample period, based upon equation (R-19). Moreover, it certainly predicts the severe recession of 1974–1975 in terms of the unemployment rate. From 1971.I through 1974.IV, the root mean square error (RMSQE) was 0.27, it was less than the standard error. Which one of the big models can predict as well outside the sample period, and uses as little information? The monetary policies followed during the period produced the severe rise in unemployment in 1975.

During the period of price controls, the official rate of inflation was determined by fiat. When the prices were freed of these controls, they moved to levels predicted accurately by my model.

From equations (R-19), (R-20), derive the steady-state rate of price change $\pi_e$. This is done by setting $U(t) = U(t-3) = U_e$, $\pi(t) = \pi(t-3) = \pi_e$, and solving the resulting equations for $\pi_e$. The sample period is 1962.IV–1970.IV.

TABLE R-3
Prediction of the unemployment rate from 1971.I to 1975.III, outside the sample period 1962.IV–1970.IV.

| Date | Actual | Predicted |
|---|---|---|
| 1971.I | 5.97% | 6.13% |
| II | 5.97 | 6.16 |
| III | 6. | 6.42 |
| IV | 5.93 | 6.23 |
| 1972.I | 5.9 | 6.1 |
| II | 5.7 | 5.7 |
| III | 5.6 | 5.1 |
| IV | 5.3 | 4.9 |
| 1973.I | 5 | 4.3 |
| II | 4.9 | 4.3 |
| III | 4.7 | 4.3 |
| IV | 4.7 | 4.4 |
| 1974.I | 5.2 | 5.0 |
| II | 5.5 | 5.4 |
| III | 5.8 | 5.9 |
| IV | 6.6 | 7.1 |
| | RMSQE = 0.27 | |
| 1975.I | | 7.5 |
| II | | 8.1 |
| III | | 9.4 |

Equation (R-21) is derived:[6]

$$\pi_e = 1.5 + 0.6(\mu - 0.6). \tag{R-21}$$

Table R-4 contains the rates of monetary expansion and rates of price change from: 1947 to 1974.IV, a twenty-seven-year span; 1954 to 1974.IV, a twenty-year period; and from 1969.IV to 1974.IV, a five-year period. The object is to predict the price level in 1974.IV, or the rate of inflation between each pair of dates, on the basis of equation (R-21). Our expectation is that the more widely separated are the dates, the better the steady-state rate of price change approximates the observed rate of price change.

[6] In my paper, I used $\pi_e = 1.5 + 0.7\ (\mu - 0.6)$ based upon column 1 in tables 4 and 5. It is a less accurate predictor than equation (R-21) above.

TABLE R-4
Long-range prediction of the 1974.IV price level.

| | 1947–74.IV (27 yrs.) | 1954–74.IV (20 yrs.) | 1969.IV–74.IV (5 yrs.) |
|---|---|---|---|
| Rate of monetary expansion $\mu$ | 3.4% p.a. | 3.8% p.a. | 6.6% p.a. |
| Actual rate of price change $\pi$ | 3.2 | 3.4 | 6.1 |
| Predicted steady-state rate of price change $\pi_e$ | 3.2 | 3.4 | 5.1 |
| Predicted price level in 1974.IV | 176.1 | 177.6 | 168.4 |
| Actual price level in 1974.IV | 177.7 | 177.7 | 177.7 |

In 1974.IV the *GNP* deflator was 177.7. The long-range predictions 1947–1974 and 1954–1974 are remarkably accurate; but the five-year prediction of the rate of inflation was one percentage point below the actual rate. Our conclusion is that the data are consistent with the basic monetarist proposition that: as the length of period increases, the rate of price change is overwhelmingly determined by the rate of monetary expansion.[7]

The inescapable conclusion is that the inflation and recessions that we have experienced is overwhelmingly due to the monetary policy that we have followed not to external random events.

> This is the excellent foppery of the world, that when we are sick in fortune, often the surfeit of our own behavior, we make guilty of our disasters the sun, the moon, and the stars: as if we were villains by necessity, fools by heavenly compulsion. . . .

[7] In the stagflation paper cited, I used revised money stock data to estimate the unemployment rate equation during the 1961.III–1973.IV period. It was:

$$U(t) = \underset{(3.5)}{1.27} + \underset{(14.1)}{0.74}U(t-3) + \underset{(4.4)}{0.23}\pi(t-3) - \underset{(-3.8)}{0.003}DG(t-\delta) - \underset{(-6.2)}{0.15}\mu(t-\delta); \quad \text{S.E.} = 0.33,$$

where "$t$" are in parentheses. The predictions outside the sample period are as follows:

| | | |
|---|---|---|
| 1974.I 4.92% | 1975.I 6.44% | 1976.I 9.09% |
| II 5.13 | II 7.09 | II 8.35 |
| III 5.47 | III 8.19 | |
| IV 6.31 | IV 9.4 | |

For 1975–1976, it seems that I may be two quarters out of phase.

Chapter 4

# LONG-RUN EFFECTS OF FISCAL AND MONETARY POLICY ON AGGREGATE DEMAND

James TOBIN and Willem BUITER

## 1. Introduction: The Setting of the Problem

This paper is a theoretical exercise addressed to a rather esoteric and artificial question in the logic of aggregate demand. Does expansionary fiscal policy raise aggregate demand permanently or at best only temporarily? The controversy is reminiscent of the Pigou–Keynes–Lerner controversy on the efficacy of reduction of money wages and prices in expanding aggregate demand, where also much was made of the distinction between short-run impacts and ultimate cumulative effects. The trouble with such discussions, including this one, is that a long run constructed to track the ultimate consequences of anything is a never-never land. For that abstraction we apologize in advance.

A characteristic monetarist proposition is that pure fiscal policy does not matter for aggregate real demand, nominal income, and the price level. The course of aggregate nominal demand, stochastic influences aside, depends solely on the path of the quantity of money somehow defined. Although increases in this monetary aggregate may frequently in practice be associated with budget deficits, the central bank always can break this link and very often does. The fiscal policies alleged not to matter are variations of government expenditure, transfer payments, and taxes while the quantity of money or its path over time remain unchanged.

We have stated this monetarist proposition baldly for the purpose of theoretical discussion. We realize that monetarists, Professor Friedman in particular, usually soften their assertions with qualifying adjectives and adverbs "minor", "almost", etc. After all, no one would wish to have his salvation depend on the literally complete independence of any two variables in a complex interdependent economy. Hedges of this order really do not alter the monetarist message for theory and policy, and they are not intended to. Therefore, let us hope that we can discuss the strong proposition without semantic and textual quarrel about the strength and purity with which it has been asserted.

Non-monetarists have argued on numerous occasions that a necessary condition for the proposition is zero elasticity of demand for money with respect to interest rates, and we have offered against the proposition the theoretical reasons and empirical evidence for believing this elasticity is not zero. In the comparative statics of short-run macro-equilibrium this condition appears as a vertical *LM* curve. When the condition is not met, the analysis indicates that a shift in the *IS* curve, – which could be brought about by an increase in the rate of government expenditures or transfers or by reduction in the flow of tax revenues – will raise aggregate real demand.

The extent to which this expansion evokes an increase in supply depends on how close the economy is to its productive capacity. Perhaps we should stress the point that no one is contending that fiscal policy can increase output when production is supply-constrained. Neither can monetary policy. Moreover, this particular debate is not about the existence or size of the natural rate of unemployment. Logically the natural rate proposition is distinct from the monetarist propositions about fiscal policy; one could accept either one without the other.

Even when output is supply-constrained issues concerning aggregate demand remain. The monetarist proposition then is that expansionary fiscal policy – purged of incidental and extrinsic monetary expansion – does not affect the price level. Basically the assertion is that government cannot change, by its own spending behavior or by measures designed to affect that of taxpayers and other citizens, the income velocity of money.

On its face this is a very surprising assertion. If those present at the conference were to decide to lower our average cash holdings while maintaining our spending, we would all agree that national income velocity would rise, though the change would hardly be detectible by our measuring devices. If the Fortune 100 did likewise, it would be detectible. Why not when the federal government does so– especially considering that the measure of velocity includes its spending in the numerator but excludes its cash from the denominator?

Monetarists argue that their proposition holds whether or not the *LM* curve is vertical. Friedman (1972, pp. 915–917) reaffirmed this view in his rejoinder to Tobin's comments on his "theoretical framework" articles. He says that fiscal effects are "certain to be temporary and likely to be minor", and that our difference of opinion is "mostly, whether one considers only the impact effect of a change or the cumulative effect". He agrees that the impact effect of a rise in government expenditure or reduction in taxes is expansionary; there is a once-for-all shift of "*IS*" and this pulls up income and interest rate along a non-vertical *LM* locus. By labelling this effect on income not only "minor" but "temporary" he seems to be saying that non-monetary financing of the accompanying budget deficits moves *LM* to the left, cancelling the expansionary shift of *IS*. But he does not say this explicitly, stressing instead that monetary financing of the same fiscal program would be more and longer expansionary than the issue of interest-bearing debt.

Anyway, the issue we wish to discuss is whether and when the impact effects typified by *IS–LM* statics are reversed, modified, or amplified by shifts in those curves. But we have a few more general observations in prelude.

First, how relevant is this issue to the policy controversy which generated the theoretical debate in the first place? The policy controversy concerns such practical matters as the effects of the 1964 tax cut, the anti-inflationary content of the 1968 tax surcharge, the role of the escalation of war spending in escalating inflation in 1966, the importance of budget economy in fighting inflation or accentuating recession in 1974. In cases like these, advocates of fiscal measures were looking for short-term effects on aggregate demand, without committing themselves to changes of expenditures and taxes never to be repeated or reversed. They were certainly not contemplating that the stock of money should remain forever constant while the stocks of other assets grow. When Walter Heller argued that the tax cut of 1964 would increase demand and reduce unemployment he was talking about what would happen in 1965. He was not talking about what would happen in 1970 or 1980 if the tax cut were even then the only change from pre-1964 monetary and fiscal policies. In this context it was no answer to say that years of accumulation of debt in exclusively non-monetary form would be contractionary. It *was* an answer, right or wrong, to say that demand for money is interest-inelastic.

Second, the claim that growth of non-monetary government debt has the same qualitative effects as reduction of money supply depends on a particular view about asset preferences – roughly that non-monetary debt is a closer substitute in portfolios for capital than for money. This is the traditional view, shared by Keynes. In his "Essay on the Principles of Debt Management" Tobin (1971) distinguished between fiscal or flow effects of government budgets and deficits and the monetary or stock effects of the accumulated debt. He pointed out that, for a one-time change of budgetary program, the flow effect is one-shot while the stock effect cumulates. A corollary is that the flow effect is reversed when the budgetary change is reversed, while the stock effect persists. But at the same time Tobin entertained the possibility that the stock effect of non-monetary debt may be expansionary, that such assets are in investors' eyes closer to money than to capital. If so the growth of non-monetary debt would shift the *LM* curve to the right rather than to the left. (The relevant interest rate on the Hicks diagram would be in this case the true Modigliani–Miller cost of equity capital, which would diverge from the rates on government securities.) We mention this here because we shall not pursue the matter in this paper, where we shall acquiesce in an extreme version of the traditional assumption, namely that government securities and capital are perfect substitutes in portfolios.

Third, there is some tendency to couple the monetarist proposition with a general attack on the use of equilibrium analysis and comparative statics, particularly the *IS–LM* apparatus, in short-run macro-economics. The attack has some justification, because it is generally true that the *incomplete* stock–flow equilibrium determined in such models implies changes in some stocks whose assumed constancy was a condition of the flow equilibrium itself. What is not true is that recognition of the temporary nature of the "equilibrium" invalidates all the propositions of such analysis or validates contrary propositions.

Keynes explicitly restricted his *General Theory* to a time period in which the stock of capital is for practical purposes constant. Yet a Keynesian equilibrium generally involves non-zero net investment, implying changes in capital stock and thus quite possibly in the investment function and other behavioral equations of his model. The same short-run assumption applies to other stocks and flows, including government debt and deficit: the analysis does not apply to a "run" long enough for the flow to make a significant change in the stock. Careful teachers of *IS–LM* and all that have never allowed their students to use the apparatus on questions like "the effects of an increase in government spending financed by printing money" because they knew that the change in money stock was indeterminate and time-dependent. Unfortunately they seldom get around to dynamic models in which the question makes sense.

## 2. The Plan and Notation of the Paper

In a pioneering paper, Blinder and Solow, inspired by the same questions which concern us, have presented a model of long-run equilibrium similar to the one we shall discuss below.[1] Our reasons for offering another version are two. First, we wish to consider some additional ways of modelling fiscal and monetary policy. Second, we wish to structure the long-run demands for wealth, capital, and money somewhat more definitely and explicitly than Blinder and Solow did, especially in their original article. We shall discuss the differences in some detail in section 3.

[1] Blinder and Solow (1973). A summary, with an important amendment, is given by the same authors in Blinder and Solow (1974, pp. 45–58). The amendment is to include income $Y$ in the investment function; we discuss its significance below in section 3. Blinder and Solow appear to have contributed the first systematic treatment of long-run effects of fiscal policy in an economy without binding labor constraints on output. Of course, growth theory has treated the long-run effects of fiscal and monetary policies in economies with full employment and flexible prices. Even there, fiscal and monetary measures are generally so intertwined that "money-growth" models shed little light on the issues concerning "pure" fiscal and monetary effects.

Like Blinder and Solow, we shall consider a Pigovian stationary state. The advantage of this abstraction is that it allows in a simple manner for adjustments of stocks of capital and other assets. It avoids the possible flow–stock inconsistencies of the short-run equilibrium models. It therefore permits us to consider the monetarist claim that the apparent power of fiscal policy in those models depends wholly on such inconsistencies. Yet the model is artificial in several respects. To be relevant to the issue at hand, the model must permit unemployment even in long-run stationary equilibrium; and this requires the implausible indefinite persistence of wage and price rigidities. We shall also, however, consider the effects of fiscal policy on the price level in a long-run equilibrium with full employment and flexible prices.

The plan of the rest of the paper is as follows: Section 3 discusses briefly the Blinder–Solow contributions. Section 4 discusses the long-run comparative statics and stability properties of pure fiscal measures in economies with unemployed labor. In Model I the instrument of fiscal policy is $G'$, government purchases of goods and services plus debt interest net of taxes on such interest. We trace the effects of once-for-all changes of $G'$, while both the money stock and the proportional tax rate remain constant. As net debt interest changes, government purchases are adjusted dollar for dollar in the opposite direction to hold $G'$ at its policy-determined level.

In Model II, the parameter of fiscal policy is $G$, government purchases, as it is in Blinder–Solow. This means that the fiscal stimulus varies endogenously as the volume of debt and the interest rate change.

Finally, section 4 analyzes briefly the use of the tax rate $\theta$ as an instrument of fiscal policy.

Section 5 takes up, still in the context of long-run unemployment, the effects of changing the quantity of money. Two kinds of monetary change are considered. One is a change in the quantity of money via open market operations, while fiscal instruments, $\theta$ and $G$ or $G'$ are held constant. The second is monetary change linked to fiscal policy: budget deficits consequent to a change in $G$ or $G'$ are financed by printing money while the non-monetary public debt is fixed.

Section 6 shifts from the Keynesian world of long-run unemployment to the neo-classical long run of full employment and flexible prices. Once again the questions are how variation of $G'$ affects the long-run equilibrium and whether the equilibrium is stable.

The variables of our models are as follows:

$Y$ = real net national product,
$K$ = capital stock,
$N$ = employment of labor,
$\overline{N}$ = labor force,

$D$ = nominal government interest-bearing debt,
$R$ = nominal rate of return on debt,
$r = R(1 - \theta)$, after-tax rate of return,
$G$ = real government expenditure, not including debt interest,
$G'$ = real government expenditure, including net debt interest,
$M$ = nominal monetary debt of government,
$\theta$ = tax rate,
$W$ = real private wealth, $K + \{(D + M)/p\}$,
$\alpha$ = capital share in income,
$p$ = price level,
$x$ = expected rate of inflation.

In the unemployment models of sections 4 and 5, employment $N$ is always less than labor force $\overline{N}$, the price level $p$ is assumed constant, and expected inflation $x$ is zero. In the full employment model of section 6, $N$ is equal to $\overline{N}$, and both $p$ and $x$ are endogenous.

Non-monetary debt is modelled like bills of short maturity, indeed strictly like interest-bearing deposits. It is always valued at par although its yield is market-determined and varies. The only convenient alternative, the one adopted by Blinder and Solow, is to go to the opposite extreme and to assume that all government debts are perpetuities with constant coupons but variable prices. The difference is not consequential for the questions of interest. More realistic specifications, with debts of finite maturity, enmesh dynamic analysis in a morass of complex bookkeeping which is not worth the trouble.

It is assumed throughout that production of $Y$ obeys a constant-returns-to-scale function of capital $K$ and labor $N$, with the usual neo-classical properties. In equilibrium the marginal product of capital derived from the production function, is equal to the real before-tax rate of return on debt ($R$ in sections 4 and 5, $R - x$ in section 6). As previously stated, we follow – without endorsing – the Keynesian assumption that debt and capital are perfect substitutes in portfolios. At times of disequilibrium the marginal product of capital may differ from the return on debt. Their divergence is the signal and incentive for net investment or disinvestment in capital.

## 3. The Blinder–Solow Models of Fiscal Effects

Blinder and Solow present first a "long-run" model with a fixed capital stock but variable government debt, and then a model in which both stocks are endogenous. The first has at best expository relevance, since it is unrealistic and potentially misleading to assume that over a horizon in which wealth and government debt change no capital accumulation can occur. For that reason, we will confine our comments and comparison to their variable-capital model. $B$ will denote the number of bonds and the money value of current debt service. (Bonds are consols with a coupon of one unit of money.) Using our own notation where possible, we can write their model as follows:

$$Y = C[Y + B - T(Y + B), M + (B/R) + K] + I(R, K) + G; \qquad 0 < C_Y < 1, \quad C_W > 0, \tag{1}$$

$$M = L[R, Y, M + (B/R) + K]; \qquad 0 < T' < 1, \tag{2}$$

$$\dot{K} = I(R, K); \qquad I_R < 0, \quad I_K < 0, \tag{3}$$

$$\dot{B} = [G + B - T(Y + B)]R; \qquad L_R < 0, \quad L_Y > 0, \quad 0 < L_W < 1. \tag{4}$$

$C$ and $T$ are, respectively, consumption and tax functions. $Y = F(B, K)$ and $R = H(B, K)$ are the *IS–LM* solutions for income and interest rate, respectively.

The main differences between this model and ours are in the specification and in policy options considered:[2]

(a) We have opted to put more explicit structure on the stationary state demand functions for stocks of wealth and capital. Our short-run saving and investment functions are derived from these demand functions via mechanisms of adjusting actual to desired stocks. In the Blinder–Solow model, in contrast, the long-run desired stocks are implicit in the consumption and investment equations [by setting $C + G = Y$ and $I = 0$ in (1) and (3)].

(b) The investment function (3), in the original Blinder–Solow, is poorly motivated. They argue that the function "is in line with modern investment theory, which envisions an equilibrium demand for capital stock and a disequilibrium demand for investment" [Blinder–Solow (1973, p. 330)]. Yet the omission of $Y$ from the function vitiates this rationalization for a model in which $Y$ is endogenous. The omission is corrected in their second exposition [Blinder–Solow (1974, p. 55)]. The investment function here is $\dot{K} = I(R, Y, K)$, presumably with $I_Y > 0$. However, the stability conditions repeated in the second version are those derived for the model with the misspecified investment equation.

[2] An inessential difference, the modelling of government debt as perpetuities, has already been mentioned.

In their original model, sufficient conditions for stability are

$$F_B > (1 - T')/T' \quad \text{and} \quad I_K + C_W < 0,$$

($F_B$ is the reduced form impact multiplier of an increase in the number of bonds held by the private sector). It can be shown that in this model stability implies $\mathrm{d}B/\mathrm{d}G > 0$ and vice versa [if $F_B > (1 - T')/T'$]–the new equilibrium number of bonds after an increase in government spending on goods and services is larger than the old equilibrium number of bonds if, and only if, the equilibrium is stable.

In the model with the amended investment function, two things happen: First, the stability conditions become very much more stringent–the linearized system is now

$$\begin{bmatrix} \dot{B} \\ \dot{K} \end{bmatrix} = \begin{bmatrix} R(1 - T' - T'F_B) & R(-T'F_K) \\ I_R H_B + I_Y F_B & I_K + H_K I_R + F_K I_Y \end{bmatrix} \begin{bmatrix} (B - B^*) \\ (K - K^*) \end{bmatrix}.$$

$(1 - T')/T' < F_B$ and $F_K < 0$ $[C_W + I_K < 0]$ are no longer sufficient for stability, since the determinant condition is no longer necessarily satisfied.

Second, stability of the system now isn't sufficient to guarantee $\mathrm{d}B/\mathrm{d}G > 0$, or vice versa. If $\mathrm{d}B/\mathrm{d}G < 0$, the long-run multiplier for bond-financed deficit spending no longer exceeds that for money-financed deficit spending [Blinder–Solow (1973, p. 327)]. It is even possible that $\mathrm{d}B/\mathrm{d}G$ is negative and so large numerically that it causes

$$\frac{\mathrm{d}Y}{\mathrm{d}G} = \left(1 + (1 - T')\frac{\mathrm{d}B}{\mathrm{d}G}\right)\Big/T'$$

to become negative. This comparative-static result can obtain whether or not the equilibrium is stable.

In the stable case, this intuitively implausible result would require the government to run more surpluses than deficits along the adjustment path, even though the initial impact of higher government spending may be to create deficits. This problem arises because Blinder and Solow do not restrict, by their consumption function, the long-run equilibrium relationship of wealth to income. It may turn out that, when the public is content with the fixed money stock and has adjusted both capital and wealth to desired magnitudes, there is less, not more, room in portfolios for debt. This possibility is evaded by their original investment function, which implies an equilibrium capital stock independent of $Y$, but it can occur when desired $K$ rises with $Y$.

(c) As regards the fiscal policy options considered, Blinder and Solow deal exclusively with our Model II. The possibility that the long-run government spending multiplier is negative under bond-financed deficits arises only in that regime. In our Model I the multiplier for $G'$ is always positive.

## 4. Analysis of Effects of Debt-Financed Government Expenditures

Variations of fiscal policy are characterized by changes in government outlays, with the tax rate $\theta$ and the money stock $M$ held constant. In Model I the parameter of policy is $G'$; in Model II, it is $G$. The former is simpler analytically and in a sense more plausible in examining the long-run consequences of a one-step change of the parameter. Model I assumes that if debt interest increases purchases are curtailed correspondingly.[3] Model II, as in Solow–Blinder, credits a given fiscal policy with expansionary effect just because interest rate increases or deficits raise outlays for debt interest. Some might regard this procedure not as a constant fiscal policy but as an ever more expansionary policy.

### 4.1. *Comparative Statics in the Two Models*

Here are the long-run equilibrium equations for Models I and II:

$$W = \mu(Y - RK)(1 - \theta) = \mu(1 - \theta)(1 - \alpha)Y = \hat{\mu}Y. \tag{5}$$

This is the condition for zero private saving. On life cycle principles, wealth is a multiple of disposable labor income. For simplicity, $\mu$ and $\alpha$ and thus $\hat{\mu}$, are taken to be constants, but they could made functions of $R$.

$$\text{(I)} \qquad G' - \theta Y = 0,$$

$$\text{(II)} \qquad G + R(1 - \theta)D - \theta Y = 0. \tag{6}$$

This is the condition for zero government saving, a balanced budget. The tax rate $\theta$ applies to wages, capital income, and debt interest.

$$M = L(r, Y/W)W = L(r, 1/\hat{\mu})\hat{\mu}Y; \qquad L_1 < 0, \;\; \hat{\mu}L > L_2 > 0. \tag{7}$$

The fraction of wealth held in money is inversely related to the after-tax return on alternative assets and positively related to the income/wealth ratio, which is

[3] An alternative which would be more plausible would to be aim fiscal policy for budget balance at a target income level $Y^*$, fixing the level of government exhaustive expenditures at $G$, and letting $\theta$ vary with debt interest so as to maintain budget balance at $Y^*$. We investigated such a model, but the analysis is too messy to report.

constant in equilibrium. Since debt and capital are perfect substitutes, (7) is a complete description of portfolio allocation.

$$K = F(R)Y, \qquad K = (\alpha/R)Y. \tag{8}$$

Technologically, the capital/output ratio is inversely related to the rate of return on capital.

$$W = K + D + M. \tag{9}$$

This is the definition of private wealth given above.

The stationary-state equilibrium of this model has the following properties. At the equilibrium $Y$ the public has the desired amount of wealth $W$. Some of it is in money, the amount of which is the constant $M$. The interest rate $r$ is such that the public is willing to hold the fraction $M/W$ of its wealth in monetary form. Some of the public's wealth is in capital $K$, namely an amount such that the return on capital is $R$. The rest of the public's wealth is in non-monetary government debt $D$. These conditions can be met for any $Y$. But the budget-balance equation for the government is necessary to keep $D$ fixed, and the addition of this requirement determines the equilibrium $Y$.

The models can be condensed into two relations of $Y$ and $R$, taking as given $G'$ or $G, M$, and $\theta$.

$$L(r, 1/\hat{\mu})\hat{\mu}Y = M. \tag{10}$$

This is the long-run "$LM$" curve, which we shall denote $LLM$.

$$\text{(I)} \quad G' - \theta Y = \dot{D} = 0,$$

$$\text{(II)} \quad r(\hat{\mu}Y - M - F(R)Y) + G - \theta Y = \dot{D} = 0. \tag{11}$$

This is the long-run budget-balance equation, to be denoted as $GT$. It also takes into account full adjustment of $W$ and $K$ to $Y$ and $R$, which with $M$ given implies a value for $D$. But this $D$ does not meet portfolio preferences unless (10) is also satisfied.

The slope of $LLM$ is given by

$$\left(\frac{\partial R}{\partial Y}\right)_{LLM} = -\frac{M/Y}{L_1\hat{\mu}Y(1-\theta)} > 0. \tag{12}$$

The slope of $GT$ is

$$\text{(I)} \quad \left(\frac{\partial R}{\partial Y}\right)_{GT} = \infty,$$

$$\text{(II)} \quad \left(\frac{\partial R}{\partial Y}\right)_{GT} = \frac{(G - rM)/Y}{(1-\theta)(D - RF'(R)Y)}. \tag{13}$$

For non-negative $D$, the denominator of the slope for Model II is certainly positive. The numerator is also positive if $G$ exceeds the hypothetical after-tax interest on the money stock, negative otherwise. $(G - rM)/Y$ is equal to $\theta - \hat{\mu}r + \alpha(1 - \theta)$, and is the rate at which an increase of $Y$ raises the budget surplus with $R$ constant, starting from a position of budget balance.

We are interested in the shift of $GT$ for an increase of $G'$ or $G$.

$$\text{(I)} \quad \left(\frac{\partial Y}{\partial G'}\right)_{GT} = \frac{1}{\theta},$$

$$\text{(II)} \quad \left(\frac{\partial Y}{\partial G}\right)_{GT} = \frac{1}{(G - rM)/Y}. \tag{14}$$

In Model I the long-run "multiplier" is simply the reciprocal of the tax rate. In Model II the multiplier is positive if $GT$ is upward sloping, but $GT$ shifts left if it is downward sloping. With non-negative $D$, $GT$ always shifts downward;

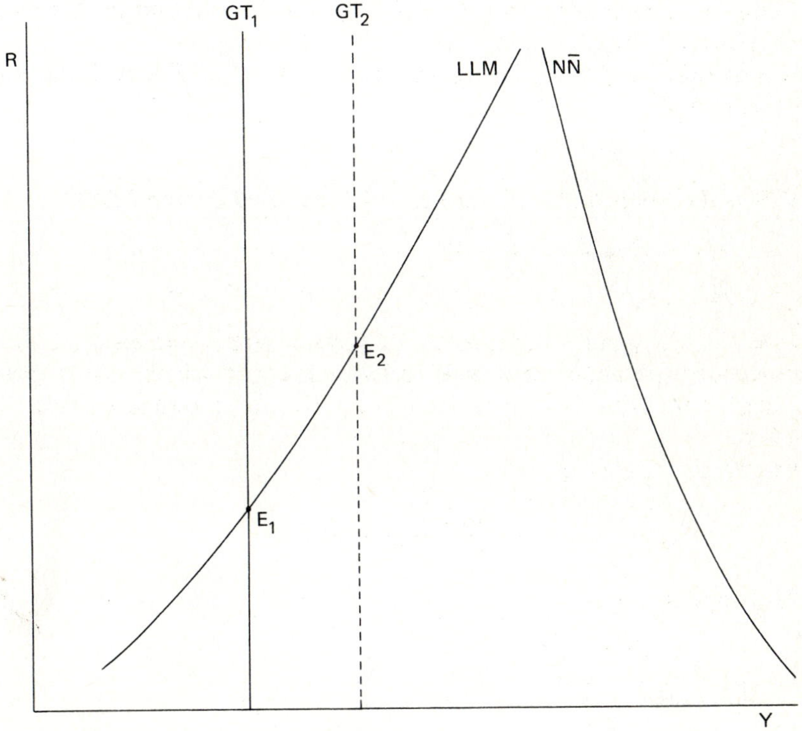


FIGURE 1. Long-run equilibria for Model I.

when $G$ increases, $R$ must decrease in order to lower debt interest and keep the budget balanced.

Model I is pictured in figure 1. To the right of $GT$, the budget deficit $\dot{D}$ is negative; to the left, it is positive. Above $LLM$ – given $M$ and assuming that $W$ and $K$ are fully adjusted to $R$ and $Y$ – the stock of debt $D$ is too small; the public would like to exchange money for debt. Below $LLM$, $D$ is too large. As the shift of $GT$ illustrates, an increase of $G'$ leads to higher equilibrium values for both $Y$ and $R$.

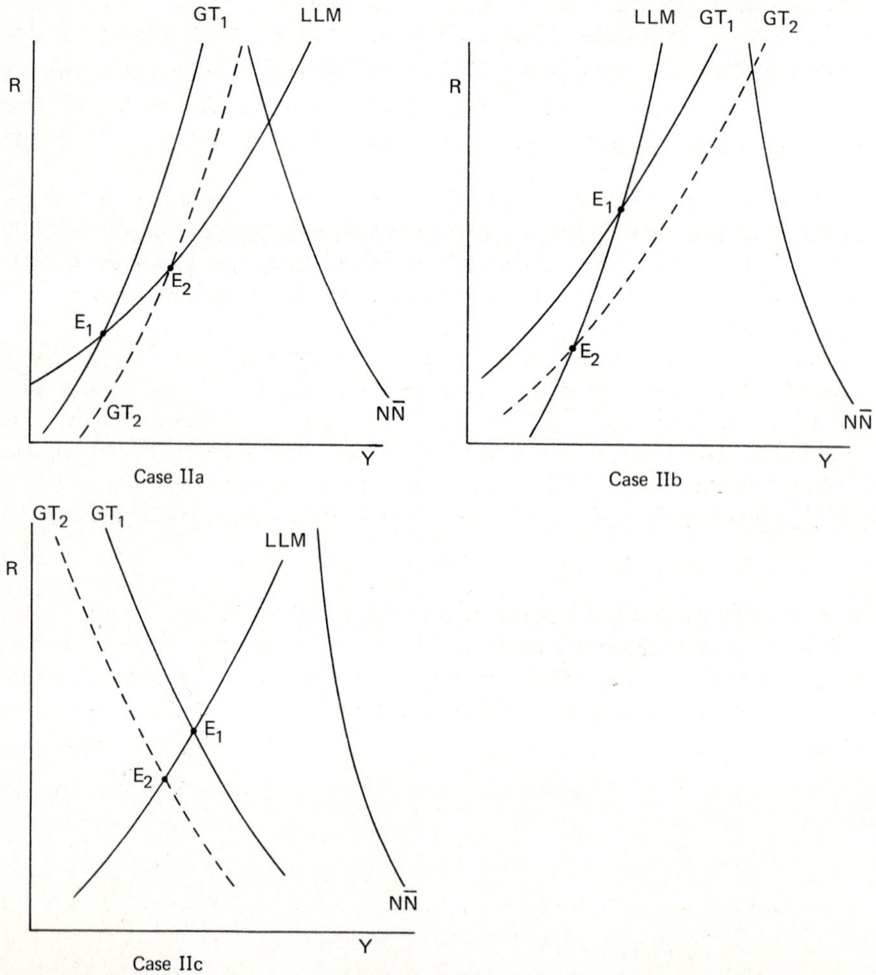


FIGURE 2. Long-run equilibria in Model II.

Model II is pictured in the three panels of figure 2. Case IIa is little different from Model I. In case IIb, the *LLM* curve is the steeper. The comparative statics suggests that fiscal expansion diminishes $Y$ and $R$, but perverse results of this type make one doubt the stability of the equilibria. In case IIc, *GT* is negatively sloped, the comparative static result is again "perverse" and there is reason to doubt stability.

These comparative statics apply, of course, only for $N \leqq \bar{N}$. Equilibrium demand for labor depends directly not only on $Y$ but also on $R$, because higher $R$ means use of labor-intensive technique. The full employment ceiling to $Y$ is shown in figures 1 and 2, as $N\bar{N}$. A demand equilibrium on the far side of $N\bar{N}$ means an inflationary gap. One way it can be eliminated is reduction of the real stock of money by inflation; we discuss this case in section 6.

### *4.2 Temporary Solutions and Dynamics: Stability in Model I*

Our dynamic story is the familiar *IS–LM* tale. We postulate conventional *IS* and *LM* loci for the Keynesian short run, i.e., for given stocks of wealth, debt, capital, and money. The solution of this system determines the momentary values of $Y$ and $R$. As the stocks change, the solution changes. The question is whether this process leads to the stationary equilibrium.

The short-run *LM* relation is implicit in the equation $L(r, Y/W)W = M$, holding $W$ constant. Its short-run slope, $-L_2/\{L_1(1 - \theta)W\}$, is less steep than its long-run slope, $\{-L(r, 1/\hat{\mu})\hat{\mu}\}/\{L_1(r, 1/\hat{\mu})(1 - \theta)W\}$, on the usual assumption, empirically supported, that the short-run income elasticity of demand for money, $L_2 Y/LW$ is less than unity. It is convenient to put the *LM* curve in explicit form (suppressing $\theta$ so long as it is being held constant),

$$R = R(Y, W, M); \qquad R_1, R_2, > 0; \quad R_3 < 0. \tag{15}$$

The short-run slope is $R_1$; the long-run slope is $R_1 + \hat{\mu}R_2$.

The short-run *IS* locus is derived from the usual identity that capital accumulation equals the sum of private and public saving. Since asset revaluations have been assumed away, private saving is equal to $\dot{W}$. The identity differs between Models,

$$\begin{aligned} &(\mathrm{I}) \quad \dot{K} + G' = \dot{W} + \theta Y, \\ &(\mathrm{II}) \quad \dot{K} + G = \dot{W} + \theta Y - rD. \end{aligned} \tag{16}$$

We assume investment and saving functions of the stock-adjustment type,

$$\begin{aligned} \dot{K} &= i(F(R)Y - K), \\ \dot{W} &= s(\hat{\mu}Y - W). \end{aligned} \tag{17}$$

The *IS* curves are combinations of (16) and (17),

$$\begin{aligned} &\text{(I)} \quad Y(s\hat{\mu} + \theta - iF(R)) = G' + sW - iK, \\ &\text{(II)} \quad Y(s\hat{\mu} + \theta - iF(R)) - Dr = G + sW - iK. \end{aligned} \tag{18}$$

The coefficient of $Y$ in (18) is the reciprocal of the conventional multiplier $m$. We assume throughout that $\hat{\mu}$ exceeds $F(R)$ in the range of relevant values: the desired wealth/income ratio exceeds the desired capital/output ratio. Indeed we shall assume that $1/m$ is positive even if $i > s$. We wish to bypass questions of short-short-run dynamics and instability. Nevertheless, in Model II the *IS* curve may become upward sloping for high stocks of debt. This can be seen from

$$\begin{aligned} &\text{(I)} \quad \left(\frac{\partial R}{\partial Y}\right)_{IS} = \frac{1/m}{YiF'(r)} < 0, \\ &\text{(II)} \quad \left(\frac{\partial R}{\partial Y}\right)_{IS} = \frac{1/m}{YiF'(R) + D(1-\theta)}. \end{aligned} \tag{19}$$

Consider first the dynamics of Model I. Figure 3 duplicates figure 1 for *LLM* and *GT* curves, and in addition shows the short-run $LM_1$ and $IS_1$ curves corresponding to the initial equilibrium at $E_1$, i.e., corresponding to the equilibrium stocks $W, K, D, M$ at $E_1$ and to the initial value of $G'$. The short-run loci naturally intersect at $E_1$. Now suppose that $G'$ is increased in one step, shifting the *GT* locus and indicating a new long-run equilibrium $E_2$.

The immediate impact is to shift the *IS* curve to $IS_{12}$, producing a short-run solution $S_{12}$. This is evanescent, of course, because stocks do not remain at their initial $E_1$ values. The question now is whether the configuration of figure 1 is stable.

At the new equilibrium $E_2$, with higher $Y$ and $R$, the public will hold more wealth, but smaller fractions of wealth in money and in capital ($\partial L/\partial R$ and $\mathrm{d}F/\mathrm{d}R$ are both negative). Consequently the volume of debt will be higher, both absolutely and as a proportion of wealth and income. A dynamic path from $E_1$ to $S_{12}$ to $E_2$ must involve deficits which achieve this accumulation of debt.

As figure 3 is drawn, $IS_{12}$ is shifted horizontally from $E_1$ by less than the shift of *GT*. This means that the short-run multiplier $m$ is less than the long-run multiplier $1/\theta$, and it guarantees that at $S_{12}$ the budget is in deficit. It is conceivable that $m$ exceeds $1/\theta$, if the short-run marginal propensity to invest $iF(R)$ is high. But $m$ would have to exceed $1/\theta$ by some margin to place $S_{12}$ in the budget surplus region to the right of $GT_2$.

Taking $m < 1/\theta$ as pictured, at $S_{12}$ both $W$ and $D$ are increasing. *LM* will be shifting up. The growth of wealth also tends to shift *IS* up (via the $sW$ term). We

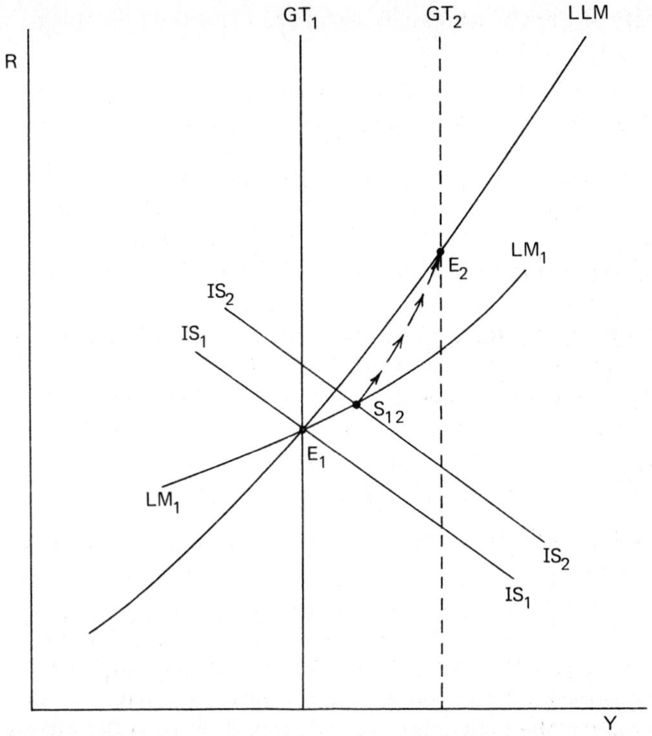


FIGURE 3. Short- and long-run equilibria in Model I.

cannot be sure whether $\dot{K}$ is positive or negative at $S_{12}$. Compared with $E_1$, the increase in $Y$ raises the demand for capital but the increase in $R$ lowers it.

A path from $S_{12}$ to $E_2$ in figure 3 seems plausible. On such a path stocks of assets other than $M$ are increasing and shifting upward both $IS$ and $LM$. But the dynamics are not easy to display graphically, and the pictured path is not the only possibility. We turn to formal stability analysis.

The system consists of four equations in $(K, D, Y, R)$:

$$\left.\begin{aligned} \dot{K} &= i(F(R)Y - K) \\ \dot{D} &= G' - \theta Y \\ 0 &= Y(s\hat{\mu} + \theta - iF(R)) - sM - sD - (s-i)K - G' \\ 0 &= R - R(Y, M + D + K, M) \end{aligned}\right\} \qquad (20)$$

The local stability of the system can be analyzed from the following characteristic quadratic equation in $\lambda$:

$$\begin{vmatrix} -i-\lambda & 0 & iF(R) & iYF'(R) \\ 0 & -\lambda & -\theta & 0 \\ -(s-i) & -s & 1/m & -iYF'(R) \\ -R_2 & -R_2 & -R_1 & 1 \end{vmatrix} \tag{21}$$

Here $1/m$ is as before shorthand for the coefficient of $Y$ in the third equation of (20).

Considering (21) as $(a\lambda^2 + b\lambda + c = 0)$, sufficient and necessary conditions for local stability – the real parts of both roots negative – are that both $b/a$ and $c/a$ exceed zero. Both conditions are met on assumptions already made, that the multiplier $m$ is positive, that $\hat{\mu} > F(R)$ (so that there is room in portfolios for assets other than capital), that $F'(R) \leqq 0$, and that $R_1$ and $R_2$ are both positive. It turns out that

$$\begin{aligned} a &= (1/m) - R_1 iYF'(R) > 0, \\ c &= \theta is > 0, \\ b &= \theta s + \theta i + is(\hat{\mu} - F(R)) - isF'(R)Y(R_1 + \hat{\mu}R_2). \end{aligned} \tag{22}$$

All the terms of $b$ are positive under the assumptions. Note that, in contrast to the Blinder–Solow conditions, no restriction on the relative sizes of $s$ and $i$, other than the one required to keep the multiplier positive, is part of the sufficient conditions for stability.

### 4.3. Stability in Model II

The system of four equations is

$$\left.\begin{aligned} \dot{K} &= i(F(R)Y - K) \\ \dot{D} &= G + rD - \theta Y \\ 0 &= Y(1/m) - sM - (s+r)D - (s-i)K - G \\ 0 &= R - R(Y, M+K+D, M) \end{aligned}\right\}. \tag{23}$$

The characteristic equation is

$$\begin{vmatrix} -i-\lambda & 0 & iF(R) & iYF'(R) \\ 0 & r-\lambda & -\theta & D(1-\theta) \\ -(s-i) & -(s+r) & 1/m & -iYF'(R) - D(1-\theta) \\ -R_2 & -R_2 & -R_1 & 1 \end{vmatrix} = 0. \tag{24}$$

Calling this equation $a'\lambda^2 + b'\lambda + c'$,

$$a' = a - R_1 D(1 - \theta) = (1/m) - R_1(iYF'(R) + D(1 - \theta)), \tag{25}$$

$$b' = b + r(s\hat{\mu} - iF(R)) + rR_1 iYF'(R) - D(1 - \theta)(s\hat{\mu}R_2 + (s + i)R_1),$$

$$c' = is(\theta - r\hat{\mu} + rF(R)\} - is(R_1 + \hat{\mu}R_2)(D(1 - \theta) - rYF'(R)).$$

For interpretation, we recall the slopes of *GT* and *LLM* given above in (12) and (13) and restate them in the symbols of this section of the paper,

$$\left(\frac{\partial R}{\partial Y}\right)_{LLM} = R_1 + R_2\hat{\mu}, \tag{12'}$$

$$\left(\frac{\partial R}{\partial Y}\right)_{GT} = \frac{\theta - \hat{\mu}r + rF(R)}{D(1 - \theta) - rF'(R)Y}. \tag{13'}$$

Given the non-negativity of the denominator in (13′) and the expression for $c'$ in (25),

$$\left(\frac{\partial R}{\partial Y}\right)_{GT} \gtreqless \left(\frac{\partial R}{\partial Y}\right)_{LLM}$$

as

$$(\theta - \hat{\mu}r + F(R)) - (R_1 + \hat{\mu}R_2)(D(1 - \theta) - rF'(R)Y) \gtreqless 0,$$

i.e., as $c' \gtreqless 0$. Hence in case IIa, $c'$ is positive, while in cases IIb and IIc, $c'$ is negative.

The value of $a'$ is the effect of $G$ on the short-run solution $Y$, specifically $\partial Y/\partial G$ calculated from the third equation of (23). The normal expectation is that it is positive; indeed the issue under discussion is whether this positive effect is temporary or not. With positive $a'$, we know that in cases IIb and IIc one of the roots $\lambda$ is positive. With normal short-run effects, therefore, the stationary equilibrium is unstable in those cases, as previously conjectured.

As for case IIa, with $a'$ positive the equilibrium will be stable if $b'$ is positive, unstable otherwise. Now even with $D$ low enough to make $a'$ positive, $b'$ may be negative. Thus IIa may be either stable or unstable.

A negative value of $a'$ seems at first glance to reverse these stability findings, making IIb and IIc possibly stable. Then one might conclude that fiscal expansion is contractionary both in short run and long run! But this conclusion is illusory. The *IS–LM* solution itself is unstable under usual assumptions about short-run dynamics. This may be seen as follows:

Let the *IS* slope [equation (19), Model II] be $(1/m)/z$. Then $a' = 1/m - R_1 z$. $R_1$ is the *LM* slope. Here are the possibilities:

| | $m > 0$ | $m < 0$ |
|---|---|---|
| $z < 0$ | (i) $a' > 0$ | (iii) if $a' < 0$ <br> $(1/m)/z > R_1 > 0$ |
| $z > 0$ | (ii) if $a' < 0$ <br> $0 < (1/m)/z < R_1$ | (iv) $a' < 0$ <br> $(1/m)/z < 0 < R_1$ |

(i) is the normal case already discussed. In case (ii) an increase in $G$ shifts the $IS$ curve right; it is upward sloping but flatter than $LM$. In cases (iii) and (iv) an increase in $G$ shifts the $IS$ curve left. In (iii) it is upward sloping but steeper than $LM$. In (iv) it is downward sloping. The four cases are pictured in figure 4. The short-run dynamics indicated by the arrows follow the usual assumption that $R$ always moves towards $LM$, while $Y$ moves towards $IS$ if $m > 0$ and away from it if $m < 0$. On this assumption, case (i) is the only stable configuration. (Cases not shown, which are also stable, involve $a' > 0$, $z < 0$.)

### 4.4. *Variation in Tax Rate*

We briefly consider the long-run effects in Model I of a third type of pure fiscal policy: changing the tax rate $\theta$, keeping $G'$ constant and financing temporary deficits by debt issue.

A reduction in $\theta$ shifts the vertical $GT$ line of Model I to the right. The long-run multiplier $\partial Y/\partial\theta$ is $-Y/\theta$. But the $LLM$ curve is not invariant to this type of fiscal action. It may shift either way. On the one hand, a tax reduction increases, for given $R$ and $Y$, the opportunity cost of holding money; this effect moves $LLM$ right. On the other hand, tax reduction increases after-tax human wealth and therefore, other things equal, raises $\hat{\mu}$. This effect moves $LLM$ left. The net effect is uncertain, and so we cannot exclude the possibility that equilibrium $R$ will be lower with lower $\theta$. The stability analysis is the same as in section 4.2.

## 5. Monetary Policy in the Long Run

Of the several possible meanings of monetary policy in this framework, we shall consider two. The first is a one-shot open market purchase. The second is a combination of fiscal and monetary expansion, a once-for-all increase in government expenditure with deficits financed by printing money instead of issuing interest-bearing debt.

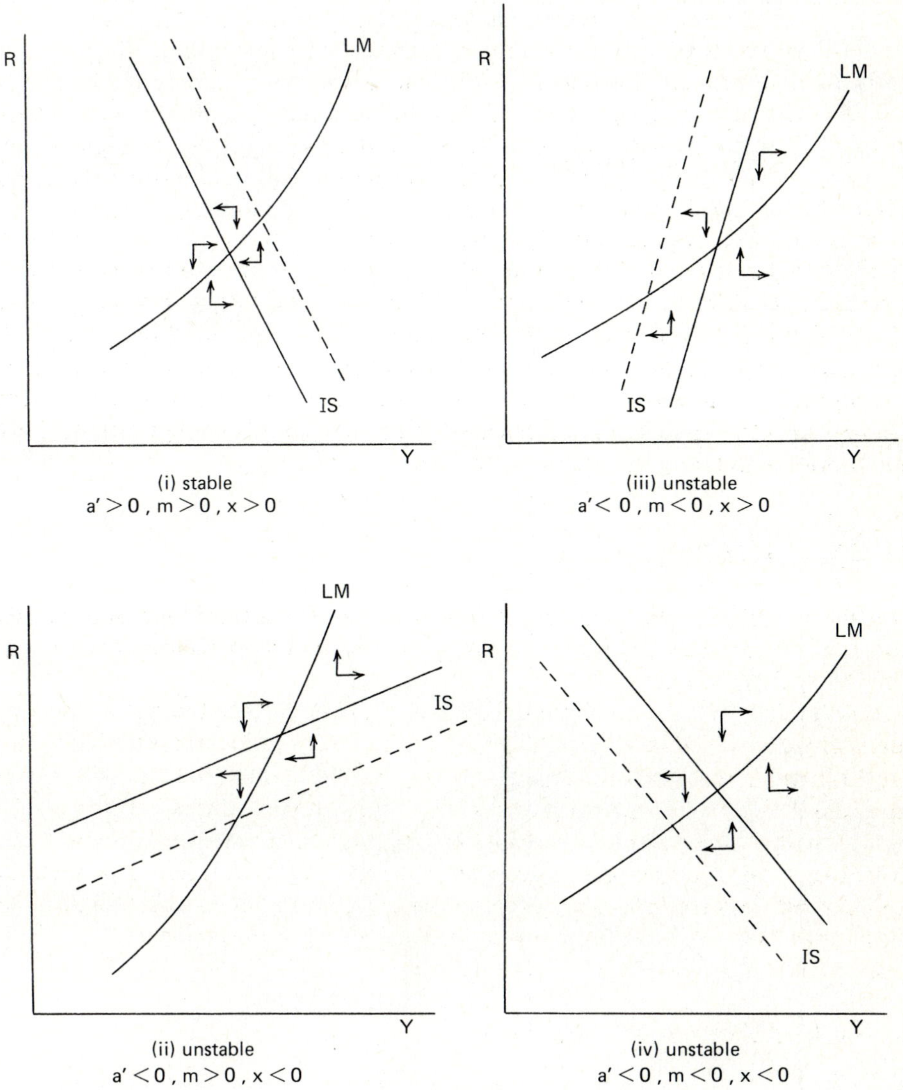


FIGURE 4. Stability or instability of short-run *IS–LM* solution.

### *5.1. Open Market Purchase of Bonds*

The story of the open market purchase is pictured in figure 5. The framework is Model I, in which $G' = G + rD$ is the parameter of budget policy. The economy starts in long-run equilibrium $E_1$, with the associated short-run curves $LM_1$ and $IS_1$. The new long-run curve $LLM_2$ implies a new equilibrium $E_2$, with unchanged $Y$ and lower $R$. The new stock equilibrium involves the same wealth $W = \hat{\mu}Y$, but a different portfolio. At $E_2$ the public will hold more money, and less debt-cum-capital, than at $E_1$. But they will also hold more capital, because the

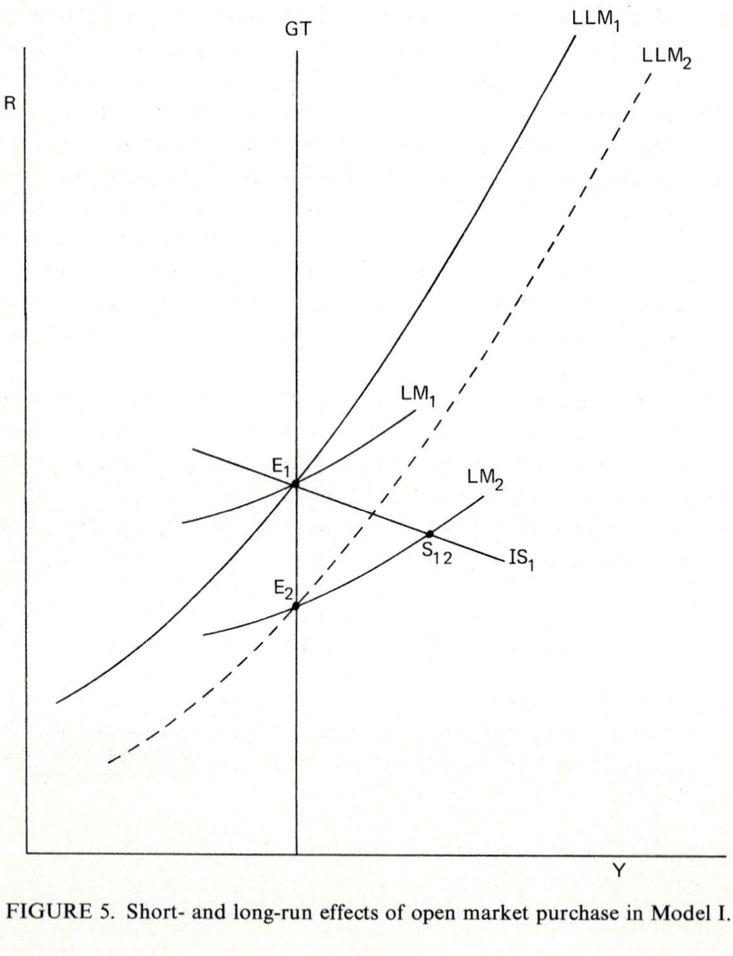


FIGURE 5. Short- and long-run effects of open market purchase in Model I.

desired capital/output ratio $F(R)$ is increased by the reduction in $R$. Thus ultimately there are two substitutions against debt, one of money in the initial open market operation and one of capital during the process of adjustment.

The shift of short-run $LM$ accomplished by the open market purchase reflects only a money-for-debt substitution. The subsequent capital-for-debt substitution does not affect the $LM$ curves. That is why $LM_2$ and $LLM_2$ cross the vertical $GT$ line at the same point. The $IS$ curve is unaffected by the initial operation. (If capital gains on bonds were taken into account, as in Blinder–Solow, $IS$ would shift up because of the increase in wealth.) The first impact of the monetary expansion is the short-run solution $S_{12}$. But the increase in income is temporary. The government is now running a surplus, and, as we have already seen, the contraction of debt brings income down. Meanwhile the public is also saving more (wealth is below $\hat{\mu}Y$) and investing more [capital is less than $F(R)Y$]. The temporary increase in wealth retards the decline of $R$, and is reversed once capital and wealth catch up with income, which is on its way down.

In Model II, higher interest rates and debt accumulation have an expansionary fiscal effect because they enlarge the budget deficit. The story for case IIa is essentially the same as for Model I, except that the open market purchase shifts the initial $IS$ curve down. $E_2$ represents a *smaller* output than $E_1$. It may seem paradoxical that monetary expansion is, in the long run, contractionary. We do not think the result should be taken seriously, given that it depends on the assumption that monetary expansion entails a fiscal contraction via reduction of debt interest transfers.

In case IIb, $E_2$ is at higher levels of $Y$ and $R$ than $E_1$. But there is no way to get there. The open market purchase shifts down the short-run $LM$ curve, increases $Y$, and decreases $R$. But from this point the dynamic previously described moves the temporary solution down and to the left.

In case IIc it is quite possible that the dynamics lead to the new equilibrium $E_2$ with higher $Y$ and lower $R$.

### *5.2. Fiscal Expansion with Money-Financed Deficits*

We turn briefly to the monetary financing of deficits combined with expansionary fiscal policy. The previous discussion of fiscal policy is now altered by holding $D$ constant instead of $M$. In Model I, the long-run $GT$ locus is unchanged, still vertical. But the $LM$ locus becomes

$$\hat{\mu}Y - L(r,1/\hat{\mu})\hat{\mu}Y - F(R)Y = D, \tag{26}$$

$$\left(\frac{\partial R}{\partial Y}\right)_{LLM} = \frac{D/Y}{L_1(1-\theta)\hat{\mu}Y + F'(R)Y} < 0. \tag{27}$$

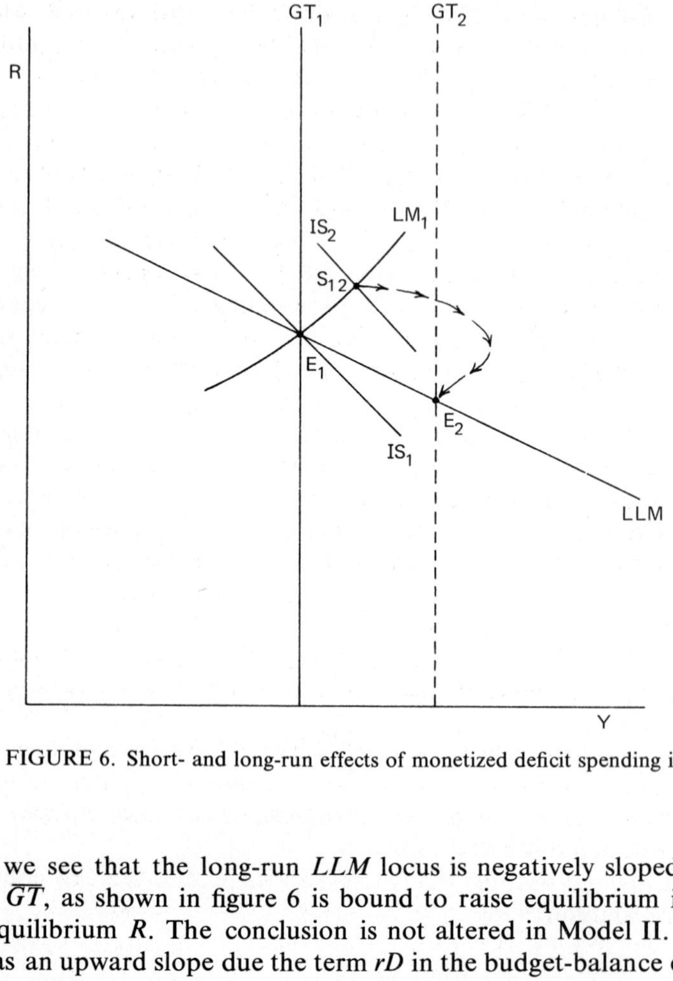


FIGURE 6. Short- and long-run effects of monetized deficit spending in Model I.

Thus we see that the long-run *LLM* locus is negatively sloped. A rightward shift of $\overline{GT}$, as shown in figure 6 is bound to raise equilibrium income *Y* and lower equilibrium *R*. The conclusion is not altered in Model II. There the *GT* locus has an upward slope due the term *rD* in the budget-balance equation, even though *D* is constant. But it is still true that a rightward shift in *GT* raises equilibrium *Y* and lowers *R*.

The dynamics are as follows: the short-run *LM* locus is

$$W - L(R(1-\theta), Y/W)W - K = D. \tag{28}$$

It is upward sloping, because *M* does not increase until a budget deficit actually appears,

$$\left(\frac{\partial R}{\partial Y}\right)_{LM} = -\frac{L_2}{L_1(1-\theta)\,W} > 0. \tag{29}$$

The short-run *IS* curve, defined as before, shifts to the right with the increase of $G'$, but on usual assumptions not as far as the *GT* line. The temporary solution is at $S_{12}$. But now there is a budget deficit: $M$ increases, $W$ increases, *IS* moves up, *LM* moves down. When the solution crosses $GT_2$ budget surpluses appear and arrest the expansion.

For formal analysis of the dynamics of this case, it is convenient to express the short-run model in terms of the four variables $K$, $W$, $Y$, and $R$,

$$\left.\begin{aligned} \dot{K} &= i(F(R)Y - K) \\ \dot{W} &= s(\hat{\mu}Y - W) \\ 0 &= Y(s\hat{\mu} + \theta - iF(R)) - sW + iK - G' \\ 0 &= R - R(K,W,Y) \end{aligned}\right\} . \tag{30}$$

Here the function $R(K,W,Y)$ is implicit in (28), and its partial derivatives are

$$\left.\begin{aligned} R_1 &= \frac{-1}{L_1(1-\theta)W} > 0 \\ R_2 &= \frac{1 - L + L_2(Y/W)}{L_1(1-\theta)W} < 0 \\ R_3 &= \frac{-L_2}{L_1(1-\theta)W} > 0 \end{aligned}\right\} . \tag{31}$$

The characteristic equation is

$$\begin{vmatrix} -i-\lambda & 0 & iF(R) & iF'(R)Y \\ 0 & -s-\lambda & s & 0 \\ i & -s & 1/m & -iF'(R)Y \\ -R_1 & -R_2 & -R_3 & 1 \end{vmatrix} = 0. \tag{32}$$

In the quadratic equation $a\lambda^2 + b\lambda + c$ all three coefficients $a$, $b$, $c$ are unambiguously positive, confirming that the comparative static story of figure 6 makes sense.

## 6. Effects of Fiscal Policy with Full Employment and Flexible Prices

The standard short-run *IS–LM* analysis applies to situations of full employment as well as unemployment, and in this section we extend our long-run analysis to conditions of full employment and flexible prices and wages. In the short run, output is fixed by the full employment labor supply. The standard short-run comparative statics is familiar: Expansionary fiscal policy, with constant nominal money stock, always raises the interest rate. Unless the demand for money is interest-inelastic and the *LM* curve vertical, it also raises the velocity of money and the price level. Increased real government expenditure "crowds out" private investment, and possibly also private consumption, to the extent necessary to equate total real demand to fixed real supply. But the short-run analysis does not trace the further effects of these changes in the rates of growth of capital and government debt.

Our long-run full employment model resembles as closely as possible both the long-run models of the previous sections and the standard short-run full employment version of *IS–LM* analysis. But differences necessarily arise. Once the price level is made endogenous in a long-run model, we must explicitly consider price expectations and distinguish real and nominal rates of return. Moreover, in a long-run full employment model the capital stock is endogenous. Output is not fixed, as it is in the short run, by labor supply; output per worker varies with the capital/output ratio and the real interest rate, as illustrated by the $N\bar{N}$ curves of figures 1 and 2.

Capital and bonds are, as before, perfect substitutes in portfolios. The portfolio choice of money vs. bonds-and-capital depends on the real after-tax rate of return differential between money and bonds. The nominal rate of return on money balances is institutionally fixed at zero. If $x$ is the expected instantaneous proportional rate of change of the price level $p$, and $R$ the nominal rate of return on bonds, the real rate of return on bonds is $R - x$, and the real after-tax rate of return differential is $R(1 - \theta)$.

Portfolio balance is therefore given by

$$L\left(R(1-\theta),\, Y\Big/\frac{M+D}{P}+K\right)\left(\frac{M+D}{p}+K\right)=\frac{M}{p}. \tag{33}$$

The production function is, as throughout the paper, a well-behaved constant returns to scale neoclassical production function in capital and labor, $N$,

$$Y = Nf(K/N); \qquad f' > 0, \qquad f'' < 0. \tag{34}$$

Labor is supplied inelastically and is always fully employed. Since we are only considering stationary states we choose units such that $N = 1$.

Rather than specifying the investment function as $I = i[F(R - x)f(K) - K]$, we shall now find it convenient to write it as

$$I = I(f'(K) - (R - x)), \qquad I(0) = 0, \quad I' > 0. \tag{35}$$

This function makes the rate of investment an increasing function of the difference between the rate of return obtainable from investing a dollar in the production of new capital goods and the rate of return on existing assets.

We shall consider 3 simple mechanisms for generating price expectations:

Static expectations: $x(t) = 0,$ (36a)

Myopic perfect foresight: $x(t) = \dot{p}(t)/p(t),$ (36b)

Adaptive expectations: $\dot{x}(t) = \beta[(\dot{p}/p) - x(t)]; \quad \beta > 0.$ (36c)

Government consumption expenditure is fixed in real terms. With bond-financed deficits, the government budget restraint is therefore given by

$$\text{(I)} \qquad \dot{D}/p = G' - \theta f(K), \tag{37a}$$

$$\text{(II)} \qquad \dot{D}/p = G + (1 - \theta)R\,(D/p) - \theta f(K). \tag{37b}$$

For reasons of space we shall consider only Model I.

### 6.1. The Long-Run Equilibrium

The complete dynamic model is

$$(IS) \qquad I[f'(K) - R + x] + G' - \theta f(K) - s\left[\hat{\mu} f(K) - \left(\frac{M + D}{p}\right) - K\right] - x\left(\frac{M + D}{p}\right) = 0. \tag{38}$$

The last term in (38) represents expected additions, positive or negative, to wealth, due to changes in the real values of nominal stocks of money and debt. It is assumed that current saving from income is adjusted correspondingly.

$$(LM) \qquad L\left[R(1 - \theta), \frac{pf(K)}{M + D + pK}\right]\left[\frac{M + D}{p} + K\right] = \frac{M}{p}, \tag{39}$$

$$\left(\frac{\dot{D}}{p}\right) = G' - \theta f(K) - \frac{\dot{p}}{p}\frac{D}{p}, \tag{40}$$

$$\left(\frac{\dot{M}}{p}\right) = -\frac{\dot{p}}{p}\frac{M}{p}, \tag{41}$$

$$\dot{K} = I[f'(K) - R + x], \tag{42}$$

$$x = 0, \tag{43a}$$

$$x = \frac{\dot{p}}{p}, \tag{43b}$$

$$\dot{x} = \beta\left[\frac{\dot{p}}{p} - x\right]. \tag{43c}$$

In a stationary long-run equilibrium, expectations are realized, momentary equilibrium holds at each point of time, and real stocks and flows remain constant. Since we are considering only fiscal policies with a constant nominal quantity of money, actual and expected rates of inflation must be zero in long-run equilibrium. In summary,

$$\dot{p}/p = x = \dot{x} = \dot{D} = \dot{K} = 0.$$

The choice of expectations function is irrelevant for the comparative static results of the model, although it crucially affects the dynamics. The stationary state equilibrium is completely described by the following four equations, which as it happens are recursive, in $K$, $R$, $p$ and $D$,

$$(GT) \qquad G' = \theta f(K), \tag{44}$$

$$R = f'(K), \tag{45}$$

$$(LLM) \qquad L\left[R(1-\theta), \frac{1}{\hat{\mu}}\right]\hat{\mu}f(K) = \frac{M}{p}, \tag{46}$$

$$\hat{\mu}f(K) = \frac{M+D}{p} + K. \tag{47}$$

Equation (45) gives a stationary state relationship between $K$ and $R$,

$$K = g(R), \qquad g'(R) = 1/f'' < 0.$$

We can therefore represent the long-run equilibrium in $R - p$ space by the $GT$ and $LLM$ curves,

$$G' = \theta f(g(R)),$$

$$L\left[R(1-\theta), \frac{1}{\hat{\mu}}\right]\hat{\mu}f(g(R)) = \frac{M}{p}.$$

These are illustrated in figure 7.
The slope of the $LLM$ curve is

$$\left(\frac{\mathrm{d}R}{\mathrm{d}p}\right)_{LLM} = \frac{-Mf''(K)}{[\hat{\mu}f(K)L_1(1-\theta)f''(K) + L\hat{\mu}f'(K)]p^2} > 0.$$

The slope of the $GT$ curve is

$$\left(\frac{\mathrm{d}R}{\mathrm{d}p}\right)_{GT} = 0.$$

An increase in $G'$ from $G'_1$ to $G'_2$ shifts the $GT$ curve down along the $LLM$ curve

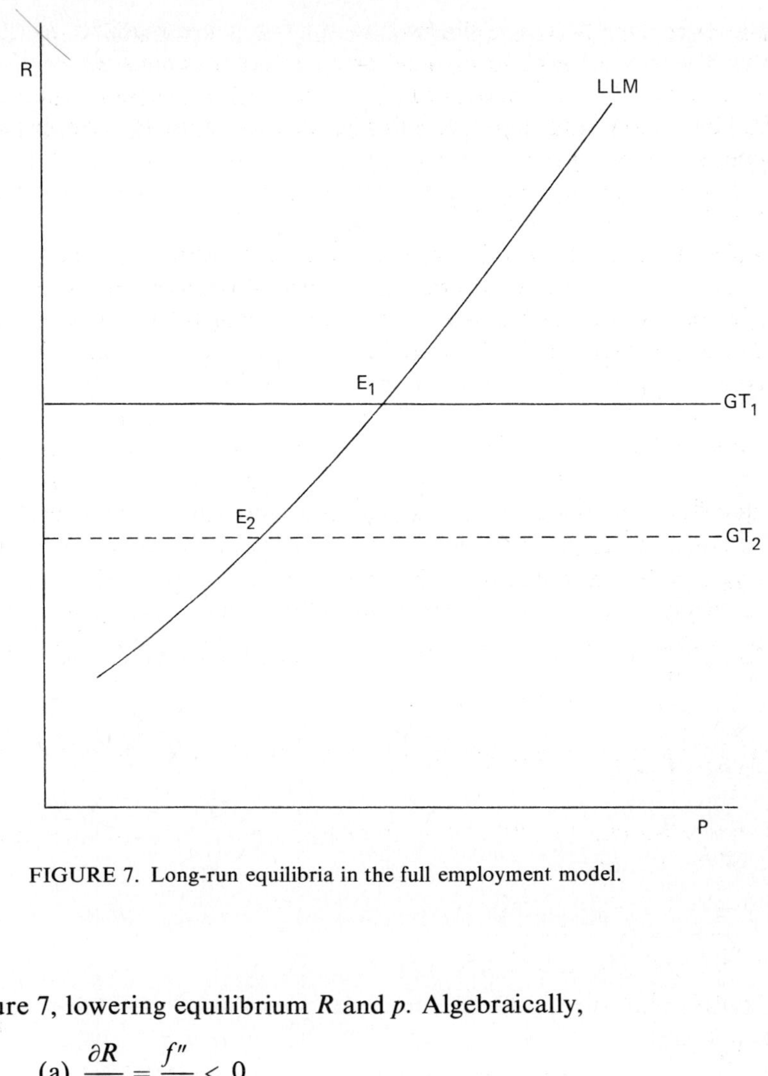


FIGURE 7. Long-run equilibria in the full employment model.

in figure 7, lowering equilibrium $R$ and $p$. Algebraically,

$$\text{(a)}\ \frac{\partial R}{\partial G'} = \frac{f''}{\theta f'} < 0, \qquad (48)$$

$$\text{(b)}\ \frac{\partial p}{\partial G'} = -\frac{L_1 \hat{\mu} f f''(1-\theta) + L\hat{\mu} f'}{\theta f'(K)\,(M/p^2)} < 0.$$

Note that even in the full employment model $\partial Y/\partial G' > 0$; the reason here, however, is capital deepening rather than the elimination of unemployment of labor.

Note also that the effectiveness of fiscal policy here is not at all dependent on the fact that government interest-bearing debt has been counted as part of private sector net worth. Even if the capitalized value of future taxes "required" to service the debt were exactly equal to the value of these bonds – and there are many sound economic reasons for arguing against such a complete offset – the balanced budget condition: $G' = \theta f(K)$ will guarantee the long-run effectiveness of fiscal policy, in a comparative-static sense.

The intuitive story behind equations (16) is simple: An increase in $G'$ requires, given $\theta$, a higher level of income to balance the budget. With full employment and a fixed labor force, this means a larger capital stock. This in turn requires a lower $R$ and a higher stationary state level of wealth. The *LLM* curve shows that both these effects will increase the demand for real money balances. Since the nominal stock of money is fixed, the price level must be lower to increase the real value of the fixed nominal quantity of money. Prima facie these results would seem to be unstable. As we observed at the outset of this section, the impact effect of an increase in $G'$ is to shift the short-run *IS* curve to the right and to raise $R$ and $p$. For the long-run equilibrium to be stable, these impact effects have to be reversed, implying that the economy "overshoots" in the short run. Nevertheless, under certain conditions, which depend crucially on the expectations mechanism and on the precise numerical values of certain coefficients, the model may be stable.

### 6.2. *The Impact Effects*

Figure 8 shows the impact effect of an increase in government expenditure $G'$. The slope of the *IS* curve is

$$\left(\frac{\mathrm{d}R}{\mathrm{d}p}\right)_{IS} = -\frac{(s - x)(M + D)}{I'p^2}.$$

When we are considering the *IS* curve that goes through the long-run equilibrium, $x = 0$ and

$$\left(\frac{\mathrm{d}R}{\mathrm{d}p}\right)_{IS} = -\frac{s(M + D)}{I'p^2} < 0.$$

The impact effect of an increase in $G'$ will be to shift the *IS* curve to the right,

$$\left(\frac{\partial R}{\partial G'}\right)_{IS} = \frac{1}{I'} > 0.$$

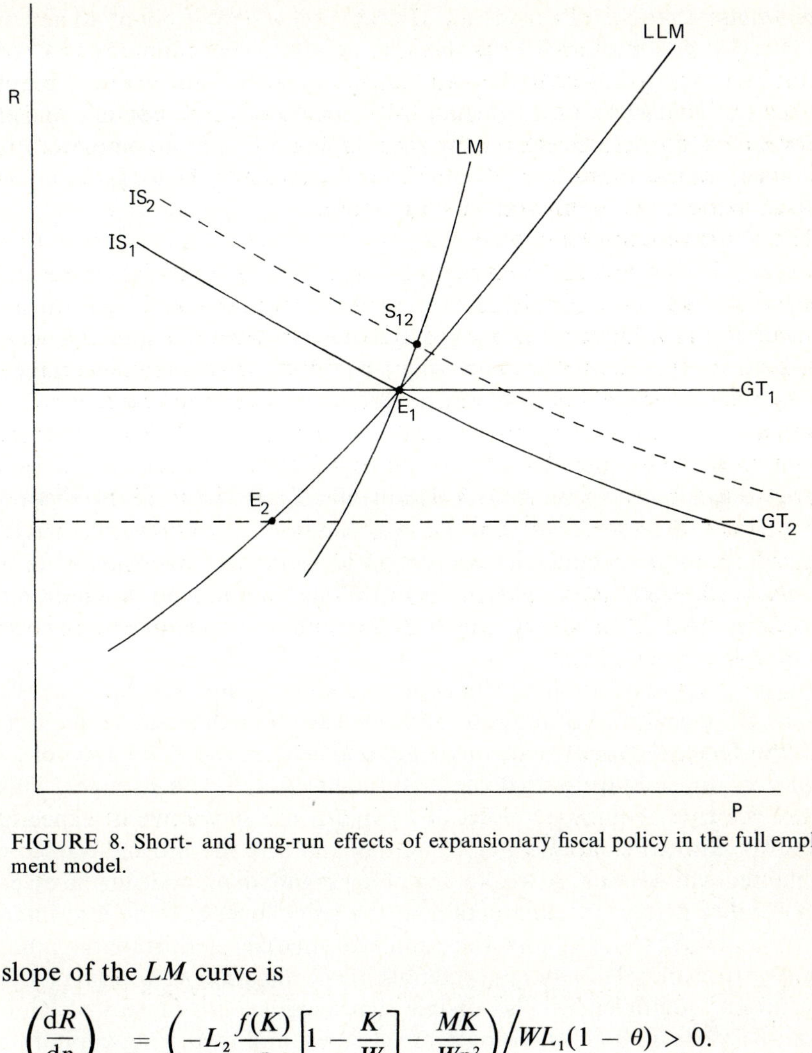


FIGURE 8. Short- and long-run effects of expansionary fiscal policy in the full employment model.

The slope of the *LM* curve is

$$\left(\frac{\mathrm{d}R}{\mathrm{d}p}\right)_{LM} = \left(-L_2\frac{f(K)}{p}\left[1 - \frac{K}{W}\right] - \frac{MK}{Wp^2}\right)\Big/ WL_1(1 - \theta) > 0.$$

The impact effect of an increase in $G'$ – given $M, D, K, x, \theta$ and the new higher level of $G'$ – is a new temporary equilibrium, as shown in figure 8, (before stocks and expectations have had time to change) at $S_{12}$ with higher $p$ and $R$. At $S_{12}$, $D$ will be increasing and $K$ will be decreasing. Except in the case of static expectations, $\dot{x}$ will be positive. The new long-run equilibrium, however, is at $E_2$, with lower $R$ and $p$ than at $E_1$.

### 6.3. Stability

The tedious mathematics of the local stability conditions for the full employment model are relegated to the appendix. To summarize, the long-run equilibrium is unstable in case of static expectations [(43a)] (6.11a) and potentially but not necessarily stable in cases of myopic perfect foresight [(43b)]. In the intermediate case of adaptive expectations [(43c)], stability requires but is not guaranteed by a finite minimum speed of adaptation.

These results may seem paradoxical. Usually static expectations are considered stabilizing, while quick translation of actual price experience into expectations is considered destabilizing. The opposite conclusion here is related to the difference in direction between short- and long-run effects, as exhibited in figure 8. This means that some over-shooting is necessary for the long-run equilibrium to be stable.

The apparent paradox arises from the endogeneity of $K$ and $Y$, and the related endogeneity of $\dot{D}$ and $D$. At a position like $S_{12}$ in figure 8, the Pigou effect is pulling consumption down, and the increase in $R - x$ is unfavorable to investment. On the other hand, the real deficit is positive and $D$ is growing, an effect accentuated as real tax revenues decline along with the capital stock $K$ and real income $Y$. The latter effect, which is the source of instability, is absent from the short-run story. The expected rate of inflation itself has two effects on short-run aggregate demand along the adjustment path. One is to raise investment by lowering the real rate of interest, and the other is to increase saving to make up for expected real capital losses on money and debt. A necessary, but not sufficient, condition for stability is that the investment effect is the stronger. This means that if the rate of inflation slows down and if the slowdown is translated fairly promptly into expectations, aggregate demand and the income-related demand for money will weaken. A weakening of aggregate demand leads, in an economy with flexible prices, to a reduction in the price level and the real interest rate and to an increase in capital stock and real income. Unfortunately, the issue of stability turns on relatively minor details of specification and on small differences in values of coefficients. It is possible that fiscal expansion sets off an unstable spiral of inflation, deficits, rising interest rates, and dwindling capital stock and output. It is also possible that is the start of an oscillation that converges to an equilibrium with lower price level, lower interest rate, higher capital stock and income.

## 7. Conclusion

Nothing in the analysis of this paper supports the claim that expansionary fiscal effects on aggregate demand are only transitory. To investigate the question, the main section of this paper focussed on the pure logic of aggregate demand. Supply constraints were assumed away – there is always labor available to produce the output demanded. In this situation, an increase in government expenditure either leads to a new long-run equilibrium with higher real income or, in unstable cases, to an explosive increase in income and interest rate. We do not stress the latter possibility, since it depends on built-in fiscal expansion via debt interest payments and since the economy would sooner or later hit a full employment ceiling.

Interest-inelasticity of demand for money seems to be crucial for the strong monetarist proposition after all. A fiscally driven expansion could, of course, occur but vanish if the short-run *LM* curve is not vertical while the long-run *LLM* curve is vertical. We are not aware that this argument has been made.

In future work on this subject, not motivated by any particular propositions, monetarist or otherwise, we would embed the moving short-run equilibria in a growth model rather than a stationary state. (The growth model is more confining. A stationary-state equilibrium just requires zero changes of stocks, and there are lots of configurations of stocks consistent with that condition. An equilibrium growth path requires that flows stand in the same relation to each other as the corresponding stocks.) Moreover, we would find more congenial a model which allows debt and capital to be imperfect substitutes with distinct rates of return. Clearly a more satisfactory model would also recognize that even when the economy is not at full employment nominally denominated stocks change in real value from price movements as well as from fiscal and monetary policies.

In section 6 we considered the long-run effects of fiscal expansion in an economy with full employment and flexible prices. Here there is a striking difference between impact and ultimate effects. The new long-run equilibrium, after a permanent increase of government expenditure, has larger real income and capital stock but lower price level and interest rate. But such equilibria are stable, if at all, only if price expectations adapt fairly quickly to price experience.

Finally, we observe again that it is disturbing that the qualitative properties of models – the signs of important system-wide multipliers, the stability of equilibria – can turn on relatively small changes of specification or on small differences in values of coefficients. We do not feel entitled to use the "correspondence principle" assumption of stability to derive restrictions on structural equations and parameters. There is no divine guarantee that the economic system is stable.

## Appendix: Stability in the Full Employment Model

We solve the short-run *LM* and *IS* equations for $R$ and $P$ as functions of $D$, $K$ and $x$, given $M$, $G'$ and $\theta$ and evaluate these solutions at the long-run equilibrium ($D^*$, $K^*$, 0),

$$R = h^1(D, K, x; M, G', \theta), \tag{A-1a}$$

$$P = h^2(D, K, x; M, G', \theta). \tag{A-1b}$$

The reduced-form impact multipliers are solved for from

$$\begin{bmatrix} -I' & \dfrac{-s(M+D)}{p^2} \\ WL_1(1-\theta) & \dfrac{L_2 f(K)}{p}\left(1 - \dfrac{K}{W}\right) + \dfrac{MK}{Wp^2} \end{bmatrix} \begin{bmatrix} \mathrm{d}R \\ \mathrm{d}P \end{bmatrix}$$

$$= \begin{bmatrix} \dfrac{-s}{p}\mathrm{d}D + ((\theta + s\hat{\mu})f'(K) - I'f''(K) - s)\mathrm{d}K - \left(I' - \dfrac{(M+D)}{p}\right)\mathrm{d}x \\ \left(\dfrac{L_2 f(K)}{pW} - \dfrac{L}{p}\right)\mathrm{d}D + \left(-L_2 f'(K) + \dfrac{L_2 f(K)}{W} - L\right)\mathrm{d}K \end{bmatrix}$$

The signs of these derivatives are not all determined, given the a priori restrictions we have imposed so far,

$h^1_D > 0$,
$h^1_K$ is undetermined; if $(\theta + s\hat{\mu})f' - I'f'' - s < 0$, $h^1_K > 0$,
$h^2_D$ is undetermined,
$h^2_K$ is undetermined; if $(\theta + s\hat{\mu})f' - I'f'' - s > 0$, $h^2_K < 0$,
$h^1_x$ is undetermined; $h^1_x > 0$ if and only if $I' - (M + D)/p > 0$,
$h^2_x$ is undetermined; $h^2_x > 0$ if and only if $I' - (M + D)/p > 0$.

We now consider stability for the three mechanisms for generating expectations:

*Static expectations:* $x = 0$

The dynamic equations are

$$\dot{D} = p[G' - \theta f(K)], \tag{A-2a}$$

$$\dot{K} = I[f'(K) - R]. \tag{A-2b}$$

Substituting (A-1a) and (A-1b) into these equations, and taking the linear approximation at the long-run equilibrium $(D^*, K^*)$ we get

$$\begin{bmatrix} \dot{D} \\ \dot{K} \end{bmatrix} = \begin{bmatrix} 0 & -p\theta f' \\ -I'h^1_D & I'[f'' - h^1_K] \end{bmatrix} \begin{bmatrix} D - D^* \\ K - K^* \end{bmatrix}. \tag{A-3}$$

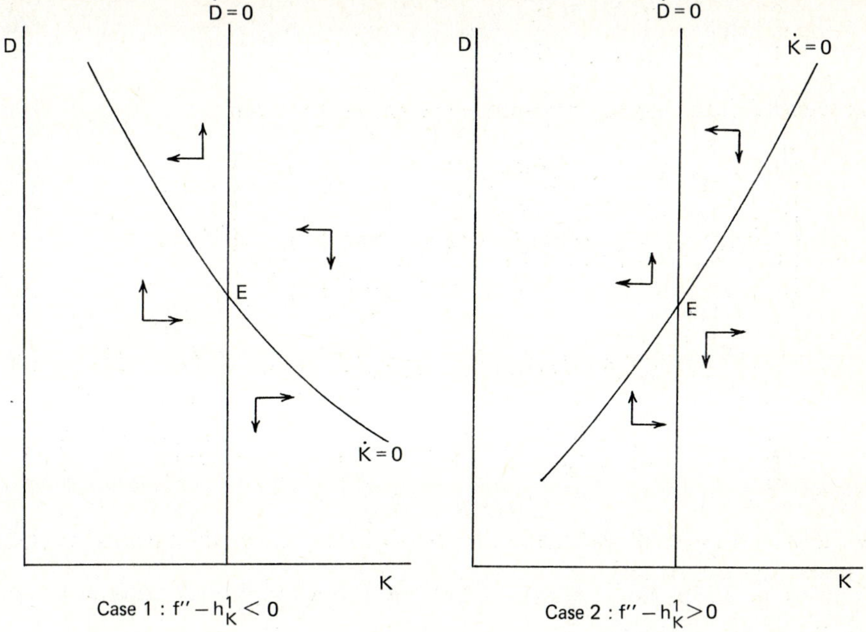


FIGURE 9. Stability in the full employment model under static expectations

Necessary and sufficient conditions for stability are

$$I'(f'' - h^1_K) < 0, \tag{A-4a}$$

$$-I'h^1_D p\theta f' > 0. \tag{A-4b}$$

(A-4a) may be satisfied, (A-4b) never is; the long-run equilibrium is unstable under static expectations. Figure 9 illustrates this instability with the familiar phase diagram in $D$, $K$ space.

*Myopic perfect foresight:* $\dot{p}/p = x$

The complete dynamic system can in this case be written as

$$I\left[f'(K) - R + \frac{\dot{p}}{p}\right] + G' - \theta f(K)$$

$$- s\left[\hat{\mu} f(K) - \frac{M + D}{p} - K\right] - \frac{\dot{p}}{p}\frac{M + D}{p} = 0, \tag{A-5a}$$

$$L\left[R(1-\theta), \frac{pf(K)}{M+D+pK}\right]\left[\frac{M+D}{p}+K\right] = \frac{M}{p}, \tag{A-5b}$$

$$\dot{D} = p[G' - \theta f(K)], \tag{A-5c}$$

$$\dot{K} = I\left[f'(K) - R + \frac{\dot{p}}{p}\right]. \tag{A-5d}$$

We solve (A-5b) for $R$ as a function of $p$, $K$ and $D$, given $M$ and $\theta$,

$$R = R(p, D, K), \tag{A-5b$'$}$$

$$R_p = \left(\frac{-L_2 f(K)}{p}\left[1 - \frac{K}{W}\right] - \frac{MK}{Wp^2}\right)\Big/ WL_1(1-\theta) > 0, \tag{A-6a}$$

$$R_D = \left(\frac{L_2 f(K)}{pW} - \frac{L}{p}\right)\Big/ WL_1(1-\theta) > 0, \tag{A-6b}$$

$$R_K = \left(-L_2 f'(K) + \frac{L_2 f(K)}{W} - L\right)\Big/ WL_1(1-\theta) > 0. \tag{A-6c}$$

Substituting (A-5b) into (A-5a), (A-5c) and (A-5d) and linearizing at the equilibrium ($K^*$, $D^*$, $p^*$) gives

$$\begin{bmatrix} \dot{p} \\ \dot{D} \\ \dot{K} \end{bmatrix} = \begin{bmatrix} \dfrac{\left[I'R_p + s\dfrac{(M+D)}{p^2}\right]p}{I' - \dfrac{M+D}{p}} & \dfrac{\left[-\dfrac{s}{p} + I'R_D\right]p}{I' - \dfrac{M+D}{p}} & \dfrac{[-I'f''(K) + I'R_K + \theta f'(K) + s\hat{\mu}f'(K) - s]p}{I' - \dfrac{M+D}{p}} \\ 0 & 0 & -p\theta f'(K) \\ \dfrac{I'\dfrac{M+D}{p}\left[R_p + \dfrac{s}{p}\right]}{I' - \dfrac{M+D}{p}} & \dfrac{\dfrac{I'}{p}[R_D(M+D) - s]}{I' - \dfrac{M+D}{p}} & \dfrac{I'\left[-f''(K)\dfrac{M+D}{p} + R_K\dfrac{M+D}{p} + \theta f'(K) + s\hat{\mu}f'(K) - s\right]}{I' - \dfrac{M+D}{p}} \end{bmatrix} \begin{bmatrix} p - p^* \\ D - D^* \\ K - K^* \end{bmatrix} \tag{A-7}$$

The characteristic equation of the coefficient matrix can be written as

$$a_0\lambda^3 + a_1\lambda^2 + a_2\lambda + a_3 = 0; \qquad a_0 > 0.$$

Necessary and sufficient for all characteristic roots to have negative real parts are

$$\begin{aligned} a_1 &> 0, \\ a_2 &> 0, \\ a_3 &> 0, \\ a_1 a_2 - a_0 a_3 &> 0, \end{aligned}$$

One of the first two inequalities can be eliminated since it is implied by the remaining three.

The characteristic equation of the system is

$$\lambda^3 + \left( \frac{-I'\left[\frac{(M+D)}{p}(R_K - f'') + f'(\theta + s\hat{\mu}) - s\right] - \left[I'R_P + s\frac{(M+D)}{p^2}\right]p}{I' - \dfrac{M+D}{p}} \right)\lambda^2$$

$$+ I'\left( \frac{\theta f'[R_D(M+D) - s] + R_P[f'(\theta + s\hat{\mu}) - s]p + \frac{s}{p}(M+D)(f'' - R_K)}{I' - \dfrac{M+D}{p}} \right)\lambda$$

$$+ \frac{s\theta I' f'[pR_P + (M+D)R_D]}{I' - \dfrac{M+D}{p}} = 0.$$

A detailed analysis of the necessary and sufficient conditions for stability would require a lot of space for rather little additional insight; some brief remarks will suffice:

$a_3 > 0$, requires $I' - (M + D)/p > 0$: the effect of an increase in the expected rate of inflation is to create excess demand in the goods market. As we shall see this condition is also necessary for stability in the adaptive expectations case.

$a_1, a_2 > 0$, these two conditions set rather strict bounds on the permissible values of $s$; it has to be large enough to make the numerator of $a_1$ positive, but small enough to make the numerator of $a_2$ positive.

$a_1a_2 - a_0a_3 > 0$, no great intuitive insight can be obtained from this condition; it does not contradict any a priori sign restrictions on the coefficients; stability however becomes a rather detailed empirical question.

*Adaptive expectations:* $\dot{x} = \beta\left(\frac{\dot{p}}{p} - x\right)$

This case too, will turn out to be at least potentially stable. Substituting (A-la) and (A-lb) into the dynamic equations, we get

$$\dot{D} = p[G' - \theta f(K)],$$
$$\dot{K} = I[f'(K) - h^1(D, K, x) + x],$$
$$\dot{x} = \left(\beta\,\frac{\dot{h}^2(D, K, x)}{h^2(D, K, x)} - x\right).$$

A linear approximation at the equilibrium $(D^*, K^*, 0)$ gives

$$\begin{bmatrix} \dot{D} \\ \dot{K} \\ \dot{x} \end{bmatrix} = \begin{bmatrix} 0 & -p\theta f' & 0 \\ -I'h^1_D & I'(f'' - h^1_K) & I'(1 - h^1_x) \\ \dfrac{-\beta h^2_K I' h^1_D}{p - \beta h^2_x} & \dfrac{p\beta}{p - \beta h^2_x}\left[-h^2_D\theta f' + \dfrac{h^2_K}{p} I'(f'' - h^1_K)\right] & \dfrac{p\beta}{p - \beta h^2_x}\left[\dfrac{h^2_K}{p} I'(1 - h^1_x) - 1\right] \end{bmatrix} \begin{bmatrix} D - D^* \\ K - K^* \\ x - 0 \end{bmatrix} \tag{A-8}$$

The characteristic equation is

$$\lambda^3 - \left\{ I'(f'' - h^1_K) + \frac{p\beta}{p - \beta h^2_x}\left[\frac{h^2_K}{p} I'(1 - h^1_x) - 1\right]\right\} \lambda^2$$
$$- \left\{ I'(f'' - h^1_K)\frac{p\beta}{p - \beta h^2_x} - I'(1 - h^1_x)\frac{p\beta}{p - \beta h^2_x} h^2_D \theta f' + I' h^1_D p\theta f' \right\} \lambda$$
$$- I' h^1_D p\theta f' \frac{p\beta}{p - \beta h^2_x} = 0.$$

The linearized version of the static expectations model (A-3) is found back as the UPPER LEFT $2 \times 2$ submatrix in the linearized version of the adaptive expectations model (A-8). The static expectations model can therefore be regarded as a limiting case of the adaptive expectations model, when $\beta = 0$ [and terms like $h_x^1$ and $h_x^2$ are irrelevant because $x \equiv 0$],

$$a_3 = -I'h_D^1 p\theta f' \frac{p\beta}{p - \beta h_x^2} > 0$$

is necessary for stability. Since $h_D^1 > 0$, $a_3 > 0$ iff $p = \beta h_x^2 < 0$, i.e., only if $h_x^2 > 0$; the impact effect of a rise in inflationary expectations is to increase the price level. $h_x^2 > 0$ iff $I' - [(M + D)/p] > 0$ which is the condition we derived for myopic perfect foresight. It is clear that with $\beta = 0$ [the static expectations case] $a_3 = 0$ and the system won't be stable.

## Bibliography

Blinder, A. S. and R. M. Solow, 1973, Does fiscal policy matter?, Journal of Public Economics 2, pp. 319–337.

Blinder, A. S. and R. M. Solow, 1974, The economics of public finance (Brookings Institution, Washington, D.C.)

Friedman, M., 1972, Comments on the critics, Journal of Political Economy, Sept.

Tobin, J., 1971, Essays in economics, vol. I: Macroeconomics (North-Holland, Amsterdam) pp. 378–455.

# 1. COMMENTS ON TOBIN AND BUITER

Milton FRIEDMAN

## 1. Introduction

Three different issues are involved in James Tobin's continuing skirmish with the allegedly "characteristic monetarist proposition ... that pure fiscal policy does not matter for aggregate real demand, nominal income, and the price level".

(A) The theoretical conditions under which this assertion would be rigorously and precisely correct for both impact and long-run effects.

(B) The empirical importance of the effects of "pure fiscal policy" arising from the failure of these conditions to be satisfied perfectly; i.e., whether, as a practical matter, sufficiently correct results will be obtained by treating them *as if* they were perfectly satisfied.

(C) The difference between the impact and the cumulative effects of a change in government spending or taxation.

Tobin's and Buiter's paper is directed mostly to analyzing the third issue for a specific model (or pair of models). I shall leave detailed criticism of that analysis to the other discussants of the paper, on grounds both of their greater competence for this task, and my tentative conclusion that these models do not cast much light on whatever real issues may divide economists labeled monetarists from economists labeled Keynesian. The models may be useful, and the results enlightening, for other purposes. On that question, I express no judgment.

I shall restrict my comments therefore primarily to the first two issues, which means, to the initial more general pages of the Tobin–Buiter paper, where the authors use my views as a springboard (or straw man?) for their analysis. I shall then add some general comments on what seem to me the real issues that need resolution.

One man's "characteristic monetarist proposition" is not another's. In my reply to Tobin's earlier comments on my two J.P.E. articles on a monetary framework, I explicitly refused to accept as characteristically monetarist a slightly different variant of the proposition that Tobin and Buiter now describe in these terms.[1] I suspect that our difference is a byproduct of my Marshallian approach to theory, which leads me to regard issue (B) as fundamental, versus Tobin's Walrasian approach, which makes it difficult for him to recognize issue (B) as a meaningful issue at all.

## 2. The Purely Theoretical Issue

Whether that be correct or not, it is desirable to get the purely theoretical issue straight. Tobin and Buiter state that "a necessary condition for the proposition [that pure fiscal policy does not matter for aggregate real demand, nominal income, and the price level] is zero elasticity of demand for money with respect to interest rates". This is clearly wrong, even on the level of the most elementary *IS–LM* model.[2] A horizontal *IS* curve is a sufficient condition for the stated result, whatever the shape of the *LM* curve. And a horizontal *IS* curve has as much claim to consideration on theoretical and empirical grounds as a vertical *LM* curve (or a horizontal *LM* curve of liquidity trap fame). Frank Knight consistently treated an infinitely elastic demand for new investment, which implies a horizontal *IS* curve, as a key element of his capital theory. One historical observation that is no less surprising than it is well documented is the relative constancy of the real interest rate over long periods of time, which could be regarded as reflecting a "roughly" horizontal *IS* curve for given price expectations.

On a purely theoretical level, it is interesting to note that much "practical Keynesianism" has treated the *LM* curve as if it were horizontal, the *IS* curve as if it were vertical; whereas much "practical monetarism" has treated the *LM* curve as it were vertical, the *IS* curve as if it were horizontal. In this sense, the two can be regarded as polar opposites. On this same level, it is interesting that in one of their longer-term models intended to demonstrate the necessity of a vertical *LM* curve for the long-run ineffectiveness of fiscal policy, Tobin and Buiter introduce the counterpart of a vertical *IS* curve (their *GT* curve in Model I).

## 3. The Practical Issue

Tobin and Buiter explicitly reject issue (B) as of any significance by noting that "monetarists ... usually soften their assertions with qualifying adjectives and

[1] These articles, comments by the critics, and my reply are all now available in Robert J. Gordon (1974). On the present point, see pp. 78, 138.

[2] I have examined this issue on a broader level in my "Interest Rates and the Demand for Money" [Friedman (1966)].

adverbs 'minor', 'almost', etc." and then adding "hedges of this order really do not alter the monetarist message for theory and policy".

From my Marshallian point of view, such "hedges" are highly relevant to both the theory that we find useful and the policy measures that we recommend. I continue to believe that the fundamental differences among us are empirical, not theoretical; that what we really differ on are precisely what effects are and are not "minor", not on whether an effect is precisely zero.

Despite their rejection of issue (B), Tobin and Buiter devote much attention to my words "certain to be temporary and likely to be minor". They treat these words from a 1967 *Newsweek* column of mine as referring to "a rise in government expenditures or reduction in taxes", whereas they were actually written in reference to an increase in taxes designed to halt inflation. That is a trivial point, involving only a change of sign, except that it has implications for the initial conditions implicit in the analysis. A more important point is that Tobin and Buiter state that I used these words to refer to "fiscal effects" but do not specify what "fiscal effects" I was referring to. In the original column, these words referred to the "net decrease in spending from these sources", and "these sources" are (1) that "some of the funds not borrowed by the Federal government may be added to idle balances rather than spent or loaned", and (2) "it takes time for borrowers and lenders to adjust to reduced government borrowing" [see Gordon (1974, pp. 139–140)]. Is this "net decrease in spending" all the "fiscal effects" that there are? For example, this statement does not say that lower interest rates are temporary – though on a fuller analysis they might be. And later, on the same page of my J.P.E. reply, interpreting my *Newsweek* statement, I assert, "once the new velocity is reached there is no further downward pressure". Is the lowered velocity not a "fiscal effect"?

My point here is not to defend my analysis as correct or my *Newsweek* statements as unambiguous. In view of Tobin's and Buiter's interpretation of them, the statements are clearly not unambiguous, and no doubt if I were writing the passage today, I would write it differently.[3] My point is only that I was quite explicit, certainly in my J.P.E. exegesis, in rejecting the view that the "fiscal effects" are precisely zero, so that Tobin's and Buiter's examination of my statement must be regarded as dealing with issue (B), not issue (A), despite their disclaimer.

Even more puzzling is Tobin's and Buiter's further statement: "by labelling

[3] In particular, I would distinguish more sharply (as Stanley Fischer suggested in his verbal comments) between the once-for-all effect of shifting to a new velocity, which would produce a once-for-all decline in the price level, and the absence of any continuing effect on inflation thereafter, even though the higher level of taxes were maintained, which would mean that the "braking effect on the economy" which the column was analyzing would be temporary.

this effect on income not only 'minor' but 'temporary' he *seems to be saying* that non-monetary financing of the accompanying budget deficits moves *LM* to the left, cancelling the expansionary shift of *IS*" (my italics). As it happens, there is no need for Tobin and Buiter to conjecture what I meant since I was painfully explicit – though, of course, possibly wrong. Let me quote (with apologies for repeating myself): "Why 'certain to be temporary'? Because the left-ward shift in the *IS* curve is a once-for-all shift. ... Put in monetarist terms, the lowered interest rate resulting from the federal government's absorbing a smaller share of annual savings will reduce velocity; the transition to the lower velocity reduces spending for a given money stock ..., but once the new velocity is reached there is no further downward pressure".

"Why 'likely to be minor'? Because the monetarist view is that 'saving' and investment have to be interpreted much more broadly than the Keynesians tend to interpret it. ... Hence even a fairly substantial tax increase will produce only a minor shift in the *IS* curve.[9] [Footnote 9 in J.P.E.: Note that what is at issue is not primarily the 'elasticity' of saving or investment, though monetarists would probably set that elasticity higher than neo-Keynesians, but rather the absolute magnitude affected (the position of the relevant investment and savings curves).]"[4]

Let me make two comments here. First, clearly judgments about the slope of the *IS* curve and not merely of the *LM* curve enter into my belief that, for a given money supply, the effect of higher taxes on inflation is likely to be minor. This is related to the theoretical point made above with reference to issue (A). Second, my analysis up to this point was on a superficial level, since it did not take into account the effect of the accumulation of government debt and decumulation of private debt. However, I did comment on this point as well, in connection with a deficit financed by borrowing, the opposite of the case considered above, and again Tobin and Buiter do not refer to this comment. Let me therefore repeat it: "As Tobin says, 'is a "rain" of Treasury bills ... of no consequence for the price level, while a "rain" of currency inflates prices proportionately'? The answer is that the evidences of government debt are largely in place of evidences of private debt – people hold Treasury bills instead of bills issued by, for example, U.S. Steel. The total nominal volume of debt grows by less – and I believe much less – than the size of the deficit. Moreover, even this growth is offset by two other factors: the increase expected in future tax liabilities accompanying the growth of the government debt, which Tobin refers to; and the reduction in the physical volume of assets created because of lowered private productive investment. On the other hand, the dollar bills are a net addition to the total nominal volume of assets."

[4] Gordon (1974, pp. 140–141).

"This analysis is, of course, greatly oversimplified. The effects of changes in asset structure are far more complex. . . . Yet, I believe that even these brief remarks indicate that they are of a different order than the effect of financing deficits by creating money.[10] [Footnote 10 in *J.P.E.*: In terms of real rather than nominal magnitudes, the difference can be interpreted as reflecting the effect of using different tax structures to finance government expenditures.]"[5]

Once again, the issue between us is largely empirical rather than theoretical. Treasury bills could be a sufficiently better substitute for money than U.S. Steel bills to raise appreciably desired velocity, or for that matter, conversely. I was expressing the empirical judgment that this was not so plus the theoretical argument that changes in Treasury bills could not be considered separately from the related changes in the whole structure of assets.

On the particular issue Tobin and Buiter raise, if I am asked whether changes in government spending and taxation which do not affect the money supply can in principle have effects on velocity, total money income, interest rates, real income, etc., my answer is unambiguously, "Of course". But I will hasten to add, so can changes in the relative price of oil produced by an international cartel or in the relative price of food produced by crop failures or in the relative price of computer services produced by technological change and so on and on. I would add further that in all these cases, I believe that the major effect is on the allocation of resources, or the distribution of income, and that the effects in each case on aggregate income and the price level are minor compared with the effects of a comparable change in the quantity of money (i.e., a change in the quantity of money over a given period equal in dollar amount to the extra or deficient government spending or taxation or the extra cost of oil). In addition, I would not deny that the cumulative effect of the continuous stream of such changes accounts for a sizable fraction of short-term fluctuations in nominal income. (As Franco Modigliani recalled, my estimate has generally been that about 50 percent of the variance of nominal income over quarterly or annual periods can be attributed to fluctuations of velocity. This is an upper estimate of the fraction attributable to the effect of non-monetary forces, since some of these fluctuations in velocity may be the delayed effect of earlier monetary changes not fully accounted for in my calculations.)

## 4. The Ambiguity of "Fiscal" Measures

As something of a digression from the main theme, let me note the ambiguity that attaches to "fiscal" measures and in particular to the concept "government

[5] Gordon (1974, pp. 1–2).

spending". In econometric work, government spending is usually equated to national income account spending on goods and services. This is a defective measure of the relevant theoretical concept. Suppose the government had imposed a special excise tax on automobiles and had used the proceeds to pay for the anti-pollution equipment on automobiles that it now requires each of us to pay for separately. That would have been economically equivalent to the present requirement, yet it would have shown up in the national income accounts as government rather than private spending. Suppose current relief recipients were relabeled government civil servants assigned to child care duties. That would raise both recorded government spending and recorded total income. In general, I believe much too sharp a distinction has been drawn between "transfers" and "expenditures on goods and services". As a final example, what of off-budget governmental guaranteed financing by F.H.A. insurance of mortgages, or through Fannie May or Freddie Mac? Should the implicit interest subsidy be regarded as part of government expenditures? Or total capital expenditures? Or what? I believe these problems are not merely intellectual puzzles but of very great empirical importance for econometric studies using "government spending" as a variable.

I have long been impressed with the empirical ambiguities in the application of the Keynesian apparatus – most of the controversy surrounding the paper that I wrote some years ago with Meiselman centered on how to define autonomous expenditures, almost none on how to define money. The similar growing ambiguity about what "government expenditures" means reinforces my scepticism about the value of using these concepts to analyze the determinants of aggregate income and the price level, or the division of changes in aggregate income between changes in real income and in prices.

## 5. The Fundamental Differences Among Us

I continue to believe, to return to Tobin's and Buiter's paper and the general subject, that the fundamental differences among us are empirical, not theoretical. But this does not mean that we all use the same theory. It means that our differences do not arise from analytical mistakes in manipulating theory. No one can use in practice a fully comprehensive theory. We must all work with simplified theories. Different empirical presumptions make different simplifications appropriate and thereby make different theoretical structures (different analytical filing cases) most useful. I must plead guilty to having contributed to confusion on this score. In the attempt to communicate, I have tried for example to present monetarist analysis in *IS–LM* terms, even though recognizing that this was a cumbrous theoretical structure for this purpose, that the quantity theory structure was much more convenient.

In concluding, let me comment briefly in very general terms on what I believe to be the major areas in which there are important empirical differences of judgment that need to be resolved. Like Thomas Mayer, I do not believe that these give rise to a dichotomy between "monetarists" and "non-monetarists", that people who share the same views in one area necessarily do so in other areas.

(1) *Money versus credit*. For the monetarist/non-monetarist dichotomy, I suspect that the simplest litmus test would be the conditioned reflex to the question, "What is the price of money"? The monetarist will answer, "The inverse of the price level"; the non-monetarist (Keynesian or central banker) will answer, "the interest rate". The key difference is whether the stress is on money viewed as an asset with special characteristics, or on credit and credit markets, which leads to the analysis of monetary policy and monetary change operating through organized "money", i.e., "credit", markets, rather than through actual and desired cash balances. Though not so obvious, the answer given also affects attitudes toward prices: whether their adjustment is regarded as an integral part of the economic process analyzed, or as an institutional datum to which the rest of the system will adjust.

(2) *Build up or down*. A second dichotomy, not at all identical with the first, is between the view that the best approach to analyzing aggregate change is from the top down – that is, analyzing the behavior of aggregates and then perhaps supplementing that analysis with an examination of the determinants of how the aggregate is divided among components – or from the bottom up – that is, analyzing directly each component and constructing the aggregate as a sum of components. This is essentially the little versus big model issue. It clearly cuts across the money-credit issue. For example, Keynes, like me, was clearly in the top-down category. And someone who believed that the quantity of money was critical could perfectly well believe that it was necessary to look at its influence, along with other forces, in disaggregated form.

(3) *Stocks and flows*. Here I believe the key issue is whether one considers stock–flow relations as more stable and predictable in the short run than flow–flow relations (in the long run all stocks and flows must be in equilibrium). Again this cuts across the other categories, since different groups may regard different capital–flow ratios or flow–flow ratios as important. For example, monetarists regard the money–income ratio as of special importance; some development theorists, the capital–output ratio. Keynesians regard the consumption–income ratio as critical. Sidney Weintraub, the wages–income ratio.

(4) *Substitution versus wealth effects.* The Pigou effect, of which James Tobin was one of the independent discoverers and certainly one of the first to see its theoretical significance [see his contribution to Seymour Harris (1947)], is of great importance on a purely analytical level, as one way to eliminate an apparent "flaw in the price system", i.e., to show that in principle there are enough equations to solve for all the unknowns, including the level of employment. However, I have never myself thought that wealth effects of changes in the quantity of money, or of price changes which altered the real quantity of money, were of any empirical importance for short-run economic fluctuations. I have always believed that substitution effects were the important way in which changes in money exerted influence. That is why, for example, I have never attributed great empirical importance to the inside–outside money distinction. Here is again a dichotomy which, as Thomas Mayer emphasized, cuts across the others.

Recent years have seen a convergence of professional judgments in each of these areas, particularly the first and third. The papers included in this volume – most notably to my mind, Stein's –, and the empirical and theoretical work they stimulate, will, I trust, accelerate this trend.

## Bibliography

Friedman, M., 1966, Interest rates and the demand for money, Journal of Law and Economics 9, Oct. Reprinted in: 1969, Optimum quantity of money and other essays (Aldine, Chicago, Ill.) ch. 7.

Gordon, R. J., ed., 1974, Milton Friedman's monetary framework (University of Chicago Press, Chicago, Ill.).

Harris, S. E., ed., 1947, The new economics (Kelley, Clifton, N. J.).

## 2. COMMENTS ON TOBIN AND BUITER

Phillip CAGAN

Compared with the dark ages of monetarism in the first years following World War II, when no one outside of a few die–hards attached any importance to the quantity of money and when fiscal measures monopolized discussions of macro-policy, monetarism today is relatively triumphant. The present discussion can be viewed as a commemoration of that triumph, in which the only thing left to be determined is the final score. From the papers and proceedings today I gather that one score to be determined is what role to assign to dethroned fiscal policy.

The Tobin – Buiter paper deals with the long-run effect of fiscal measures. In the usual analysis of the intermediate-run effect, based on *IS–LM* curves, an autonomous increase in government expenditures financed by the issue of bonds shifts the *IS* curve upward to produce a new equilibrium point at a higher rate of interest and a higher level of net national product. A crucial assumption is that the *LM* curve is not vertical but reflects a reduction in the demand for money at higher interest rates. In addition to this usual result. Tobin and Buiter's model includes a negative effect of total wealth on saving and a positive effect of net national product on tax revenues (for given tax rates). Consequently, the government deficit, which exists in the preceding intermediate-run equilibrium, adds to the stock of outstanding government bonds and raises wealth; this in turn gradually reduces the propensity to save out of income, which further raises the rate of interest and the level of aggregate expenditures. As net national product rises, tax revenues increase to gradually eliminate the deficit. At the final equilibrium in which the budget is again in balance, the higher rate of interest corresponds to a higher marginal product of capital associated with a decline in the capital–output ratio. Government bonds have replaced private capital and bonds in the public's portfolio. (Prices are assumed fixed in this analysis, which admittedly would otherwise give somewhat different results.) The conclusion is that, in the long run, the fiscal effect on aggregate demand is larger than it is in the intermediate run.

So far as I can see, this result is the same as that which follows an autonomous increase in private investment, except that then the capital–output ratio would rise. The only other difference is that the public might, in the former case, discount part of the future tax liabilities from the increase in government debt payments and so increase saving sufficiently to absorb the new issues of debt; as has been pointed out in the literature, if future tax liabilities on the debt were fully discounted, there would be no effect on the interest rate and net national product at all. But no one wants to press that possibility.

The Tobin–Buiter long-run effect of fiscal policy, which comes over and above the usual intermediate-run effect, depends on increasing wealth, which does not occur if the crucial assumption of an interest-elastic demand for money balances is not satisfied; for then the government bonds would "crowd out" private debt completely, and wealth would not grow faster with a government deficit than without it. Except for its short-run impact, therefore, a permanent effect of fiscal policy is made to depend on the interest elasticity of the demand for money balances.

The theoretical dependence of fiscal policy on this elasticity had been pointed out before the 1940's; yet in the late 1940's, and even much later in textbooks, the multiplier effect was described in practical terms as simply the reciprocal of the marginal propensity to save out of income, which implicitly assumed that the interest elasticity of money demand was infinite – that is, implying the well-known and convenient (for fiscal analysis) liquidity trap.

Those earlier robust wings of fiscal policy have been clipped quite a bit, because the multiplier is considerably smaller when it is based on the interest-elasticity of money demand. The value of this elasticity is widely estimated to be around $-1/2$ or less. If the intermediate-run response of investment to the interest rate is fairly elastic, the intermediate-run fiscal multiplier will be considerably below the reciprocal of the marginal propensity to save. Moreover, the growth of money substitutes does not appear to have enlarged the interest elasticity, as Anna Schwartz and I find in a study forthcoming in the *Journal of Money, Credit and Banking*.

There are grounds for believing that these estimates may even overstate the true interest elasticity of money demand. The usual estimates do not allow for any indirect payment of interest on demand deposits, so that the single interest rate used in the regressions could act as a proxy for other cyclical effects. I do not claim that the true interest elasticity is zero, only that it is low. And it could become even lower. Suppose that interest payments on demand deposits were legalized (or, equivalently, that banks find better means of evading the prohibition). The difference in yields between deposits and other assets would tend to remain constant in the long run, despite changes in the general level of interest rates. Then the slope of the *LM* curve would depend on the lack of interest paid on currency! There would still be a short-run impact from a change in government expenditures, but the long-run effect of fiscal policy in Tobin and Buiter's model would become very small. (This could offset some of the intermediate-run effects of monetary policy too, but would not eliminate them completely or change the very long-run effects.)

This reminds me of the unease I have always had with the standard counter–argument to the Keynesian liquidity trap. Pigou's wealth effect to extricate the economy from the trap came to depend upon the effect of price deflation on outside money (since government bonds could be discounted by taxpayers of future interest payments), and outside money in the United States consists of currency only, a slender base indeed to launch such a major assault. Fiscal policy could someday find itself in the same box, and the possibility is not such a far-fetched theoretical curiosity as the liquidity trap.

Let me, as a friendly gesture, come to the aid of fiscal policy!

A change in government expenditures financed by borrowing (and given a constant money stock) is likely to have a much stronger effect on aggregate demand in the short run than in the long run. I am skeptical of the results of econometric models which show the effect as continuing to increase for many years. They incorporate subsequent accelerator effects on investment which may not adequately hold the money stock constant. The reasons for expecting a larger short-run effect are that an increase in government expenditures produces an immediate increase in aggregate expenditures and ensuing multiplier effects on household expenditures while the various offsets take longer: (1) The rise in interest rates due to the increased government borrowing implies a cutback in business investment, but this effect will be slow in coming for the same reason that monetary open-market operations affect investment expenditures slowly. (2) The full effect of the government borrowing on interest rates, which under (1) crowds out private investment, will not occur immediately because substitutions between money and bonds may for a while absorb the shock impact of portfolio changes. (3) If, as mentioned above, the implicit interest payment on demand deposits partially responds in the longer run to a change in the level of interest rates, the initial rise in the yield differential on bonds over money will be reduced. (4) Any tendency of the public to discount future tax liabilities will increase saving and offset the increase in government expenditures.

It is not necessary to conclude that the long-run effect of fiscal policy is zero in order to argue that, contrary to the Tobin–Buiter model, the effect rises to a peak in the intermediate run and thereafter decays appreciably. But, far from a disgrace, this humped pattern is very appealing for policy purposes. It complements the long lag of monetary policy and provides a useful short-run counter-cyclical tool for mild business cycles. Policy-makers can push the fiscal button to stimulate the economy in a recession and not worry that it will overstimulate the economy in the ensuing cyclical recovery. Indeed, it is possible to imagine a combination of fiscal and monetary actions whose combined pattern of effects over time is almost rectangular, thus dovetailing and offsetting the lags in both.

Frequent and rapid changes of monetary policy in the short run have come under criticism in recent years because of the complicated and uncertain lag pattern of the effects, which makes a steady policy much more feasible to manage without serious error. Since fiscal policy has a complicated train of effects, it also loses its usefulness for short-run stabilization purposes. Many of us have lost interest in fiscal measures as an effective stabilization tool, not through any esoteric theoretical arguments, but because it has proved too difficult to execute in a timely manner. Changes in government expenditures are hard to administer quickly and effectively, much less broadly; and tax changes are too slow to be enacted, not to mention their uncertain effects on spending if thought by the public to be temporary.

Recent experiences with monetary restraint have enhanced the attractiveness of combining it with fiscal surpluses to mitigate the initial effects on financial markets. (This is a second best solution, for it would be better to remove the regulatory and institutional arrangements which unduly strike at housing and other sectors in periods of financial stringency.) Sophisticated combinations of fiscal and monetary policy have been proposed to help mitigate financial stringencies; here the fact that fiscal effects decay over time is an attribute. But the political difficulties of engineering fiscal surpluses have precluded this intriguing marriage of fiscal and monetary measures.

The main proposition of monetarism is that a proper growth rate of the money stock is crucial to a stable growth path of output and prices and that a flexible monetary policy to counteract short-run fluctuations is dificult to execute and best avoided or at least not overdone. I do not see that any prevailing views on fiscal policy challenge this proposition. Fiscal measures cannot substitute for a proper monetary growth in the long run; and, while they might be considered as a substitute for monetary policy for short-run stabilization purposes, they are subject to the same errors and difficulties. In making practical policy decisions, I do not see a basic conflict between monetary and fiscal policy.

## 3. COMMENTS ON TOBIN AND BUITER

Stanley FISCHER*

### 1. Introduction

The paper by James Tobin and Willem Buiter (henceforth TB) contains a number of interesting and provocative results. However, the authors fail to emphasize sufficiently that the basic source of those results is the long-run government budget constraint and that the effectiveness of fiscal policy is guaranteed in any stable model incorporating that constraint.

Since the TB paper opens with a description of supposed monetarist views on fiscal policy, I begin this comment by reviewing in section 2 some of Milton Friedman's written views on fiscal policy and the significance of the postulate that the demand for money is interest-elastic (henceforth "the postulate"). Friedman's theoretical analysis of the short-run effects of fiscal policy is no different from that of most Keynesians. The disagreement between monetarists and Keynesians on the use of fiscal policy as a counter-cyclical stabilization device is indeed largely empirical; accordingly it is the Ando–Modigliani paper which is most relevant to that argument. Nonetheless, Friedman's analysis of the long-run effects of fiscal policy is at best sketchy, so that the TB paper is directed to a partly, but certainly not entirely,[1] unexplored and unsettled issue. In section 3, I discuss some specifics of the TB paper, and in section 4, I consider more general questions raised by the paper.

### 2. Monetarism and the Interest-Elasticity of the Demand for Money

In at least two recent papers, Friedman has discussed the questions of the effectiveness of fiscal policy and of the significance of the postulate for monetary and

*I am grateful to James Tobin and William Buiter for comments on an earlier version of these comments.

[1]See Alan S. Blinder and Robert M. Solow (1974). The burden of the debt literature is concerned with a similar issue.

fiscal policy. In "Interest Rates and the Demand for Money," Friedman (1969) asserts that no fundamental issues in monetary policy depend on whether interest rates enter the demand for money function, and also presents a perfectly standard Keynesian analysis of the short-run effects of fiscal policy. He asks first whether the money stock alone determines nominal income and the price level if interest rates do not affect the demand for money. The answer is yes, so long as no other real factors affect velocity. Second he asks whether money is necessarily non-neutral if the postulate holds. The answer is no: in the full-employment flexible price *IS–LM* model, as all readers of Patinkin know, money is neutral, even if the demand for money is interest-elastic. Further, Friedman (1969, footnote 24) notes that money is not neutral in the fixed price version of the *IS–LM* model if the postulate holds; he also asserts in the text that fiscal policy can and does affect the price level in the full-employment version of the *IS–LM* model (p. 153). On these theoretical points then, there is no disagreement.

Some confusion could arise from Friedman's use of the word "stable." In discussing the first question referred to in the preceding paragraph, Friedman asserts that "if interest rates are stable, [for which I read constant – say with a horizontal *IS* curve] knowledge of interest rates is not necessary to predict changes in nominal income or in prices" (p. 146). The paper concludes that the "important consideration for monetary theory and policy is whether the demand for money can be treated as a reasonably stable function of a fairly small number of variables . . ." (p. 155). The two statements are not identical; the effects of monetary policy have to be predictable if it is to be useful, and instability of the velocity function clearly precludes that possibility, whether or not the postulate holds.

In his "Comments on the Critics", Friedman (1972, especially pp. 914–915) provides an analysis of the effects of a tax surcharge with which, as he notes, a Keynesian would agree up to a point. The point is that at which he states:

> (4) 'However, any net decrease in spending from these sources [increases in the demand for money arising from lower interest rates and lags in the response of investment demand to lower interest rates] is certain to be temporary and likely to be minor.'
> (5) 'To have a significant impact on the economy, a tax increase must somehow affect monetary policy – the quantity of money and its rate of growth.' [Friedman (1972, p. 915)]

And then Friedman goes on to argue for his empirical proposition (4).

Essentially the argument comes down to two points. First, the one-time shift in the *IS* curve produced by a tax increase reduces the price level relative to what it would otherwise have been, but does not affect the underlying long-run rate of inflation if the rate of monetary growth is unaffected. Second, consider a one-time increase in taxes reversed after a year: if the reduced deficit leads to a reduction in the stock of money, the price level is lower than it would be if the reduced deficit leads to a reduction in the stock of government bonds. This is correct, but not relevant for the issue at hand.

Again, Keynesians should agree with both propositions, though they might dispute Friedman's implied empirical estimates of the resulting price level difference arising from the difference between reductions in the money stock and the stock of bonds.

Why then the persistent disagreements between Keynesians and monetarists of fiscal policy and the role of the postulate? Among the possible reasons are:

(i) Reduced form estimates, typically used by monetarists, show little impact of fiscal policy whereas structural models, typically used by Keynesians, do indicate substantial effects for fiscal policy.
(ii) Friedman has generally approached the question of the significance of the postulate as it relates to the effectiveness of monetary policy – for which it is not crucial – whereas Keynesians discuss the postulate to ask what it implies about fiscal policy – for which it appears to be crucial (though see the last paragraph of this comment).
(iii) The time perspectives of the two groups differ. Keynesians emphasize the short run; as TB note, the arguments about fiscal policy in the sixties (and probably those soon to occur) were not about the long run. Someone wanting to reduce the rate of inflation over the next year might well want to use fiscal measures even if these had no long-run effects on the rate of inflation. Monetarists tend to be sceptical about the predictability of the effects of any counter-cyclical stabilization policies and thus concentrate on the determinants of the longer-run performance of the economy.

The agreements and disagreements outlined in this section set the scene for two of the papers of this volume. Agreement on the short-run theoretical implications of fiscal policy but disagreement on its short-run empirical effectiveness lead to the Ando–Modigliani paper. And the issue of the long-run effects of fiscal policy – not analyzed in depth by Friedman – is taken up by TB. I should add that there does not seem to me to be any underlying policy issue of importance hinging on the TB paper: if fiscal policy had significant short-term effects on the price level and nominal income but no long-run effects it would be an ideal stabilization tool. It is the weakness and uncertainty of the effects of fiscal policy in the St. Louis model rather than the zero long-run fiscal multiplier which makes monetary policy a more effective stabilization device in that model than fiscal policy [see Cooper and Fischer (1974)].

## 3. The TB Paper Close-Up

The major focus of the TB paper is the relationship between the long-run effectiveness of fiscal policy and the interest elasticity of the demand for money. The paper also contains a number of surprising results, the source of which is the steady state government budget constraint. Among the surprises are: expansionary fiscal policy may require a reduction in government spending on goods and services; expansionary monetary policy may lead to lower employment; expansionary fiscal policy in a full-employment model leads to a lower price level; rapidly adjusting expectations are stabilizing.

In this section of the comment, I take the TB framework and assumptions as given in discussing their results. To avoid complications I consider only the TB Model I in which the fiscal policy variable $G'$ is the sum of government expenditure on goods and services ($G$) and net (of taxes) debt interest. In so doing, I probably oversimplify their analysis, since the analysis of Model II, in which $G$ is the policy variable, is considerably more difficult. Model I embodies the steady state government budget constraints,

$$G' = \theta Y, \tag{TB-6}$$

and

$$G' = \theta f(k), \tag{TB-44}$$

in the fixed price and flexible price versions, respectively.

These constraints directly imply an almost well-known multiplier relationship which says that the long-run government expenditure multiplier is the reciprocal of the tax rate,[2] provided that income in fact converges to the values implied by the constraints. This result holds independently of the rest of the model: it is indeed so simple that it is possible to overlook the fact that it alone essentially guarantees the long-run effectiveness of fiscal policy, defined as changes in $G'$.

Model I, with fixed prices, is stable, so long as the demand for money is interest elastic. If the postulate does not hold, the *LLM* curve in TB's figure 4–3 is vertical, and no long-run equilibrium exists unless the *LLM* and *GT* schedules coincide.

Two comments on the fixed price version of Model I. First, it is possible that an expansionary fiscal policy, initiated by an increase in $G$, government expenditure on goods and services, ultimately implies that $G$ be lower than in the initial steady state if the demand for money has low interest elasticity. This reduction in $G$ can occur because an initial increase in $G$ leads to larger deficits and a higher

[2] Blinder and Solow (1974, p. 49). Parenthetically, while the TB discussion of the Blinder–Solow paper suggests that the latter authors commit an egregious error in omitting income from the investment function, it is far from settled whether income should be included in that function.

interest rate, implying increased debt interest payments. It is in situations where $G$ is required to fall as part of an expansionary policy that Model II – in which $G$ is the policy variable – is unstable.

Second, the TB valuation of capital in transitions between steady states is incorrect. "The" interest rate is determined in the short run by the *IS–LM* model, in which bonds and capital are perfect substitutes. The marginal product of capital can – and when capital is being accumulated, does – differ from the interest rate in transitions. Yet TB do not revalue capital during these processes. Fortunately, it turns out that if the price of capital (Tobin's famous "$q$") is adjusted so that the instantaneous yield on bonds and capital are always equal (but ignoring capital gains) essentially the same results obtain, except that the condition for positivity of the Keynesian multiplier becomes more rigorous. The revised condition is

$$s\hat{\mu} + \theta - (i + s)F(R) > 0.$$

The role of the interest elasticity of the demand for money is unchanged.

The long-run effects of an open-market purchase discussed in section 5.1 appear strange. An open-market purchase, while expansionary for the short run, actually reduces employment in the long run in the fixed price version of Model I. Their budget constraint (TB-6) is again responsible. Given (TB-6), monetary policy cannot affect the level of nominal income, but an open-market purchase does reduce the interest rate, thereby increasing the capital stock. With higher capital stock and unchanged income, employment falls. More testimony to the power of the government budget constraint.

The surprising results of the long-run growth model discussed in section 6 are again due to the strength of the budget constraint. Why does an increase in government spending reduce the price level? Examine their (TB-44): an increase in $G'$ increases real income and the capital stock, thereby reducing the real interest rate. Hence the demand for real balances increases; since the nominal money stock is unchanged, the price level has to fall. As the authors point out, the short-run results are precisely the opposite of the long-run results, and they use this fact to provide a persuasive explanation of their stability results.[3]

Thus, on closer examination, the surprises in the TB paper are due almost entirely to the power of the long-run government budget constraint. Indeed that constraint, $G' = \theta Y$, bears a striking similarity to a famous equation $MV = Y$, except that this time the coefficient on $Y$ is fixed by law. It is clear that $G' = \theta Y$ and $MV =$

[3] The TB stability analysis can be simplified. Consider for example the fixed price version of Model I. Solve first for the instantaneous *IS–LM* equilibrium to obtain $R$ and $Y$ as functions of $K$ and $D$. Then work with a $2 \times 2$ linearized system for $K$ and $D$ as functions of $K$ and $D$ using the reduced forms derived from the *IS–LM* analysis.

$Y$ cannot coexist in the long run unless $M$ and $G'$ (or $\theta$) are appropriately chosen or unless $\theta$ or $V$ can vary, and in Model I $\theta$ is not allowed to vary.

## 4. The TB Paper at a Distance

In this section I comment on some of TB's assumptions and their relationship to their stability analysis.

The assumption of long-run price inflexibility is extraordinary. No one, Keynesian or monetarist, has any good reason to believe prices are inflexible in the long run. The authors apparently need the assumption to study the long-run effects of fiscal policy on aggregate demand; if they do, that suggests the question of the long-run effects of fiscal policy is ill posed. If prices do adjust slowly to excess demand, then that adjustment process should be explicit in the model, so that the stability analysis is done correctly.

The stability analysis of section 4.2 of the TB paper, where the short-run stability of the *IS–LM* mechanism is invoked to rule out interest in certain comparative static results, is inconsistent with the stability analysis of the rest of the paper. Either TB have instantaneous adjustment of $R$ and $Y$, as they assume in most of the paper, or they do not – in which case they should model the dynamics of the adjustment of the interest rate and income along with that of the capital stock and the government debt.[4]

Given the crucial role of stability analysis in the paper, the authors' unease about the correspondence principle, with which they conclude, is justified. There are many points at which behavioral functions and adjustment processes other than those of TB, for instance those implicitly referred to in the preceding paragraph, could have been written down with equal plausibility. Thus TB's warning about the fragility of the stability results should be treated seriously.

Finally, I should point out that the interest elasticity of the demand for money does not, after all, appear to be crucial for the long-run effectiveness of fiscal policy, even in a model very similar to that of TB. If the wealth income ratio is a declining function of the interest rate, then *LLM* in TB's figure 3 is upward sloping even if the interest rate does not directly affect the demand for money, and the model is stable for some ranges of parameter values. Of course, the variable wealth–income ratio makes the long-run demand for

[4] It is tempting to conjecture that the TB procedure can be justified if $R$ and $Y$ adjust very rapidly relative to $K$ and $D$. Examination of a $4 \times 4$ linear system in which speeds of adjustment for two variables are much greater than those for the other two does not suggest the conjecture is correct.

money an indirect function of the interest rate. It is the essence of the TB paper that, if $M/Y$ is constant and $M$ is unchanged, then changes in $G'$ cannot, in the long run, lead to a new steady state $Y$ even if $G' = \theta Y$.

## Bibliography

Blinder, A. S. and R. M. Solow, 1974, Analytical foundations of fiscal policy, in: The economics of public finance (Brookings Institution, Washington, D.C.).

Cooper, J. P. and S. Fischer, 1974, Monetary and fiscal policy in the full stochastic St. Louis econometric model, Journal of Money, Credit and Banking, Feb., pp. 1–22.

Friedman, M., 1969, The optimum quantity of money and other essays (Aldine, Chicago, Ill.).

Friedman, M., 1972, Comments on the critics, Journal of Political Economy, Sept.–Oct., pp. 906–950.

# 4. COMMENTS ON TOBIN AND BUITER

William BOMBERGER

Tobin–Buiter and Stein have provided us with two similar models which have been devised to answer the same question but with different motives. The question is: "Will an increase in government expenditures produce a significant and permanent increase in nominal output if the time path of the money supply is held constant?"

Stein's motive is to isolate a key parameter the sign of which will determine the answer to the above question. He seeks to identify monetarists and non-monetarists but their opinion as to that sign.

The Tobin–Buiter (TB) motive is to demonstrate that reasonable assumptions lead to an unambiguous answer of "yes" to the above question.

Remarkably, both appear to succeed. One need not agree that the answer to this question is all that divides monetarists from others in order to be curious about this result. A world in which the answer to this question is "no" has a distinctly more monetarist flavor than a world in which the answer is "yes". It is, therefore, of at least some interest to identify those characteristics of the models which lead them to different conclusions.

Within the Stein framework, the effectiveness of fiscal policy depends upon the result of one hypothetical experiment: An individual discovers a treasury bill in his mailbox. Finding himself wealthier, he puts in an order for a Cadillac. Finding his portfolio now glutted with bonds, he places a sell order on a Pennsylvania Turnpike bond he owns. This causes disequilibrium in the market for financial assets and an eventual decrease in capital good purchases somewhere. When all the smoke has cleared aggregate demand has either risen or fallen ($P_5$ is either positive or negative). If it has fallen one may assume that any increase in government expenditures will not be expansionary in such a world.

Within the TB framework the result of that experiment is irrelevant. Fiscal policy is always expansionary. One notes that an increase in government expenditures must be matched by an equal increase in tax receipts if a balanced budget equilibrium is to be restored. Hence *if* equilibrium is restored output must rise. This is not particularly controversial.

However, this assumption does not empty the model of content. Suppose that the Stein monetarist condition holds ($P_5 < 0$). Suppose further that one begins in a balanced budget equilibrium and that there is a disturbance which lowers output slightly. Tax receipts fall and a slight deficit occurs. Private holdings of government bonds rise slightly and the effect is contractionary causing a further fall in output and a larger deficit.

Thus if $P_5$ is negative the Tobin–Buiter equilibrium ought to be unstable. In TB's figure 1 the shift of equilibrium from $E_1$ to $E_2$ as a result of an increase in $G$ does not yield the Tobin–Buiter result. Output will rise but eventually it will fall back accompanied by rising interest rates. The economy drifts to the northwest in the $R$ versus $Y$ diagram and $E_2$ will never be reached. The trajectory is identical to that envisioned by the monetarists of Stein's model.

Why, then, is the stability of the TB model not dependent on the sign of $P_5$? The possibility of a negative $P_5$ does not seem to be excluded by the portfolio adjustment equation:

$$R = R(Y, W, M); \qquad R_1, R_2 > 0, \quad R_3 < 0, \tag{TB–15}$$

which is quite consistent with that of Stein,

$$\rho = g(U, \pi^*, m, \theta); \qquad g_1, g_3 < 0, \quad g_2, g_4 > 0. \tag{S–15}$$

Despite some superficial differences the models are more similar than they appear. The essential differences are the result of the different motives of their creators.

Because the answer to the original question is empirical within the Stein framework, he develops a model which is appropriate for estimation. He eschews the fixed-wage labor market of TB in favor of a more realistic model of price, wage, and expectations adjustment. He also avoids assuming an endogenous capital stock and thereby bypasses the necessity of measuring the capital stock or rates of return on capital.

The difference in labor markets does not contribute to the variance of the models' results. Had TB assumed flexible wages and prices and an exogenous labor supply, this result would have been precisely the same as regards the original question. A rise in nominal government expenditures would have an unambiguously positive effect on nominal income of amount $\Delta G/\theta$ in Model I. The rise would be totally in the form of a price rise and the model would remain stable.

The crucial assumption involves the endogeneity of the capital stock. To see this one can assume an exogenous capital stock and examine the stability of the Tobin–Buiter Model I under that assumption. A quick reexamination of their (20) and (21) yields the result:

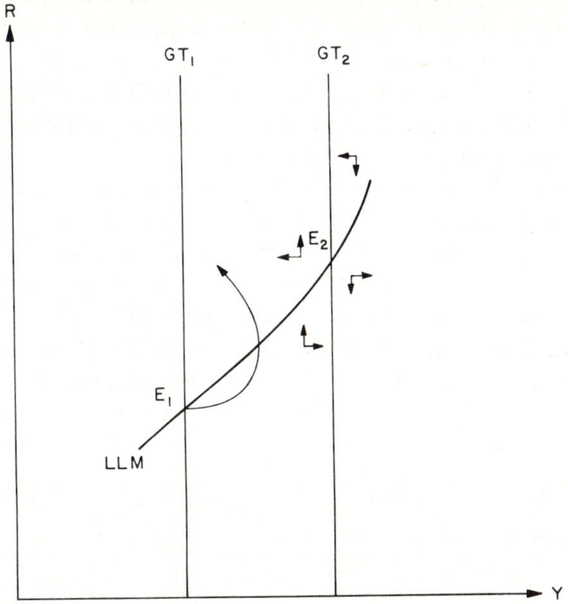


FIGURE 1. Model I of Tobin and Buiter if $K$ is exogenous and $R_2 iYF'(R) + s < 0$.

$$\lambda = -\theta\{R_2 iYF'(R) + s\}/\{(1/m) - R_1 iYF'(R)\}.$$

Note that the term $R_2 iYF'(R) + s$ is precisely $P_5$, and is of ambiguous sign. If it is negative, $\lambda$ is positive, the TB model is unstable and one observes trajectories of income and interest rate consistent with the Stein monetarist position. If it is positive, Stein's non-monetarist trajectory is restored.

It thus appears that the strict dichotomy of results depending upon one parameter estimate was the result of allowing the stock of debt to adjust to current flows while preventing the capital stock from doing the same. Unfortunately for those of us who would like to see the disputes among economists narrowed to differences on specific empirical questions, this means that the strict dichtomy will likely disappear when Stein extends his model to a growth model.

If this is true it will not mean that the model will cease to be of interest or of empirical usefulness. Relatively monetarist or non-monetarist results will depend upon different parameter values, especially in the short run. Stein has provided a framework in which these parameters may be estimated without considerable disaggregation; as well as a framework within which economists of varying views may feel comfortable. The model will simply not yield the very convenient either/or results of the present version.

**REPLY**

## Is Friedman a Monetarist?

James TOBIN

I alone am responsible for section 1 of our joint paper and for any misinterpretation of Milton Friedman's monetarism which it contains. If there is guilt, none of it falls on Willem Buiter.

On a previous occasion I wrote:

> Milton Friedman's work on money is important and influential: it commands the attention of economists, policy-makers, journalists, and men of affairs throughout the world. That is why it deserves and receives serious critical discussion. I am continually perplexed by Friedman's propensity in professional debate to evade by verbal quibbling the responsibility and the credit for the characteristic propositions of 'monetarism' associated with his name. [Tobin (1970a, p. 329)]

This time I have the following specific comments:

(1) Friedman is quite right that a horizontal *IS* locus, derived from infinite elasticity of investment or consumption with respect to the real interest rate, will sustain what I termed the "characteristic monetarist proposition". I should have recognized this alternative to the vertical *LM* locus. But I could not take it very seriously for short-run macro-economic analysis, even if I were to agree to Frank Knight's view that the demand for capital stock is infinitely elastic in the long run. Real interest rates, whether on fixed-nominal-value obligations or on equities, do vary in the short run.

(2) Our main differences may be empirical, not theoretical, as Friedman says. But the purpose of this discussion, as of the "Theoretical Framework" exchange, was to focus on theoretical differences. This focus also has an empirical purpose. Jerry Stein wanted to carry out my hope that we might "agree on which values

of which parameters in which behavior relations imply which policy conclusions, then ... concentrate on the evidence regarding the values of those parameters" [Tobin (1972, p. 852)]. This approach is a needed supplement to the empiricism of quasi-reduced-forms and of large macro-models, which have not been conclusive. It is regrettable that Friedman will not state his theory in a way which makes Stein's approach possible.

(3) Friedman chides me for implying that his words "certain to be temporary and likely to be minor" refer to *all* fiscal effects. He says that the words refer only to the two sources enumerated earlier in the same paragraph of his *Newsweek* column. But the full paragraph begins with a sentence that makes clear that these are the *only* sources of "any *net* effect on private spending". Of course the lower velocity is a fiscal effect, as he says. But it is not a new source; he had already listed it as the first of the sources of "temporary" and "minor" effects, additions to idle balances.

I must say that it did not occur to me that "temporary" could mean "once-for-all". No one has argued – except for unstable situations inviting "pump-priming" – that a one-time permanent reduction in government spending or increase in taxes causes velocity to decline continuously and indefinitely.

(4) In the same *Newsweek* (January 30, 1967) article, Friedman said:

> To have a significant impact on the economy, a tax increase must somehow affect monetary policy – the quantity of money and its rate of growth. It clearly need not have any such effect. The Federal Reserve can increase the quantity of money by precisely the same amount with or without a tax rise. However, a tax rise may embolden the Fed politically to hold down the quantity of money, because such a policy would then be more consistent with lower interest rates than if taxes were kept unchanged.
>
> The tax reduction of 1964 had this effect – in the opposite direction. It encouraged the Fed to follow a more expansionary policy. This monetary expansion explains the long-continued economic expansion. And it is the turnabout in monetary policy since April 1966 that explains the growing signs of recession.
>
> The level of taxes is important – because it affects how much of our resources we use through government and how much we use as individuals. It is not important as a sensitive and powerful device to control the short-run course of income and prices.

Indeed he quoted the first sentence of this passage in his J.P.E. comment [Friedman (1972, p. 915)].

In a previous exchange I quoted the first part of this passage in support of the following sentences:

> Milton Friedman asserts that changes in the supply of money *M* are the principal cause of changes in money income *Y*. In his less guarded and more popular expositions, he comes close to asserting that they are the unique cause. [Tobin (1970b, p. 301)]

Friedman objected strongly to the first sentence but said (1970, p. 319) that the second "does give the right flavor of my views, and I have no wish to quibble over wording." Speaking of the *Newsweek* passage cited above, he said also (1970, pp. 318–319), "The excerpt . . . says that a *tax increase* will not have a significant impact on normal income unless it somehow affects the quantity of money and its rate of growth. *This does say that taxes by themselves are unimportant for the course of nominal income* (my italics), it does not say that variables other than taxes and money may not have important effects on money income."

(5) I am at fault for some misunderstandings because I took for granted but did not explicitly state that there are, in addition to the systematic effects on velocity attributable to changes in the exogenous – policy or non-policy – variables of a macro-model, unsystematic or random variations in velocity. Friedman says that "about 50% of the variance of nominal income. . . can be attributed to fluctuations of velocity", although he notes that this exaggerates the fraction attributable to non-monetary forces. He includes fiscal policies in the same category as relative price changes, technological developments, and other events which are from a macro-economic vantage point the sources of unsystematic noise in the time series of velocity.

For me this is enough to justify the amazing claim of section 1 of our paper: Friedman is a monetarist. The Pope is a Catholic.

(6) Whether fiscal policy has a significant systematic effect on monetary velocity or is a source of minor noise is important in evaluating fiscal policy. But it is important for the conduct of monetary policy too. If fluctuations in velocity – other than those related to current and past money stock – are unsystematic and unpredictable, the Federal Reserve might as well follow a fixed monetary rule. But if there are important systematic effects attributable to fiscal policies, export surpluses, or other causes, the "Fed" should try to measure them, predict them, and to modify its policies accordingly.

(7) I believe that my language made clear my uncertainty about Friedman's views on the longer-run demand effects of accumulation of stocks of money or government debt. His J.P.E. comment does claim that growth of monetary debt is

much more expansionary than growth of non-monetary debt, but beyond that it is not explicit.

I pointed out a possible rationalization of the assertion that fiscal impacts are temporary. The absorption of non-monetary debt into portfolios might raise interest rates, enough eventually to cancel out the one-time fiscal impact. This sequence of events would also be consistent with Friedman's statement that growth of government debt occurs "largely" at the expense of growth of private debt. Otherwise, it is hard to understand such "crowding out" in an economy *not* fully employed. At any rate the possibility that debt accumulation shifts *LM* to the left seemed worth investigating, as a route by which the monetarist conclusion could be reached without a vertical *LM* curve.

(8) I recognize that an even more fundamental question is the effect of growth of government debt on saving. I discussed this briefly in my J.P.E. comment, but it is not the subject of our paper. Is the public satisfying any part of its desire for wealth when it purchases Treasry bonds? If not, its consumption spending will be the same whether a given budget of government expenditure is financed by taxes or by non-monetary borrowing. This is a central argument in a very recent *Newsweek* article (January 27, 1975), where Friedman is once again a monetarist, opposing proposals to stimulate recovery by tax reduction without equivalent expenditure cuts. Note that the argument that government debt issues, like taxes, crowd out consumption, is not consistent with the claim that it crowds private borrowers and investors out of the capital markets.

(9) While strong monetarism survives in *Newsweek* and in the pronouncements of the Shadow Open Market Committee, the monetarism of professional conferences is pretty tame. Monetarists certainly give different policy recommendations from other economists, but they have a hard time grounding those recommendations in their theories or even differentiating their theories from other models. I see nothing particularly monetarist, as I used to understand the word, in the Brunner–Meltzer paper. I certainly cannot accept their imperialist claim that concern for long-run equilibrium and for stock and balance sheet equilibrium is an invention and exclusive possession of "monetarists".

Friedman's own litmus paper test, "What is the price of money?" is fun at cocktail parties. But some of my friends are good enough capital theorists to question the question. They can recognize *both* the purchasing power value of a dollar bill and the per annum opportunity cost of holding a dollar bill rather than some other asset. Others are good enough Marshallians or Walrasians to reject Friedman's favorite money–credit dichotomy. They suspect that "monetary policy and monetary change" operate *both* through credit markets and through "actual and desired cash balances".

(10) Distinctively monetarist policy recommendations stem less from theoretical or even empirical findings than from distinctive value judgments. The preferences revealed consistently in those recommendations are for minimizing the public sector and for paying a high cost in unemployment to stabilize prices. Maybe at the next conference we should discuss those basic issues.

## Bibliography

Friedman, M., 1970, Comment on Tobin, Quarterly Journal of Economics, May.
Friedman, M., 1972, Comments on the critics, Journal of Political Economy, Sept.–Oct.
Tobin, J., 1970a, Rejoinder, Quarterly Journal of Economics, May.
Tobin, J., 1970b, Money and income: Post hoc ergo hoc?, Quarterly Journal of Economics, May.
Tobin, J., 1972, Friedman's theoretical framework, Journal of Political Economy, Sept.–Oct.

## A MODEST PROPOSAL

Carl F. CHRIST

*Whereas*, participants at this conference seem increasingly persuaded to the view that changes in the rate of growth of the money stock have important effects extending over several years, and

*Whereas*, participants seem increasingly persuaded also to the view that the important effects of fiscal policy changes are rather short-lived, so that fiscal policy would appear to be the better countercyclical policy, and

*Whereas*, the Federal Reserve can act quickly and has in the past permitted rather prompt and frequent changes in the rate of growth of the money stock, and

*Whereas*, the Congress moves slowly and has in the past made only ponderous and infrequent changes in fiscal policy,

*Now therefore be it resolved*, that control of the rate of growth of the money stock be given to the Congress and control of fiscal policy be given to the Federal Reserve.

## INDEX